THE HISTORY OF MEN'S MAGAZINES

VOLUME 2: POST-WAR TO 1959

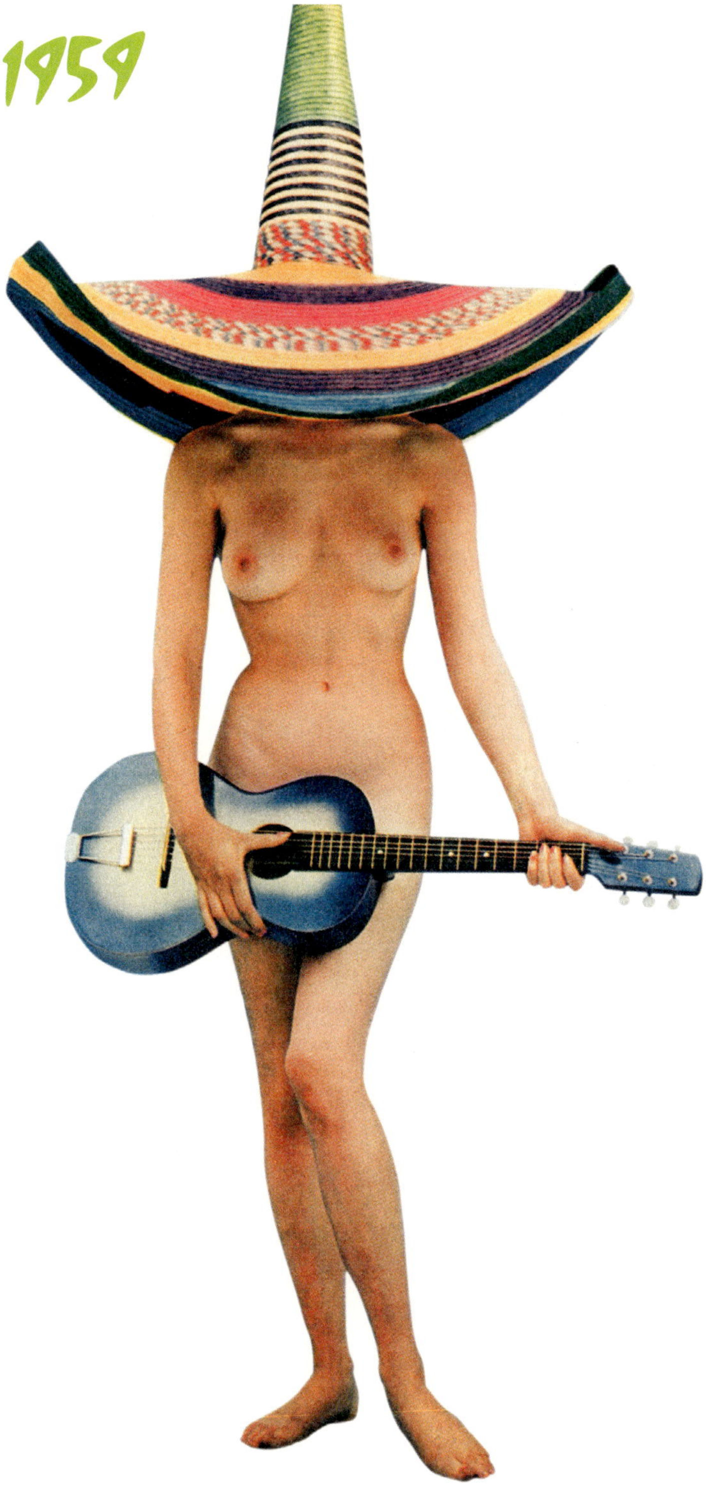

VOL.2

DIAN HANSON'S: THE HISTORY OF MEN'S MAGAZINES

VOLUME 2: POST-WAR TO 1959

TASCHEN

KÖLN LONDON LOS ANGELES MADRID PARIS TOKYO

To stay informed about upcoming TASCHEN titles, please request our magazine at www.taschen.com or write to TASCHEN, Hohenzollernring 53, D-50672 Cologne, Germany, Fax: +49-221-254919. We will be happy to send you a free copy of our magazine which is filled with information about all of our books.

Edited by Dian Hanson
Text by Dian Hanson except as otherwise noted
German translation by Harald Hellmann, Cologne (Text) and Thomas J. Kinne, Nauheim (Captions); French translation by Philippe Safavi, Paris
Cover design and typography by Sense/Net, Andy Disl and Birgit Reber, Cologne
Design by Andy Disl/Birgit Reber, Cologne, additional design by Keith Kinsella, Los Angeles
Production by Stefan Klatte, Cologne

Printed in Germany
ISBN 3-8228-2625-1

Page 1:
Year: **1959.** Title: **Jem.** Country: **USA.**
Page 2:
Year: **1957.** Title: **Jem.** Country: **USA.**
Page 5:
Year: **1952.** Title: **Flirt.**
Artist: **Peter Driben.** Country: **USA.**

A Timeline of History with Men's Magazines

1900 – 1957

Year: **1957.** Title: **Man to Man.** Country: **USA.**

1900
... Sigmund Freud publishes *The Interpretation of Dreams.*
... Max Planck presents the quantum theory of radiation.
... Germany's Benz & Company produces its first automobile.
... *Le Frou-Frou* and other French magazines celebrate the new cancan craze.

1901
... *Kraft und Schönheit*, Germany first nudist magazine debuts.
... Pablo Picasso begins his "*blue period*."
... Huge oil fields are discovered in Texas, making the gasoline-powered automobile economically feasible in America.

1902
... The Ten Commandments are found on papyrus and determined to be the oldest Biblical writing in existence.
... *L'Etude Academique* is already presenting unretouched French nudes as art.

1903
... Alfred Stieglitz publishes *Camera Work* to promote photography as art.
... Lenin becomes the head of the Bolsheviks.
... Orville and Wilbur Wright make the first manned airplane flight.
... *Vanity Fair* magazine in New York arouses the beast in its readers with actresses in tight men's trousers.

1904
... A Mercedes car reaches 97.25 mph to smash the world speed record.

1905
... Albert Einstein publishes his theory of relativity.
... Richard Strauss's shocking opera *Salome* presents the dance of the seven veils.
... The first detective magazines thrill readers on both sides of the Atlantic.

1906
... Richard Ungewitter of Germany publishes *Die Nacktheit* (*The Nakedness*), a pamphlet advocating nudism and Life Reform.
... 75,000 subscribers cancel the American *Ladies Home Journal* over venereal disease articles.

1907
... Florenz Ziegfield thrills New York with his first annual Paris-inspired Follies.
... Plastic is invented.
... Picasso introduces Cubism.

1908
... Artist Gustav Klimt paints *The Kiss*.
... Henry Ford's Model T automobile is introduced.
... *Le Sourire* becomes France's most popular racy humor magazine.

1910
... The Singapore Sling cocktail is invented at Raffle's Hotel in Singapore.
... America passes its first drunk-driving law.
... The Mexican Revolution begins.
... Cheap pulp paper makes crime and romance magazines increasingly affordable and thus popular with the working classes.

Year: **1958.** Title: **Hi-Life.** Country: **USA.**

SCAMP

THE SPARKLING COMPANION FOR MEN

You've All Got Three Heads
by JOE E. LEWIS

MAY
FIFTY CENTS

A British Beauty's Success Story:
HOLLYWOOD OR BUST—IN FULL COLOR

Every Man's a Romeo at Sea:
THE CAROUSING IN CRUISING

1915: America's postal censor Anthony Comstock retires after burning "60 train cars" of books, photos, magazines and drawings

1911

... Rotogravure technique allows magazines to print high quality color photos.
... Roald Amundsen discovers the South Pole.
... Danish actress Asta Nielsen cross-dresses on film.

1912

... The Titanic sinks, killing 1502.

1913

... Hollywood becomes America's movie production center.
... D. H. Lawrence's autobiographical *Sons and Lovers* deals openly with sex.

1914

... Archduke Franz Ferdinand is assassinated in Sarajevo; World War I begins.

1915

... America's postal censor Anthony Comstock retires after burning "60 train cars" of books, photos, magazines and drawings he personally deemed obscene.
... Actress Audrey Munson is first to take her clothes off in a commercial motion picture.
... Franz Kafka writes *The Metamorphosis*.
... Lenny Burtman, future publisher of *Exotique*, is born.

1916

... Rasputin is murdered.
... Margaret Sanger leads the international birth control movement.
... The Dada art movement begins.

1917

... Tsar Nicholas abdicates; Lenin leads the Bolshevik Revolution.
... Police in Japan order cinemas to separate seats for men and women in the name of decency.

1918

... Bolsheviks murder Tsar Nicholas and his family.
... The world's worst influenza epidemic kills 20 to 40 million people worldwide.
... Kaiser Wilhelm abdicates; World War I ends; the Weimar Republic is founded.
... Disillusioned Germans make Berlin the Sin Capital of the World.

1919

... In New York, the Algonquin Round Table of writers holds its first luncheon, just as the 18th Amendment takes away Americans' right to drink alcohol.
... Walter Gropius establishes the Bauhaus at Weimar, Germany.
... Dr. Magnus Hirschfeld opens the world's first sexological institute, the Institute for Sexual Science, in Berlin.
... The Freikörperkultur (Free Body Culture) movement springs up in Germany in opposition to the decadence of Berlin. Dozens of politically motivated nudist magazines follow.
... In Japan the first bondage magazines are published.
... *Capt. Billy's Whiz Bang* debuts in America as the country's first avowed men's magazine.
... Elmer Batters, future father of "leg art" magazines, is born.

1920

... The 19th Amendment gives American women the right to vote.
... "Négritude", the French language anti-colonial literary movement begins.

Year: **1957.** Title: **Dazzle.** Country: **USA.**

... A husband/wife Hungarian photography team called Manassé produces exotic art deco nudes for the new French "art" magazines.
... D. H. Lawrence's *Women in Love* examines sexual, psychological relationships.

1921

... Mahatma Gandhi starts his Civil Disobedience Movement in India.
... Britain's influential *The New Statesman* writes glowingly of German nudism; *Health & Efficiency* fitness magazine adopts nudist format, becomes England's first nude magazine.

1922

... Hollywood censors itself with own film review board, the Hays Office, in reaction against nude and decadent films.
... James Joyce's *Ulysses* is published.
... In America a police car is designed featuring a machine gun mounted on the hood.

Year: **1959.** Title: **Scamp.** Country: **USA.**

1921: Britain's influential *The New Statesman* writes glowingly of German nudism; *Health & Efficiency* fitness magazine adopts nudist format, becomes England's first nude magazine.

...American magazine delivery drivers are also carrying guns; organized crime has infiltrated and taken control of the distribution business.

1923
..."Empress of the Blues" Bessie Smith records her first song, *Down Hearted Blues*, as the Jazz Age begins.

1924
...The Surrealists paint a sensual dream world.
...The first Berlin-based nudist magazines debut with an openly sexual orientation.
...Reuben Sturman, future American Godfather of Pornography, is born.

1925
...F. Scott Fitzgerald writes *The Great Gatsby*.
...Adolf Hitler writes *Mein Kampf*.
...The first motel opens in California, providing motorists with convenience and privacy.
...Racy *Dawn* magazine is published in New York, combining "eugenics, nudism and art studies".

1926
...The British Empire becomes a Commonwealth.
...Hugh Marston Hefner is born.
...Dawn Publishing introduces *Sex* magazine in America. Birth control advocate Margaret Sanger is rumored to be secret publisher.
...Samuel Roth pirates, prints and distributes James Joyce's banned *Ulysses* in the US and goes to prison.

1927
...Charles Lindbergh lands at Le Bourget airfield near Paris, the first man to cross the Atlantic Ocean in an airplane.
...The final volume of Marcel Proust's *Remembrance of Things Past* is published — five years after his death.
...First electronic television is invented.

YEAR: **1959**. TITLE: **The Dude**. COUNTRY: **USA**.

1928
...Anthropologist Margaret Mead titillates and outrages with *Coming of Age in Samoa*.
...D. H. Lawrence publishes *Lady Chatterley's Lover*, quickly banned almost everywhere.
...Alexander Fleming discovers penicillin.
...Edwin Bower Hesser photographs Jean Harlow, Louise Brooks and other Hollywood starlets nude for new magazines combining film news and "art studies".

1929
...The American stock market crashes; The Great Depression begins.
...Dr. Magnus Hirschfeld publishes *Die Aufklärung*, the most perverse Berlin sex magazine to date.
..."Estrone", the first recognized sex hormone, is discovered.
...Tijuana Bibles, 16-page hardcore comics, appear in US.

1930
...Grant Wood paints *American Gothic*.
...The Chrysler Building is completed in New York City.
...Bob Guccione, future publisher of *Penthouse* magazine, is born.

1931
...In Berlin, eccentric genius Konrad Zuse invents a computer, but is ignored by scientific community.
...In the US, *Scrabble* word game is invented.
...China's Yangtze River floods, killing 3.7 million people from disease, starvation, and drowning.
...IBM introduces a machine that can do multiplication.

1932
...Lindbergh's baby is kidnapped and killed.
...Aldous Huxley writes *Brave New World*.
...First *Spicy* pulp fiction magazines are published by Culture Publications in New York; destined to become the most valuable men's magazines ever made.

1933
...President Roosevelt toasts the end of American prohibition with a Martini.

YEAR: **1953**. TITLE: **Adam**. COUNTRY: **USA**.

Adam©
A MAN'S MAGAZINE
APRIL • 25 CENTS
Exclusive Photos and Intimate Facts on
THE STRIP TEASE QUEENS
UNIQUE POLICE WEAPON REVEALED FOR FIRST TIME
Detective tells how he catches world's worst criminals

1936: England's King Edward VIII gives up his throne to marry an American divorcee. It's rumored that kinky sex is her allure.

YEAR: **1957**. TITLE: **The Gent**. COUNTRY: **USA**.

...Hitler is named Chancellor of Germany.
...Nazi youth raid Dr. Magnus Hirschfeld's Institute for Sexual Science. They gather half a ton of books, pamphlets, and magazines to be destroyed at the May 10th book burning.
...All German magazines are purged of sexual content.
...*The Nudist*, America's first nudist magazine, debuts.

1934
...The concept of the atomic bomb is patented by Hungarian scientist Leo Szilard
...Argentina publishes sophisticated sex and humor magazine *Caricatura*.
...Henry Miller's *Tropic of Cancer* is published in Paris.
...Several thousand Americans attend a pro-Nazi rally in Queens, New York.
...Fulgencio Batista takes over the government of Cuba. His relationships with American organized crime turn Havana into a renowned center of gambling and sexual entertainment.

1935
...French men's magazine publishing reaches its zenith, with titles including *Beauté*, *Fantasio*, *Paris Sex Appeal*, and *Paris Plaisirs*, coinciding with the rise of the Popular Front and better living conditions for workers.
...Dr. Magnus Hirschfeld dies in exile.
...Alvin Goldstein, future publisher of *Screw*, is born.

1936
...Irish law bans advertising of all birth control devices.
...England's King Edward VIII gives up his throne to marry an American divorcee. It's rumored that kinky sex is her allure.
...The first successful reconstruction of an amputated penis takes place.
...The Summer Olympics are held in Berlin.
...Porsche perfects the first Volkswagen.
...Henry Havelock Ellis completes *Studies in the Psychology of Sex*.
...The first franchise drive-in restaurant, *Bob's Big Boy*, opens in Glendale, CA

1937
...The Spanish Civil War begins.
...Pablo Picasso paints *Guernica*, showing the horrors of that war.
...Japan invades China.
...Risque humor magazines gain popularity in the US and England.

1938
...Jean-Paul Sartre writes his first novel, *Nausea*.
...Culture Publications acquires *Superman*, launches Action Comics, sidelines *Spicy* titles.
...Mexico produces the elegant European style *VEA* men's magazine.

1939
...German troops invade Poland; World War II begins.
...*London Life* magazine gains fame for its extremely fetishistic reader letters' column.

1940
...German troops enter Paris.
...The Occupation of Paris closes the French fashion houses, but *La Vie Parisienne* and *Paris Sex Appeal* continue publishing through the war.

1940s
...Wilhelm Reich suggests that cancer results from repressed sexual desires.

1941
...In New York the first television commercial is broadcast.
...General Hideki Tojo becomes the prime minister of Japan.
...Japan bombs Pearl Harbor in Hawaii; the US declares war on Japan.
...In the US non-nude patriotic men's magazines replace the sophisticated nude titles of the 1930s.
...Robert Harrison publishes the first of his distinctive magazines, *Beauty Parade*.

1942
...The US enters the European war.
...Daimler-Benz suspends manufacture of Mercedes cars in favor of tanks.
...Kodak invents the first true color negative film.

YEAR: **1957**. TITLE: **Bachelor**. COUNTRY: **USA**.

Bachelor

MAY

35c

CONFESSIONS OF A SINFUL ROMAN

A CRAZY AFTERNOON WITH PAPA HEMINGWAY

GIRLS WHO TAKE ONE TOO MANY

1948: Alfred C. Kinsey publishes his groundbreaking *Sexual Behavior in the Human Male*.

... Future *Hustler* magazine publisher Larry Flynt is born.

1943
... *Being and Nothingness*, explaining Sartre's philosophy of existentialism, is published.
... English magazine *Men Only* includes discreet nudes to raise military morale.
... Italy surrenders.

1944
... Paris is liberated.
... An American attempt at high-altitude bombing of Japan leads to discovery of the jet stream.
... Irving Klaw inherits the family magazine store in New York, notices his customers seek nude glamour photos and starts providing them.

1945
... Germany surrenders unconditionally in Reims, France; Hitler commits suicide.
... The US drops atomic bombs on Hiroshima and Nagasaki; Japan surrenders.
... English pilot John Sutcliffe is so traumatized by the devastation of Japan he develops protective clothing fetish; later leading him to publish *Atomage* magazine.
... ENIAC, the first electronic computer, is built.
... The United Nations Organization is formed.
... *Neues Kriminalmagazin*, a sexy crime fan magazine inspired by the pre-war *Kriminalmagazin*, is published in Munich, ending a twelve-year absence of German sex magazines.

1946
... Paris is inspired by the American atomic tests on Bikini Atoll in the South Pacific to introduce the bikini bathing suit.
... The Cannes Film Festival debuts.
... The first issue of *Paris-Hollywood* is published; its editor is Maurice Bessy, future administrator of the Cannes festival.
... Winston Churchill's "Iron Curtain" speech marks the beginning of the Cold War.
... Juan Peron is elected president of Argentina.
... John Willie publishes the first issue of *Bizarre* magazine.

1947
... Jackie Robinson becomes the first black American to play in major league baseball.
... Gandhi's Civil Disobedience Movement drives the British out of India.
... Last *Spicy* pulp fiction and patriotic magazines cease publishing in America as topless nudity returns.

1948
... Alfred C. Kinsey publishes his groundbreaking *Sexual Behavior in the Human Male*.
... The South African government launches a system of apartheid, limiting the rights of black citizens.
... The state of Israel is founded.
... In America the Frisbee is invented.

1949
... The People's Republic of China is established under the leadership of Mao Zedong.

Year: **1954**. Title: **Bare**. Country: **USA**.

... Network television is established in the U.S.
... Sexy, sophisticated digest magazines appear in Paris; soon there are dozens of competing titles, with *Paris Tabou* the best.
... In England kinky *Fads and Fancies* takes over from *London Life*.

1950
... American Senator Joseph McCarthy claims to have a list of "known" Communists in the US government, starting a decade of "Red" hunts and accusations.
... The Korean War begins.
... *Paris-Hollywood* magazines are judged too hot for the French newsstand and must be sold under the counter.

1950s
... Abstract Expressionism debuts.

Year: **1956**. Title: **He**. Country: **USA**.

EVELYN WEST: THE NAKED TRUTH!
15c
HE
MAGAZINE FOR MEN
MARCH 1956
SHOCKING STORY:
DO YOU NEED A PROSTITUTE?
SHOULD YOU WHIP YOUR WIFE?

SWANK

IND.

MAR.

35¢

a heel confesses:

LIFE and LOVES of a GIRL HOUND

Suspense thriller:

SOME OF MY BEST FRIENDS ARE DEAD

1957: *Duke*, America's first men's magazine made by and for black men has a six issue run.

1951
... Stiletto high heels are invented by Charles Jourdan.
... The Swedish film *One Summer of Happiness* sparks new sexual openness.
... Lenny Burtman publishes first issue of *Exotique*.
... Samuel Roth publishes *American Aphrodite*, a highbrow erotic quarterly.

1952
... In London, England 4,000 people die in The Great Smog, when pollution blankets the city.
... Humphrey Osmond, researching schizophrenia, coins the term "psychodelic".
... A boy from the Bronx, New York, goes to Denmark and comes back Christine Jorgensen, the world's first public transsexual.
... Body building titan Joe Weider inscrutably publishes early US gay magazines *Adonis*, *Body Beautiful* and *Muscle Teens*, followed by girlie magazine *Jem*.
... Robert Harrison's *Confidential*, the first scandal magazine, debuts.

1953
... Winston Churchill wins the Noble Prize for literature.
... *Spick* and *Span* and many other mildly sexy digests begin publishing in England.
... Josef Stalin dies.
... Alfred C. Kinsey publishes *Sexual Behavior in the Human Female*.
... Hugh Hefner's *Playboy* magazine debuts.
... Samuel Roth is arrested for sending *American Aphrodite* and new magazine *Good Times* through the US mail.

1954
... William Masters begins his sex research; Virginia Johnson soon joins him.
... Color television sets go on sale in America.
... Art nude magazines enjoy a strong resurgence in America.
... Nudist digests are the first "men's interest" magazines to appear in Scandinavia.

1955
... Vladimir Nabokov's scandalous *Lolita* is published.
... American Senator Estes Kefauver censors comic books, leading to the fall of the entire American pulp magazine industry.
... Dictator Juan Peron is forced to flee Argentina.
... Buenos Aires produces an abundance of cheap burlesque and humor magazines.

1956
... "We will bury you" threat made by Khrushchev to Western diplomats.
... Elvis Presley becomes the world's first rock star.
... Sweden's first openly sexual magazines *Top Hat* and *Cocktail* debut.

1957
... Belgium, France, Italy, Luxembourg, the Netherlands, and West Germany form the European Economic Community (EEC).
... Ingmar Bergman makes *Wild Strawberries*.
... Denmark publishes its first nudist and art nude digests.
... The Soviet Union launches Sputnik, the first satellite to orbit Earth.

YEAR: **1956**. TITLE: **Rogue**.
ARTIST: **L. N. Rognan**. COUNTRY: **USA**.

... England's George Harrison Marks produces his first issue of *Kamera* magazine.
... *Duke*, America's first men's magazine made by and for black men has a six issue run.
... In Japan *Club Kitan*, the first high quality post-war bondage magazine, appears.
... The US Supreme Court finally reaches a decision in Samuel Roth's obscenity case. Roth goes to prison, but his case forces a new definition of obscenity, known as the Roth Test, which results in previously unknown publishing freedom. Within the next year a record number of new men's magazines will appear on America's newsstands.

YEAR: **1958**. TITLE: **Swank**. COUNTRY: **USA**.

THE BALL THAT
BEATS 'EM ALL
PUBLICISTS

Zeittafel: Geschichte und Männermagazine

1900 – 1957

1900
... Sigmund Freud veröffentlicht *Die Traumdeutung*.
... Max Planck stellt seine Quantentheorie vor.
... Die deutsche Firma Benz & Cie. produziert das erste Automobil.
... *Le Frou-Frou* und andere französische Zeitschriften feiern den neuen Modetanz Cancan.

1901
... *Kraft und Schönheit*, die erste deutsche Nudistenzeitschrift, erscheint.
... Pablo Picassos „*blaue Periode*" beginnt.
... In Texas werden riesige Erdölvorkommen entdeckt; erst dadurch wird das benzinbetriebene Automobil in den USA ökonomisch sinnvoll.

1902
... Ein Papyrus mit den Zehn Geboten wird entdeckt.
... *L'Etude Académique* zeigt unretuschierte weibliche Akte.

1903
... Alfred Stieglitz verlegt die Zeitschrift *Camera Work*.
... Lenin übernimmt die Führung der Bolschewisten.
... Orville und Wilbur Wright gelingt der erste gesteuerte Motorflug.
... Die Zeitschrift *Vanity Fair* aus New York bringt ihre Leser mit Bildern von Schauspielerinnen in engen Männerhosen zur Raserei.

1904
... Ein Mercedes bricht mit 156 km/h den Geschwindigkeitsweltrekord.

1905
... Albert Einstein veröffentlicht seine Relativitätstheorie.
... In der skandalösen Oper *Salome* von Richard Strauss wird der Schleiertanz gezeigt.
... Beiderseits des Atlantiks erscheinen die ersten Kriminalmagazine.

1906
... Richard Ungewitter veröffentlicht in Deutschland *Die Nacktheit*, ein Pamphlet für Nudismus und Lebensreform.
... Nach Veröffentlichung von Artikeln über Geschlechtskrankheiten kündigen 75.000 Leser ihr Abonnement des amerikanischen *Ladies Home Journal*.

1907
... Florenz Ziegfeld zeigt in New York seine ersten, von Frankreich inspirierten Follies.
... Plastik wird erfunden.
... Picasso wendet sich dem Kubismus zu.

1908
... Gustav Klimt malt *Der Kuss*.
... Henry Fords „Model T" kommt auf den Markt.
... *Le Sourire* wird Frankreichs beliebtestes pikantes Magazin.

1910
... Im Raffle's Hotel in Singapur wird der Cocktail Singapore Sling erfunden.
... Die USA erlassen das erste Gesetz gegen Alkohol am Steuer.
... In Mexiko bricht die Revolution aus.
... Billiges Pulppapier macht Hefte mit Kriminal- und Liebesgeschichten für die breite Masse erschwinglich.

YEAR: **1947**. TITLE: **Bits of Beauty.** COUNTRY: **USA.**

YEAR: **1958**. TITLE: **Ace.** COUNTRY: **USA.**

1915: Amerikas Zensurpapst Anthony Comstock geht in den Ruhestand. Er rühmt sich „60 Waggons“ mit Büchern, Fotos, Magazinen und Zeichnungen vernichtet zu haben.

1911

... Kupfertiefdruck macht es möglich, in Magazinen Farbfotos in guter Qualität abzudrucken.

... Roald Amundsen erreicht den Südpol.

... Die dänische Schauspielerin Asta Nielsen zeigt sich in einem Film in Männerkleidung.

1912

... 1502 Menschen finden beim Untergang der Titanic den Tod.

1913

... Hollywood wird zum Zentrum der Filmproduktion in den USA.

... D. H. Lawrence nimmt in seinem autobiografischen Roman *Söhne und Liebhaber* zum Thema Sexualität kein Blatt vor den Mund.

1914

... Erzherzog Franz Ferdinand wird in Sarajewo ermordet; Beginn des Ersten Weltkriegs.

1915

... Amerikas Zensurpapst Anthony Comstock geht in den Ruhestand. Er rühmt sich „60 Waggons“ mit Büchern, Fotos, Magazinen und Zeichnungen vernichtet zu haben, die er als obszön empfunden habe.

... Die Schauspielerin Audrey Munson zieht sich als Erste in einem Film aus.

... Franz Kafka schreibt *Die Verwandlung*.

... Lenny Burtman, der spätere Verleger von *Exotique*, wird geboren.

1916

... Rasputin wird ermordet.

... Margaret Sanger macht sich für die Geburtenkontrolle stark.

... Dada wirbelt die Kunstwelt durcheinander.

1917

... Der russische Zar dankt ab; Lenin wird Kopf der russischen Revolution.

... Kinobesitzer in Japan werden von der Polizei angehalten, aus Gründen der Sittsamkeit Frauen und Männer getrennt voneinander zu platzieren.

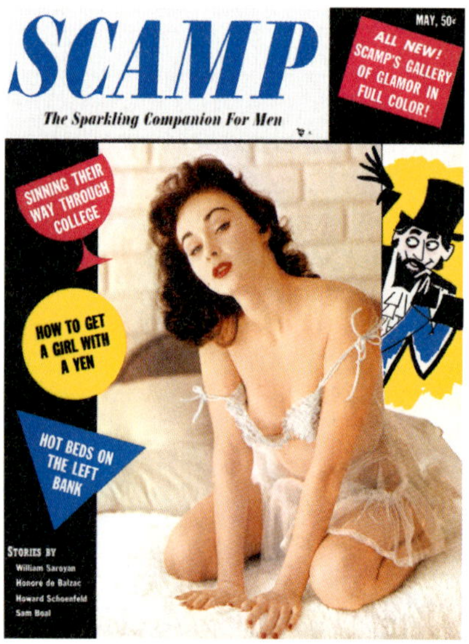

YEAR: **1957**. TITLE: **Scamp**. COUNTRY: **USA**.

1918

... Die Bolschewisten ermorden die Zarenfamilie.

... Die schlimmste Grippe-Epidemie der Welt fordert weltweit 20–40 Millionen Todesopfer.

... Ende des Ersten Weltkrieges; Kaiser Wilhelm dankt ab; Gründung der Weimarer Republik.

... Berlin wird zur sündigsten Stadt der Welt.

1919

... Pünktlich zum Beginn der Prohibition findet sich im New Yorker Hotel Algonquin erstmals der illustre gleichnamige Autorenstammtisch um Dorothy Parker ein.

... Walter Gropius begründet in Weimar das Bauhaus.

... Dr. Magnus Hirschfeld eröffnet in Berlin das Institut für Sexualwissenschaft, das erste Institut seiner Art auf der Welt.

... In Deutschland entsteht aus Opposition zum dekadenten Berlin die Freikörperkultur.

... In Japan erscheinen die ersten Bondage-Magazine.

... Mit *Capt. Billy's Whiz Bang* erscheint Amerikas erstes Männermagazin.

... Elmer Batters, der Vater der „Leg Art“, wird geboren.

1920

... Der 19. Zusatzartikel zur Verfassung bringt den amerikanischen Frauen das Wahlrecht.

... In Frankreich beginnt die unter dem Namen Négritude bekannt gewordene antikolonialistische Literaturbewegung.

... Ein ungarisches Fotografenehepaar produziert unter dem Namen Manassé exotische Art-déco-Akte für die neuen französischen „Kunstmagazine“.

... D. H. Lawrence analysiert in dem Roman *Liebende Frauen* Paarbeziehungen.

1921

... Mahatma Gandhi startet in Indien seine Bewegung des zivilen Ungehorsams.

... Die renommierte englische Zeitschrift *The New Statesman* berichtet begeistert über den deutschen Nudismus;

YEAR: **1956**. TITLE: **Rave**. COUNTRY: **USA**.

MARILYN MONROE'S TRUE STORY!
NEVER BEFORE PUBLISHED—28 PAGES!
UGUST
25¢
PDC
RAVE
who kissed her here?
who kissed her here?
who kissed her here?
who kissed her here?
Anita Ekberg
Kim Novak
Sammy Davis, Jr.
Ed Sullivan

1921: Die renommierte englische Zeitschrift *The New Statesman* berichtet begeistert über den deutschen Nudismus; *Health & Efficiency* macht sich die nudistische Idee zu eigen und wird Englands erstes Nacktmagazin.

YEAR: **1955**. TITLE: **Eyeful.** COUNTRY: **USA**.

Health & Efficiency macht sich die nudistische Idee zu Eigen und wird Englands erstes Nacktmagazin.

1922

... Hollywood führt mit dem Hays Office die Selbstzensur ein.
... *Ulysses* von James Joyce erscheint.
... In den USA wird der erste Polizeiwagen entworfen; auf der Motorhaube ist ein Maschinengewehr montiert.
... In den USA tragen auch die Auslieferungsfahrer für Zeitschriften Waffen; das organisierte Verbrechen kontrolliert die Vertriebe.

1923

... Bessie Smith, die Königin des Blues, nimmt *Down Hearted Blues*, ihre erste Platte auf; das Zeitalter des Jazz beginnt.

1924

... Breton veröffentlicht sein Surrealistisches Manifest.
... In Berlin erscheint die erste Nudistenzeitschrift, die den Nudismus nicht entsexualisiert.
... Reuben Sturman, der spätere Pate der Pornografie in den USA, wird geboren.

1925

... F. Scott Fitzgerald schreibt *Der große Gatsby*.
... Adolf Hitler schreibt *Mein Kampf*.
... In Kalifornien wird das erste Motel eröffnet.
... In New York erscheint die Zeitschrift *Dawn*, die sich der „Eugenik, dem Nudismus und dem künstlerischen Akt" verschrieben hat.

1926

... Aus dem britischen Empire wird das Commonwealth.
... Hugh Marston Hefner wird geboren.
... Obwohl das Werk in den USA verboten ist, vertreibt Samuel Roth eine Raubkopie von *Ulysses* und muss dafür ins Gefängnis.
... Dawn Publishing stellt in den USA das Magazin *Sex* vor; hinter der Veröffentlichung soll Margaret Sanger, die Befürworterin der Geburtenkontrolle, stehen.

1927

... Charles Lindbergh überquert im Alleinflug als Erster den Atlantik.
... Der letzte Band von Marcel Prousts *Auf der Suche nach der verlorenen Zeit* wird veröffentlicht – fünf Jahre nach seinem Tod.
... Erfindung des elektronischen Fernsehens.

1928

... Die Anthropologin Margaret Mead erregt mit *Coming of Age in Samoa* Aufsehen.
... D. H. Lawrence veröffentlicht den Roman *Lady Chatterley*, der nahezu überall verboten wird.
...Alexander Fleming entdeckt das Penicillin.
... Edwin Bower Hesser fotografiert Jean Harlow, Louise Brooks und andere Hollywood-Starlets nackt für ein neues Magazin, das Berichte aus der Filmbranche und „künstlerische Aktstudien" verbindet.

1929

... Börsenkrach in den USA; Beginn der Depression.
... Dr. Magnus Hirschfeld veröffentlicht *Die Aufklärung*.
... Als erstes Sexualhormon wird Östrogen identifiziert.
... In den USA erscheinen die so genannten Tijuana Bibles, kleine, 16-seitige Hardcore-Comics.

1930

... Grant Wood malt *American Gothic*.
... In New York wird das Chrysler Building fertig gestellt.
... Bob Guccione, der spätere *Penthouse*-Herausgeber, wird geboren.

1931

... Der exzentrische Erfinder Konrad Zuse baut in Berlin den ersten Computer, wird jedoch von der Fachwelt ignoriert.
... In den USA wird das Spiel *Scrabble* erfunden.
... Ein Hochwasser des Jangtsekiang kostet in China 3,7 Millionen Menschen das Leben.
... IBM stellt eine Maschine vor, die multiplizieren kann.

YEAR: **1953**. TITLE: **Whisper.**
ARTIST: **Peter Driben**. COUNTRY: **USA**.

SUMMER LOVE PLAYGROUNDS!
PDC
WHISPER
The STORIES BEHIND THE HEADLINES
JAN.
25¢
• CAP, GOWN & LACE PANTIES!
• PASSION IN THE DESERT!
• FEMME SABER FIGHTERS!
• UNCENSORED: THE GIRL FRIENDS OF MURDER, INC.!
PETER DRIBEN

MORE COLOR—MORE PAGES

caper

MARCH 50 CENTS CDC

CAPER VISITS A HAREM

A KID'S FIRST FIGHT

HOT GIRLS IN THE COOL PACIFIC

1936: Der englische König Edward VIII. tritt zurück, um eine geschiedene Amerikanerin zu heiraten. Außergewöhnliche Sexualpraktiken machen angeblich ihren besonderen Reiz aus.

1932

... Entführung und Ermordung des Lindbergh-Babys.

... Aldous Huxley schreibt *Schöne neue Welt*.

... Culture Publications aus New York

YEAR: **1956**. TITLE: **Carnival.** COUNTRY: **England.**

veröffentlichen die erste Nummer des Pulp-Magazins *Spicy*, heute das kostbarste Männermagazin, das es je gab.

1933

... Präsident Roosevelt stößt mit einem Martini auf das Ende der Prohibition an.

... Hitler wird Reichskanzler.

... Das Hirschfeld-Institut in Berlin wird von Nazis verwüstet. Eine halbe Tonne an Büchern und Zeitschriften wird bei der Bücherverbrennung am 10. Mai Opfer der Flammen.

... Alle deutschen Zeitschriften werden von sexuellen Inhalten gesäubert.

... Mit *The Nudist* erscheint die erste Nudistenzeitschrift der Vereinigten Staaten.

1934

... Der ungarische Wissenschaftler Leo Szilard lässt sich das Grundmodell für eine Atombombe patentieren.

... In Argentinien wird das anspruchsvolle Sex- und Satiremagazin Caricatura veröffentlicht.

... Henry Millers *Wendekreis des Krebses* erscheint in Paris.

... Mehrere Tausend Amerikaner nehmen an einer nazifreundlichen Kundgebung in Queens, New York teil.

... In Kuba kommt General Fulgencio Batista an die Macht. Dank seiner Verbindungen zum organisierten Verbrechen in den USA wird Havanna zu einem Zentrum des Glücksspiels und der Prostitution.

1935

... Blütezeit der französischen Männermagazine, darunter Titel wie *Beauté*, *Fantasio*, *Paris Sex Appeal* und *Paris Plaisirs*; eine Regierung der Volksfront gelangt an die Macht und verbessert die Lebensbedingungen der Werktätigen.

... Dr. Magnus Hirschfeld stirbt im Exil.

... Der spätere *Screw*-Verleger Alvin Goldstein wird geboren.

1936

... Irland verbietet jegliche Werbung für Mittel zur Geburtenkontrolle.

... Der englische König Edward VIII. tritt zurück, um eine geschiedene Amerikanerin zu heiraten. Außergewöhnliche Sexualpraktiken machen angeblich ihren besonderen Reiz aus.

... Erstmals wird ein abgetrennter Penis erfolgreich wiederhergestellt.

... Olympische Sommerspiele in Berlin.

... Porsche baut den ersten Volkswagen.

... Henry Havelock Ellis beendet die Arbeit an seinen *Sexualpsychologischen Studien*.

... In Glendale in Kalifornien eröffnet mit *Bob's Big Boy* das erste Drive-In-Restaurant einer Restaurantkette.

1937

... Beginn des spanischen Bürgerkriegs.

... Pablo Picasso malt *Guernica*.

... Japan überfällt China.

... Schlüpfrige Witzblätter werden in den USA und in England immer beliebter.

1938

... Jean-Paul Sartre schreibt *Der Ekel*.

... Culture Publications erwirbt die Rechte an *Supermann*, startet die Action Comics und baut die *Spicy*-Titel aus.

... In Mexiko erscheint nach europäischem Vorbild das elegante Männermagazin *VEA*.

1939

... Deutscher Überfall auf Polen; Beginn des Zweiten Weltkriegs.

... Die englische Zeitschrift *London Life* wird berüchtigt für die fetischistische Tendenz ihrer Leserbriefseite.

1940

... Deutsche Truppen marschieren in Paris ein.

... Die Pariser Modehäuser werden geschlossen, doch *La Vie Parisienne* und *Paris Sex Appeal* erscheinen auch während der Besatzungszeit weiter.

YEAR: **1959**. TITLE: **Caper.** COUNTRY: **USA.**

1948: Alfred C. Kinsey veröffentlicht sein bahnbrechendes Werk über *Das sexuelle Verhalten des Mannes.*

1940er
... Wilhelm Reich vertritt die Meinung, dass unterdrückte sexuelle Triebe Krebs auslösen.

1941
... Erste Ausstrahlung eines TV-Werbespots in New York.
... General Hideki Tojo wird Premierminister von Japan.
... Überfall auf Pearl Harbor; USA erklären Japan den Krieg.
... In den USA verdrängen patriotische Männermagazine die Titel der 30er Jahre.

YEAR: **1958**. TITLE: **Submission in Leather.** ARTIST: **Eric Stanton**. COUNTRY: **USA**.

... Robert Harrison veröffentlicht *Beauty Parade*.

1942
... Die USA treten in den Zweiten Weltkrieg ein.
... Daimler-Benz stellt die PKW-Produktion zugunsten der Panzer-Produktion ein.
... Kodak erfindet den ersten echten Farbfilm.
... *Hustler*-Verleger Larry Flynt wird geboren.

1943
... Sartre beschreibt in *Das Sein und das Nichts* seine Philosophie des Existenzialismus.
... Zweeks Steigerung der Wehrtüchtigkeit druckt das englische Magazin *Men Only* dezente Aktbilder ab.
... Kapitulation Italiens.

1944
... Paris wird befreit.
... Der Versuch, Tokio aus großer Höhe zu bombardieren, führt zur Entdeckung des Jet Streams.
... Irving Klaw übernimmt den Laden seiner Familie in New York und versorgt die Kundschaft mit Nacktfotos von Filmstars.

1945
... Bedingungslose Kapitulation Deutschlands in Reims; Selbstmord Hitlers.
... Atombomben auf Hiroshima und Nagasaki; japanische Kapitulation.
... Der englische Pilot John Sutcliffe ist von den Zerstörungen in Japan so traumatisiert, dass er Schutzkleidung zum Fetisch erhebt; später wird er das Magazin *Atomage* herausgeben.
... ENIAC, der erste elektronische Computer, wird gebaut.
... Gründung der UNO.
... In München erscheint angelehnt an den Vorkriegstitel *Kriminalmagazin* das Sex & Crime-Blatt *Neues Kriminalmagazin* und beendet Deutschlands 12-jährige Abstinenz auf dem Sektor der Männermagazine.

1946
... Nach den amerikanischen Atomtests auf dem Bikini-Atoll wird in Frankreich ein neuer Badeanzug Bikini getauft.
... Erste Filmfestspiele in Cannes.
... Die erste Nummer von *Paris-Hollywood* erscheint; Verleger ist Maurice Bessy, der zukünftige Leiter der Filmfestspiele von Cannes.
... Winston Churchills Rede über den „Eisernen Vorhang" markiert den Beginn des Kalten Krieges.
... In Argentinien wird Juan Peron zum Präsidenten gewählt.
... John Willie veröffentlicht die erste Ausgabe von *Bizarre*.

1947
... Jackie Robinson wird der erste Afroamerikaner im professionellen Baseball.
... Indien wird unabhängig.
... Die *Spicy*-Pulps und patriotischen Magazine verschwinden bei der Rückkehr der Oben-ohne-Magazine.

1948
... Alfred C. Kinsey veröffentlicht in den USA sein bahnbrechendes Werk über *Das sexuelle Verhalten des Mannes*.
... Die südafrikanische Regierung grenzt die Rechte der Schwarzen durch das System der Apartheid ein.
... Gründung des Staates Israel.
... In den USA wird das Frisbee erfunden.

1949
... Gründung der Volksrepublik China unter Mao Tse-tung.
... In den USA entsteht das Network-Fernsehen.

YEAR: **1950s**. TITLE: **Escape into Bondage**. ARTIST: **Eric Stanton**. COUNTRY: **USA**.

1957: *Duke*, das erste amerikanische Magazin von und für afroamerikanische Männer, bringt es auf sechs Ausgaben.

... In Paris werden anspruchsvolle, kleinformatige Sexmagazine verlegt; das beste von ihnen heißt *Paris Tabou*.
... In England entsteht nach Vorbild der Leserbriefe aus *London Life* die Zeitschrift *Fads and Fancies*.

1950
... Senator Joseph McCarthy beginnt in den USA seine „Hexenjagd".
... Beginn des Koreakriegs.
... *Paris-Hollywood* darf nicht mehr offen verkauft werden.

1950er
... Der abstrakte Expressionismus beginnt.

1951
... Charles Jourdan erfindet die Stilettos.
... Der schwedische Film *Sie tanzte nur einen Sommer* gibt den Anstoß zu einem offeneren Umgang mit der Sexualität.
... Lenny Burtman veröffentlicht die erste Nummer seines Magazins *Exotique*.
... Samuel Roth verlegt *American Aphrodite*, ein anspruchsvolles, vierteljährlich erscheinendes Erotikmagazin.

1952
... In London sterben bei der großen Smogkatastrophe ca. 4.000 Menschen.
... Bei der Untersuchung von Schizophrenie prägt Humphrey Osmond den Begriff „psychodelic".
... Ein Junge aus der Bronx geht nach Dänemark und kommt als Christine Jorgensen zurück, der erste öffentlich bekannte Fall von Geschlechtsumwandlung.
... Der Bodybuilding-Papst Joe Weider verlegt mit *Adonis*, *Body Beautiful* und *Muscle Teens* frühe amerikanische Gay-Magazine und lässt den Girlie-Titel *Jem* folgen.
... Robert Harrisons *Confidential*, Prototyp aller Skandalmagazine, erscheint erstmals.

1953
... Winston Churchill bekommt den Nobelpreis für Literatur.
... In England erscheinen *Spick* und *Span* und zahlreiche weitere, dezent erotische Magazine im Kleinformat.
... Tod Stalins.
... Alfred C. Kinsey veröffentlicht *Das sexuelle Verhalten der Frau*.
... Erste Ausgabe von Hugh Hefners *Playboy*.
... Samuel Roth muss ins Gefängnis, weil er *American Aphrodite* und die neue Zeitschrift *Good Times* mit der Post verschickt hat.

1954
... William Masters beginnt mit seinen Forschungen zur Sexualität; Virginia Johnson schließt sich ihm bald an.
... Die ersten Farbfernsehgeräte sind in den USA erhältlich.
... Neue Blüte der Magazine für den künstlerischen Akt in den USA.
... In Skandinavien erscheinen Nudistenzeitschriften als erste „Männermagazine".

1955
... Vladimir Nabokovs skandalöser Roman *Lolita* erscheint.
... Senator Estes Kefauver zensiert Comichefte und führt so den Untergang der kompletten amerikanischen Pulp-Industrie herbei.
... Diktator Juan Peron wird aus Argentinien vertrieben.
... In Buenos Aires werden zahllose billige Burlesk-Magazine produziert.

1956
... Chruschtschow droht dem Westen: „Wir werden euch zu Grabe tragen".
... Elvis Presley wird der erste Rockstar der Welt.
... *Top Hat* und *Cocktail*, Schwedens erste echte Sexmagazine, erscheinen.

1957
... Belgien, Frankreich, Italien, Luxemburg, die Niederlande und die BRD gründen die EWG.
... Ingmar Bergman dreht *Wilde Erdbeeren*.
... Dänemark verlegt die ersten Nudistenzeitschriften und Magazine für den künstlerischen Akt.
... Die Sowjetunion schießt Sputnik, den ersten Satelliten, ins All.
... In England veröffentlicht George Harrison Marks die erste Ausgabe von *Kamera*.
... *Duke*, das erste amerikanische Magazin von und für afroamerikanische Männer, bringt es auf sechs Ausgaben.
... In Japan erscheint mit *Club Kitan* der erste ansprechende Bondage-Titel nach dem Krieg.
... Der US-Supreme Court findet endlich zu einer Entscheidung im Pornografieverfahren gegen Samuel Roth. Roth muss in Haft, aber hat eine neue Definition von Obszönität, den sog. Roth-Test, erwirkt, der bislang ungeahnte verlegerische Freiheiten gestattet. Im nächsten Jahr sollte eine noch nie da gewesene Menge von Männermagazinen an die amerikanischen Zeitschriftenstände gelangen.

YEAR: **1956**. TITLE: **Sir!** COUNTRY: **USA**.

ND.
RE NUDISTS PSYCHOPATHIC?
SIR!
A MAGAZINE FOR MAL
September 25¢
DRUG CURE FOR ALCOHOLISM
SEE PAGE 32
"WHY I POSE FOR ART STUDENTS"
SEE PAGE 26
CANNIBALISM IN COLORADO
SEE PAGE 44

Chronologie des événements mondiaux et de la presse masculine

1900 – 1957

1900
... Sigmund Freud publie *L'interprétation des rêves*.
... Max Planck présente sa théorie des quanta.
... L'Allemand Benz & Co. produit sa première automobile.
... *Le Frou-Frou* et d'autres magazines français célèbrent la mode du cancan.

1901
... Lancement du premier magazine nudiste allemand, *Kraft und Schönheit*.
... Picasso entame sa « période bleue ».
... D'immenses champs pétrolifères sont découverts au Texas, rendant l'automobile alimentée à l'essence rentable aux Etats-Unis.

1902
... Découverte d'un papyrus sur lequel sont écrits les dix commandements. Il est considéré comme l'écrit biblique le plus ancien connu.
... En France, *L'Etude Académique* présente déjà des nus non retouchés en tant qu'art.

1903
... Alfred Stieglitz publie *Camera Work* pour promouvoir la photographie en tant qu'art.
... Lénine prend la tête du mouvement bolchevique.
... Orville et Wilbur Wright réalisent le premier vol en avion.
... A New York, le magazine *Vanity Fair* réveille la bête chez ses lecteurs en montrant des actrices portant des pantalons d'hommes moulants.

1904
... Une Mercedes atteint 156 km/h, pulvérisant le record du monde de vitesse.

1905
... Albert Einstein publie sa théorie de la relativité.
... L'opéra *Salomé* de Richard Strauss fait scandale avec sa danse des sept voiles.
... Le premier magazine d'histoires policières fait fureur des deux côtés de l'Atlantique.

1906
... L'allemand Richard Ungewitter publie *Die Nacktheit (la nudité)*, un pamphlet prônant le nudisme et la réforme de la vie.
... Aux Etats-Unis, 75 000 lecteurs annulent leur abonnement au *Ladies Home Journal* après qu'il a publié des articles sur les maladies vénériennes.

1907
... Florenz Ziegfield ravit New York avec ses premières Follies annuelles inspirées des revues parisiennes.
... Invention du plastique.
... Picasso crée le cubisme.

1908
... Gustav Klimt peint *Le Baiser*.
... Lancement de la Model T d'Henry Ford.

Year: **1952**. Title: **Paris Life.** Country: **USA**.

... *Le Sourire* devient le magazine d'humour grivois le plus populaire de France.

1910
... Invention du cocktail Singapore Sling à l'hôtel Raffle à Singapour.
... Les Etats-Unis adoptent leur première

Year: **1950**. Title: **C'est Paris.** Country: **France**.

1915: Aux Etats-Unis, le censeur des postes Anthony Comstock prend sa retraite après avoir brûlé « 60 wagons » de livres, de photos, de magazines et de dessins qui lui paraissaient obscènes.

loi sur la conduite en état d'ivresse. Début de la révolution mexicaine.
... Le papier pulpe rend les magazines sentimentaux et de faits divers meilleur marché et donc populaires auprès des classes ouvrières.

1911
... La technique de la rotogravure permet aux magazines de publier des photos en couleurs.

YEAR: **1958**. TITLE: **Frolic**. COUNTRY: **USA**.

... Roald Amundsen découvre le pôle Sud.
... L'actrice danoise Asta Nielsen se travestit dans un film.

1912
... Naufrage du Titanic, faisant 1 502 victimes.

1913
... Hollywood devient le centre de production cinématographique des Etats-Unis.
... Le roman autobiographique de D. H. Lawrence *Amants et fils* parle ouvertement de sexualité.

1914
... L'archiduc François-Ferdinand est assassiné à Sarajevo ; début de la Première Guerre mondiale.

1915
... Aux Etats-Unis, le censeur des postes Anthony Comstock prend sa retraite après avoir brûlé « 60 wagons » de livres, de photos, de magazines et de dessins qui lui paraissaient obscènes.
... Audrey Munson est la première actrice à se déshabiller dans un film grand public.
... Franz Kafka écrit *La métamorphose*.
... Naissance de Lenny Burtman, futur éditeur d'*Exotique*.

1916
... Raspoutine est assassiné.
... Margaret Sanger conduit le mouvement international pour le contrôle des naissances.
... Début du mouvement Dada.

1917
... Abdication du tsar Nicolas II ; Lénine conduit la révolution bolchevique.
... Au Japon, la police ordonne aux cinémas de séparer les hommes et les femmes au nom de la décence.

1918
... Les bolcheviques assassinent le tsar Nicolas et sa famille.
... Une terrible épidémie de grippe fait 20 à 40 millions de morts dans le monde.
... L'empereur Guillaume dépose la couronne impériale ; fin de la Grande Guerre ; naissance de la république de Weimar.
... Les Allemands désabusés font de Berlin la capitale mondiale du péché.

1919
... A New York, les auteurs membres de l'Algonquin Round Table tiennent leur premier déjeuner, alors même que le 18e amendement ôte aux Américains le droit de consommer de l'alcool.
... Walter Gropius fonde le Bauhaus à Weimar, en Allemagne.
... Le professeur Magnus Hirschfeld ouvre le premier centre de sexologie du monde, « l'Institut pour la science sexuelle », à Berlin.
... En Allemagne, le mouvement Freikörperkultur (culture du corps libre) apparaît en réaction à la décadence berlinoise. Des dizaines de magazines nudistes politisés fleurissent.
... Au Japon, publication des premiers magazines de bondage.
... Lancement de *Capt. Billy's Whiz Bang* aux Etats-Unis, premier magazine américain ouvertement pour hommes.
... Naissance d'Elmer Batters, futur père des magazines de « Leg Art ».

1920
... Le 19e amendement accorde le droit de vote aux Américaines.
... Naissance de « Négritude », mouvement littéraire anticolonial francophone.
... Un couple de photographes hongrois, les Manassé, réalise des nus exotiques Art déco pour les nouveaux magazines « artistiques » français.
... *Femmes amoureuses* de D. H. Lawrence explore les relations sexuelles et psychologiques.

YEAR: **1958**. TITLE: **Ace**. COUNTRY: **USA**.

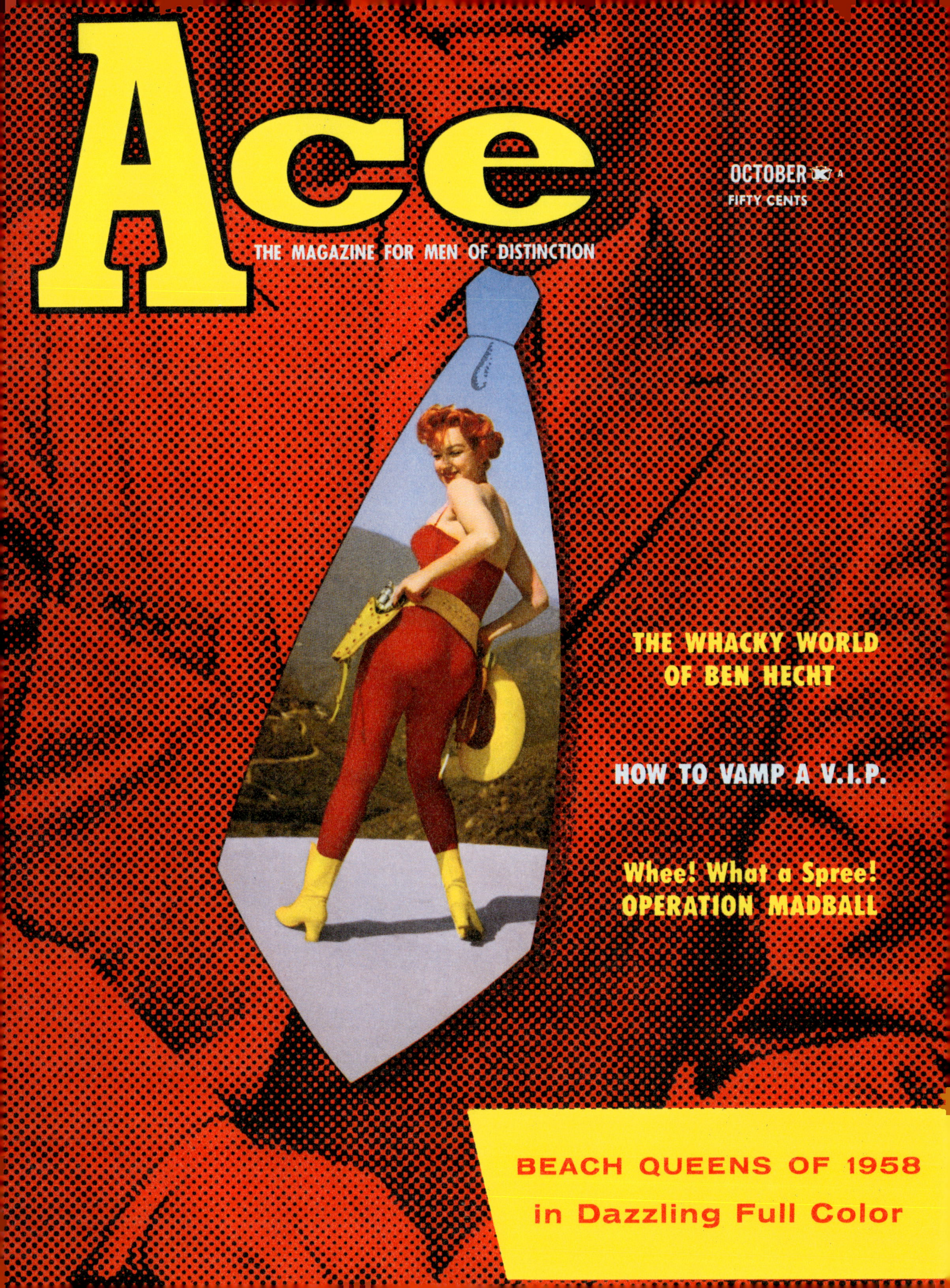
Ace
THE MAGAZINE FOR MEN OF DISTINCTION
OCTOBER
FIFTY CENTS
THE WHACKY WORLD OF BEN HECHT
HOW TO VAMP A V.I.P.
Whee! What a Spree! OPERATION MADBALL
BEACH QUEENS OF 1958
in Dazzling Full Color

WINK
A Whirl of Girls
PDC
APR.
25¢
GAY
Nighties

1921: L'influent journal britannique *The New Statesman* chante les louanges du nudisme allemand; le magazine de santé et de sports *Health & Efficiency* adopte le format nudiste, devenant le premier du genre en Grande-Bretagne.

1921

... Le Mahatma Gandhi lance le mouvement de désobéissance civile en Inde.

... L'influent journal britannique *The New Statesman* chante les louanges du nudisme allemand ; le magazine de santé et de sports *Health & Efficiency* adopte le format nudiste, devenant le premier du genre en Grande-Bretagne.

1922

... Hollywood s'autocensure avec sa propre commission d'évaluation, le Hays Office, pour réagir contre la nudité et la décadence dans les films.

... Publication d'*Ulysse* de James Joyce.

... Conception de la première voiture de police aux Etats-Unis, avec une mitraillette sur le capot.

... Les livreurs des messageries de presse américaines circulent armés; le syndicat du crime s'est infiltré et a pris le contrôle de la distribution.

1923

... Bessie Smith, la « reine du blues », enregistre sa première chanson, *Down Hearted Blues*, inaugurant l'ère du jazz.

1924

... Les Surréalistes peignent un monde onirique et sensuel.

... Parution des premiers magazines nudistes berlinois avec une franche orientation sexuelle.

... Naissance de Reuben Sturman, futur parrain américain de la pornographie.

1925

... F. Scott Fitzgerald publie *Gatsby le magnifique*.

... Adolf Hitler écrit *Mein Kampf*.

... Ouverture du premier motel en Californie, offrant aux automobilistes confort et intimité.

... Parution de *Dawn* à New York, un magazine osé conjuguant « eugénisme, nudisme et études artistiques ».

1926

... L'empire britannique devient une « communauté d'États souverains », ou Commonwealth.

... Naissance d'Hugh Marston Hefner.

... Dawn Publishing lance le magazine *Sex* aux Etats-Unis. On raconte que Margaret Sanger, chantre du contrôle des naissances, en serait secrètement l'éditrice.

... Samuel Roth pirate, imprime et distribue aux Etats-Unis le livre interdit de James Joyce, *Ulysse*, et se retrouve en prison.

1927

... Charles Lindbergh, premier homme à traverser l'Atlantique en avion, atterrit au Bourget près de Paris.

... Le dernier volume de l'œuvre *A la recherche du temps perdu* de Marcel Proust est publié cinq ans après sa mort.

... La première télévision électronique est inventée.

1928

... L'anthropologue Margaret Mead titille et scandalise avec *Coming of Age in Samoa*, une étude sur les rites initiatiques de la puberté sur les îles Samoa.

... D. H. Lawrence publie *L'amant de lady Chatterley*, rapidement interdit presque partout.

... Alexander Fleming découvre la pénicilline.

... Edwin Bower Hesser photographie Jean Harlow, Louise Brooks et d'autres starlettes d'Hollywood nues pour les nouveaux magazines associant les nouvelles sur le cinéma et les « études artistiques ».

1929

... Krach de Wall Street; début de la Grande Dépression.

... Le professeur Magnus Hirschfeld publie *Die Aufklärung*, le magazine érotique berlinois le plus pervers à ce jour.

... Découverte de l'œstrone, première hormone sexuelle connue.

... Les bibles de Tijuana, des bandes dessinées pornographiques de 16 pages, apparaissent aux Etats-Unis.

1930

... Grant Wood peint *American Gothic*.

... Achèvement de la construction du Chrysler Building à New York.

... Naissance de Bob Guccione, futur éditeur de *Penthouse*.

1931

... A Berlin, le génie excentrique Konrad Zuse invente un ordinateur, mais la communauté scientifique ne lui prête aucune attention.

... Aux Etats-Unis, invention du *Scrabble*.

... En Chine, la crue du Yangzijiang fait 3,7 millions de victimes succombant aux maladies, à la famine ou à la noyade.

... IBM présente une machine capable de faire des multiplications.

1932

... Enlèvement et assassinat du bébé des Lindbergh.

... Aldous Huxley écrit *Le meilleur des mondes*.

... Culture Publications publie à New

YEAR: **1955**. TITLE: **Wink**. COUNTRY: **USA**.

C'EST PARIS

Numéro Spécial — Le Pantalon

REVUE MENSUELLE — FRENCH-CANCAN — AVRIL 1951 . PRIX 120 FR

1936: Le roi d'Angleterre Edouard VIII abdique pour épouser une divorcée américaine. On raconte qu'elle a des pratiques sexuelles très spéciales.

York les premiers magazines « pulps » *Spicy* ; ils deviendront un jour les magazines pour hommes les plus recherchés des collectionneurs.

1933

... Roosevelt, président des Etats-Unis, célèbre la fin de la prohibition en portant un toast avec un Martini.
... Hitler est nommé chancelier de l'Allemagne.
... La jeunesse nazie fait une rafle à l'Institut pour la science sexuelle du professeur Magnus Hirschfeld. Elle confisque une demi-tonne de livres, pamphlets et magazines pour les brûler lors de l'autodafé du 10 mai.
... Les magazines allemands sont purgés de tout contenu sexuel.
... Lancement de *The Nudist*, le premier magazine nudiste américain.

1934

... Le concept de la bombe atomique est breveté par le physicien d'origine hongroise Leo Szilard.
... L'Argentine publie *Caricatura*, un magazine sophistiqué d'érotisme et d'humour.
... Publication à Paris du *Tropique du Cancer* d'Henry Miller.
... Plusieurs milliers d'Américains participent à une manifestation pronazie dans le Queens à New York.
... Fulgencio Batista prend la tête du gouvernement cubain. Ses relations avec le syndicat du crime américain transforment La Havane en un centre réputé du jeu et sexe.

1935

... La presse masculine française connaît un apogée avec des titres tels que *Beauté*, *Fantasio*, *Paris Sex Appeal* et *Paris Plaisirs*, coïncidant avec la montée du Front Populaire et une amélioration des conditions de vie des ouvriers.
... Le professeur Magnus Hirschfeld meurt en exil.
... Naissance d'Alvin Goldstein, futur éditeur de *Screw*.

1936

... La loi irlandaise interdit toute publicité pour des méthodes contraceptives.
... Le roi d'Angleterre Edouard VIII abdique pour épouser une divorcée américaine. On raconte qu'elle a des pratiques sexuelles très spéciales.
... Première chirurgie réparatrice réussie sur un pénis amputé.
... Jeux olympiques d'été à Berlin.
... Porsche achève la construction de la première Volkswagen.
... Henry Havelock Ellis achève *Studies in the Psychology of Sex*.
... Ouverture du premier restaurant drive-in franchisé, *Bob's Big Boy*, à Glendale (Californie).

1937

... Début de la guerre civile espagnole.
... Pablo Picasso peint *Guernica*, montrant les horreurs de la guerre d'Espagne.
... Le Japon envahit la Chine.
... Les magazines grivois sont de plus en plus appréciés en Grande-Bretagne et aux Etats-Unis.

1938

... Jean-Paul Sartre écrit son premier roman, *La nausée*.
... Culture Publications rachète Superman, lance Action Comics, supplante les titres Spicy.

YEAR: **1958**. TITLE: **La Vie Parisienne.** COUNTRY: **France.**

... Le Mexique produit l'élégant *VEA*, un magazine pour hommes à l'européenne.

1939

... Les nazis envahissent la Pologne ; déclenchement de la Seconde Guerre mondiale.
... Le magazine *London Life* devient célèbre pour son courrier des lecteurs extrêmement fétichiste.

1940

... Les troupes allemandes entrent dans Paris.
... Sous l'occupation, les maisons de couture parisiennes ferment mais *La Vie Parisienne* et *Paris Sex Appeal* continuent de paraître tout au long de la guerre.

YEAR: **1951**. TITLE: **C'est Paris.** COUNTRY: **France.**

1948: Alfred C. Kinsey publie son ouvrage révolutionnaire *Le comportement sexuel de l'homme*

1940S
... Wilhelm Reich laisse entendre que les désirs sexuels refoulés pourraient provoquer le cancer.

1941
... A New York, diffusion de la première télévision commerciale.
... Le général Hideki Tojo devient le Premier ministre du Japon.
... Le Japon bombarde Pearl Harbor à Hawaï ; les Etats-Unis déclarent la guerre au Japon.
... Aux Etats-Unis, les magazines patriotiques, sans nudité, remplacent les titres sophistiqués des années trente qui contenaient du nu.
... Robert Harrison publie le premier de ses magazines, *Beauty Parade*.

1942
... Entrée en guerre des Etats-Unis.
... Daimler-Benz suspend la fabrication des automobiles Mercedes pour privilégier celle des tanks.
... Kodak invente le premier vrai négatif couleur.
... Naissance de Larry Flynt, futur éditeur d'*Hustler*.

1943
... Sartre publie *L'être et le néant* expliquant sa philosophie de l'existentialisme.
... Le magazine anglais *Men Only* inclut quelques nus discrets pour remonter le moral des troupes.
... L'Italie capitule.

1944
... Paris est libérée.
... Une tentative américaine de bombardement du Japon depuis une haute altitude entraîne la découverte du jet-stream.
... Irving Klaw hérite de la boutique familiale à New York, remarque que ses clients s'intéressent aux photos glamour de nu et commence à leur en procurer.

1945
... L'Allemagne capitule sans conditions à Reims ; Hitler se suicide.
... Les Etats-Unis lâchent des bombes atomiques sur Hiroshima et Nagasaki; capitulation du Japon.
... Le pilote britannique John Sutcliffe, traumatisé par la dévastation du Japon, développe des tenues protectrices fétichistes ; il publiera plus tard le magazine *Atomage*.
... Construction d'ENIAC, le premier ordinateur électronique.
... Création de l'Organisation des Nations unies.
... *Neues Kriminalmagazin*, un magazine policier sexy inspiré par *Kriminalmagazin*, publié avant la guerre, paraît à Munich, mettant un terme à douze ans d'absence de magazines érotiques allemands.

1946
... Inspirée par les essais atomiques américains dans le Pacifique Sud, Paris lance le bikini, d'après l'atoll du même nom.
... Premier festival international du film de Cannes.
... Maurice Bessy, le futur directeur du festival de Cannes, lance le premier numéro de *Paris-Hollywood*.
... Le discours de Winston Churchill dit « du rideau de fer » marque le début de la guerre froide.
... Juan Perón est élu président de l'Argentine.
... John Willie publie le premier numéro de *Bizarre*.

1947
... Jackie Robinson devient le premier Noir américain à jouer dans une équipe de baseball de première division.
... Le mouvement de désobéissance civile de Gandhi chasse les Britanniques d'Inde.
... Fin des pulps *Spicy* et des magazines patriotiques, détrônés par le retour des images de seins nus.

1948
... Alfred C. Kinsey publie son ouvrage révolutionnaire *Le comportement sexuel de l'homme*.
... Le gouvernement sud-africain instaure un système d'apartheid, limitant les droits des citoyens noirs.
... Fondation de l'Etat d'Israël.
... Invention du frisbee aux Etats-Unis.

1949
... Proclamation de la république populaire de Chine par Mao Tsê-Tung.
... Etablissement du réseau télévisuel aux Etats-Unis.
... Des digests sexy et sophistiqués fleurissent à Paris ; ils sont bientôt des dizaines à se concurrencer, *Paris Tabou* étant le meilleur.
... En Grande-Bretagne, le bizarre *Fads and Fancies* prend le relais de *London Life*.

1950
... Le sénateur américain Joseph McCarthy affirme détenir un liste de communistes « avérés » au sein du

YEAR: **1957**. TITLE: **Monsieur.** COUNTRY: **USA.**

THE MAGAZINE OF ENTERTAINMENT FOR MEN
K
MONSIEUR
OCT./50¢
TEXAS TAKES IT OFF— SEX IN THOSE WIDE OPEN SPACES!
J. ROSMINI

50¢
sir Knight
VOL. 1 NO. 5
ADULTS ONLY!
Special Las Vegas Issue!

1957: *Duke*, le premier magazine américain conçu par et pour des hommes noirs paraît pendant six numéros.

gouvernement, inaugurant une décennie d'accusations et de chasse aux « rouges ».
... Déclenchement de la guerre de Corée.
... *Paris-Hollywood*, jugé trop osé pour les kiosques français, est vendu sous le comptoir.

1950s:
... L'expressionnisme abstrait début.

1951
... Les talons aiguilles sont inventés par Charles Jourdan.
... Le film suédois *Hon Dansade en Sommer* (« Un été de bonheur ») déclenche une nouvelle conscience de la sexualité.
... Lenny Burtman édite le premier numéro d'*Exotique*.
... Samuel Roth publie *American Aphrodite*, une ambitieuse revue érotique trimestrielle.

1952
... A Londres, le « grand smog », la chape de pollution qui recouvre la ville, fait 4 000 victimes.
... Humphrey Osmond, qui fait des recherches sur la schizophrénie, invente le terme « psychodélique ».
... Un garçon né dans le Bronx, à New York, se rend au Danemark et revient sous le nom de Christine Jorgensen, le premier transsexuel affirmé au monde.
... Le baron du culturisme, l'obscur Joe Weider, publie les premiers magazines gays américains, *Adonis*, *Body Beautiful* et *Muscle Teens*, puis le titre de pin-up *Jem*.
... Robert Harrison lance le premier journal à scandales *Confidential*.

1953
... Winston Churchill reçoit le prix Nobel de littérature.
... *Spick*, *Span* et de nombreux autres digests modérément érotiques commencent à paraître en Grande-Bretagne.
... Mort de Joseph Staline.
... Alfred C. Kinsey publie *Le comportement sexuel de la femme*.
... Hugh Hefner lance le premier numéro de *Playboy*.
... Samuel Roth est arrêté pour avoir envoyé *American Aphrodite* et le nouveau magazine *Good Times* par la poste.

1954
... William Masters commence ses recherches sur la sexualité ; Virginia Johnson le rejoint bientôt.
... Premiers postes de télévision couleur aux Etats-Unis.
... Les magazines de nu artistique jouissent d'un fort regain d'intérêt aux Etats-Unis.
... Les digests nudistes sont les premiers magazines « d'intérêt masculin » à apparaître en Scandinavie.

1955
... Parution du sulfureux *Lolita* de Vladimir Nabokov.
... Le sénateur américain Estes Kefauver censure les comics, entraînant la mort de tout le secteur des « pulps ».
... Le dictateur Juan Perón est contraint de fuir l'Argentine.
... Buenos Aires produit une abondance de magazines bon marché de burlesque et d'humour.

1956
... Khrouchtchev menace les diplomates occidentaux : « On vous enterrera ».
... Elvis Presley devient la première rock star du monde.
... Lancement des premiers magazines suédois ouvertement érotiques *Top Hat* et *Cocktail*.

1957
... La Belgique, la France, l'Italie, le Luxembourg, les Pays-Bas et l'Allemagne de l'Ouest forment la Communauté économique européenne (CEE).
... Ingmar Bergman réalise *Les fraises sauvages*.
... Le Danemark publie ses premiers digests de nudisme et de nu artistique.
... L'Union soviétique lance Spoutnik, le premier satellite en orbite autour de la terre.
... En Grande-Bretagne, George Harrison Marks lance le premier numéro de *Kamera*.
... *Duke*, le premier magazine américain conçu par et pour des hommes noirs paraît pendant six numéros.
... Au Japon, parution de *Club Kitan*, le premier magazine bondage de qualité de l'après-guerre.
... La Cour suprême des Etats-Unis rend enfin un jugement dans l'affaire de Samuel Roth, accusé d'obscénité. Roth ira en prison mais son procès donne lieu à une nouvelle définition de l'obscénité, connue sous le nom de « test Roth », qui autorise une liberté éditoriale sans précédent. Au cours de l'année suivante, un nombre record de nouveaux magazines pour hommes apparaîtront dans les kiosques.

YEAR: **1958**. TITLE: **Sir Knight**. COUNTRY: **USA**.

PETER
DRIBEN-

Robert Harrison's Whirl of Girls

Robert Harrisons Mädchenparaden
La ronde des girondes de Robert Harrison

In America, conversion from patriotica to peace-time men's magazines wasn't entirely easy. Robert Harrison entered publishing near the end of the war and his titles *Wink*, *Titter*, *Eyeful*, *Beauty Parade* and *Whisper* supplied the bridge. Beginning with *Beauty Parade* in 1942, Harrison's formula took the patriotic theme common to all American men's magazines during World War II and added luridly painted pin-up covers and photo stories straight from the burlesque stage. There was no nudity, but the fetishistic costumes of his stripper

Robert Harrison

In den USA verlief die Umstellung von Patriotika auf Männermagazine in Friedenszeiten nicht ganz reibungslos. Gegen Ende des Krieges erschien Robert Harrison auf der Szene und schlug mit seinen Magazinen *Wink*, *Titter*, *Eyeful*, *Beauty Parade* und *Whisper* eine Brücke. Er begann 1942 mit *Beauty Parade* und ergänzte den patriotischen Grundtenor, den alle Magazine während des Krieges gemein hatten, mit knalligen Pin-up-Illustrationen auf dem Cover und Fotostorys aus dem Varietémilieu. Es gab keine Nackten, aber die fetischistischen Kostüme der Stripperinnen-Modelle machten das mehr als wett.

Es war die Ära des Beines, schon allein deswegen, weil das der einzige erotische Teil einer Frau war, den man von Gesetz wegen enthüllen durfte. Die Beine wurden herausgestellt und glorifiziert, in Netzstrümpfe gehüllt und auf High Heels gestellt, von deren luftigen Höhen sie in Harrisons Magazinen auch gerne abstürzten. Seine Fotos waren reiner Slapstick, bei dem Frauen in extravaganter Unterwäsche mit Peitsche, Gewehr und Lasso ausgestopfte Raubtiere bändigten, von Küchenstühlen in Pappmachéozeane sprangen, miteinander boxten, rangen und sich gegenseitig fesselten – wenn sie nicht gerade Harrison selbst fesselten.

Wie viele Girlie-Verleger nach ihm hatte Robert Harrison eine exhibitionisti-

Après leur élan patriotique, les magazines de charme américains eurent quelques difficultés à se réadapter à la paix. Robert Harrison entra dans l'édition à la fin de la guerre et ses titres, *Wink*, *Titter*, *Eyeful*, *Beauty Parade* et *Whisper* assurèrent la transition. Se lançant avec *Beauty Parade* en 1942, Harrison reprit le thème patriotique commun à toutes les revues pendant la seconde guerre mondiale auquel il ajouta des couvertures aux pin-up joyeusement colorées et des histoires en photos directement empruntées au théâtre burlesque américain. Il n'y avait pas de nudité mais cette absence était large-

Harrison took the patriotic theme and added luridly painted pin-up covers.

ment compensée par les tenues fétichistes des modèles. C'était l'ère de la jambe, uniquement parce que c'était le seul aspect érotique de la femme que l'on pouvait dévoiler légalement. Les jambes étaient exagérées et glorifiées, enveloppées dans des bas résille et juchées sur des talons vertigineux. Dans les magazines d'Harrison, elles trébuchaient souvent.

YEAR: **1954.** TITLE: **Flirt.**
ARTIST: **Peter Driben.** COUNTRY: **USA.**

Year: **1954.** Title: **Wink.**
Artist: **Peter Driben.** Country: **USA.**

There was no nudity, but the fetishistic costumes of his stripper models more than made up for it.

models more than made up for it. This was the age of the leg, only because it was the one erotic aspect of a woman that could be legally revealed. Legs were exaggerated and glorified, covered in fishnets and propped on the highest heels. And in Harrison's magazines they routinely toppled off those heels. His photos were all slapstick skits where women in flamboyant undies tamed taxidermied beasts with whip, gun and lariat, dived off kitchen chairs into crepe paper oceans, boxed and wrestled and tied each other up – when they weren't tying up Harrison himself. Robert Harrison, like many girlie publishers to follow, had an exhibitionist streak. He loved playing the baggy-panted buffoon in his own photo shoots, teased and spurned by Bettie Page, Carole Landis, Dagmar, and Lili St Cyr, the comic loser familiar to all burlesque fans.

By the 50s Harrison's brand of burlesque was looking dated. Men expected photo covers and nudity. Rather than change his style Harrison gave up girlies altogether for what would be his biggest success, and total undoing. The prototype was *Whisper*. Its first issue had a Peter Driben-painted cover like Harrison's other magazines, but mixed in with the burlesque were stories of real sleaze and scandal. When his other girlies began to falter, *Whisper* prospered. And when the US government began a very public investigation of organized crime in 1952, Harrison noted *Whisper's* success and was inspired to start a new magazine based entirely on the burlesque of real life: crime, scandal and celebrity gossip. He called it *Confidential*, and by 1956 it was selling four million copies a month. It was also spawning lawsuits.

Year: **1948.** Title: **Eyeful.** Artist: **Peter Driben.** Country: **USA.**

sche Ader. Er liebte es, in seinen Fotostories den Clown in sackartigen Hosen zu spielen, der von Bettie Page, Carole Landis, Dagmar oder Lili St Cyr angeheizt und dann verschmäht wurde – der tollpatschige Verlierertyp, der allen Varietégängern vertraut war.

Als die Fünfziger anbrachen, wirkte burlesker Stil überholt. Die Männerwelt verlangte nun Fototitel und Nackte. Statt an seinen Girlie-Magazinen etwas zu ändern, gab er sie ganz auf, zugunsten seines größten Erfolgs und letztlichen Ruins.

Der Prototyp war *Whisper*. Die erste Nummer hatte eine Coverillustration von Peter Driben wie Harrisons andere Magazine, doch unter die komischen Bildgeschichten mischten sich Storys über echte Skandale. Während seine anderen Magazine schon kränkelten, blühte *Whisper* auf. Als die US-Regierung dann 1952 eine sehr öffentlichkeitswirksame Unter-

Ses photos présentaient des gags où des femmes portant des dessous extravagants domptaient des bêtes féroces empaillées à l'aide de fouets, de revolvers ou de lassos, s'élançaient depuis des chaises de cuisine dans des océans de papier crépon, boxaient, luttaient et se ligotaient, quand elles ne ligotaient pas Harrison lui-même. Robert Harrison, comme de nombreux autres éditeurs de revues de charme après lui, avait un penchant exhibitionniste. Dans ses propres photos, il aimait se mettre en scène en pitre en culotte bouffante, aguiché puis éconduit par Bettie Page, Carole Landis, Dagmar et Lili St. Cyr, incarnant le looser cher aux amateurs de comique burlesque.

Dans les années cinquante, ce type de farce était tombé en désuétude. Les hommes voulaient des photos en couverture et de la nudité. Plutôt que de changer de style, Harrison abandonna alors complètement les pin-up pour ce qui allait être son plus grand succès … et sa perte. Le prototype fut *Whipser*. Son premier numéro arborait une illustration de Peter Driben en couverture, comme les autres magazines d'Harrison, mais ses gags burlesques se mêlaient à des faits divers sordides et des scandales. Lorsque ses autres magazines de charme périclitèrent, *Whipser* prospéra. Puis, quand le gouvernement américain monta une enquête très publique sur le crime organisé en 1952, Harrison, fort du succès de *Whisper*, décida de lancer un nouveau titre basé entièrement sur le côté vaudevillesque de la vie : crimes, scandales et potins de célébrités. Il le baptisa *Confidential*. Dès 1956, il en vendait quatre millions d'exemplaires par mois. Il s'attira aussi des procès. Harrison apprit vite l'inconvénient de cibler des stars : elles avaient les

WINK
A Whirl of Girls
PDC
FEB.
25¢
SORRY WRONG NUMBER
SORRY WRONG NUMBER
BANNED...IN PARIS!
See Page 12

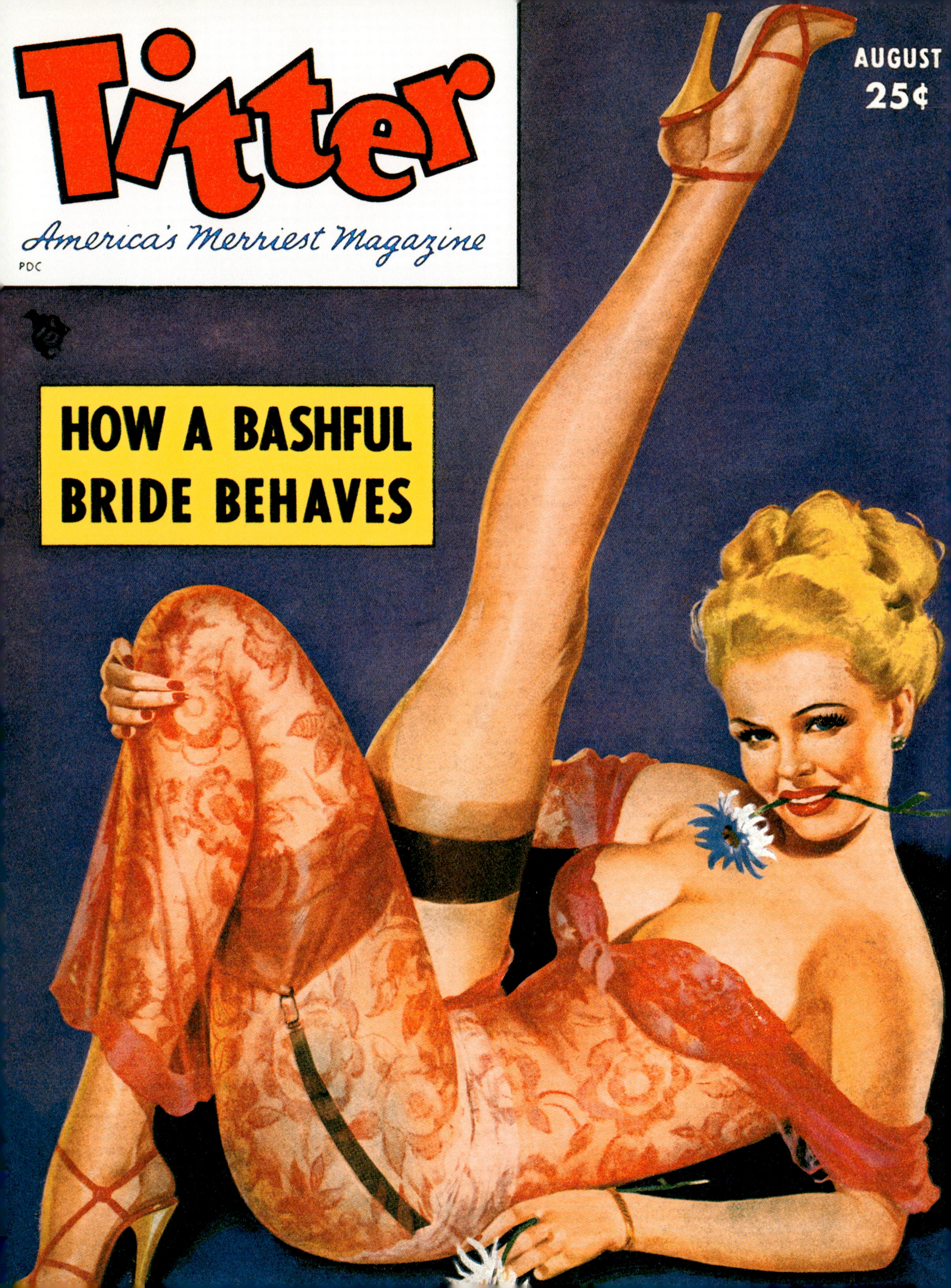
Titter
America's Merriest Magazine
PDC
AUGUST
25¢
HOW A BASHFUL BRIDE BEHAVES

Year: **1952.** Title: **Titter.**
Artist: **Peter Driben.** Country: **USA.**

Legs were exaggerated and glorified, covered in fishnets and propped on the highest heels.

Harrison soon learned the downside of targeting celebrities: they could afford good lawyers. In 1958, facing financial ruin, he was forced to sell *Confidential* and *Whisper*. His other magazines had already been retired. Harrison's final years were spent cranking out one shots; single issue specialty magazines on the scandal of the moment. It's tempting to say he died a bitter man, but by the time of his death he had slipped into such obscurity his state of mind is not known.

All Harrison publications are ardently collected today. Most buy them just for the cover art by pin-up legends Earl Moran, Peter Driben and Billy De Vorrs, but to frame these magazines is to lose out on all the raucous, quirky pleasure contained within. Open your magazines, turn the oversized pages, and see Robert Harrison's peculiar personality, with all its tics and obsessions, come back to life.

Year: **1955.** Title: **Beauty Parade.** Country: **USA.**

suchung über das organisierte Verbrechen einleitete, besann sich Harrison auf den Erfolg von *Whisper* und kam auf die Idee, ein neues Magazin zu publizieren, das sich ganz der Burleske des wirklichen Lebens widmete: Verbrechen, Skandalen und Tratsch über Prominente. Er nannte es *Confidential*, und 1956 lag die verkaufte Auflage bereits bei vier Millionen Heften im Monat.

Allerdings zog es auch Prozesse nach sich. Harrison musste bald erfahren, dass es seine Schattenseiten hatte, wenn man Prominente attackierte: die konnten sich erstklassige Rechtsanwälte leisten. Den finanziellen Ruin vor Augen, musste er 1958 *Whisper* und *Confidential* verkaufen. Seine anderen Magazine waren da bereits eingestellt.

In seinen letzten Jahren brachte Harrison nur noch so genannte One-Shots auf den Markt, Sonderausgaben, die sich einem aktuellen Skandal widmeten. Man wäre versucht zu sagen, dass er als verbitterter Mensch starb, doch zur Zeit seines Todes war er bereits so in Vergessenheit geraten, dass niemand etwas über seine seelische Verfassung weiß.

Alle Publikationen von Robert Harrison sind heute heiß begehrte Sammlerstücke. Die meisten kaufen sie in erster Linie wegen der Titelbilder von legendären Pin-up-Künstlern wie Earl Moran, Peter Driben oder Billy de Vorrs, aber wenn man sich diese Magazine einrahmt, entgehen einem die ganzen derben, schrulligen Späße darin. Schlagen Sie die Hefte auf und erleben Sie, wie Robert Harrisons seltsame Persönlichkeit mit all ihren Marotten und Obsessionen wieder zum Leben erwacht.

Year: **1954.** Title: **Whisper.** Country: **USA.**

moyens de s'offrir de bons avocats. En 1958, menacé de faillite, il dut vendre *Confidential* et *Whisper*. Ses autres magazines avaient déjà disparu. Harrison passa ses dernières années à tenter de refaire surface, lançant des numéros uniques de magazines spécialisés dans le dernier scandale du jour. Il est tentant de dire qu'il est mort rongé par l'amertume mais, en vérité, à l'époque de son décès, il avait sombré dans l'anonymat le plus complet et on ignore son état d'esprit.

Aujourd'hui, toutes les publications d'Harrison sont très prisées des collectionneurs. On les recherche surtout pour leurs couvertures de pin-up signées d'illustrateurs de légende tels qu'Earl Moran, Peter Driben et Billy De Vorrs. Toutefois, les encadrer serait perdre tout le plaisir décalé et chahuteur contenu entre leurs pages. Ouvrez-les donc, feuilletez leurs grandes pages et découvrez la personnalité singulière de Robert Harrison, avec ses tics et ses obsessions.

Show Girl

Cowgirl

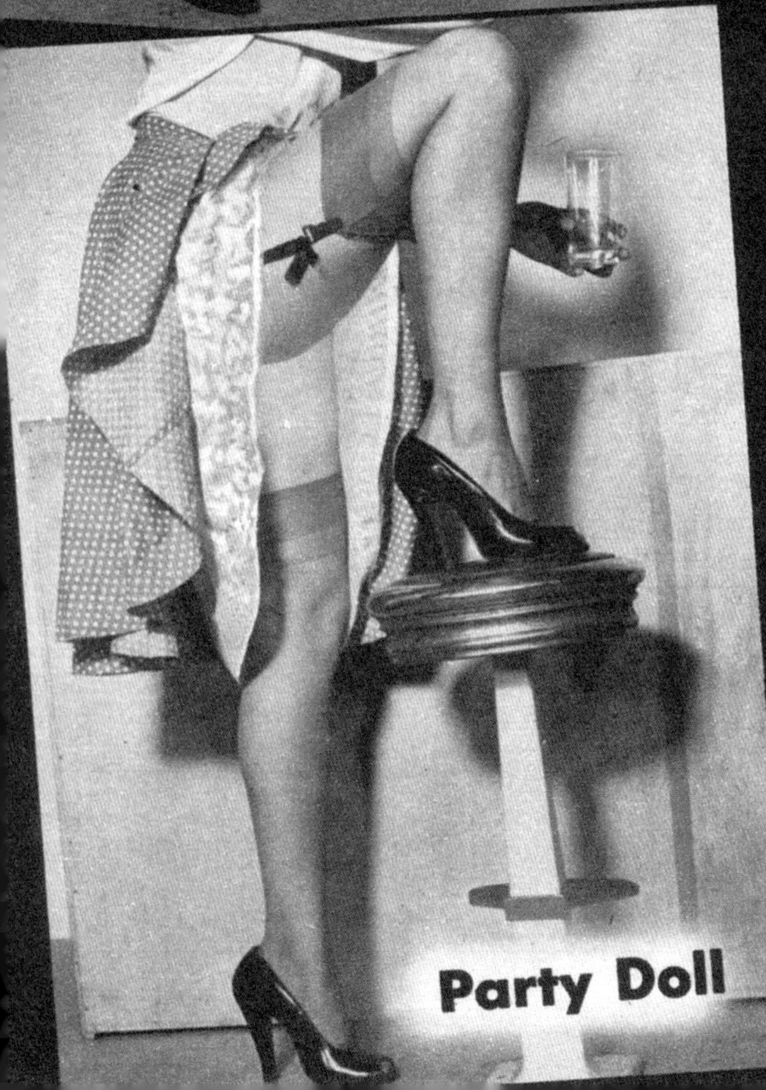

Party Doll

Career Girl

Peter Driben lacked the celebrity credentials of pin-up artists Vargas and Petty, but his leggy covers, this from 1946, boosted Robert Harrison to newsstand dominance.

Peter Driben war nicht so prominent wie die Pin-up-Künstler Vargas und Petty, aber seine beinbetonten Titelbilder, wie dieses von 1946, verhalfen Robert Harrison zum Siegeszug an den Zeitungskiosken.

Peter Driben n'avait pas le statut de célébrité des créateurs de pin-up Vargas et Petty, mais ses filles aux longues jambes en couverture des publications de Robert Harrison (ici, en 1946) leur assurèrent la première place dans les kiosques.

Year: **1946.** Title: **Wink.** Artist: **Peter Driben.** Country: **USA.**

Year: **1940s.** Title: **Wink.** Country: **USA.**

Year: **1949.** Title: **Wink.** Artist: **Peter Driben.** Country: **USA.**

Year: **1955.** Title: **Beauty Parade.** Artist: **Peter Driben.** Country: **USA.**

Year: **1952.** Title: **Flirt.** Artist: **Peter Driben.** Country: **USA.**

Year: **1946.** Title: **Eyeful.** Artist: **Peter Driben.** Country: **USA.**

YEAR: **1947.** TITLE: **Wink.** ARTIST: **Peter Driben.** COUNTRY: **USA.**

PAGE 52 + 53:
YEAR: **1954.** TITLE: **Flirt.** COUNTRY: **USA.**

Eat-iquette

HERE ARE THE LATEST SOUPED-UP RULES ON HOW TO FEED YOUR FACE!

Like pie? Well, keep your eyes open at pie time. There may be a practical joker near!

Corn on the cob is messy, but with Prof. Nutt's new gadget (only $5.59) anybody can manage the stuff!

GET ENOUGH TO EAT these days, chum? Know how to eat it? Sure? Styles of eatin' are changing, pal, so you better listen and get hep!

For instance, soup. It's almost impossible to eat it with a spoon without half of it falling on the old vest!

Now, with our new method, injectin' the tricky stuff into your arm, you avoid that!

Try these new methods, and save yourself headaches!

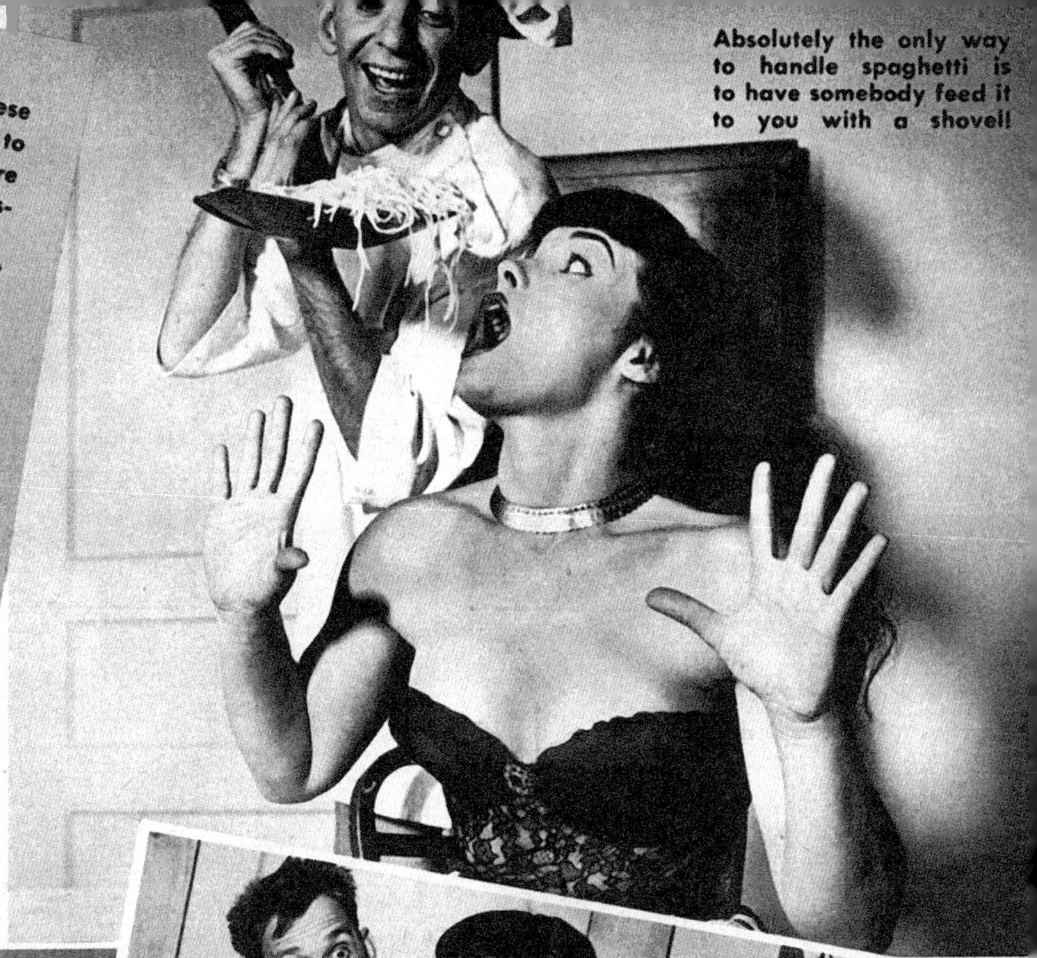

Absolutely the only way to handle spaghetti is to have somebody feed it to you with a shovel!

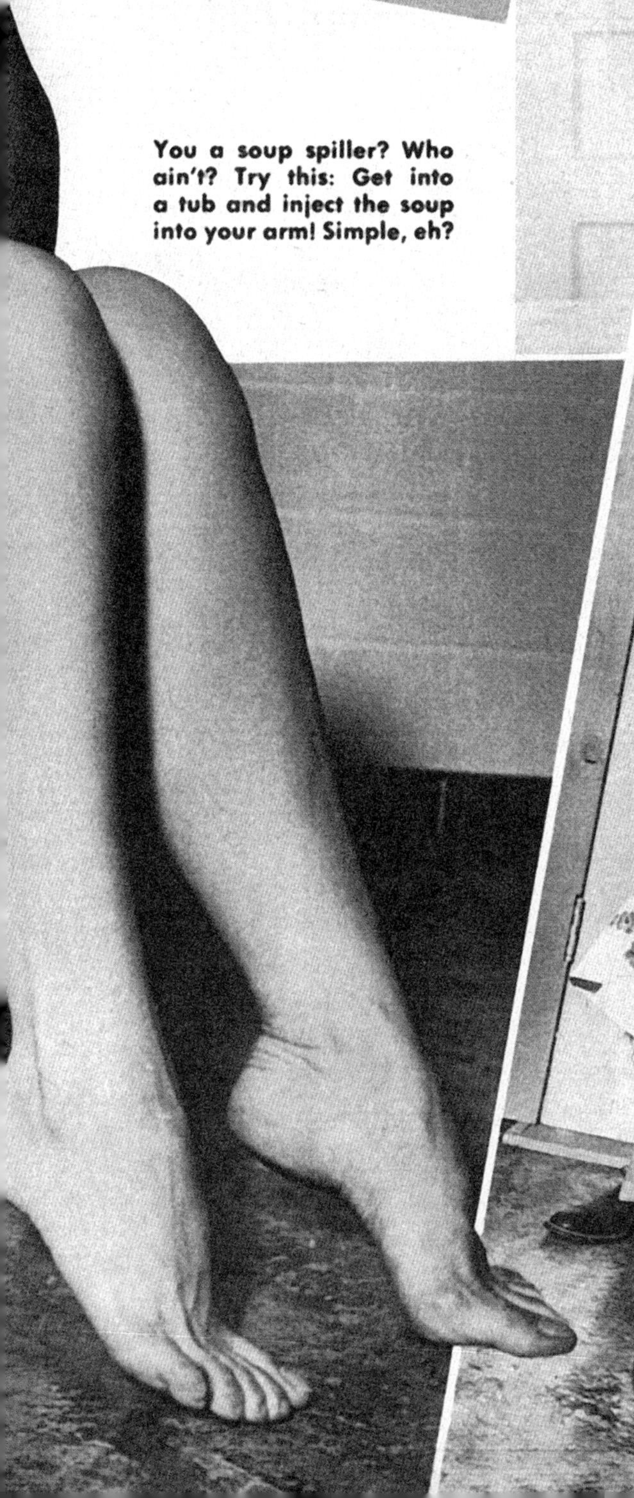

You a soup spiller? Who ain't? Try this: Get into a tub and inject the soup into your arm! Simple, eh?

Like apples? Why not try ducking for them 'n have fun while you eat, chum?

Flirt, Wink, Titter et al were in decline by the time of this 1954 issue, with more sophisticated magazines like Playboy replacing the slapstick burlesque titles.

Flirt, Wink, Titter und Konsorten waren bereits alle auf dem absteigenden Ast, als diese Ausgabe von 1954 erschien: anspruchsvollere Magazine wie Playboy nahmen den Platz der burlesken Varietétitel ein.

Flirt, Wink, Titter et les autres étaient tous sur le déclin à l'époque de ce numéro de 1954, des magazines plus sophistiqués comme Playboy prenant le pas sur les titres de blagues et de gags.

YEAR: **1954.** TITLE: **Flirt.** ARTIST: **Peter Driben.** COUNTRY: **USA.**

YEAR: **1947.** TITLE: **Flirt.**
COUNTRY: **USA.**

This is the end! I spank I go home!
Never mind her man, baby. You'll be happier when you've picture own!

YEAR: **1954.** TITLE: **Flirt.** COUNTRY: **USA.**

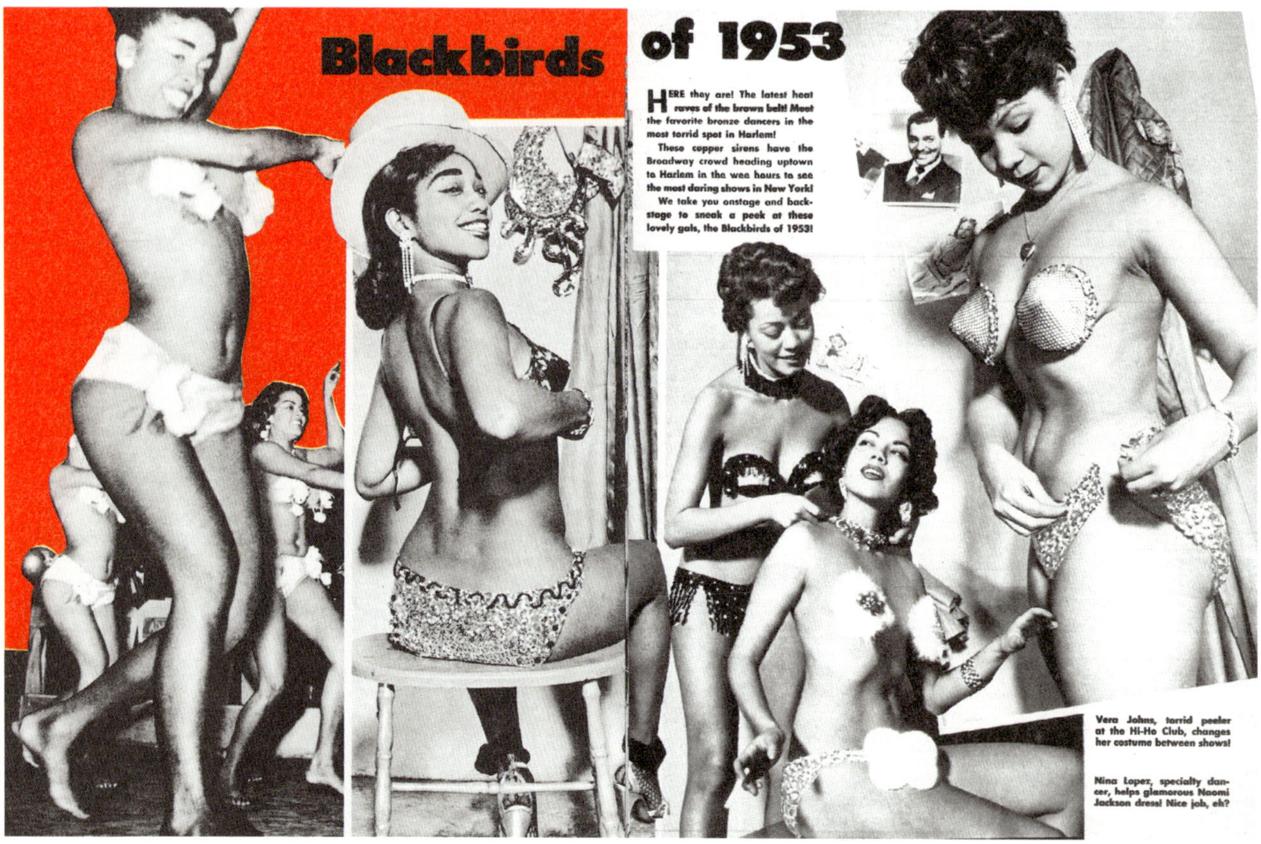

YEAR: **1954.** TITLE: **Flirt.** COUNTRY: **USA.**

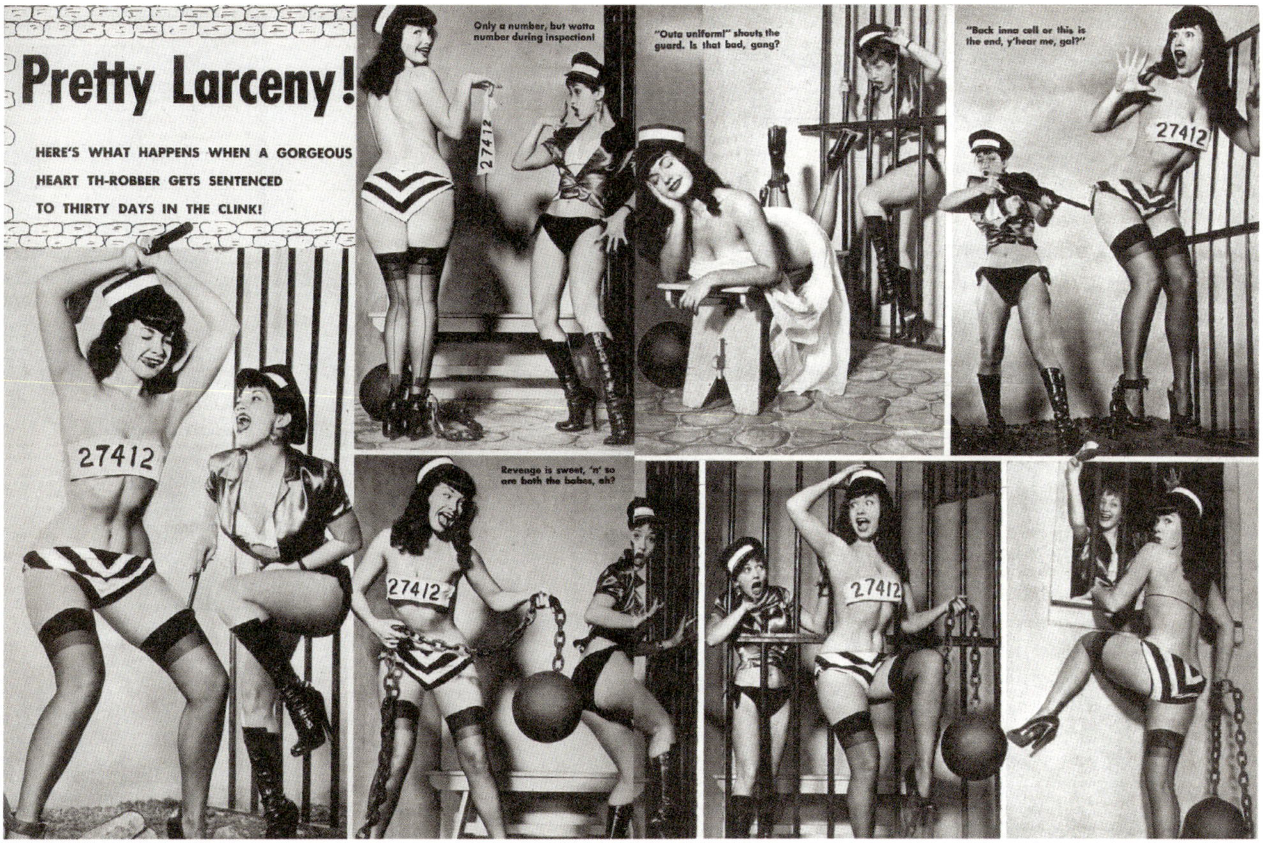

YEAR: **1950s.** TITLE: **Whisper.** COUNTRY: **USA.**

YEAR: **1946.** TITLE: **Wink.** COUNTRY: **USA.**

WILD WOMEN OF BORNEO!
PDC
WHISPER
The STORIES BEHIND THE HEADLINES
JULY
25¢
Exposed:
SULTRY SPIES OF BIG BUSINESS
PETER DRIBEN
• TRIBE TRIES GIRL GYPSY FOR SIN!
• WHITE SLAVERY ON THE HIGH SEAS!
• PRICE OF LOVE AROUND THE WORLD!

Whisper was the prototype for Confidential, the first celebrity scandal magazine and Harrison's biggest success.

Whisper war Vorläufer und Vorbild für Confidential, das erste Promi-Skandalblatt und Harrisons größter Erfolg.

Whisper était le prototype de Confidential, le premier magazine de ragots de stars et le plus gros succès d'Harrison.

YEAR: **1952.** TITLE: **Flirt.** ARTIST: **Peter Driben.** COUNTRY: **USA.**

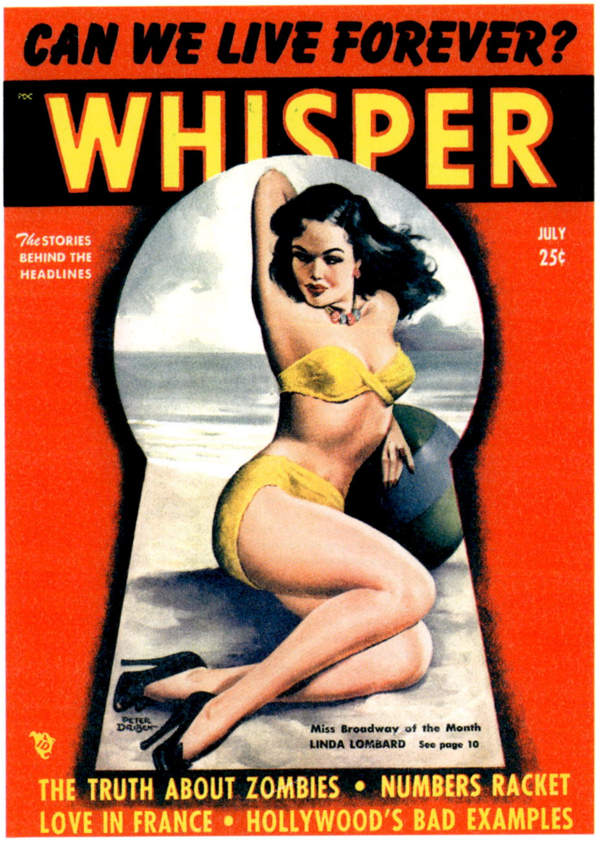

YEAR: **1950.** TITLE: **Whisper.** ARTIST: **Peter Driben.** COUNTRY: **USA.**

YEAR: **1953.** TITLE: **Beauty Parade.** ARTIST: **Peter Driben.** COUNTRY: **USA.**

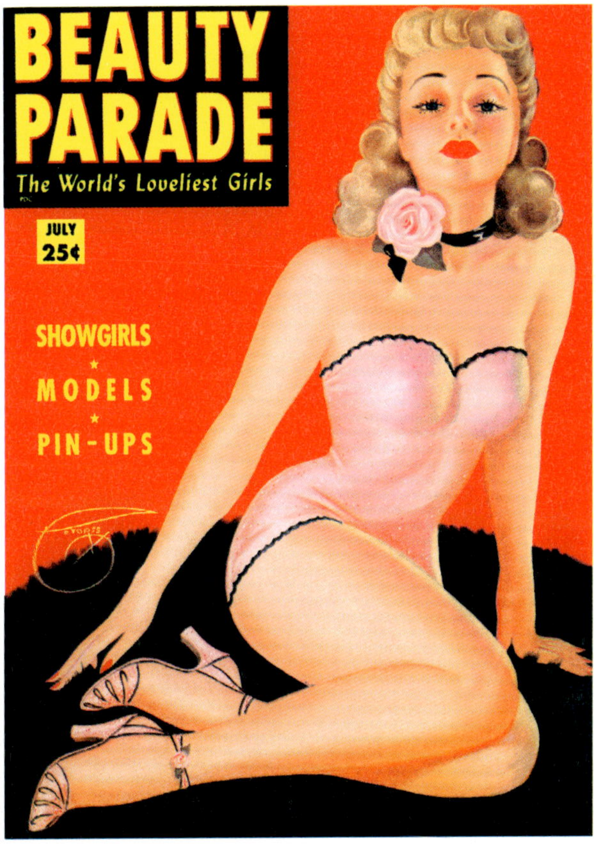

YEAR: **1955.** TITLE: **Beauty Parade.** ARTIST: **Billy De Vorrs.** COUNTRY: **USA.**

PAGE 60 + 61: YEAR: **1952.** TITLE: **Titter.** COUNTRY: **USA.**

LEFT: YEAR: **1953.** TITLE: **Whisper.** ARTIST: **Peter Driben.** COUNTRY: **USA.**

1

"Gooneth! Lookth like I've caught Thoulders with his panth down. I'll twail thith cwook!"

2

"This wist wadio'

Dixie Twaythie!

DIXIETH'S the darling of the detective forth, fellers, and when thith female Therlock gothe out to get her man, she sure followth him around! In facth, she's only a shadowth of her fwormer thelf, twyin' to twap a nathty cwook namethed Thoulders, in thith exthiting melodwama called, "The Cathe of the Mithing Panth!!!"

Thith Girl Detective Gothe for Bad Guys!

"wing me a polithe car!"

"He muth be around here. I thmell a skunkth!"

"Oh dear, he'th got himthelf barrelled!"

5

"Don't beg for merthy! It's the hoothgow next!"

"l alwayth knew he had althie thoulderths ! !"

I WAS A WHITE SLAVE IN HARLEM
WHISPER
PDC
THE STORIES BEHIND THE HEADLINES
NOV.
25c
SPAIN'S CULT OF MOON VIRGINS
MEN WHO SLEEP WITH CORPSES
THRU the KEYHOLE

Year: **1953.** Title: **Confidential.** Country: **USA.**

Year: **1950.** Title: **Whisper.** Country: **USA.**

Below: Year: **1954.** Title: **Wink.** Country: **USA.**

Left: Year: **1954.** Title: **Whisper.** Country: **USA.**
Page 64 + 65:
Year: **1952.** Title: **Whisper.** Country: **USA.**
Year: **1952.** Title: **Titter.** Country: **USA.**

A WHISPER HEADLINE FEATURE

Island-studded Celebes Sea is the scene of daring raids like this by Moro warriors in sex slave racket.

WHITE SLAVERY on the High Seas

BEAUTIFUL NATIVE GIRLS STOLEN FROM VILLAGES AND SOLD AS HAREM SLAVES!

(Special to WHISPER)

SWARTHY, cold-blooded pirates, whose prey is not gold but girls, are terrorizing natives of the island-studded Celebes Sea with daring raids on unprotected villages and carrying off lovely native maidens to be sold into slavery.

This brazen sex smuggling racket is causing grave concern to authorities of two governments, who learned recently that the Moro raiders had turned from seizing copra boats and gone into a more lucrative field — that of supply-

CONFUCIUS SAY....

HANG ONTO THESE WORDS OF WISDOM, FELLERS, AND BECOME A REAL WISE GUY!

OVER 2500 years ago, fellers, a smart Chinaman named Confucius made lots of people smarter with remarks like "people who live in glass houses should pull down curtains." Old Confucius sure knew what he was talking about, so pay attention, pal, as our curvy Wing Ding and her partner, Lum Bago, show you witty wisdom!

"Man take woman for better or worse. Woman take

By 1966 Confidential *had already driven Harrison into financial ruin and dropped its celebrity emphasis due to innumerable lawsuits.*

Im Jahre 1966 hatte Confidential *Harrison wegen unzähliger Gerichtsverfahren schon in den wirtschaftlichen Ruin getrieben und längst aufgegeben, nur über Prominente zu berichten.*

En 1966, ayant conduit Harrison à la faillite à cause de ses innombrables procès, Confidential *avait cessé de mettre l'accent sur les célébrités.*

YEAR: **1953.** TITLE: **Confidential.** COUNTRY: **USA.**

YEAR: **1966.** TITLE: **Confidential.** COUNTRY: **USA.**

Confidential®
JAN.
35c
Who's Behind Those
Nudes
Bustin' Out
All Over?

CHERRIES
Those ripe red CHERRIES
Hold hidden dangers.
PRUNES
Prune is a little flirt!
Gets in jams and desserts.
X-???
X ??? An experimental fruit
Yet undeveloped.
PUMPKINS
Pumpkins — when they're round and
Firm they're best of all.
CUCUMBERS
Cucumbers look harmless but —
Are they?
COCOANUTS
Cocoanuts—It takes plenty of paring
To reach this treat.
PEACHES
Many states have PEACHES fine,
But I'll take Georgia's any time.
WATERMELONS
Watermelon — AH . . . .
So big — so satisfying!
A BUMPER CROP
APRICOTS
Apricots I love or not —
Depending on what they've got.
ORANGES
Oranges so round—rich in Vitamin C
Are good for the vision.
CRAB APPLES
Crab apples — if not too green
Are a marvelous treat.
AVOCADO
Avocados are quite all right
For the "educated" appetite.
Variety—They Say—Is
The Spice of Life
CRANBERRIES
Cranberries — every one really is
A delectable bite.
PLUMS
Give me luscious PLUMS and
Let me dream!
PEARS
Nature with man her goodness shares
In the succulent PEARS.
HONEYDEW MELON
Honeydew I love to eat
Cause it's so naturally sweet.

CELEBRITY SIN:

The Scandal Magazines

Promi-Sünden: Die Skandalmagazine
Péchés de stars : Les feuilles à scandale

Robert Harrison deserves credit for inventing the scandal magazine genre, first with *Whisper*, then with his hugely successful *Confidential*. There had been movie magazines prior to these two that dabbled in celebrity sin, particularly the spectacular *Shock* of the early 40s, and detective magazines that documented the transgressions of the infamous, but not until *Confidential* were sex and fame and shame combined to such effect. As with any successful product imitators quickly followed, many creating more sexual, more bizarre scandal magazines than Harrison's, geared to a strictly male market. *Man to Man* was around for years as a general interest men's magazine, but it realized its potential in the mid-50s when it switched to an amusing mix of scandal, flying saucer sightings, freaks

EYEWITNESS REPORT

JIMMY DONAHUE'S PRIVATE *Peek* AT CHRISTINE

. . . If you've wondered about that Jorgensen "girl", the Woolworth heir has the lowdown. Jimmy was there the night the Copenhagen cut-up actually settled, once and for all, whether she's really Christine

By RICHARD DONALDSON

IT'S BEEN YEARS since George Jorgensen went to Denmark and startled the nation by coming back Christine. Literally tons of stuff has been written about the revamped GI since then, but none of all that paper and print definitely and finally answered the big question in most American minds: Was Jorgensen truly Christine? Or was she still pretty George?

The answer's in now, though, from an eyewitness who went to considerable trouble to find out, and who loves to talk about his remarkable adventure with Chris. But it's hard to say which is the more eyebrow-raising — the results, or the fact that the romantic investigation was carried out by one of high society's top scamps, Woolworth scion Jimmy Donahue.

It's true, of course, that the balding social register playboy has always had a yen for boys who liked to be different. When not escorting the Duchess of Windsor and other top-drawer blue bloods to swank Park Avenue events, Jimmy is most often to be found in Manhattan's dimly-lit swish bars, at a table surrounded by lavender lads. On several occasions, in fact, Donahue's larks with gay blades have gotten him into brushes with the law from which only his fat bank account rescued him.

Was She a He — Or Was He a She?

But Christine was a different matter altogether. Or was she? The fact that a tantalizing mystery still exists was demonstrated not long ago when famed stripper Gypsy Rose Lee met Christine at a cocktail party tossed by the wife of columnist Bob Considine. Gypsy had a ribald suggestion for Christine.

"Save your money, honey, and buy yourself a big town house," she recommended, "then if times get bad you can always take in boarders.

"You'll never have any trouble filling the house," Gypsy added brightly. "There are too many who'd be hoping to catch you under the shower."

Presumably, Donahue would have been one of the first to sign up for such housing, because he vowed time and time again to his friends that he meant to get the answer, personally, to the questions about Chris. And just how he did it became the main topic of conversation a month or so ago at an elegant dinner party Jimmy gave in his bachelor apartment on Fifth Avenue, in the seventies.

He got his chance to swing into action one night last spring, when Miss Jorgensen opened at New York's Latin Quarter nightery for a couple of weeks of singing throaty songs and telling slightly naughty jokes about herself.

Donahue got up a party of friends, including one or two who knew Christine, and managed to wangle an introduction after the first show. She sat at his table chattering away until it was time for the second evening performance, which Jimmy also sat through. Then, rushing backstage, he started the wheels of his great investigation rolling by inviting Christine to go driving with him in Central Park. She was delighted.

In telling the story of what followed, Jimmy relates that, once in the car, he tried in vain to get Christine onto the subject of interesting operations. But la Jorgensen would have none of it. She preferred to discuss singing — or her hobby, photography.

Jimmy Had an Idea — and Chris Liked It

After a few fruitless turns about the Park, Jimmy tried a new tack. Why not wind up their captivating first meeting by stopping off at his apartment for a nightcap? Chris murmured it sounded like just what the doctor ordered.

They settled cozily on the sofa in the study of his apartment and Donahue whisked out a bucket of ice, plenty of soda and a bottle of rare old Scotch.

He kept Chris' glass loaded but the whiskey didn't work. There was *still* no talk about interesting operations, so the determined *(Continued on page 81)*

YEAR: **1955.** TITLE: **Confidential.** COUNTRY: **USA.**

Playgirl, not to be confused with the women's magazine, was a tawdry jumble of anything publisher/editor Walter Hale could find for free.

YEAR: **1956.** TITLE: **Playgirl.** COUNTRY: **USA.**

Robert Harrison gebührt die Anerkennung dafür, zuerst mit *Whisper* und mit dem ungeheuer erfolgreichen *Confidential* das Genre der Skandalmagazine erfunden zu haben. Es hatte auch vorher schon Filmzeitschriften gegeben, die sich nebenbei mit Promi-Tratsch beschäftigten, vor allem das legendäre *Shock* in den frühen Vierzigern, und Detektivmagazine, die die Sünden der Berühmt-Berüchtigten kolportierten, doch erst *Confidential* fand die wirklich durchschlagende Kombination von Sex, Ruhm und Schande. Wie bei jedem erfolgrei-

On doit à Robert Harrison d'avoir inventé le journal à scandale, d'abord avec *Whisper* puis avec l'immense succès de *Confidential*. Avant eux, des revues de cinéma avaient déjà fait quelques incursions dans ce domaine, notamment le spectaculaire *Shock* au début des années quarante, ainsi que des magazines policiers qui relataient les écarts de personnages notoires, mais il fallut attendre *Confidential* pour que le sexe, la célébrité et le scandale soient associés avec une telle efficacité. Comme dans le cas de tout produit qui fait recette, les imita-

Year: **1959.** Title: **Glance.** Country: **USA.**

The good thing about masturbation is that you don't have to dress up for it.

–Truman Capote

of nature and pin-ups. *Playgirl*, not to be confused with the later women's magazine, was a tawdry jumble of strippers, Hollywood gossip and, one suspects, anything else publisher/editor Walter Hale could find for free.

Mr. Hale, who used his publications to promote his opinions on almost everything, stated in the space usually reserved for legal and subscription information that "*Playgirl* is published solely for the edification, education, euphoria and amusement of sophisticated adults with an appreciation for the fine feminine artifices, the female figure and the feline fervor of wonderful women. Sissies are advised that the content is shocking and those unable to face the facts of femininity will find no solace in these pages."

Hale published a number of odd scandal titles in the 50s, including *Hollywood Confidential*, *Scandolls*, *Gay Paris Confidential* and *San Francisco Confidential*, providing many years of solace to stouthearted scandal fans.

Fans of nearly nude Hollywood actresses couldn't do better than *Glance*. Not only did it feature great nudist, stripper, celebrity and crime photos, but its ads were among the era's funniest. Chastity belts, sex drugs, handguns and muscle girl wrestling movies could all be had from its back pages. In 1958 the scandal genre took a big blow when Robert Harrison was convicted of printing concocted celebrity stories in *Confidential*. Other publishers backed away from Hollywood, and as the 60s produced more explicit men's magazines the scandal sheets concentrated even more on sex and less on celebrity in their bid for survival. During the 70s scandal magazines

Year: **1956.** Title: **Playgirl.** Country: **USA.**

chen Produkt folgten die Nachahmer auf dem Fuße, und viele davon produzierten im Vergleich mit Harrison sexuell offenherzigere, bizarrere und auf ein rein männliches Publikum zugeschnittene Skandalmagazine. *Man to Man* existierte bereits einige Jahre als General-Interest-Magazin, aber sein wahres Potenzial erkannte es erst Mitte der Fünfziger, als es zu einer unterhaltsamen Mischung aus Skandalen, Ufo-Sichtungen, skurrilen Naturphänomenen und Pin-ups überging. *Playgirl*, nicht zu verwechseln mit dem Frauenmagazin gleichen Namens, war ein ordinärer Mischmasch von Stripperinnen, Hollywood-Tratsch und, so wie es aussah, allem x-Beliebigen, das Verleger Walter Hale in die Finger bekam, ohne dafür zahlen zu müssen. Mr. Hale, der seine Magazine als Foren für seine Meinung zu Gott und der Welt betrachtete, erklärte in der normalerweise juristischen Hinweisen und Abonnementkondi-

teurs ne tardèrent pas à apparaître, bon nombre d'entre eux créant des magazines encore plus érotiques et bizarres s'adressant à un public exclusivement masculin. *Man to Man* circula pendant des années comme un magazine d'intérêt général pour hommes, jusqu'à ce qu'il trouve sa voie dans le milieu des années cinquante avec un amusant mélange de scandales, de témoignages sur les ovnis, d'accidents de la nature et de pin-up. *Playgirl*, à ne pas confondre avec le titre pour femmes plus tardif, était un mélange scabreux de strip-teaseuses, de potins d'Hollywood et, apparemment, de tout ce que Walter Hale, l'éditeur et rédacteur en chef, pouvait trouver gratuitement. M. Hale, qui utilisait ses publications pour diffuser son opinion sur pratiquement tout, déclara dans l'espace habituellement réservé aux informations légales et aux abonnements : « *Playgirl* est consacré exclusivement à l'édification, l'éduca-

Year: **1959.** Title: **Scandolls.** Country: **USA.**

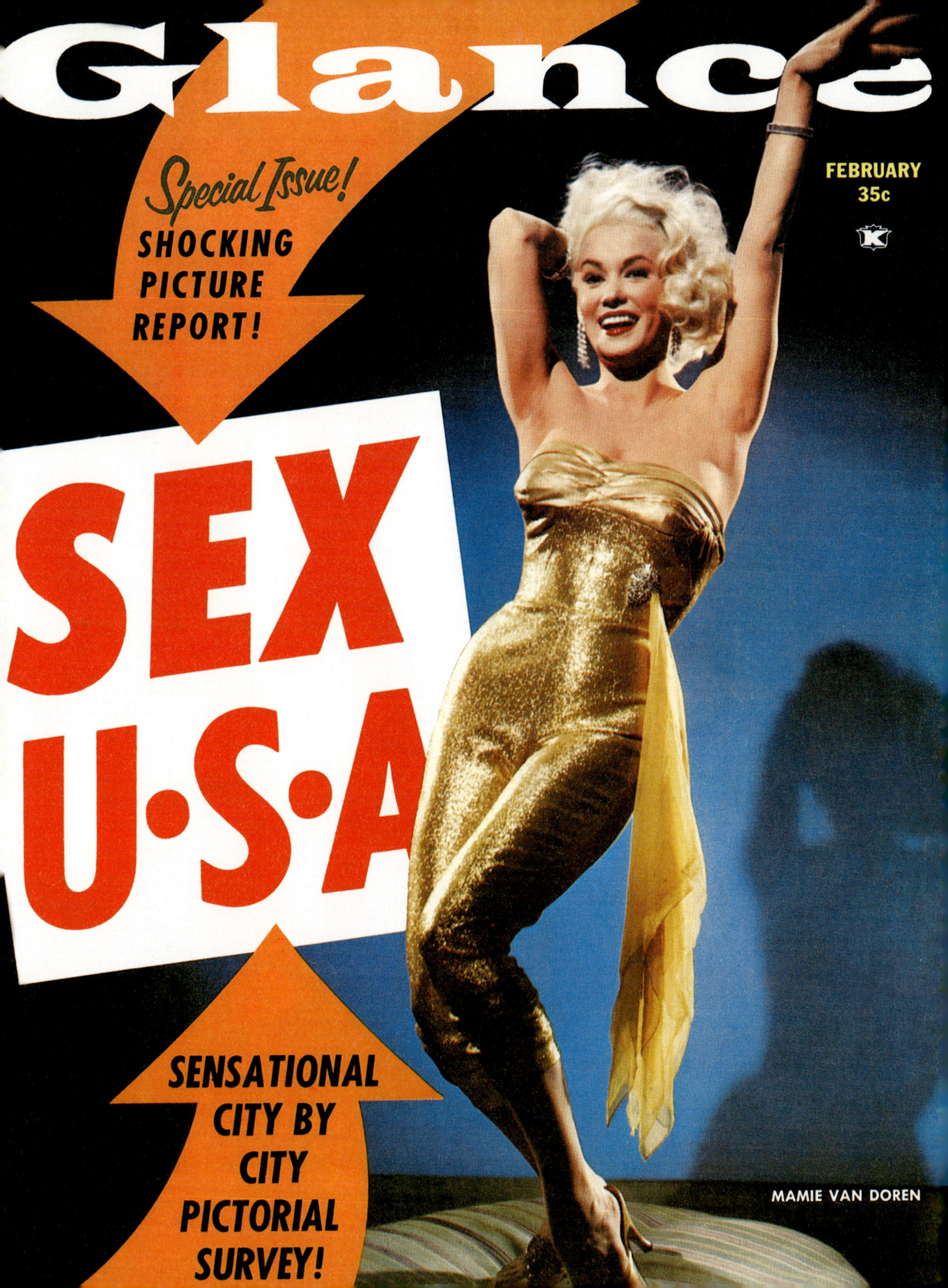
Glance
Special Issue!
SHOCKING
PICTURE
REPORT!
FEBRUARY
35c
SEX
U·S·A
SENSATIONAL
CITY BY
CITY
PICTORIAL
SURVEY!
MAMIE VAN DOREN

YEAR: **1956.** TITLE: **Playgirl.** COUNTRY: **USA.**

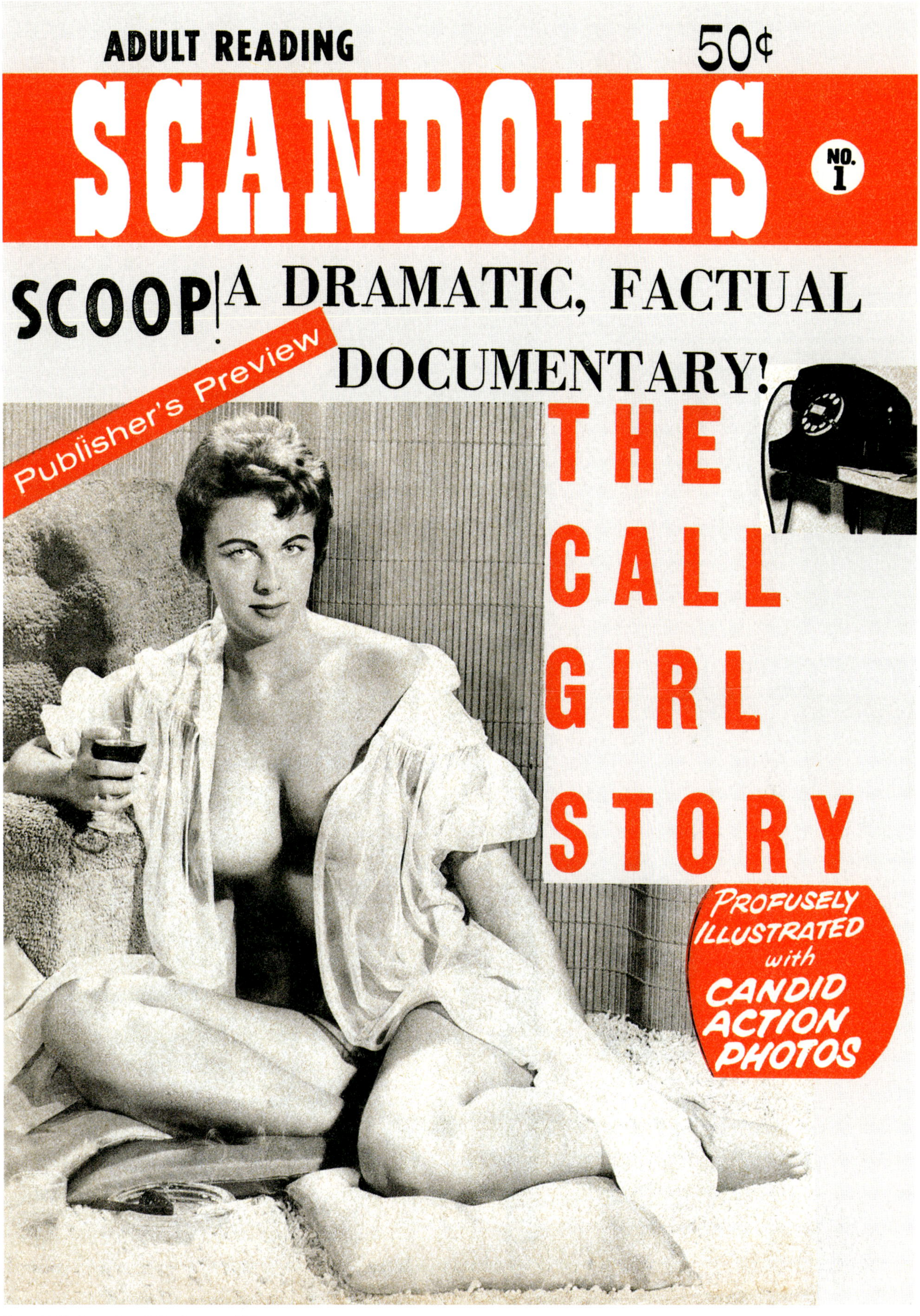

YEAR: **1959.** TITLE: **Scandolls.** COUNTRY: **USA.**

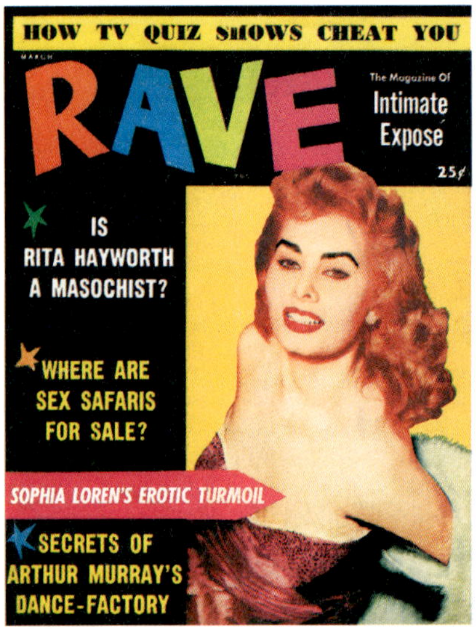

Year: **1956.** Title: **Rave.** Country: **USA.**

reinvented themselves yet again, dumping the explicit sex to become women's interest magazines. Today scandal magazines survive only in the form of supermarket tabloids aimed at America's housewives.

Imitators quickly followed, many creating more sexual, more bizarre scandal magazines, geared to a strictly male market.

tionen vorbehaltenen Rubrik: „*Playgirl* ist ausschließlich zur Erbauung, Erziehung, Unterhaltung und zum Entzücken anspruchsvoller Erwachsener gedacht, die die faszinierenden femininen Ränke, die weiblichen Formen und das katzenhafte Temperament schöner Frauen zu würdigen wissen. Hasenherzen seien gewarnt, dass der Inhalt schockierend ist, und wer davor zurückschreckt, sich dem wahren Wesen der Frau zu stellen, wird an diesen Seiten keine Freude haben.“ Hale verlegte in den Fünfzigern eine ganze Reihe absonderlicher Skandalmagazine, darunter *Hollywood Confidential*, *Scandolls*, *Gay Paris Confidential* und *San Francisco Confidential*, und spendete damit den nicht schreckhaften Skandalfans viele Jahre ebenso viel Freude und Erbauung.

Die beste Adresse für Freunde fast nackter Hollywood-Schauspielerinnen war *Glance*. Das Magazin zeigte nicht nur tolle Nudisten-, Stripperinnen- und Starfotos und Aufnahmen von Verbrechen,

tion, l'euphorie et le divertissement des adultes sophistiqués qui apprécient le raffinement des artifices féminins, la silhouette du beau sexe et la ferveur féline de femmes merveilleuses. Les chochottes sont averties que le contenu de ce magazine peut choquer et ceux incapables de faire face à la féminité n'y trouveront aucun réconfort ».

Hale publia plusieurs étranges titres à scandale dans les années cinquante, dont *Hollywood Confidential*, *Scandolls*, *Gay Paris Confidential* et *San Francisco Confidential*, offrant des années de réconfort à des amateurs de scandales au cœur bien accroché.

Les fans d'actrices hollywoodiennes presque nues ne pouvaient trouver mieux que *Glance*. Non seulement ce magazine présentait d'excellentes photos de nudistes, de strip-teaseuses, de célébrités et de faits divers, mais ses petites annonces comptaient parmi les plus drôles de l'époque. A la fin du magazine, on pouvait tout trouver : ceintures de chasteté,

Year: **1959.** Title: **Glance.** Country: **USA.**

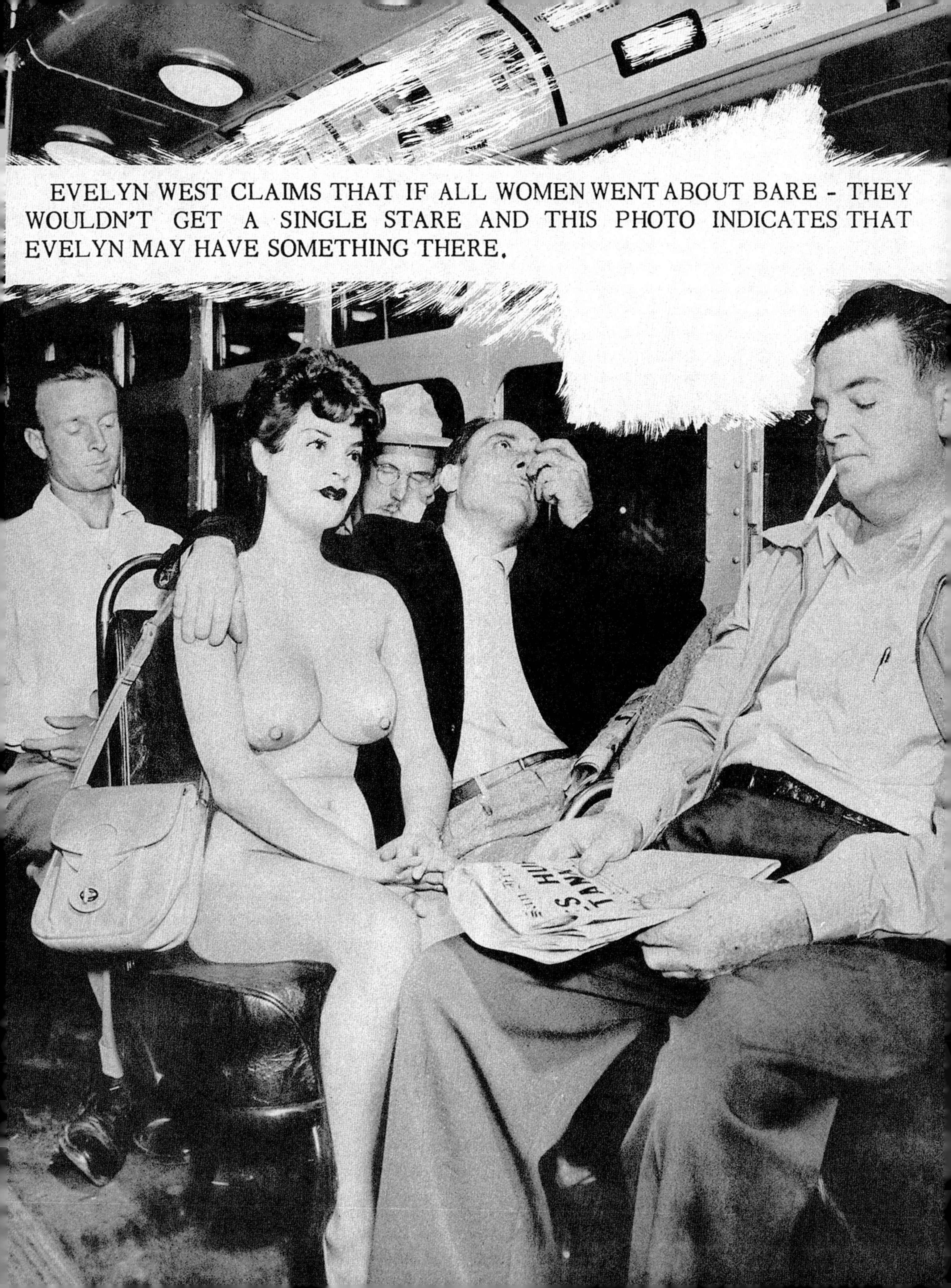

EVELYN WEST CLAIMS THAT IF ALL WOMEN WENT ABOUT BARE - THEY WOULDN'T GET A SINGLE STARE AND THIS PHOTO INDICATES THAT EVELYN MAY HAVE SOMETHING THERE.

RIGHT: YEAR: **1950s.** TITLE: **Male Cry.**
COUNTRY: **USA.**

YEAR: **1955.** TITLE: **San Francisco Confidential.**
COUNTRY: **USA.**

auch der Anzeigenteil gehörte zu den unterhaltsamsten seiner Zeit. Dort konnte man u. a. Keuschheitsgürtel, Sexdrogen, Faustfeuerwaffen und Wrestlingfilme mit Muskel-Mädchen finden. Als Robert Harrison 1958 wegen gefälschter Prominentenfotos in *Confidential* verurteilt wurde, erlitt das Genre der Skandalmagazine einen herben Rückschlag. Andere Verleger ließen lieber die Finger von Hollywood, und als in den Sechzigern offenherzigere Männermagazine auf den Markt kamen, setzten die Skandalblätter noch stärker auf Sex anstelle von Promis. In den Siebzigern lebten die Skandalblätter wieder auf, kamen jedoch vom expliziten Sex ab und mutierten zu Frauenzeitschriften. Heute existieren Skandalblätter nur noch in Form von in Supermärkten angebotenen und für Hausfrauen konzipierten Herz-Schmerz-Zeitschriften.

aphrodisiaques, armes de poing et films de lutteuses musclées.

En 1958, la presse à scandale essuya un dur revers quand Robert Harrison fut condamné pour avoir publié dans *Confidential* des commérages inventés de toutes pièces. D'autres éditeurs s'écartèrent d'Hollywood et, avec l'avènement des magazines pour hommes plus explicites, les journaux à scandale se concentrèrent davantage sur le sexe et moins sur les vicissitudes des vedettes dans leur lutte pour survivre. Dans les années soixante-dix, les journaux à scandale se réinventèrent à nouveau, laissant tomber la sexualité explicite pour devenir des magazines féminins. Aujourd'hui, ils ne survivent que sous la forme de tabloïdes de supermarchés s'adressant à la femme au foyer américaine.

As men's magazines became more explicit the scandal sheets concentrated more on sex and less on celebrity.

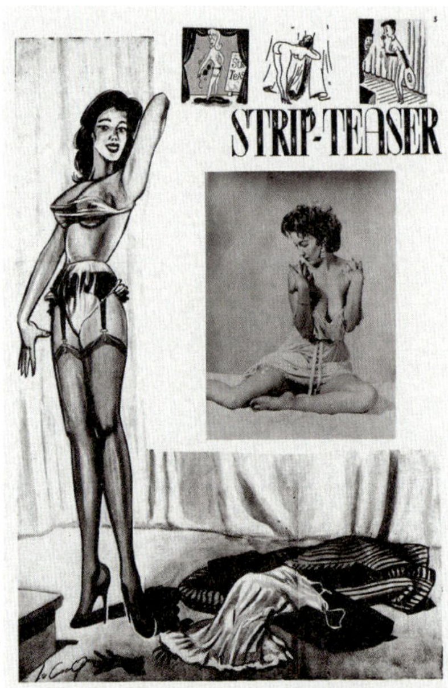

YEAR: **1950s.** TITLE: **Male Cry.** COUNTRY: **USA.**

YEAR: **1955.** TITLE: **Bare.** COUNTRY: **USA.**

The **Male Cry** Combined with

HOLLYWOOD CONFIDENTIAL

ADULT ENTERTAINMENT

PRICE ONE DOLLAR

IN THIS ISSUE:

FILMVILLE LAYS AN AWFUL EGG!

DARING FEATURES

GIRLIE PHOTOS

Sensational Exclusive!

THE SORDID STORY

girl slaves

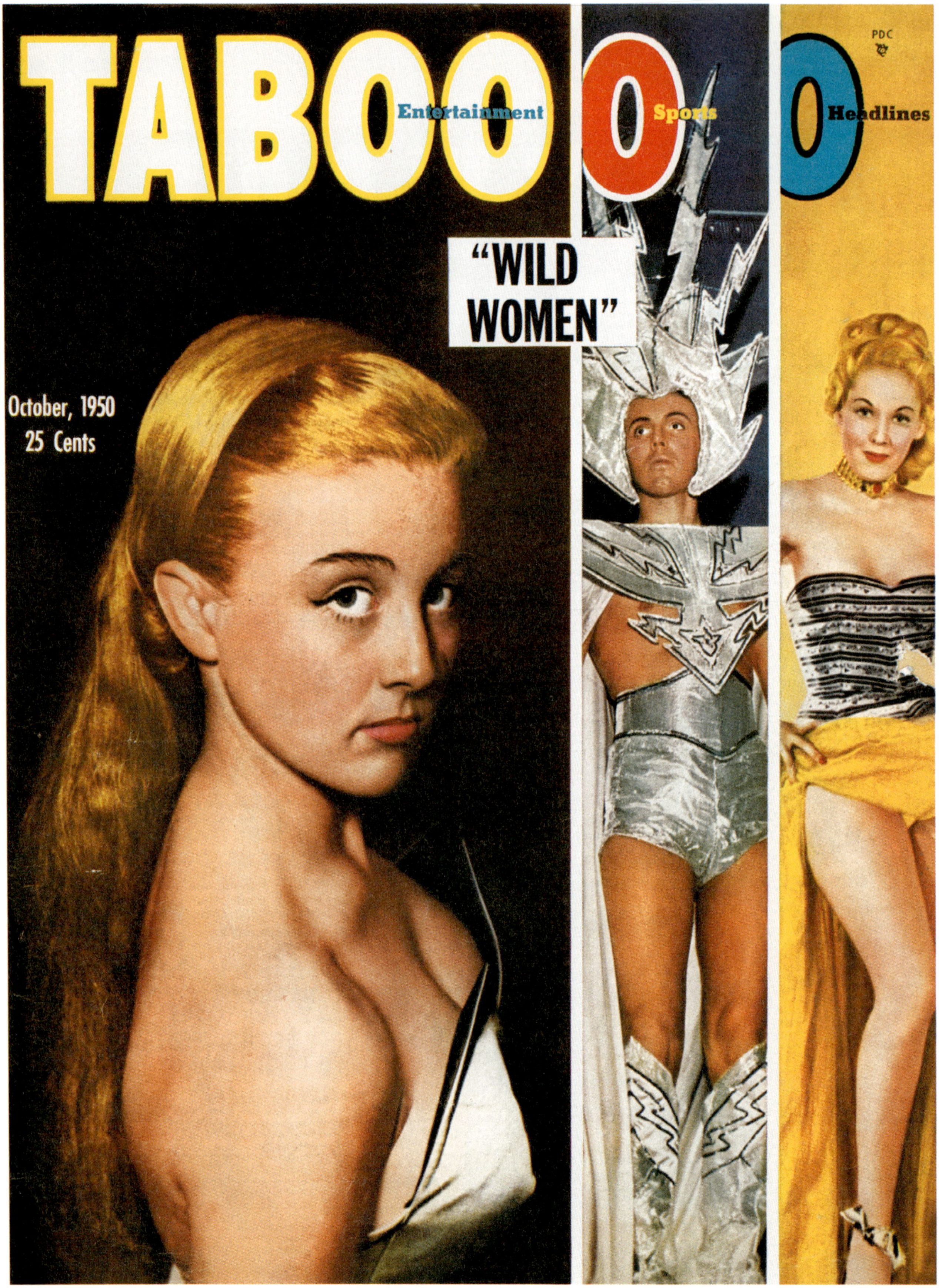

YEAR: **1950.** TITLE: **Taboo.** COUNTRY: **USA.**

YEAR: **1957.** TITLE: **Hollywood Confidential.** COUNTRY: **USA.**

HIS ISSUE: "PARLOR, BEDROOM AND BEDLAM"

HOLLYWOOD CONFIDENTIAL

★ PRICE ONE DOLLAR PER COPY IN U. S. A. ★ ADULT ENTERTAINMENT ★

YEAR: **1955.** TITLE: **Confidential.** COUNTRY: **USA.**

YEAR: **1959.** TITLE: **The Lowdown.**
COUNTRY: **USA.**

WOMEN: BEWARE OF
ESTROGEN: THE DRUG THAT CAN DRIVE YOU WILD!

THE Lowdown

April 25¢ K

THE FACTS THEY DARE NOT TELL YOU

DIANE HARTMAN: *Is She Really A* **Nymphet?**

A Bebop Special: **THE BARONESS AND THE "MONK"**

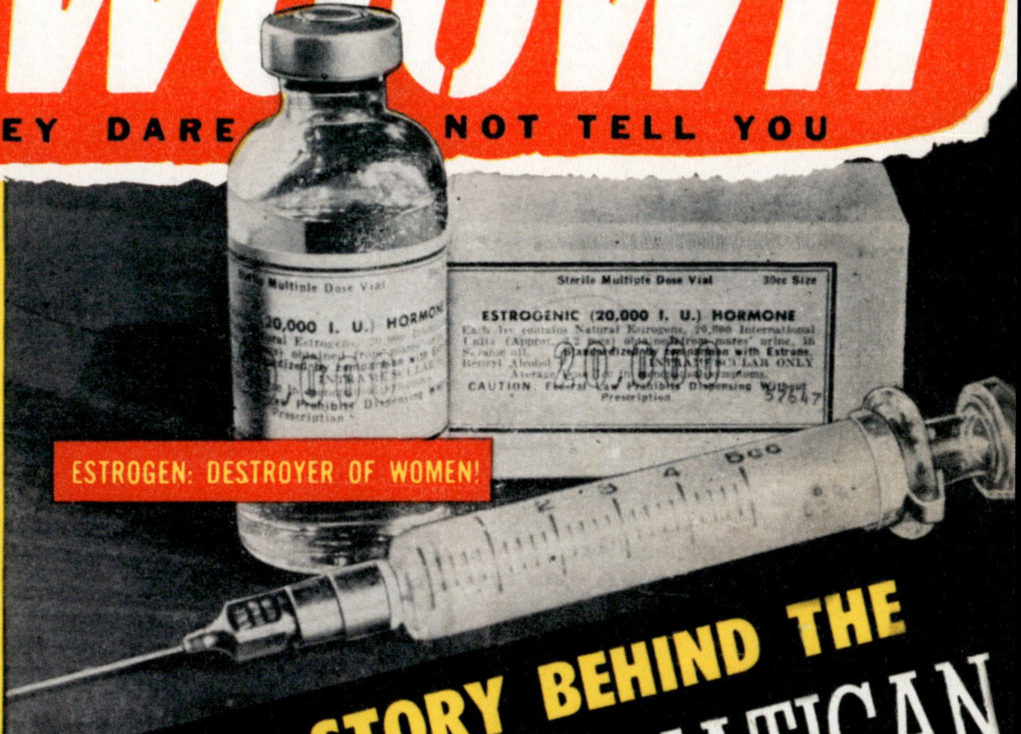

ESTROGEN: DESTROYER OF WOMEN!

EXCLUSIVE: THE PICS AND STORY BEHIND THE ROMAN ORGY that SHOCKED the VATICAN

PAT WARD: *Who Took A Whip To Her?*

ow Important Men Get Framed in the **SEX HAKEDOWN RACKET**

DIANE: SEX PERSONIFIED?

ROMAN ORGY: WHAT HAPPENED LATER?

Year: **1954.** Title: **Man to Man.** Country: **USA.**

Year: **1954.** Title: **Man to Man.**
Country: **USA.**

MAN to MAN
THE ANCIENTS KNEW OF A-BOMBS
YOU CAN STILL BUY FEMALE SLAVES
May 25¢
IS THERE SEX IN THE SPIRIT WORLD?
Lilly Christine

TEMPEST STORM

Year: **1941.** Title: **Shock.** Country: **USA.**

Year: **1940s.** Title: **Manhattan Scandals.** Country: **USA.**

Left:
Year: **1954.** Title: **Hollywood Confidential.** Country: **USA.**

Year: **1959.** Title: **The Lowdown.** Country: **USA.**

Page 86 + 87:
Year: **1954.** Title: **Man to Man.** Country: **USA.**
Year: **1956.** Title: **Crime Confessions.** Country: **USA.**

"Fallouts" of radioactive particles from the A-bomb explosions in Nevada may be dangerous to sex life

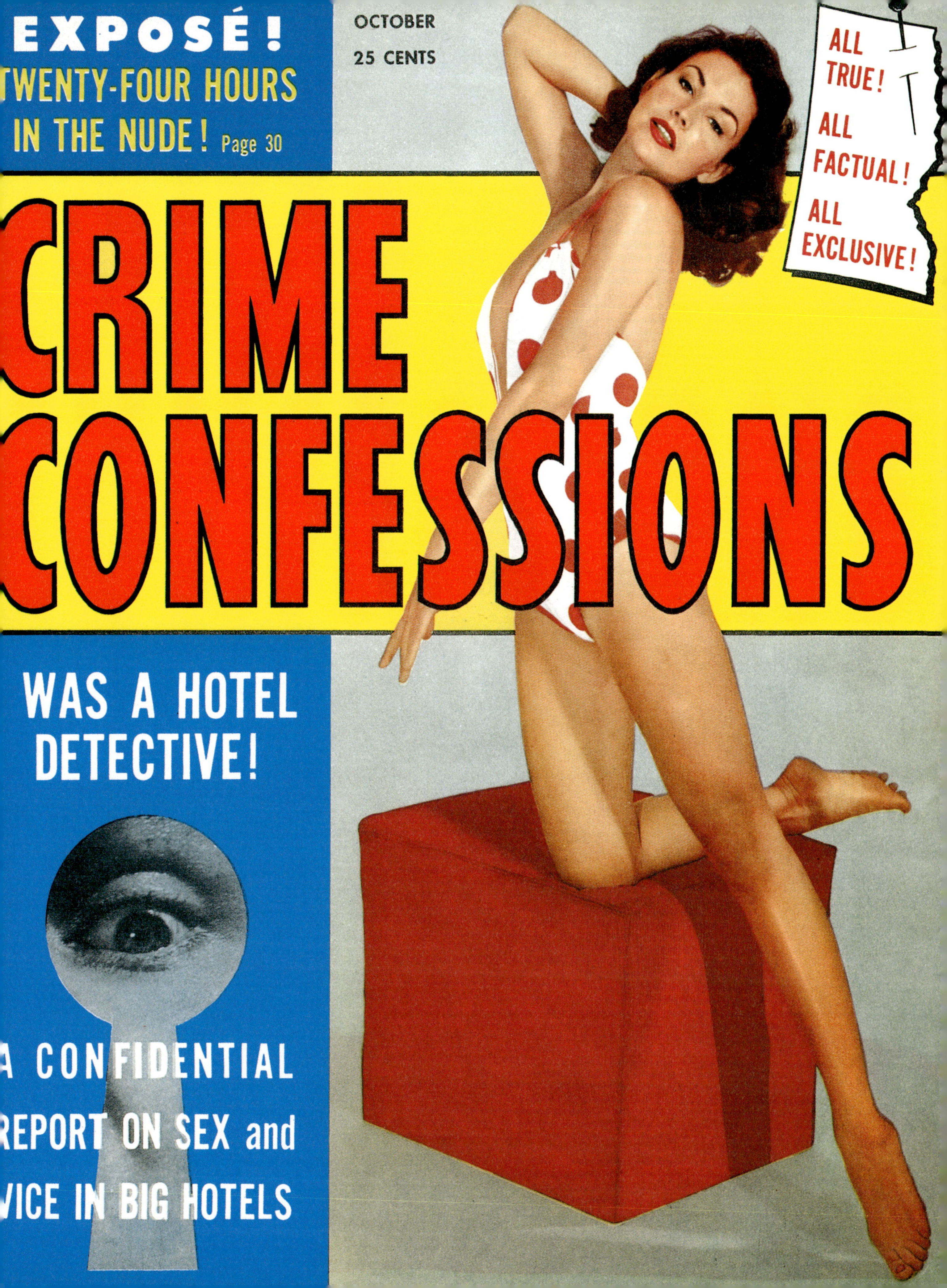
EXPOSÉ!
TWENTY-FOUR HOURS
IN THE NUDE! Page 30
OCTOBER
25 CENTS
ALL TRUE!
ALL FACTUAL!
ALL EXCLUSIVE!
CRIME
CONFESSIONS
WAS A HOTEL
DETECTIVE!
A CONFIDENTIAL
REPORT ON SEX and
VICE IN BIG HOTELS

YEAR: **1956.** TITLE: **Playgirl.** COUNTRY: **USA.**

YEAR: **1956.** TITLE: **Playgirl.**
COUNTRY: **USA.**

GIRLS
YOU
EYE-DOLIZE
NO. 15

SOUTH OF THE BORDER:

Argentina and Mexico

Verbotenes aus dem Süden: Argentinien und Mexiko
Les photos du sud : L'Argentine et le Mexique

Sometimes there seems to be no reason as to which countries produced men's magazines. I expected to find lots of magazines from salacious pre-Castro Cuba. In fact, I found two, and one was postrevolution. I also expected Brazil might be a major producer, but turned up nothing in my search. In all of Central and South America it seems just two countries supported significant publishing industries: Mexico and Argentina, with Argentina by far the leader.

On closer inspection Argentina's dominance is perfectly logical. During the late 1800s the country grew wealthy exporting meat and grain to Europe. This wealth, an excellent climate and turmoil in various European nations sparked an immigration boom that saw Argentina's population grow to 8 million by 1914. Most of the immigrants from Italy, Spain, Germany, Austria, France and the

Like Argentina, Mexico produced far more sophisticated men's magazines in the 1930s than at any time after.

YEAR: **1944.** TITLE: **VEA.**
COUNTRY: **Mexico.**

YEAR: **1956.** TITLE: **Dinamita.**
COUNTRY: **Argentina.**

Manchmal ist es schwer zu ergründen, warum bestimmte Länder Männermagazine produzieren und andere nicht. Ich hatte erwartet, auf viele Zeitschriften aus dem leichtlebigen Kuba vor Castro zu stoßen, fand aber ganze zwei, eines davon aus der Zeit nach der Revolution. Auch Brasilien hatte ich als maßgeblichen Produzenten eingeschätzt, doch ich entdeckte nichts. In ganz Mittel- und Südamerika scheint es nur zwei Länder zu geben, die in nennenswertem Umfang solche Publikationen produziert haben:

On a parfois du mal à comprendre pourquoi tel pays plutôt qu'un autre produisait des magazines pour hommes. Je m'attendais à trouver de nombreuses revues émanant de Cuba dans sa période salace pré-Castro. En fait, je n'en ai découvert que deux. Je m'attendais également à ce que le Brésil soit un grand producteur de ce genre de publications, mais mes recherches n'ont abouti à rien. Dans toute l'Amérique centrale et du Sud, deux pays seulement semblent avoir eu un secteur de publications érotiques de grande envergure : le Mexique et l'Argentine.

En y regardant de plus près, le cas de l'Argentine s'explique très bien. À la fin des années quatre-vingt du 19e siècle, le pays était entré dans une période de prospérité grâce aux exportations de viandes et de grains vers l'Europe. La conjonction de trois facteurs : richesse, climat favorable et désarroi de la population dans plusieurs pays européens, entraîna une grande vague d'immigration qui porta sa population à 8 millions en 1914. La plupart des immigrants, originaires d'Italie, d'Espagne, d'Allemagne, d'Autriche, de France et de Grande-Bretagne, s'installèrent à Buenos Aires, faisant de la ville un grand centre intellectuel et culturel. Durant la Première Guerre mondiale, le pays connut une nouvelle phase d'expansion économique en raison de la dépen-

SALUD • MORAL

Heliópolis

Revista Argentina
de LIBRECULTURA.

YEAR: **1938.** TITLE: **Heliópolis.**
COUNTRY: **Argentina.**

In Buenos Aires beautiful men's magazines appeared after the democracy fell in the 30s.

United Kingdom settled in Buenos Aires, making it a center of culture and education. World War I only helped the economy, as Europe increased its reliance on Argentine farm products. By 1920 it was one of the richest nations on earth. Argentina had a comparatively stable government at this time, which fostered a large middle class, with all that attends such a society, including a healthy publishing industry. German, Spanish, French and Italian publishers all contributed to the stylish look of early magazines. Then, as in the rest of the world, The Great Depression struck in 1929. The democracy fell in 1930, and from that time until the present, military dictatorships have been more rule than exception. It has always been acknowledged that there is one industry that

Mexiko und – viel bedeutender – Argentinien.

Eigentlich ist Argentiniens Dominanz logisch: Im späten 19. Jahrhundert wurde das Land durch den Export von Fleisch und Getreide nach Europa sehr wohlhabend. Dieser Reichtum, angenehme klimatische Bedingungen und die Unruhen in verschiedenen europäischen Ländern führten zu einer Einwanderungswelle, die Argentiniens Bevölkerung im Jahr 1914 auf 8 Millionen hatte anwachsen lassen. Die meisten Einwanderer, die aus Italien, Spanien, Deutschland, Österreich, Frankreich und Großbritannien kamen, ließen sich in Buenos Aires nieder und machten die Stadt zu einem Kultur- und Bildungszentrum. Der Zweite Weltkrieg gab der argentinischen Wirtschaft weiter Aufschwung, denn Europa

YEAR: **1929.** TITLE: **Vida Nocturna.**
COUNTRY: **Argentina.**

dance accrue de l'Europe envers ses exportations de produits agricoles. Vers 1920, l'Argentine comptait parmi les pays les plus riches du monde. Elle bénéficiait aussi à l'époque d'une certaine stabilité politique, ce qui favorisa la constitution d'une classe moyenne, avec tout ce que cela implique. Qui dit classe moyenne dit aussi secteur de l'édition florissant. Qu'ils soient allemands, espagnols, français ou italiens, tous les éditeurs ont contribué au charme raffiné des premiers magazines. Puis, en 1929, comme partout ailleurs, l'Argentine fut frappée de plein fouet par la crise économique. La démocratie s'effondra en 1930 et, depuis ce temps, les dictatures militaires se sont succédé pour ainsi dire sans discontinuer. Il est notoire qu'une seule industrie prospère en temps de crise : celle du divertissement, et tout spécialement du divertissement sexuel qui réconforte les hommes dans l'adversi-

YEAR: **1929.** TITLE: **Vida Nocturna.** COUNTRY: **Argentina.**

Year: **1944.** Title: **VEA.** Country: **Mexico.**

Year: **1952.** Title: **VEA.**
Country: **Mexico.**

VEA

MUJERES · POLITICA · TOROS Y DEPORTES

ROSITA FORNES

No. 384
MARZO 22 DE 1952
$ 1.00
MEXICO, D. F.

There were no more French nudes or political humor, just lingerie shots and "native" nudes, possibly lifted from the *National Geographic*.

thrives in economic hard times though. Entertainment, and especially sexual entertainment, helps men suffer adversity. In Buenos Aires beautiful men's magazines appeared in the 30s. Note how closely the nudist publication from 1936 resembles the magazines from Germany's Weimar period. It's no accident, Germans poured into the country to escape the Nazi regime. The sophisticated erotic humor magazine *Caricatura* predated that, mixing art deco design with French nudes and daring political humor. In 1943 Juan Peron came to power. I have been unable to discover his stance on men's magazines. Certainly he alienated the Catholic Church by legalizing gambling and prostitution, so he would seem to have been pro-sex, but I could find no magazines from his first term in office. As his power declined in the second term magazines again appeared, and many simple, low quality pin-up and humor magazines such as *Ricuritas*, *Dinamita* and *Pobre Diablo* marked the late 50s period following his ouster. The magazines of this period tell how Argentina's fortunes fell following the Depression and years of military rule. The pin-ups and some of the cartoons were pirated directly from North American magazines. There were no more French nudes or political humor, just lingerie shots and "native" nudes, possibly lifted from *The National Geographic*, and comics with vaudeville themes.

Like Argentina, Mexico produced far more sophisticated men's magazines in the 1930s than at any time after. *VEA* was a large-format lifestyle title along the lines of *La Vie Parisienne* and *Berliner Leben*. In 1938 it featured full body nudes with only the pubic region air-

musste nun noch mehr landwirtschaftliche Produkte importieren. 1920 war Argentinien eines der reichsten Länder der Erde. Argentinien hatte damals eine relativ stabile Regierung, eine starke Mittelschicht und alles, was eine solche Gesellschaft mit sich bringt, unter anderem ein blühendes Verlagswesen. Deutsche, spanische, französische und italienische Verleger – sie trugen alle zu dem durchgestylten Erscheinungsbild der frühen Zeitschriften bei. Aber 1929 bekam auch Argentinien die Folgen der Weltwirtschaftskrise zu spüren. 1930 kam das Ende der Demokratie, und seitdem waren Militärdiktaturen mehr die Regel als die Ausnahme. Man geht eigentlich immer davon aus, dass es auch in wirtschaftlich schlechten Zeiten einen florierenden Industriezweig gibt: Unterhaltung – und sexuelle Unterhaltung im Besonderen – hilft den Leuten, ihr Unglück besser zu ertragen. In Buenos Aires erschienen in den Dreißigern wunderschöne Männermagazine. Man braucht sich nur anzusehen, wie sehr die argentinischen Nudistenzeitschriften von 1936 ihren Verwandten aus dem Deutschland der Weimarer Republik ähneln. Das ist kein Zufall. Deutsche Flüchtlinge strömten ins Land, um dem Naziregime zu entkommen. Das humoristische Sexmagazin *Caricatura* ist noch etwas älter; es kombiniert europäisches Art-déco-Design und Nackte im Stil französischer Magazine mit gewagtem politischen Humor. 1943 kam Juan Peron an die Macht. Welche Einstellung er zu Männermagazinen hatte, konnte ich nirgendwo finden. Zwar hat er die katholische Kirche vor den Kopf gestoßen, indem er Glücksspiel und Prostitution legalisierte. Man sollte also annehmen, dass er „pro Sex" gewesen

té. De splendides magazines pour hommes apparurent à Buenos Aires dans les années trente. Il est intéressant de noter à quel point la publication nudiste de 1936 ressemble aux magazines allemands de l'époque de Weimar. Ce n'est pas le fruit du hasard car beaucoup d'Allemands fuyant le régime nazi trouvèrent refuge en Argentine. L'élégante revue érotique et humoristique *Caricatura*, antérieure à cette période, présentait également un graphisme Art déco combiné à des nus à la française et un humour politique impertinent.

En 1943, Juan Perón parvient au pouvoir. Malgré mes recherches, il m'a été impossible de découvrir ce qu'il pensait des magazines pour hommes. Etant donné qu'il s'était aliéné l'Eglise catholique en légalisant le jeu et la prostitution, on peut en déduire qu'il était favorable au sexe en général, mais je n'ai pu trouver de revues datant de sa première présidence.

Les magazines sont réapparus vers la fin de son second mandat présidentiel, alors que son pouvoir déclinait. A partir de la fin des années cinquante, après son éviction de la présidence, l'Argentine ne publia plus que des magazines de pin-up et d'humour peu raffinés, tels que *Ricuritas*, *Dinamita* et *Pobre Diablo*. Les revues de cette période en disent long sur l'état de l'Argentine, passées la crise économique et les années de dictature militaire. Les pin-up et certaines bandes dessinées étaient piratées sans vergogne dans des revues nord-américaines.

Finis les nus français et l'humour politique, il fallait se contenter de modèles portant de la lingerie fine et de nus « indigènes », sans doute chapardés dans les archives du *National Geographic*, et de

Dinamita
año 3 - Nº 35
$3

Year: **1944.** Title: **VEA.** Country: **Mexico.**

Year: **1945.** Title: **VEA.** Country: **Mexico.**

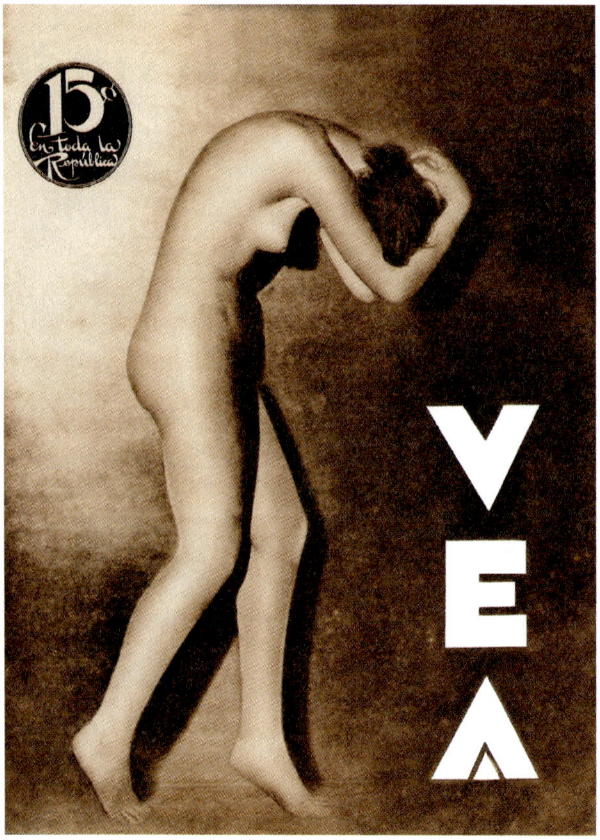

Year: **1939.** Title: **VEA.** Country: **Mexico.**

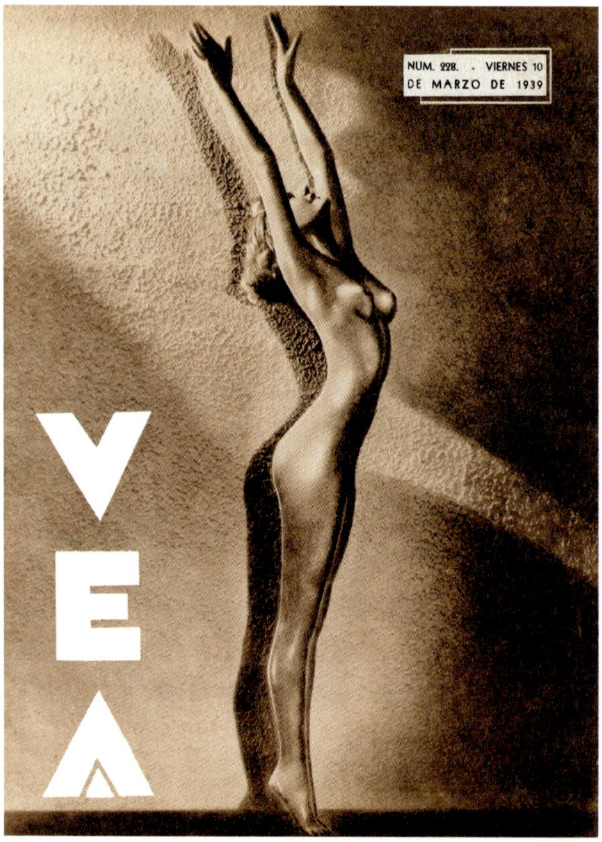

Year: **1939.** Title: **VEA.** Country: **Mexico.**

Year: **1952.** Title: **VEA.** Country: **Mexico.**

LAS FLORES dan el toque alegre al femenino departamento de la deslumbrante Estela Mary.

By 1960 the North Americans really were so rich they didn't much care if *Ja-Ja* and *Dinamita* nibbled their leftovers.

brushed. By 1945 the breasts were covered and most of the content was recycled (probably without permission) from US pin-up magazines. In the 50s *VEA* slipped still further before mercifully disappearing, its pirated photos hardly visible on the cheap pulp stock. *Vodevil* was a 1950s competitor with equally bad paper and appropriated content, but some amusing hand-tinted covers. *Ja-Ja* was the leading Mexican humor magazine of the 50s, with cartoons similar to those in *Pobre Diablo* and great painted pin-up covers, which again, may have been borrowed. By the late 50s even the cartoons were swiped from El Norte's abundant new men's magazines, with Bill Ward becoming as popular south of the border as above.

I don't believe the South Americans simply became larcenous in the 1950s. Working with minuscule budgets, the Mexican and Argentinean publishers spent where absolutely necessary – on paper and printing. When it came to content they rationalized that US publishers were producing more sexy photos than they could possibly track and that siphoning a few off for the pleasure of those less fortunate wouldn't be noticed. And while no US publisher would have sanctioned the theft of his material, by 1960 the North Americans really were so rich they didn't much care if *Ja-Ja* and *Dinamita* nibbled their leftovers.

sei. Aber ich konnte kein einziges Männermagazin aus seiner ersten Amtszeit aufspüren. Als sein Einfluss während seiner zweiten Amtszeit schwand, erschienen wieder Zeitschriften, hauptsächlich aber viele einfache, humoristische Pin-up-Magazine in sehr schlechter Qualität (z. B. *Ricuritas*). *Dinamita* und *Pobre Diablo* sind charakteristisch für die Zeit nach Perons Entmachtung in den späten Fünfzigern. Diese Zeitschriften machen deutlich, wie tief Argentinien durch die Weltwirtschaftskrise und die Militärdiktatur gesunken war. Die Pin-ups und einige der Cartoons waren direkt aus US-amerikanischen Magazinen geklaut – keine Spur mehr von französischen Nackten und politischem Humor, nur Modelle in Unterwäsche und nackte „Eingeborene", die man wahrscheinlich aus *National Geographic* gemopst hatte.

Wie in Argentinien erschienen auch in Mexiko in den Dreißigern wesentlich anspruchsvollere Männermagazine als in späteren Zeiten. *VEA* war ein großformatiges Lifestyle-Magazin im Stile von *La Vie Parisienne* oder *Berliner Leben*. Schon 1938 zeigte es komplette Akte, bei denen nur die Schamgegend retuschiert war. 1945 waren die Brüste jedoch bedeckt, und das meiste Material war (wahrscheinlich ohne Erlaubnis) aus Zeitschriften aus den USA recycelt. Statt mit einem Rest von Würde abzutreten, sank *VEA* in den Fünfzigern so tief, dass die geklauten Pin-ups auf dem billigen Papier kaum noch zu erkennen waren. *Vodevil* war in den Fünfzigern ein Konkurrenzblatt, ebenfalls auf schlechtem Papier gedruckt und mit geklautem Inhalt, hatte aber einige amüsante handkolorierte Cover zu bieten. Das führende Humormagazin in den Fünfzigern war *Ja-Ja* mit vergleich-

bandes dessinées aux histoires vaudevillesques.

Comme l'Argentine, le Mexique produisit des revues pour hommes bien plus sophistiquées dans les années trente que plus tard. *VEA* était un magazine vie moderne grand format dans la veine de *La Vie Parisienne* et de *Berliner Lieben*. En 1938, on y trouvait des nus intégraux où seul le pubis avait été retouché à l'aérographe. A partir de 1945, les seins étaient couverts et la plupart du contenu était du recyclage (probablement sans autorisation) de magazines de pin-up nord-américains. Dans les années cinquante, *VEA* périclita encore jusqu'à finalement disparaître, ses photos piratées à peine visibles sur un papier de très mauvaise qualité. *Vodevil* un des ses concurrents dans les années 1950, avait un papier aussi médiocre et un contenu à l'avenant mais il publia quelques couvertures amusantes teintes à la main. *Ja-Ja* était le magazine d'humour mexicain le plus vendu des années cinquante. Il comportait des bandes dessinées semblables à celles de *Pobre Diablo* et de belles couvertures de pin-up peintes qui, là encore, étaient peut-être empruntées. A la fin des années cinquante, même les bandes dessinées étaient volées à l'abondante presse masculine du « Norte », Bill Ward devenant aussi populaire des deux côtés de la frontière.

Je ne pense pas que les Sud-Américains soient particulièrement chapardeurs. Leurs pays comparativement pauvres vivaient dans l'ombre d'un pays très riche. Travaillant avec des budgets minuscules, les éditeurs argentins et mexicains l'investissaient dans ce qui était absolument indispensable : le papier et l'impression. Pour ce qui était du contenu, ils se disa-

VODEVIL
PARIS MEXICO
REVISTA ARTISTICA
PARA ADULTOS
No. 82
FEBRERO 11 DE 1955
$1.50
MONEDA
MEXICANA
20

Ricuritas
$ 3-
LAS MUJERES MAS HERMOSAS DEL MUNDO
June McCall

YEAR: **1956.** TITLE: **Dinamita.** COUNTRY: **Argentina.**

YEAR: **1956.** TITLE: **Dinamita.** COUNTRY: **Argentina.**

YEAR: **1956.** TITLE: **Ricuritas.** COUNTRY: **Argentina.**

YEAR: **1955.** TITLE: **Ricuritas.** COUNTRY: **Argentina.**

YEAR: **1957.** TITLE: **Ricuritas.**
COUNTRY: **Argentina.**

YEAR: **1954.** TITLE: **Vodevil.** COUNTRY: **Mexico.**

Most persons live more happily with themselves and with other persons if their sexual arousal, whenever it is of any magnitude, may be carried through to the point of orgasm.

–Sexual Behavior in the Human Female, Alfred C. Kinsey, 1953

baren Cartoons wie in *Pobre Diablo* und tollen gemalten Pin-ups auf dem Titel, die möglicherweise aber auch woanders „entlehnt“ waren. In den späten Fünfzigern waren selbst die Witzzeichnungen geklaut, und Bill Ward wurde südlich der Grenze genauso bekannt wie im Norden.

Ich glaube nicht, dass die Südamerikaner in den Fünfzigern plötzlich diebische Elstern wurden. Sie mussten einfach erleben, wie ihre Länder immer ärmer und die USA im Norden immer reicher wurden. Da sie mit minimalen Budgets haushalten mussten, investierten die mexikanischen und argentinischen Verleger ihr Geld nur dort, wo es absolut notwendig war: beim Papier und beim Druck. Wenn es um den Inhalt ging, sagten sie sich vernünftigerweise, dass die Verleger in den USA so viele sexy Fotos produzierten, dass sie kaum den Überblick behalten konnten und es nicht bemerken würden, wenn ein paar davon für die weniger vom Glück Gesegneten abgezweigt würden. Kein US-Verleger hätte den Diebstahl dieses Materials verfolgt, und bis 1960 waren die Nordamerikaner so reich, dass es ihnen ziemlich egal war, ob *Ja-Ja* und *Dinamita* ihre Brotsamen auflasen.

YEAR: **1945.** TITLE: **VEA.** COUNTRY: **Mexico.**

ient que les éditeurs nord-américains produisaient des photos plus sexy que ce qu'ils pouvaient réaliser et que personne ne le remarquerait s'ils en détournaient quelques-unes pour le plaisir des moins fortunés. Et si aucun éditeur nord-américain n'approuvait le vol de son matériel, dans les années soixante, ils étaient devenus si riches qu'ils se souciaient peu de savoir si *Ja-Ja* et *Dinamita* se nourrissaient de leurs restes.

YEAR: **1959.**
TITLE: **Dinamita.** COUNTRY: **Argentina.**

Dinamita
abril 1959
$ 6.-

Year: **1954.** Title: **Vodevil.** Country: **Mexico.**

Year: **1955.** Title: **VEA.** Country: **Mexico.**

Year: **1954.** Title: **VEA.** Country: **Mexico.**

Year: **1955.** Title: **VEA.**
Country: **Mexico.**

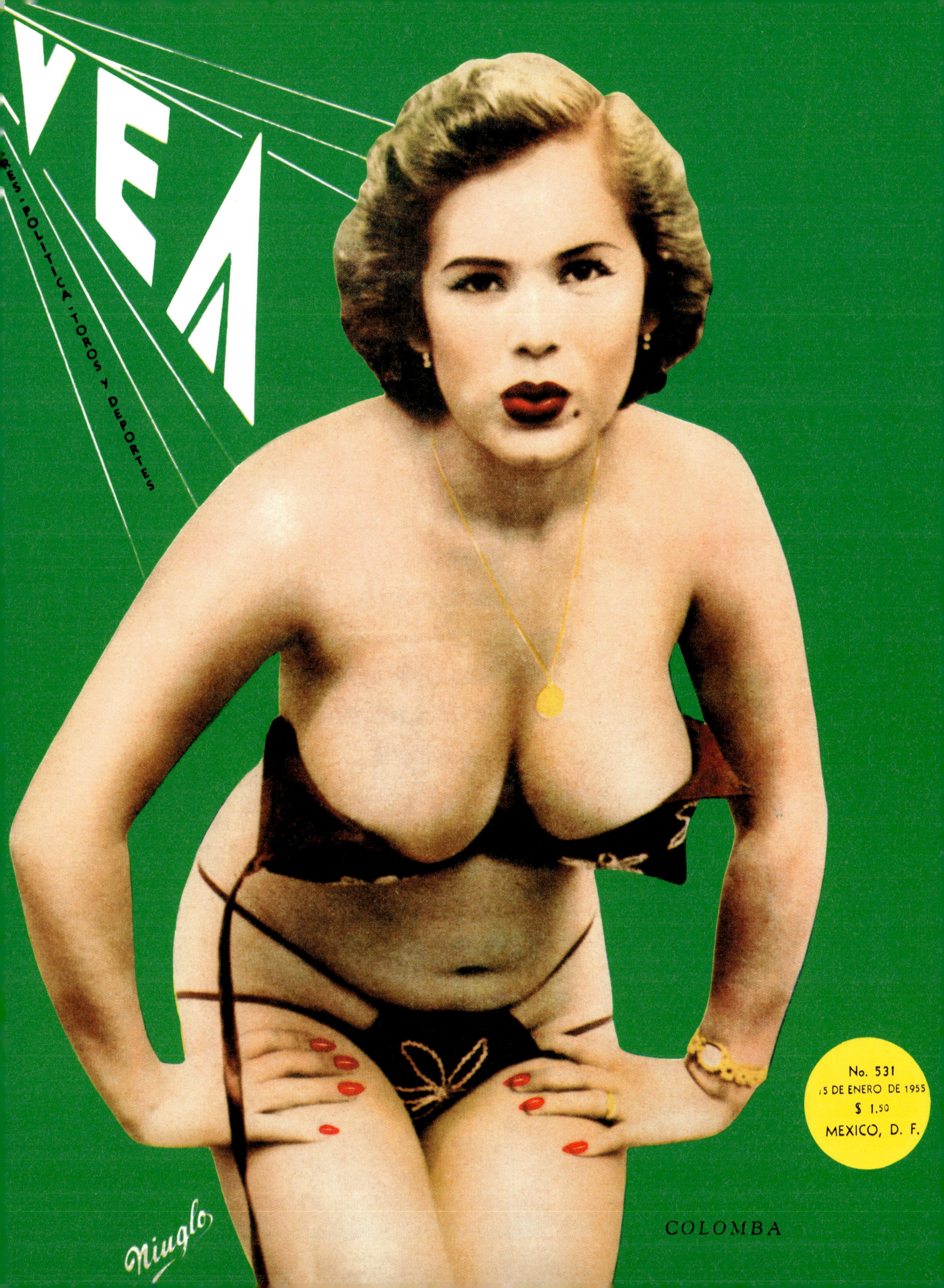
VEA
RES, POLITICA, TOROS Y DEPORTES
No. 531
15 DE ENERO DE 1955
$ 1.50
MEXICO, D. F.
Niuglo
COLOMBA

YEAR: **1955.** TITLE: **Pobre Diablo.** COUNTRY: **Argentina.**

YEAR: **1954.** TITLE: **Pobre Diablo.** COUNTRY: **Argentina.**

YEAR: **1954.** TITLE: **Pobre Diablo.** COUNTRY: **Argentina.**

YEAR: **1954.** TITLE: **Pobre Diablo.** COUNTRY: **Argentina.**

YEAR: **1955.** TITLE: **Pobre Diablo.**
COUNTRY: **Argentina.**

POBRE
DIABLO
$ 1.50
AÑO 8 Nº 487
ELISEO
PLANA.-

BIZARRE

JOHN WILLIE:

A Most Bizarre Life

John Willie: Ein bizarres Leben
John Willie : Une vie des plus bizarres

John Willie – the American word for toilet meshed with the English word for penis. A name selected from the lower classes by a member of the upper. John Willie, artist and publisher, fashion designer and photographer, father of modern fetish, creator of *Sweet Gwendoline* and *Bizarre* magazine, pervert, drunk and probable misogynist. If ever there was a man dunked in the toilet of fate by his own penis, it was John Alexander Scott Coutts, aka John Willie.

Willie started his life with all the advantages accorded the son of a wealthy British banking family and ended it broke and bitter, having lost all to lust. Born in 1902, he was truly a product of his age. Corsetry was in full flower during his sexually formative years. In his upper-class home he had ample opportunity to see women struggling for breath

> If ever there was a man dunked in the toilet of fate by his own penis, it was John Willie.

in their fashionable corsets and teetering in high-heeled kidskin boots. The hobble skirt was all the rage around the

John Willie: der amerikanische Begriff für Klo gepaart mit dem englischen Wort für Penis. Ein Name aus der Unterschicht, den sich ein Mitglied der Oberschicht suchte. John Willie, Künstler und Verleger, Modedesigner und Fotograf, der Vater des modernen Fetischismus, der Schöpfer von *Sweet Gwendoline* und *Bizarre*, Perverser, Trunkenbold und wahrscheinlich Frauenhasser. Wenn es je einen Menschen gab, der sich von seinem eigenen Penis in die Sickergrube des Schicksals ziehen ließ, dann war es John Alexander Scott Coutts alias John Willie.

Willies Leben begann mit allen Privilegien, die dem Sohn einer wohlhabenden englischen Bankiersfamilie zugute kommen, und endete in Bankrott und Verbitterung, nachdem er alles seiner Lust geopfert hatte. Geboren 1902, war er ein echtes Kind seiner Zeit. In seinen sexuell prägenden Jahren erlebte die Korsettmanie ihren Höhepunkt. In seinem begüterten Elternhaus hatte er hinreichend Gelegenheit, dabei zuzusehen, wie Frauen in ihren modischen Korsetts nach Luft rangen und auf hochhackigen Ziegenlederstiefeletten um ihr Gleichgewicht kämpften. Der Humpelrock war zur Zeit seiner Pubertät der letzte Schrei, und natürlich lernte er in seiner vortrefflichen Public School die Freuden des Rohrstocks kennen. Kein Wunder, dass dieser feinfühlige Junge sein künstlerisches

John Willie : *john* signifiant les w.-c. pour les Américains et *willie*, un zizi pour les Anglais. Un pseudonyme choisi parmi les classes populaires par un membre de la haute. John Willie était artiste, éditeur, styliste de mode, photographe, père du fétichisme moderne, créateur des revues *Sweet Gwendoline* et *Bizarre*, pervers, soûlard et sans doute misogyne. Si jamais un homme se laissa mener par le bout de son sexe jusque dans les latrines du destin, ce fut bien John Alexander Scott Coutts, alias John Willie.

Willie commença sa vie avec tous les privilèges accordés au fils d'une famille de riches banquiers anglais et la termina ruiné et amer, ayant tout perdu à cause de sa libido. À l'époque où sa sexualité se développait, le corset régnait en maître. Dans sa maison de la haute bourgeoisie, il eut tout loisir d'observer les femmes tentant de trouver leur souffle dans le dernier harnachement à la mode et vacillant du haut de leurs bottines en chevreau. Il atteignit la puberté à l'époque où la jupe entravée faisait fureur et, naturellement, son éducation dans les meilleures écoles anglaises lui enseigna les délices de la canne. On ne peut donc guère s'étonner que cet enfant sensible utilise ses talents artistiques pour dessiner des femmes pieds et poings liés. Pour soigner son vice, sa famille le bannit en Australie, mais des années dans la marine marchan-

YEAR: **1946.** TITLE: **Bizarre.**
ARTIST: **John Willie.** COUNTRY: **USA.**

ON WITH THE MOTLEY!

Robin Hood

The Burglar

Little Miss Muffet

The Dunce

PAGE 112 +113:
YEAR: **1946.** TITLE: **Bizarre.**
ARTIST: **John Willie.** COUNTRY: **USA.**

RIGHT:
YEAR: **1950s.** TITLE: **Bizarre.**
COUNTRY: **USA.**

His family banished him to Australia to cure his vice, but years in the Merchant Marine failed to undo the early influences.

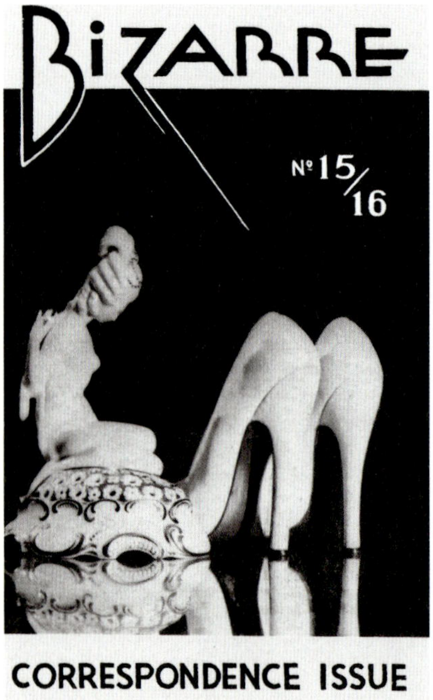

YEAR: **1955.** TITLE: **Bizarre.** COUNTRY: **USA.**

time he reached puberty and, of course, his proper public school taught him the pleasures of the cane. Little wonder this sensitive youth used his artistic skills to draw women in bondage. His family banished him to Australia to cure his vice, but years in the Merchant Marine failed to undo the early influences. He continued to perfect his fetish art and in the early 40s took it to New York City. New York was and is a publishing town with some tolerance for moral outlaws. Willie found encouragement for his fantasies there, and the means to put them on paper. He started *Bizarre* magazine in 1946 with his own savings. The paper and printing were hardest to come by, with war shortages still felt. The content was easier: Willie was artist, photogra-

Talent nutzte, um Frauen in Bondage zu zeichnen. Um ihm solche Flausen auszutreiben, schickte ihn seine Familie nach Australien, doch selbst lange Jahre in der Handelsmarine konnten seine frühen Eindrücke nicht mehr auslöschen. Er vervollkommnete seine Fetischkunst und ging in den frühen Vierzigern nach New York. New York war und ist ein Verlagsstandort, der einige Toleranz für moralische Grenzgänger aufbringt. In New York fand Willie sich in seinen Fantasien bestärkt und sah die Möglichkeit, sie zu Papier zu bringen. 1946 startete er mit seinen eigenen Ersparnissen das Magazin *Bizarre*. Das Schwierigste daran war, Papier und einen Drucker aufzutreiben, denn die kriegsbedingten Rationierungen machten sich immer noch bemerkbar. Mit dem Inhalt des Magazins war es einfacher: Willie war Zeichner, Fotograf und der Autor. Seine Frau war sein erstes Modell, und als sie ihn verließ, nahm er jede Frau als Modell, die er finden konnte, und sprach sogar Frauen auf der Straße an. Es fehlte ihm stets an Geld, um regelmäßig zu erscheinen oder einen festen Vertrieb zu finden. Wie Eric Kroll in seinem Vorwort zum TASCHEN-Reprint von *Bizarre* berichtet, stellte Willie die Magazine in seiner Lieblingsbar ins Regal hinter der Theke, und wenn eine Frau sich dafür interessierte, sprach er sie an, ob sie ihm Modell stehen wolle.

In unserer modernen Pornokratie, die jede erdenkliche Perversion zu erlauben scheint, kann man sich kaum noch vorstellen, wie schwierig es für Willie war, sein kleinformatiges Heft zu veröffentlichen. Angeblich soll er für den Fall, dass die Polizei sein Haus durchsuchte, mehrere andere Wohnungen unterhalten haben, in denen er Aufnahmen machte

de ne parvinrent à le purger de ces premières influences. Il continua à peaufiner son art fétichiste et l'emporta avec lui à New York au début des années quarante. New York était et est encore une ville d'éditeurs assez tolérante envers les hors la loi de la bonne moralité. Willie y trouva un accueil favorable pour ses fantasmes et les moyens de les coucher sur le papier. Il lança la revue *Bizarre* en 1946 avec ses propres économies. Le papier et l'impression étaient encore difficiles à trouver en raison des pénuries de la guerre. Le contenu posait moins de problème : Willie était dessinateur, photographe, écrivain. En un premier temps, sa

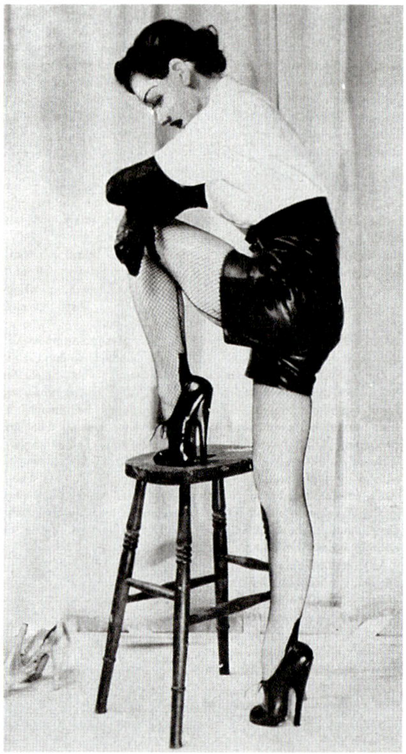

YEAR: **1956.** TITLE: **Bizarre.** COUNTRY: **USA.**

YEAR: **1955.** TITLE: **Bizarre.**
COUNTRY: **USA.**

pher and writer. His first model was his wife; when she left him he found models where he could, even approaching strangers on the street. There was never enough money to publish regularly or for any formal method of distribution. Eric

Willie found encouragement for his fantasies in New York, and the means to put them on paper.

Kroll noted in his intro to the TASCHEN reprint of *Bizarre* that Willie would stock his magazine on the racks in his favorite bars, then watch for women showing interest and ask them to model.

In the modern pornocracy, where every perversion seems legal, it's hard to imagine how Willie struggled to publish his little digest. It's said that he kept secret apartments used only for photo shoots and magazine production, in case the police raided his home. Many of his contributors were known to him only by pseudonyms, just as he was known to them only as John Willie. Even after he moved to Hollywood in 1957 the law pursued him; it was the era of Commie-bashing, government morals police and Senator Estes Kefauver's war on comic book sin. And you couldn't get much more sinful than Willie's *Sweet Gwendoline*. When the paranoia grew too great he'd destroy original art and negatives, and before his death from brain cancer in 1962 he destroyed his entire archive. In 13 years,

und sein Heft produzierte. Viele seiner Mitarbeiter kannte er nur unter Pseudonym, und sie kannten ihn nur als John Willie. Selbst als er 1957 nach Hollywood übersiedelte, saßen ihm die Behörden weiter im Nacken; es war die Zeit der Kommunistenjagd, der staatlichen Moralpolizei und des Senators Estes Kefauver und seines Feldzugs gegen die Hefte mit sündigen Comics. Und sündiger als Willies Comic *Sweet Gwendoline* konnte es kaum werden. Als die Paranoia überhand nahm, zerstörte er seine Originalzeichnungen und -negative, und ehe er 1962 an einem Gehirntumor starb, vernichtete er sein komplettes Archiv. In 13 Jahren, von 1946 bis 1959, erschienen nur 26 Ausgaben von *Bizarre*, wobei Nummer 21 möglicherweise schon die

YEAR: **1950s.** TITLE: **Bizarre.** ARTIST: **John Willie.**
COUNTRY: **USA.**

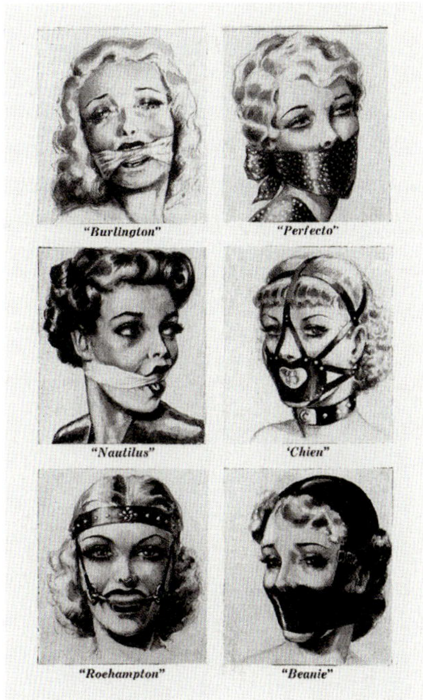

YEAR: **1952.** TITLE: **Bizarre.** ARTIST: **John Willie.**
COUNTRY: **USA.**

femme posa pour lui. Lorsqu'elle le quitta, il trouva des modèles là où il le pouvait, abordant même des inconnues dans la rue. Il n'avait les moyens ni de paraître régulièrement ni d'avoir un réseau formel de distribution. Dans son introduction à la réédition de *Bizarre* par les éditions TASCHEN, Eric Kroll raconte qu'il déposait des exemplaires de sa revue dans ses bars favoris, puis attendaient que des femmes s'y intéressent pour leur demander de poser.

Dans la pornocratie moderne où toutes les perversions semblent permises, on a du mal à imaginer les difficultés rencontrées par Willie pour publier son petit digest. On dit qu'il avait des appartements secrets qui ne servaient que pour ses séances de photos et la production de sa

Year: **1946.** Title: **Bizarre.**
Artist: **John Willie.** Country: **USA.**

from 1946 to 1959, there were only 26 issues of *Bizarre*, with no. 21 possibly the last done by Willie himself. Increasingly drunk and disillusioned, he reportedly passed the magazine on to one of his artists, Mahlon Blaine, shortly after his arrival in California. This means that in little over ten years John Willie built the reputation that would inspire every fetish artist to follow, from Bilbrew to Stanton to de Mulatta, and all fetish magazines up to the present day. In 1961 John Willie returned to a very different England to die, one that arguably could no longer create a man like him. Though his sexual orientation robbed him of a normal life and normal relationships, it also powered a genius that lifted him above the ordinary and into the pages of history.

a smart pair of knee-length black kid button boots

Year: **1946.** Title: **Bizarre.** Country: **USA.**

letzte war, die Willie selbst produzierte. Zunehmend dem Alkohol verfallen und desillusioniert soll er das Magazin kurz nach seiner Ankunft in Kalifornien Mahlon Baine, einem seiner Künstler, anvertraut haben. Das würde bedeuten, dass sich John Willie in wenig mehr als zehn Jahren einen Ruf aufgebaut hat, der von Bilbrew über Stanton bis zu de Mulatta jeden Fetischkünstler, der ihm folgen sollte, und jedes Fetischmagazin bis zum heutigen Tag inspiriert hat. Als er 1961 zum Sterben nach England heimkehrte, kam er in ein gänzlich verändertes Land, ein Land, das wohl keinen Mann wie ihn mehr hervorbringen konnte. Seine sexuelle Orientierung hat ihn zwar um ein normales Leben und normale Beziehungen gebracht, beflügelte jedoch auch ein Talent, das ihn über das Alltägliche hinaushob und Geschichte schreiben ließ.

It's said Willie kept secret apartments used only for photo shoots and magazine production in case the police raided his home.

revue au cas où la police perquisitionnerait son domicile. Il ne connaissait bon nombre de ses contributeurs que par leur pseudonyme, tout comme ils ne le connaissaient que sous le nom de John Willie. Même après son installation à Hollywood en 1957, la loi le poursuivit. C'était l'ère de la chasse aux cocos, de la police des mœurs du gouvernement et de la croisade morale du sénateur Estes Kefauver contre les bandes dessinées subversives. Or, on pouvait difficilement faire plus subversif que *Sweet Gwendoline*. Lorsque la paranoïa devenait trop pressante, il faisait disparaître ses dessins originaux et ses négatifs et, peu avant sa mort en 1962 des suites d'une tumeur au cerveau, il détruisit toutes ses archives. En 13 ans, de 1946 à 1959, il n'y eut que 26 numéros de *Bizarre*, le numéro 21 étant probablement le dernier réalisé par Willie lui-même. De plus en plus alcoolique et désabusé, il aurait transmis sa revue à l'un des ses artistes, Mahlon Blaine, peu après son arrivée en Californie. Cela signifie qu'il ne lui fallut qu'une dizaine d'années pour se construire une réputation qui inspirerait tous les artistes fétichistes après lui, de Bilbrew à Stanton en passant par de Mulatta, ainsi que tous les magazines fétichistes à ce jour. En 1961, John Willie revint mourir dans une Angleterre bien différente de celle qu'il avait laissée, une Angleterre qui ne pourrait sans doute plus créer un homme comme lui. Bien que ses goûts sexuels l'aient privé d'une vie et de relations normales, ils nourrirent un grand talent qui l'éleva au-dessus de l'ordinaire et jusque dans les pages de l'histoire.

THIRTY-FIVE CENTS

YEAR: **1953.** TITLE: **Bizarre.** ARTIST: **John Willie.** COUNTRY: **USA.**

YEAR: **1956.** TITLE: **Bizarre.** ARTIST: **John Willie.** COUNTRY: **USA.**

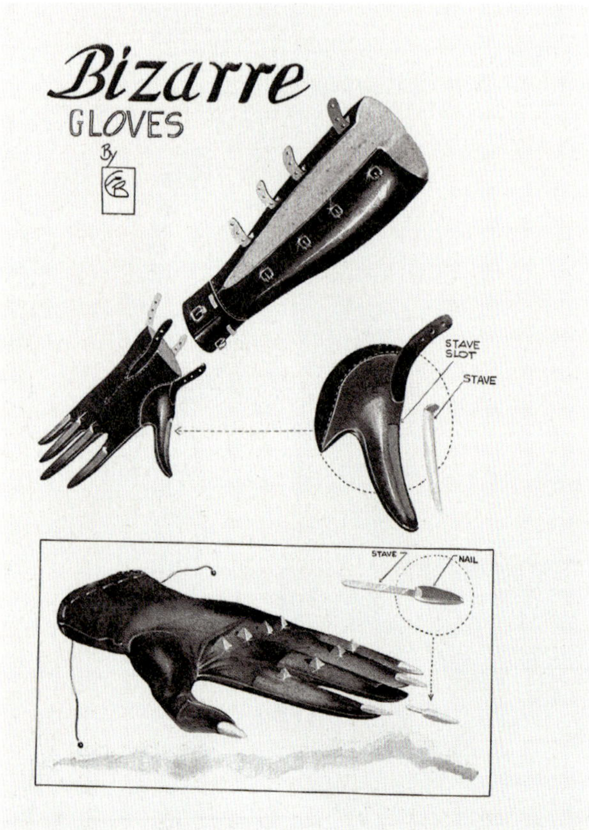

YEAR: **1956.** TITLE: **Bizarre.** ARTIST: **John Willie.** COUNTRY: **USA.**

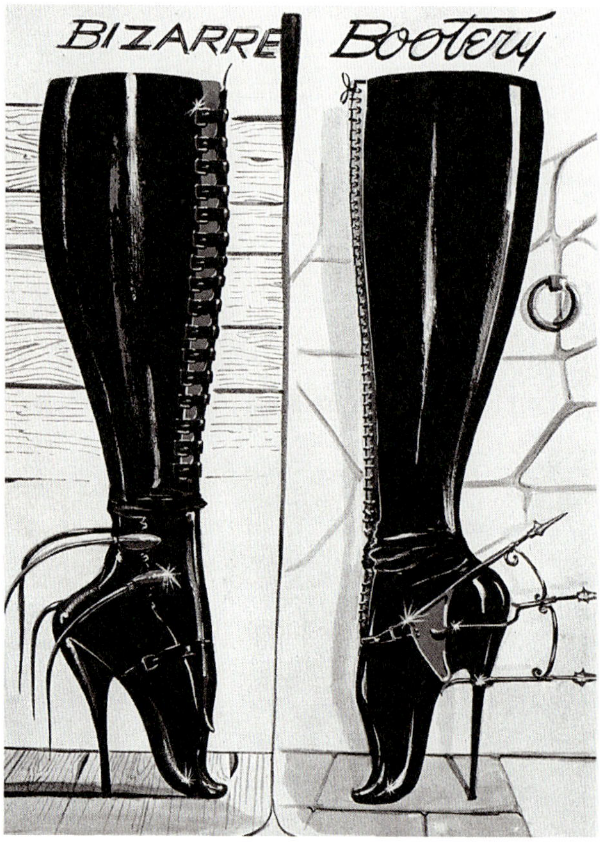

YEAR: **1950s.** TITLE: **Bizarre.** ARTIST: **John Willie.** COUNTRY: **USA.**

YEAR: **1953.** TITLE: **Bizarre.** ARTIST: **John Willie.** COUNTRY: **USA.**

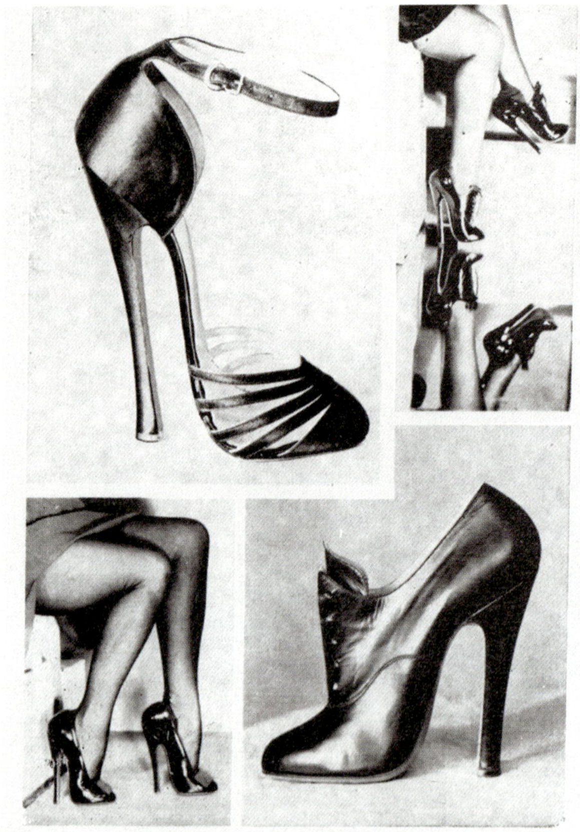

Year: **1940s.** Title: **Bizarre.** Country: **USA.**

Year: **1946.** Title: **Bizarre.** Artist: **John Willie.** Country: **USA.**

Year: **1959.** Title: **Bizarre.** Artist: **Malone Blaine.** Country: **USA.**

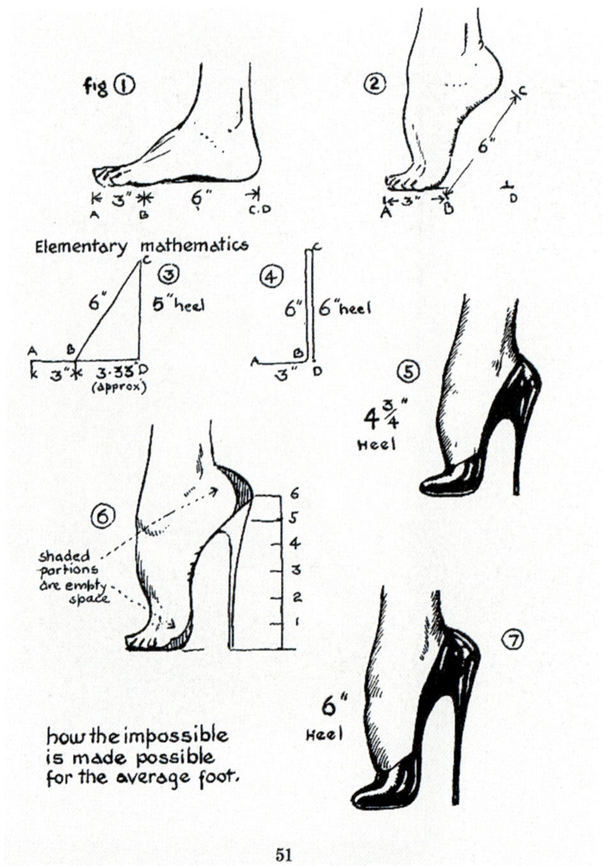

Year: **1946.** Title: **Bizarre.** Artist: **John Willie.** Country: **USA.**

Right: Year: **1940s.** Title: **Bizarre.**
Country: **USA.**

John Willie enjoyed designing his own fantasy fetish-wear and filled his Bizarre *magazines with these inventions.*

John Willie fand Spaß daran, fetischistische Kleidungsstücke zu entwerfen, und präsentierte seine Kreationen in seinem Magazin Bizarre.

John Willie aimait dessiner des tenues fétichistes issues de ses fantasmes et remplissait les pages de son magazine Bizarre *avec ses créations.*

YEAR: **1946.** TITLE: **Bizarre.** ARTIST: **John Willie.** COUNTRY: **USA.**

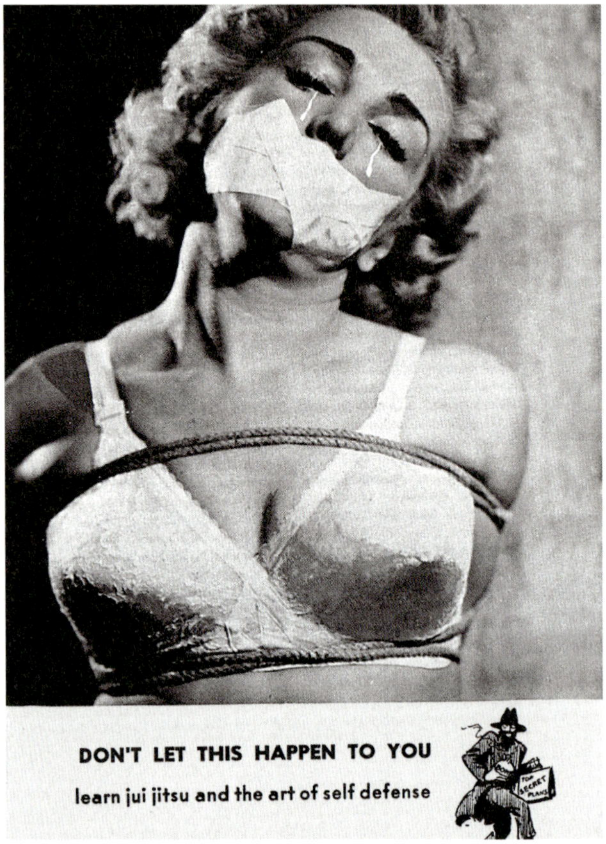

YEAR: **1956.** TITLE: **Bizarre.** COUNTRY: **USA.**

YEAR: **1956.** TITLE: **Bizarre.** COUNTRY: **USA.**

YEAR: **1946.** TITLE: **Bizarre.** COUNTRY: **USA.**

YEAR: **1956.** TITLE: **Bizarre.**
ARTIST: **John Willie.** COUNTRY: **USA.**

TEACHER
MISS MAGGIE
15
EDITOR

GB

LENNY BURTMAN:

A Yearning for the Exotique

Lenny Burtman: Die Sehnsucht nach dem Exotischen
Lenny Burtman : Une soif d'exotisme

Leonard "Lenny" Burtman was born August 8th 1915 in The Bronx, New York. Burtman did not set out to make publishing his life's work, but as he matured, for reasons unknown he developed an overwhelming and very specific fetish that demanded satisfaction. His taste was for powerful, intimidating women in exotic make-up and elaborately constructed costumes. He liked them in leather and satin and nylon. He liked them in extremely, torturously, high heels. He liked them drinking liquor and

Burtman worked like a man obsessed — which clearly he was — to spread the gospel of female dominance.

smoking cigarettes and smirking imperiously. He didn't mind the occasional whip or gun. There weren't many representations of this on American newsstands in 1950. Thus Leonard Burtman, inventor of the photographic strobe, professional scientist and amateur photographer, became a publisher. He called his

YEAR: **1950s.** TITLE: **Exotique.**
COUNTRY: **USA.**

YEAR: **1950s.** TITLE: **Exotique Photo Album.**
COUNTRY: **USA.**

Leonard „Lenny" Burtman wurde am 8. August 1915 in der Bronx in New York geboren. Man hatte Burtman das Verlegerwesen nicht in die Wiege gelegt, doch als er reifer wurde, entwickelte er aus unbekannten Gründen eine übermächtige und ganz spezielle Neigung, die nach Befriedigung verlangte. Er hatte eine Vorliebe für starke, einschüchternde Frauen in exotischem Make-up und kunstvoll konstruierten Kostümen. Sie mussten Leder,

Léonard Burtman (dit « Lenny ») naquit le 8 août 1915 dans le Bronx, à New York. L'édition n'était pas sa vocation première mais, en mûrissant il développa, pour des raisons obscures, un fétichisme spécifique et envahissant qui exigeait d'être satisfait. Il aimait les femmes puissantes, intimidantes, portant des maquillages exotiques et des tenues alambiquées. Il les voulait en cuir, satin et nylon. Il les voulait perchées sur des talons vertigi-

YEAR: **1950s.** TITLE: **Fantastique.**
ARTIST: **Gene Bilbrew.** COUNTRY: **USA.**

Year: **1950s.** Title: **Exotique.** Country: **USA.**

Year: **1950s.** Title: **Exotique.** Country: **USA.**

Year: **1950s.** Title: **Exotique.** Country: **USA.**

Year: **1950s.** Title: **Exotique.** Country: **USA.**

Year: **1950s.** Title: **Extatique.**
Artist: **Gene Bilbrew.** Country: **USA.**

INITIATION WEEK
ALL NEW PLEDGES MUST OBEY ALL ORDERS FROM MAY 15-22.
ORDERS WILL BE STRICTLY ENFORCED
INITIATION HAZING FUN
(See page 9)
No.

Year: **1960.** Title: **Fantasia.**
Artist: **Gene Bilbrew.** Country: **USA.**

first company Burmell and introduced his signature digest, *Exotique*, in 1951. *Exotique* was "dedicated to Fashions, Fads and Fancies", though the early issues mostly featured fiction. His inspirations were John Willie's *Bizarre* and an obscure English digest called *Fads and Fancies,* produced by London's Utopian Press in 1949/50. *Fads and Fancies'* subhead was "Readers' Views On Sports & Fashions", but the sports were female wrestling and the fashions every permutation of fetish, illustrated by a very talented but uncredited artist.

Burtman found artist Gene Bilbrew to illustrate *Exotique*'s letters and fiction and it was Bilbrew who gave the magazine its memorable look, while Burtman devoted most of his attention to the photo

Year: **1950s.** Title: **Exotique.**
Artist: **Gene Bilbrew.** Country: **USA.**

Samt oder Nylon tragen. Sie mussten extrem hohe, peinigende High Heels tragen. Sie mussten Alkohol trinken und rauchen und süffisant und gebieterisch lächeln. Gegen eine Peitsche oder Pistole hier und da hatte er nichts einzuwenden. An amerikanischen Zeitschriftenständen des Jahres 1950 war derartiges eher selten zu finden. Und so wurde Leonard Burtman, der Erfinder des Röhrenblitzes,

It was Gene Bilbrew who gave the magazine its memorable look, while Burtman devoted most of his attention to the photo shoots.

der Forscher und Amateurfotograf, zum Verleger. Seinen ersten Verlag nannte er Burmell, und 1951 präsentierte er sein Markenzeichen, *Exotique*, ein Magazin im Digestformat. *Exotique* widmete sich laut Untertitel „fashions, fads und fancies", allerdings boten die frühen Ausgaben vorwiegend fiktionale Texte. Seine Vorbilder waren John Willies *Bizarre* und ein obskures Blatt namens *Fads and Fancies*, das 1949/50 bei Utopian Press in London erschien. Der Untertitel von *Fads and Fancies* lautete „Reader's View On Sports & Fashions", aber bei dem Sport handelte es sich um Damenringen und bei der Mode um Fetischmode in jeder erdenklichen Spielart, illustriert

Year: **1950s.** Title: **Exotique.**
Artist: **Gene Bilbrew.** Country: **USA.**

neux, buvant de l'alcool, fumant, avec des moues narquoises et impérieuses. Il n'avait rien contre la présence occasionnelle d'un fouet ou d'une arme à feu. En 1950, on ne trouvait pas beaucoup d'images de femmes de ce genre dans les kiosques américains.

C'est ainsi que Léonard Burtman, inventeur du stroboscope, homme de science et photographe amateur, devint éditeur. Il baptisa sa société Burmell et, en 1951, lança *Exotique*, le digest qui allait bâtir sa réputation. La revue était « consacrée à la mode, aux marottes et aux masques », quoique les premiers numéros soient surtout composés de nouvelles. Il s'inspirait du *Bizarre* de John Willie et d'un obscur digest anglais intitulé *Fads and Fancies* produit à Londres par Utopian Press en 1949–50. Le sous-titre de *Fads and Fancies* était « les vues

YEAR: **1949.** TITLE: **Fads and Fancies.** COUNTRY: **England.**

Year: **1949.** Title: **Fads and Fancies.** Country: **England.**

His taste was for powerful, intimidating women in exotic make-up and elaborately constructed costumes.

shoots. This is where his fantasies were realized. He picked all the clothing for his models, even commissioning shoes to be made to his tastes. He personally posed the women and often took the photographs as well. When he married satanic stripper Tana Louise she became his constant subject, appearing in every issue. Burtman, like many a pornographer before and after him, self-distributed his magazine from the trunk of his car. Those who imagine sex magazines are made for profit alone take note: there have always been easier ways to make money than driving from newsstand to liquor store to tobacco shop begging owners to take a few magazines on credit. Burtman worked like a man obsessed – which clearly he was – to spread the gospel of female dominance. As *Exotique's* readership grew he added *Extatique*, *Fan-*

YEAR: **1950s.** TITLE: **Fantastique.** COUNTRY: **USA.**

von einem sehr begabten Künstler, der namentlich nicht genannt wurde.

Burtman gewann den Künstler Gene Bilbrew, um die Geschichten und Leserbriefe in *Exotique* zu illustrieren, und es war Bilbrew, der dem Magazin sein unverwechselbares Gesicht gab, während Burtman sich vorwiegend den Fotos widmete. Auf ihnen wurden seine Fantasien Wirklichkeit. Er suchte alle Kleidung für die Modelle aus und ließ sogar eigens Schuhe nach seinem Geschmack anfertigen. Oft stellte er die Modelle persönlich in Position und fotografierte auch selbst. Nachdem er die diabolische Stripperin Tana Louise geheiratet hatte, wurde sie sein festes Modell und war in jeder Ausgabe zu sehen. Wie so viele Pornografen vor und nach ihm fuhr Burtman persönlich mit dem Wagen herum, um sein Magazin zu vertreiben. Wer da denkt, Sexmagazine würden nur des Profits wegen hergestellt, aufgepasst: Es gab schon immer einfachere Möglichkeiten, sein Geld zu verdienen, als Kioske und Schnaps- und Tabakläden abzuklappern und die Besitzer anzubetteln, ein paar Magazine in Kommission zu nehmen. Burtman arbeitete wie ein Besessener, der er auch war, um die frohe Kunde von der weiblichen Dominanz zu verbreiten. Als die Leserschaft von *Exotique* wuchs, brachte er auch noch *Extatique*, *Fantastique*, *Masque* und eine Reihe forcierter Transvestismus-Titel heraus, ein weiteres sehr persönliches Anliegen von ihm. Ende der Fünfziger war *Exotique* so vorbildhaft auf seinem zugegebenermaßen kleinen Markt, dass viele Nachahmer die Fotos und Zeichnungen daraus kopierten. *Fantasia* war der Hauptkonkurrent und wird fälschlicherweise gelegentlich für einen Burtman-Titel gehalten. Hätte Lenny dahintergesteckt, hätte

YEAR: **1950s.** TITLE: **Exotique.** COUNTRY: **USA.**

des lecteurs sur le sport et la mode », sauf que le sport en question était la lutte féminine et la mode toutes les variantes du fétichisme, illustrées par un artiste très talentueux jamais cité.

Burtman engagea Gene Bilbrew pour illustrer les lettres et les nouvelles d'*Exotique*. Ce dernier lui donna son allure mémorable pendant que Burtman se consacrait aux prises de vue. C'était là qu'il réalisait ses fantasmes. Il dénichait toutes sortes de tenues pour ses modèles, commandant même des souliers à son goût. Il faisait lui-même poser les filles et, souvent, prenait les photos. Après qu'il eut épousé la strip-teaseuse satanique Tana Louise, il en fit son modèle de prédilection, la faisant paraître dans tous les numéros. Burtman, à l'instar de nombreux pornographes avant et après lui, distribuait lui-même son magazine de-

Year: **1950s.** Title: **Fantastique.** Country: **USA.**

125

Year: **1950s.** Title: **Guys in Gowns.** Artist: **Gene Bilbrew.** Country: **USA.**

Year: **1950s.** Title: **Guys in Gowns.** Artist: **Gene Bilbrew.** Country: **USA.**

Year: **1950s.** Title: **Masque.** Artist: **Gene Bilbrew.** Country: **USA.**

Year: **1950s.** Title: **Exotique.** Artist: **Gene Bilbrew.** Country: **USA.**

Year: **1950s.** Title: **Exotique.**
Artist: **Eric Stanton.** Country: **USA.**

YEAR: **1950s.** TITLE: **Exotique.**
COUNTRY: **USA.**

There were easier ways to make money than driving from newsstand to liquor store begging owners to take a few magazines on credit.

Lenny Burtman

tastique, *Masque* and a number of forced cross-dressing titles, another area of intense personal interest. By the late 50s *Exotique* was such a leader in its admittedly limited field it had inspired imitators that closely copied its photo and art content. *Fantasia* was the main competitor, and is sometimes mistaken for a Burtman title. Of course if Lenny had done it the title would have been *Fantasique*.

By 1960 *Exotique* wasn't looking quite so exotic. There were dozens if not hundreds of men's magazine titles produced in America by then, including the high quality, full-sized slicks coming out of California. To compete, Burtman folded his beloved *Exotique*, changed the name of his company to Selbee Associates and geared up for a new style of fetish magazine. He would spend the next 25 years of his life making large-format glossy fetish titles with names like *High Heels*, *Satana* and *Leg Show*.

das Magazin natürlich *Fantasique* geheißen.

1960 hatte *Exotique* nichts besonders Exotisches mehr. Zu dieser Zeit erschienen hunderte, wenn nicht tausende verschiedener Männermagazine in den USA, darunter auch die großformatigen, schicken Hochglanzmagazine aus Kalifornien. Um konkurrenzfähig zu bleiben, stellte Burtman sein geliebtes *Exotique* ein, änderte den Namen seines Verlags in Selbee Associates und machte sich daran, eine neue Art von Fetischmagazinen zu produzieren. In den nächsten fünfundzwanzig Jahren seines Lebens stellte Burtman ebenfalls großformatige Hochglanztitel wie *High Heels*, *Satana* oder *Leg Show* her.

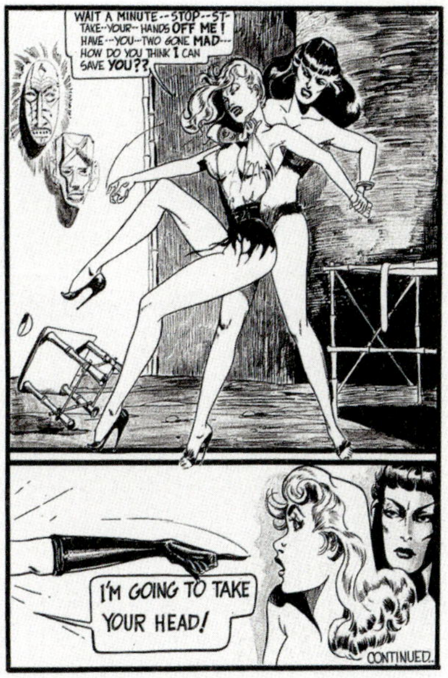

YEAR: **1950s.** TITLE: **Exotique.** COUNTRY: **USA.**

puis le coffre de sa voiture. Que ceux qui croient qu'on ne fait des magazines érotiques que pour l'argent prennent note : il y a des moyens plus faciles de faire fortune qu'en faisant du porte à porte entre les kiosques, les marchands d'alcool et les buralistes, suppliant leurs propriétaires de prendre quelques exemplaires à crédit. Burtman se démena comme l'obsédé qu'il était pour répandre l'évangile de la domination féminine. A mesure que le lectorat d'*Exotique* grandit, il y ajouta *Extatique*, *Fantastique*, *Masque* et un certain nombre de titres consacrés au travestisme, un autre domaine qui le fascinait particulièrement. A la fin des années cinquante, *Exotique* dominait tant ce créneau (il est vrai limité) que ses émules copiaient ses photos et son contenu artistique. Son principal rival était *Fantasia*, qu'on prend parfois à tort pour un des magazines de Burtman. Naturellement, si cela avait été le cas, il se serait appelé *Fantasique*.

Vers 1960 *Exotique* avait cessé de paraître si exotique. Il y avait alors aux États-Unis des dizaines, voire des centaines d'autres revues pour hommes, dont de luxueuses revues de grande qualité produites en Californie. Pour faire face à cette concurrence, Burtman ferma son cher *Exotique*, rebaptisa sa société Selbee Associates et se lança dans un nouveau style de magazines fétichistes. Il allait passer les vingt-cinq années suivantes à réaliser de grandes revues sur papier glacé tels que *High Heels*, *Satana* et *Leg Show*.

Year: **1950s.** Title: **Exotique.** Artist: **Gene Bilbrew.** Country: **USA.**

Year: **1950s.** Title: **Exotique.**
Artist: **Gene Bilbrew.** Country: **USA.**

YEAR: **1950s.** TITLE: **Exotique.** ARTIST: **Gene Bilbrew.** COUNTRY: **USA.**

YEAR: **1950s.** TITLE: **Exotique.** ARTIST: **Eric Stanton.** COUNTRY: **USA.**

YEAR: **1950s.** TITLE: **Exotique.** ARTIST: **Gene Bilbrew.** COUNTRY: **USA.**

YEAR: **1950s.** TITLE: **Exotique.** ARTIST: **Eric Stanton.** COUNTRY: **USA.**

YEAR: **1959.** TITLE: **Fantasia.** ARTIST: **Gene Bilbrew.** COUNTRY: **USA.**

YEAR: **1950s.** TITLE: **Exotique.** ARTIST: **Gene Bilbrew.** COUNTRY: **USA.**

YEAR: **1950s.** TITLE: **Exotique.** ARTIST: **Gene Bilbrew.** COUNTRY: **USA.**

YEAR: **1950s.** TITLE: **Connoisseur.** ARTIST: **Gene Bilbrew.** COUNTRY: **USA.**

YEAR: **1950s.** TITLE: **Masque.** ARTIST: **Gene Bilbrew.** COUNTRY: **USA.**

YEAR: **1950s.** TITLE: **Exotique.**
ARTIST: **Gene Bilbrew.** COUNTRY: **USA.**

GENE BILBREW

PHYLLIS
IN CENSORLAND
3/6

ENGLAND:

A Long Climb to the Top Shelf

England: Der lange Weg ins oberste Regal
Grande-Bretagne : La lente ascension vers l'étagère du haut

For all its history of caning and cross dressing, prostitutes and perversions, England started slow and advanced slower in the men's magazine market. *Tidbits of Beauty* is the first example I could find of anything remotely sexual. *Health & Efficiency*, an early physical culture magazine, adopted a particularly sexless nudist format in the early 20s. *London Life* made a name for itself in the late 30s/ early 40s not for its photos, as they went no further than bathing suited beauty queens, but for its amazingly perverse, utterly English reader letters. Rubber Macs and ruffled underpants were described and extolled in excruciating detail, as were corsets, female wrestling, amputees, long hair, high heels, silk stockings, cross-dressers and of course, the predictable caning. Actual procreative sex was off-limits. *London Opinion*, *Men Only* and *Lilliput* sprang up in the

Rubber Macs and ruffled underpants were described and extolled in excruciating detail.

YEAR: **1950s.** TITLE: **Phyllis in Censorland.**
COUNTRY: **England.**

Für seine lange Tradition in Flagellantismus und Transvestismus, Prostitution und Perversion, entdeckte England nur sehr zögernd den Markt für Männermagazine, der noch zögernder voran kam. *Tidbits of Beauty* ist das früheste Beispiel für irgendetwas auch nur ansatzweise Sexuelles, das ich finden konnte. In den Zwanzigern gab es *Health & Efficiency*, ein frühes Magazin für Körperertüchtigung und Freikörperkultur, das sich eine betont asexuelle Aufmachung zulegte. *London Life* machte sich in den späten Dreißigern beziehungsweise frühen Vierzigern seinen Namen nicht wegen der Bilder, die nie über Schönheitsköniginnen im Badeanzug hinausgingen, sondern wegen seiner erstaunlich perversen, durch und durch englischen Leserbriefe. In denen wurden Gummiregenmäntel und gerüschte Unterhöschen in ebenso schauderlicher Detailverliebtheit beschrieben und angepriesen wie Korsetts, Damenringkampf, Amputierten-Sex, lange Haare, High Heels, Seidenstrümpfe, Transvestiten und, wie sollte es anders sein, natürlich Flagellantismus. Sex zur Fortpflanzung hatte darin nichts zu suchen. *London Opinion*, *Men Only* und *Lilliput* erschienen ebenfalls erstmals in den frühen Vierzigern. Auch sie erwähnten Sex nie, aber wenn man die Magazine durchblättert, entdeckt man hier und da das deplaziert wirkende Foto einer Frau

En dépit de sa longue tradition de châtiments corporels, de travestissements, de prostituées et de perversions, l'Angleterre entra tardivement sur le marché des magazines pour hommes et évolua plus lentement qu'ailleurs. Le premier exemple de revue présentant un élément vaguement érotique que j'ai pu trouvé était *Tidbits of Beauty*. *Health & Efficiency*, un magazine de culture physique, adopta un format nudiste particulièrement asexué au début des années vingt. Entre la fin

YEAR: **1950s.** TITLE: **Phyllis in Censorland.**
COUNTRY: **England.**

MAY, 1945
London Opinion
9d
AND THE HUMORIST

YEAR: **1945.** TITLE: **London Opinion.** COUNTRY: **England.**

YEAR: **1945.** TITLE: **London Opinion.**
COUNTRY: **England.**

I little dreamed the day I chose the stage as my career
There'd always be a censor and he'd always interfere.
He started straight away by saying when he saw this pose:
"On no consideration would I pass a pair like those."

from Phyllis in Censorland

YEAR: **1950s.** TITLE: **Phyllis in Censorland.**
COUNTRY: **England.**

same early-40s war-time period. Again, these magazines made no mention of sex, but as one paged through them there'd be the occasional incongruous photo of a woman in a bathing suit, or in her underwear, or even in a topless art pose. Outside of England you'd never imagine you were reading a men's magazine. Humor helped the English considerably in handling the embarrassment of sex. *Blighty* and *Razzle* showed up in the mid to late 40s, followed by *A Basinful of Fun* around 1950. *Razzle* was the raciest, mixing discreet art nudes with the cartoons; for the others even the pen and ink girls had be to kept well covered. *Fads and Fancies* was an unusual little fetish digest directly descended from the *London Life* letters pages. It was way ahead of its time in 1950, but again, its extremity was all in words and fully dressed fetish drawings.

In this cautious way England made it all the way to the mid-50s producing only

im Badeanzug, in Unterwäsche, oder einer Oben-ohne-„Aktstudie", aber man musste schon Engländer sein, um zu bemerken, dass man ein Männermagazin in Händen hielt.

Große Hilfe beim Umgang mit dem peinlichen Thema Sex fanden die Engländer im Humor. *Blighty* und *Razzle* erschienen Mitte/Ende der Vierziger, gefolgt von *A Basinful of Fun* um 1950. *Razzle* war das gewagteste der drei Magazine und mengte den Cartoons dezente Aktstudien bei; bei den anderen mussten selbst die Mädchen aus Tusche sich züchtig bedeckt halten. *Fads and Fancies* war ein ungewöhnliches, kleinformatiges Fetischmagazin, das direkt den Leserbriefseiten von *London Life* entsprungen war. Es war 1950 seiner Zeit weit voraus, aber auch hier spielte sich das Extreme nur im Text ab, und die Zeichnungen zeigten vollständig bekleidete Mädchen in Fetischmode.

Auf diese vorsichtige Weise verfuhr England bis in die Fünfziger und produzierte nur Magazine, die jeder sehen durfte und die mithin über der Ladentheke verkauft werden konnten. 1954 oder 1957 (beide Daten werden genannt) erschien mit *Kamera* das erste Magazin, das ins oberste Regal verbannt werden musste, und schockierte die englische Öffentlichkeit so, dass sich die erste Nummer 150.000 mal verkaufte. Der Verleger, Chefredakteur und Fotograf war Harrison Marks, ein unverfrorener junger Mann, der das englische Zartgefühl noch mehr malträtierte, indem er a) seinen Namen groß und breit stolz überall ins Magazin schrieb, und b) Nacktfotos seiner Frau Pamela Green darin veröffentlichte. Obschon Marks nur Oben-ohne-Fotos zeigte, die unterhalb der Taille

des années trente et le début des années quarante, *London Life* se construisit une petite réputation, non pas sur ses photos qui n'allaient jamais au-delà de reines de beauté en maillot de bain, mais sur son courrier des lecteurs d'une perversité hallucinante et toute britannique. Les imperméables en caoutchouc et les culottes à volants y étaient décrits dans un luxe de détails, tout comme les corsets, les combats de catch féminin, les amputés, les cheveux longs, les talons hauts, les bas en soie, les travestis et, bien entendu, les incontournables fessées à coups de baguette. Le seul sujet proscrit était le sexe procréatif.

London Opinion, *Men Only* et *Lilliput* apparurent également au début des années quarante, en pleine guerre. Une fois de plus, ces magazines ne parlaient pas de sexualité mais, en les feuilletant, on tombait parfois sur la photo incongrue d'une femme en maillot de bain ou en sous-vêtements, ou même sur une photo « artistique » montrant des seins nus. Personne, hormis un Anglais, n'aurait pu imaginer qu'il s'agissait là de magazines pour hommes.

L'humour aida beaucoup les Anglais à surmonter leur gêne devant la sexualité. *Blighty* et *Razzle* firent leur apparition au milieu des années quarante, suivies vers 1950 de *A Basinful of Fun*. *Razzle* était le plus leste, associant des nus artistiques discrets à ses bandes dessinées. Dans les autres, même les filles dessinées au crayon et à l'encre restaient bien couvertes. *Fads and Fancies* était un petit digest fétichiste inhabituel, digne héritier du courrier des lecteurs de *London Life*. En 1950, il était très en avance sur son temps mais, là encore, son extrémisme s'exprimait par les mots et les dessins fé-

YEAR: **1940.** TITLE: **London Life.**
COUNTRY: **England.**

ov. 16th
1940

7d.

LONDON LIFE

YEAR: **1956.** TITLE: **Can-Can.** COUNTRY: **England.**

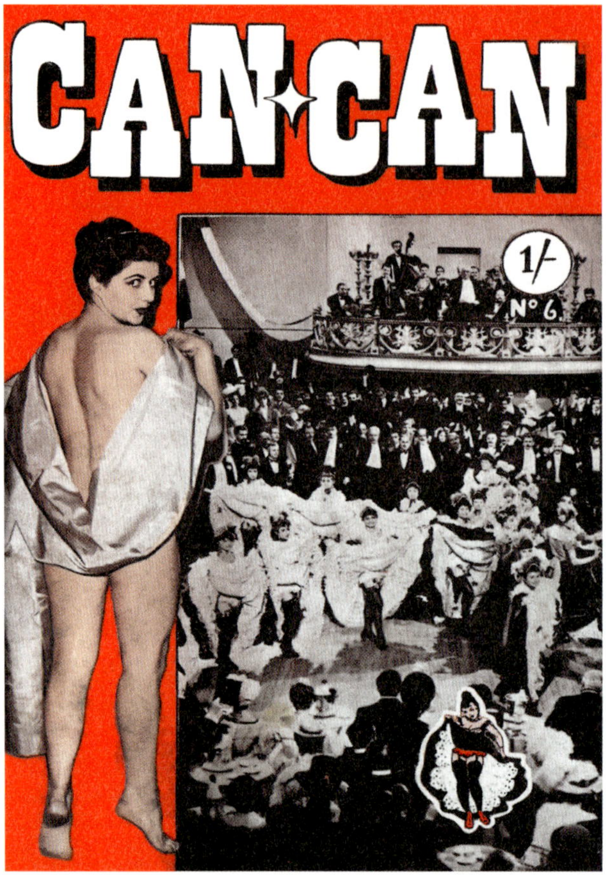

YEAR: **1956.** TITLE: **Can-Can.** COUNTRY: **England.**

YEAR: **1956.** TITLE: **Can-Can.** COUNTRY: **England.**

YEAR: **1956.** TITLE: **Can-Can.** COUNTRY: **England.**

YEAR: **1957.** TITLE: **Can-Can.** COUNTRY: **England.**

YEAR: **1957.** TITLE: **Can-Can.** COUNTRY: **England.**

Year: **1950s.** Title: **Foto.**
Country: **England.**

Table Top magazines – those that could be openly displayed for anyone to see. In either 1954 or 1957 (both dates are quoted) *Kamera*, the first Top Shelf magazine, appeared and so shocked the English public that its first issue sold 150,000 copies. Its publisher, editor and photographer was Harrison Marks, a brash young figure photographer who further tweaked English sensibilities by a) proudly plastering his name all over his magazine, and b) putting naked photos of his wife Pamela Green in it. Though Marks' photos were topless only, well airbrushed below the waist, and unquestionably tasteful in their composition, *Kamera* was lucky to even get the Top Shelf; more often it was hidden under the counter. Wherever it was positioned *Kamera* sold well and Marks soon followed with *Solo*, *Femme*, *In Focus* and *U. S. Glamour*.

With the door if not opened at least nudged ajar, a modest flood of pin-up and figure model magazines followed, including *Oh!!*, *'Nuff Sed*, *Spot On!* and *Can-Can*. Through the 1950s the men's magazine market was split between the airbrushed art nude digests and a peculiar brand of playful panty-flashing magazines typified by *Spick*, *Span* and *Beautiful Britons*. In most cultures fully dressed women wouldn't stand a chance against nudes, but England's long history of clothing fetishism, combined with an even longer history of not much caring what other cultures prefer, saw the panty-flashers often outselling the nudes. In fact, *Spick* and *Span* persevered into the 70s, when the art nude magazines of Harrison Marks and others had long since been replaced by full-sized, full-blown sex magazines.

sorgfältig retuschiert waren, hatte *Kamera* Glück, wenn es überhaupt ins oberste Regal durfte, meistens verschwand es unter der Ladentheke. Aber es verkaufte sich gut, und Marks schob bald die Titel *Solo*, *Femme*, *In Focus* und *U. S. Glamour* nach.

Nachdem die Tür einmal aufgestoßen war, folgte eine bescheidene Zahl von Pin-up- und Fotoaktmagazinen, darunter *Oh!!*, *'Nuff Sed*, *Spot On!* und *Can-Can*. In den Fünfzigern war der Markt aufgeteilt zwischen den retuschierten Aktfotografie-Titeln und einer eigentümlichen verspielten Sorte von Magazinen wie *Spick*, *Span* und *Beautiful Britons*, in denen einem Blicke auf Schlüpfer gewährt wurden. In den meisten Kulturen hätten vollständig bekleidete Frauen gegen nackte keine Chance, aber Englands ehrwürdige Tradition in der Fetischisierung von Kleidungsstücken kombiniert mit der noch ehrwürdigeren Tradition, sich nicht darum zu scheren, was andere Kulturen schätzen, sorgte dafür, dass die Schlüpfermädchen sich oft besser verkauften als die nackten. Tatsächlich hielten sich *Spick* und *Span* bis in die Siebziger, als die Aktmagazine von Harrison Marks und anderen längst durch echte Sexmagazine abgelöst worden waren.

The first Top Shelf magazine so shocked the English public it sold 150,000 copies.

tichistes où les corps étaient toujours entièrement vêtus.

La Grande-Bretagne continua jusqu'au milieu des années cinquante à ne produire que des magazines qui pouvaient trôner sur la table du salon sans embarrasser personne. Puis en 1954 ou 57 (les deux dates sont citées) parut *Kamera*, la première revue de charme. Elle choqua tant le public britannique que son premier numéro se vendit à 150 000 exemplaires. Son éditeur, rédacteur en chef et photographe s'appelait Harrison Marks, un jeune effronté qui heurta encore plus les sensibilités anglaises primo en placardant son nom partout dans sa revue, deuxio en y publiant des photos de sa femme Pamela Green nue. Bien que les photos de Marks ne montraient que des seins (le reste étant abondamment retouché) et restaient toujours de bon goût, *Kamera* devait s'estimer heureux d'être

Year: **1940s.** Title: **Lush.** Country: **England.**

Year: **1957.** Title: **Carnival.** Country: **England.**

Year: **1957.** Title: **Carnival.** Country: **England.**

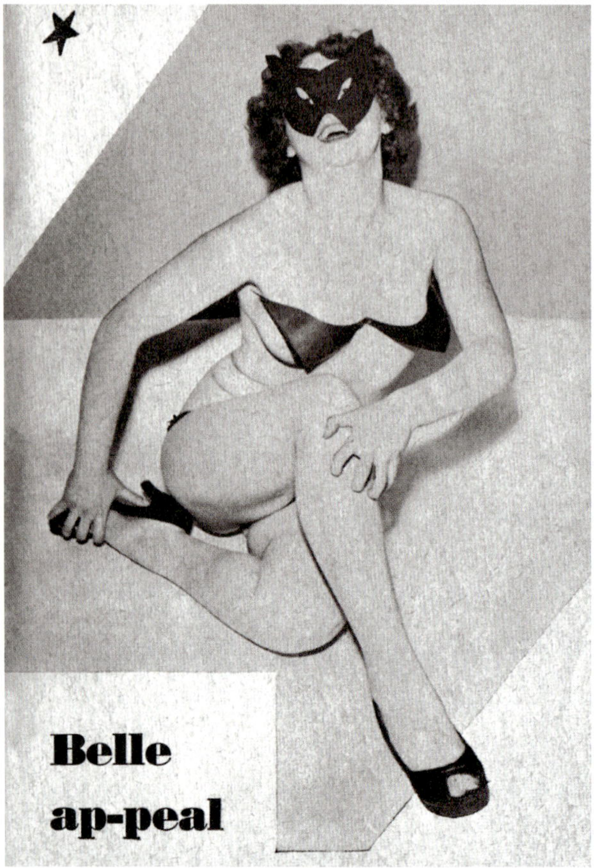

Year: **1956.** Title: **Carnival.** Country: **England.**

Year: **1956.** Title: **Carnival.** Country: **England.**

Year: **1956.** Title: **Carnival.** Country: **England.**

Year: **1950s.** Title: **Breezy.** Country: **England.**

Year: **1950s.** Title: **Breezy.** Country: **England.**

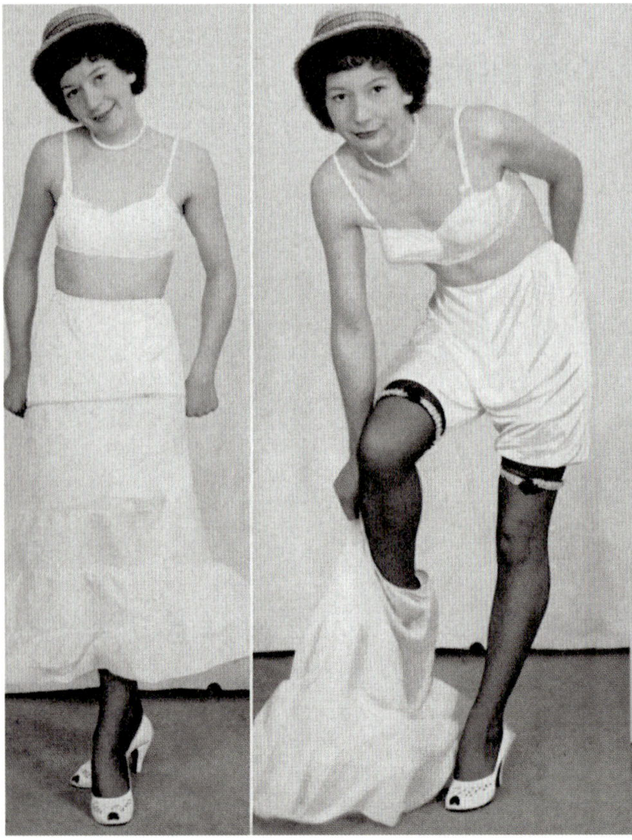

Year: **1950s.** Title: **Breezy.** Country: **England.**

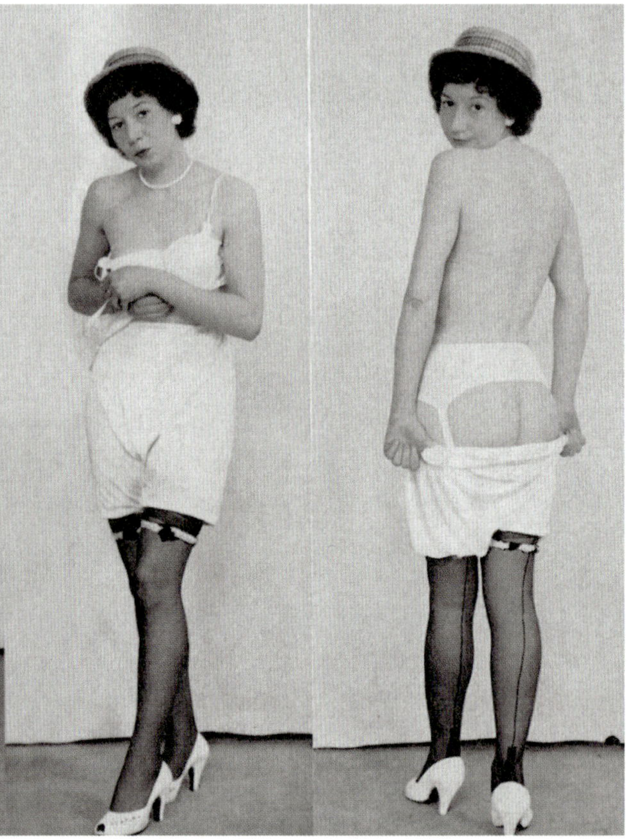

Year: **1950s.** Title: **Breezy.**
Country: **England.**

These magazines made no mention of sex, but as one paged through them there'd be the occasional incongruous photo.

YEAR: **1950s.** TITLE: **Ladies.** COUNTRY: **England.**

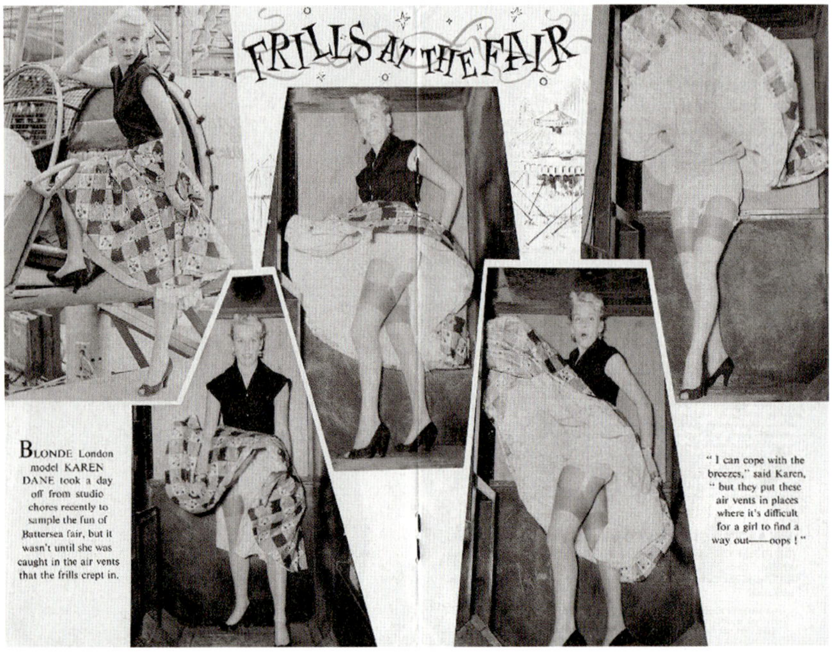

YEAR: **1950s.** TITLE: **Ladies.** COUNTRY: **England.**

vendu légalement dans les kiosques, même si elle n'était présentée que sur les étagères les plus hautes (inaccessibles aux enfants). Le plus souvent, elle était cachée sous le comptoir. Partout où elle était présentée, elle se vendait bien et Marks enchaîna rapidement avec *Solo*, *Femme*, *In Focus* et *U. S. Glamour*.

La porte n'était qu'entrebâillée mais cela suffit pour qu'une petite vague de magazines de pin-up et de nus s'y engouffre, notamment *Oh!!*, *'Nuff Sed*, *Spot On !* et *Can-Can*. Tout au long des années cinquante, le marché fut divisé entre les digests de nus artistiques retouchés à l'aérographe et une branche singulière de magazines ludiques où des filles laissaient entrevoir leurs dessous, dont *Spick*, *Span* et *Beautiful Britons*. Dans la plupart des cultures, ces femmes entièrement vêtues n'auraient pas fait long feu face aux filles nues mais la longue tradition anglaise en matière de fétichisme vestimentaire, associée à la tradition encore plus longue des Anglais de se soucier comme d'une guigne de ce qui plaît dans les autres cultures, fit que les montreuses de culottes se vendaient souvent mieux que les nus. De fait, *Spick* et *Span* survécurent jusque dans les années soixante-dix, alors que les nus artistiques de Marks avaient depuis longtemps cédé la place à des magazines érotiques grand format.

YEAR: **1950s.** TITLE: **Ladies.** COUNTRY: **England.**

LADIES
No. 6 3/6

Year: **1950s.** Title: **Magnifico.** Country: **England.**

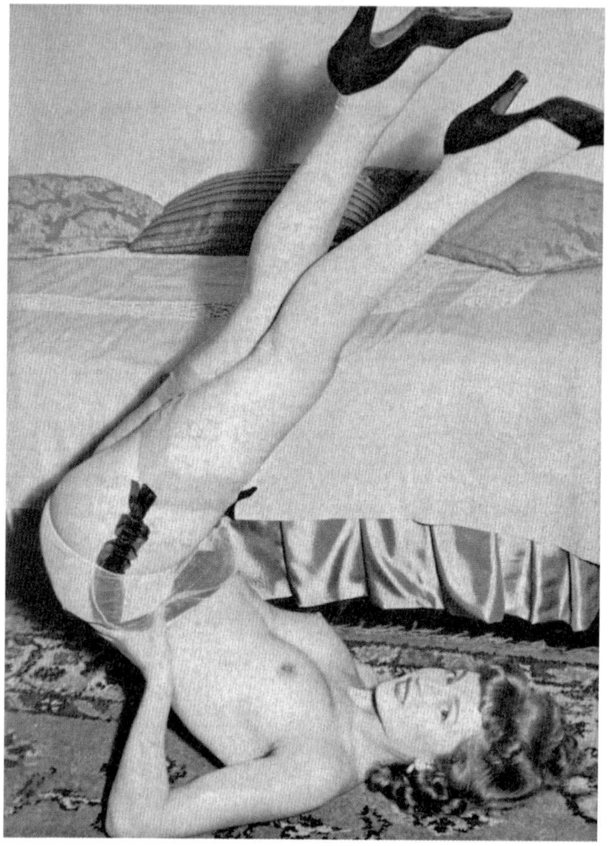

Year: **1950s.** Title: **Girly.** Country: **England.**

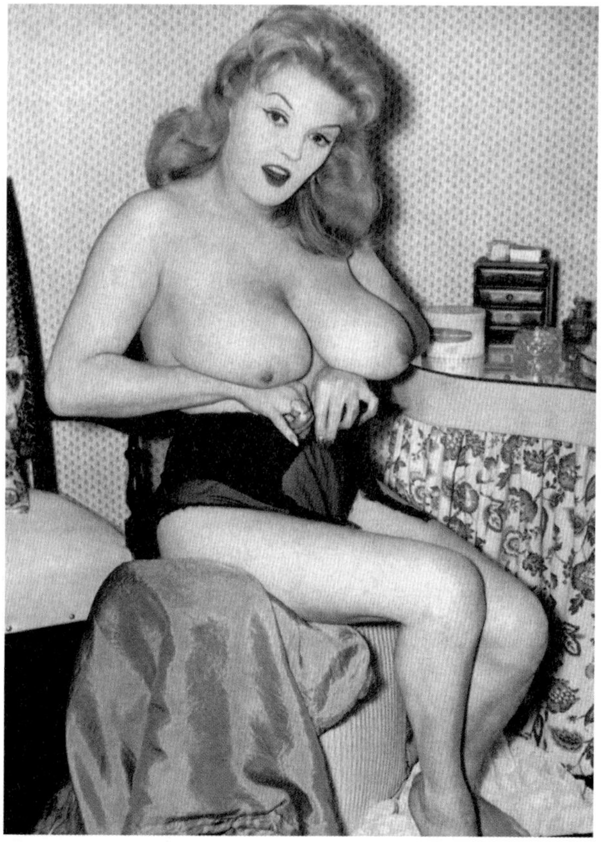

Year: **1950s.** Title: **Silky.** Country: **England.**

Year: **1950s.** Title: **Continental Keyholes.** Country: **England.**

Year: **1950s.** Title: **Magnifico.**
Country: **England.**

YEAR: **1950s.** TITLE: **Silky.** COUNTRY: **England.**

YEAR: **1950s.** TITLE: **Magnifico.**
COUNTRY: **England.**

YEAR: **1950s.** TITLE: **Spot On!** COUNTRY: **England.**

YEAR: **1950s.** TITLE: **Spot On!** COUNTRY: **England.**

YEAR: **1950s.** TITLE: **Fern.** COUNTRY: **England.**

YEAR: **1956.** TITLE: **Carnival.** COUNTRY: **England.**

HULA BLUES

Quite frankly we were so impressed by this series of photographs of lovely Lyn Shaw, submitted to us by photographer D. F. Ripsher, that we included them all. And we think our readers will agree that it was a wise move.

Not, of course, that Lyn suffers from "The Blues" at all, but—Jiminy Cricket!—when she wants to put them over, she *does* put them over. With a bang — and a loud bang, at that!

Photos by

D. F. Ripsher

Year: **1956.** Title: **Carnival.** Country: **England.**

Year: **1958.** Title: **Carnival.** Country: **England.**

Year: **1950s.** Title: **Lush.** Country: **England.**

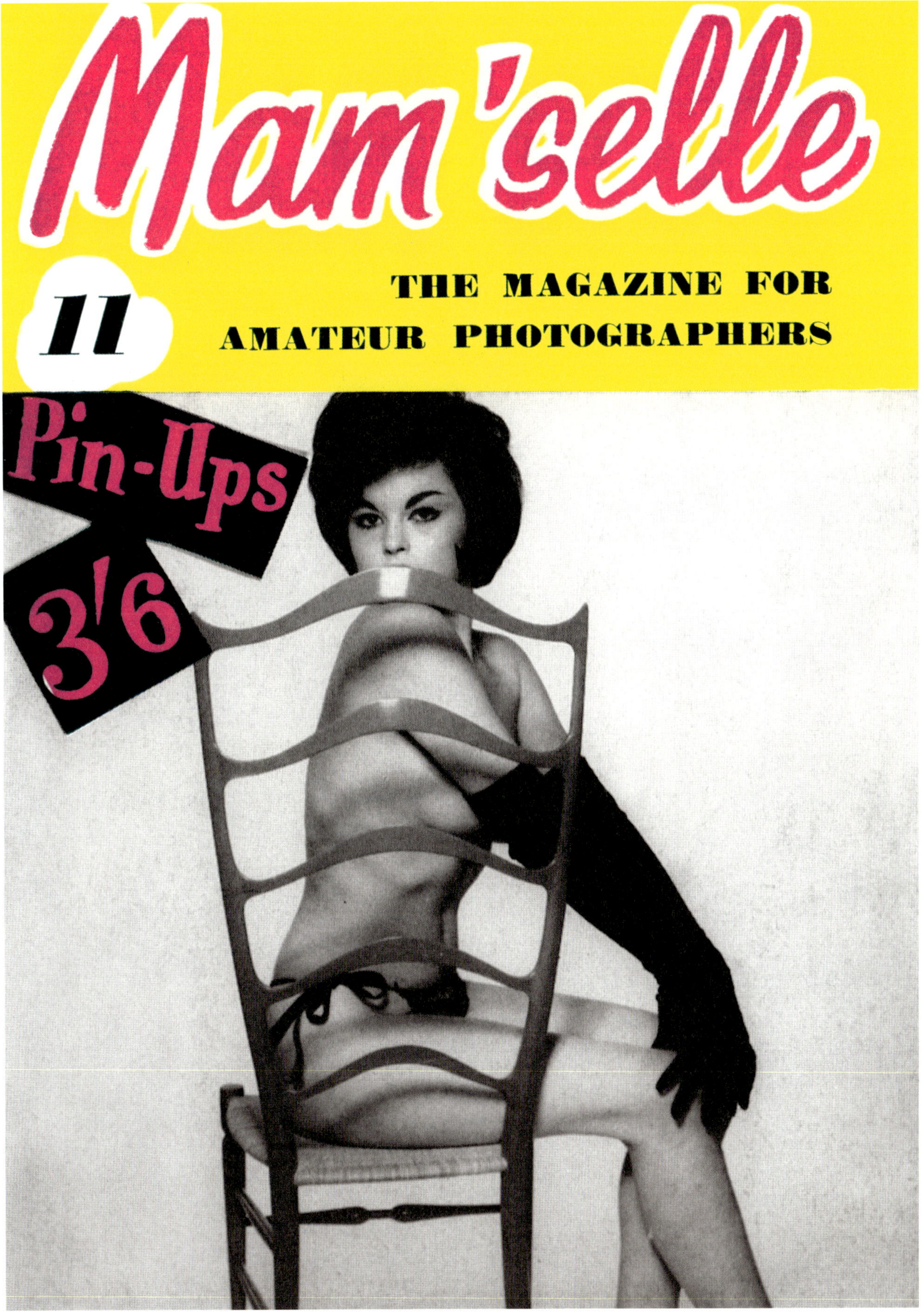

YEAR: **1950s**. TITLE: **Mam'selle**. COUNTRY: **England**.

YEAR: **1950s.** TITLE: **Model.** COUNTRY: **England.**

Year: **1950s.** Title: **Nimbus.** Country: **England.**

YEAR: **1950s.** TITLE: **Girly.** COUNTRY: **England.**

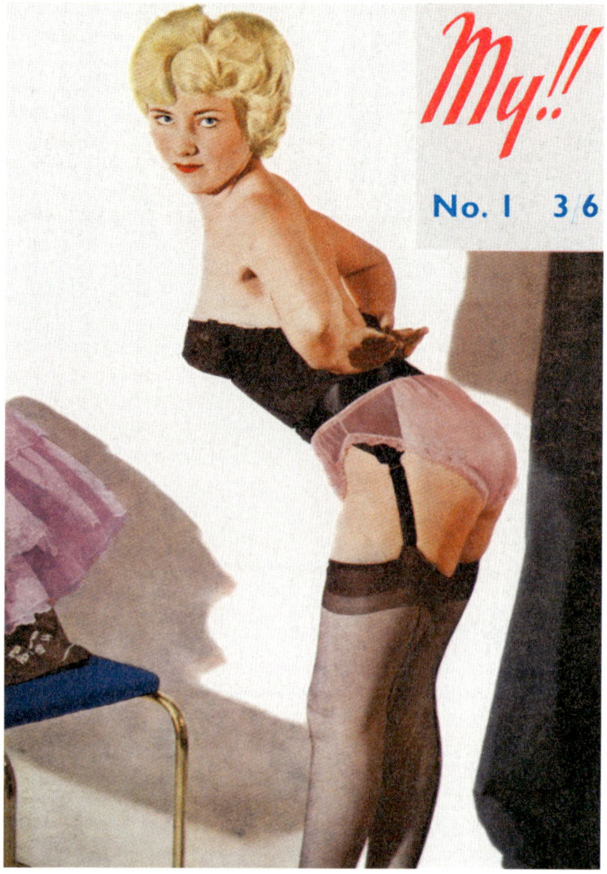

YEAR: **1950s.** TITLE: **My!!** COUNTRY: **England.**

YEAR: **1950s.** TITLE: **Oh!!** COUNTRY: **England.**

YEAR: **1950s.** TITLE: **Nu Look.** COUNTRY: **England.**

YEAR: **1950s.** TITLE: **Foto.**
COUNTRY: **England.**

Year: **1950s.** Title: **Mirage.** Country: **England.**

YEAR: **1959.** TITLE: **X for Men.** COUNTRY: **England.**

YEAR: **1959.** TITLE: **Lilliput.** COUNTRY: **England.**

YEAR: **1959.** TITLE: **X for Men.** COUNTRY: **England.**

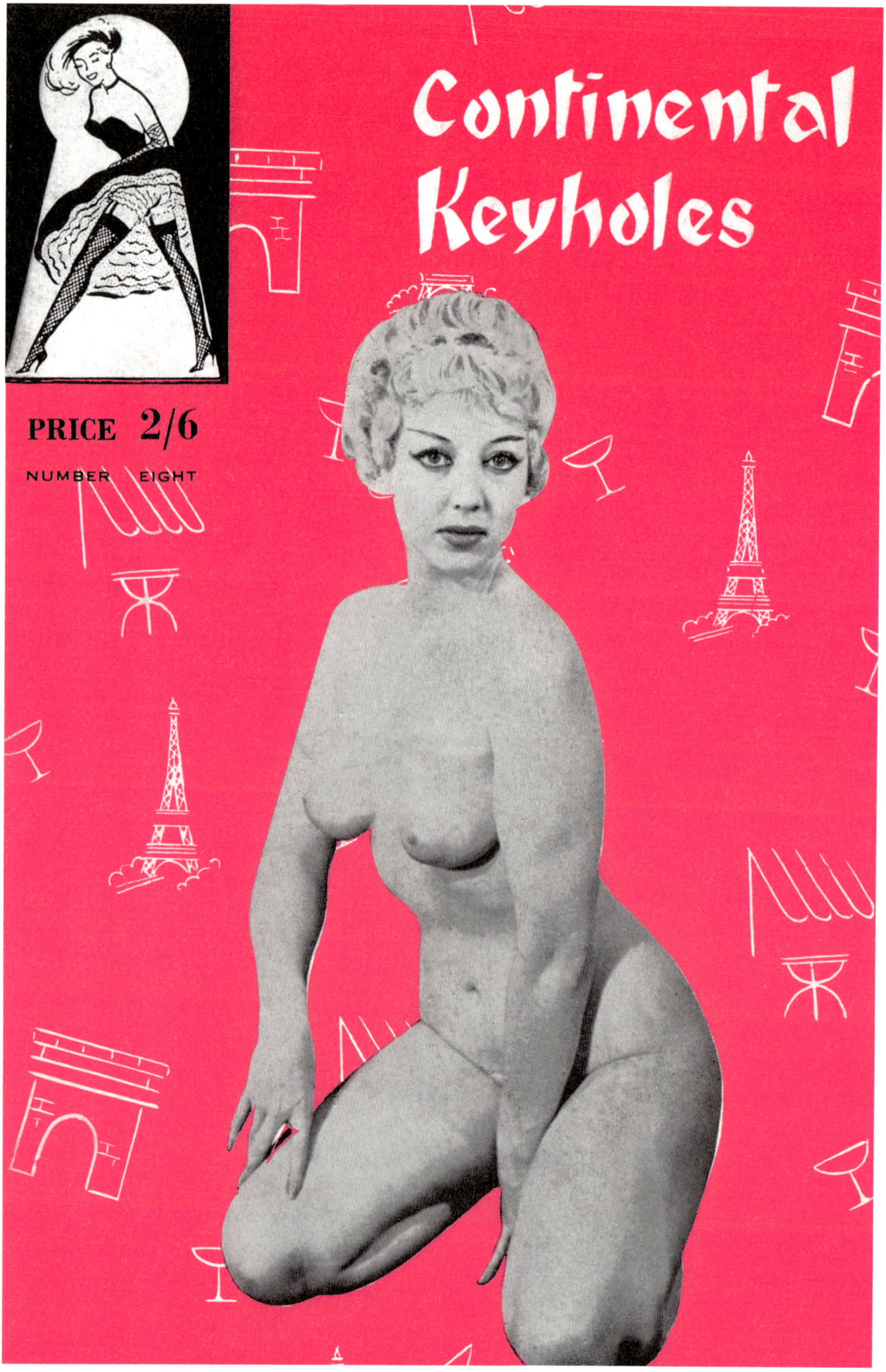

YEAR: **1950s.** TITLE: **Continental Keyholes.** COUNTRY: **England.**

YEAR: **1950s.** TITLE: **Mirage.** COUNTRY: **England.**

YEAR: **1958.** TITLE: **Stag.** COUNTRY: **England.**

Year: **1950s.** Title: **Continental Kuties.** Country: **England.**

Year: **1950s.** Title: **Paris-Vision.** Country: **England.**

Year: **1950s.** Title: **Girly.** Country: **England.**

Year: **1950s.** Title: **Lush.** Country: **England.**

THE OLD BUMP AND GRIND:

Post-War, Pre-*Playboy*

Schwingt die Hüften: Nach dem Krieg und vor dem *Playboy*
Ces bons vieux déhanchements d'antan : Après la guerre et avant *Playboy*

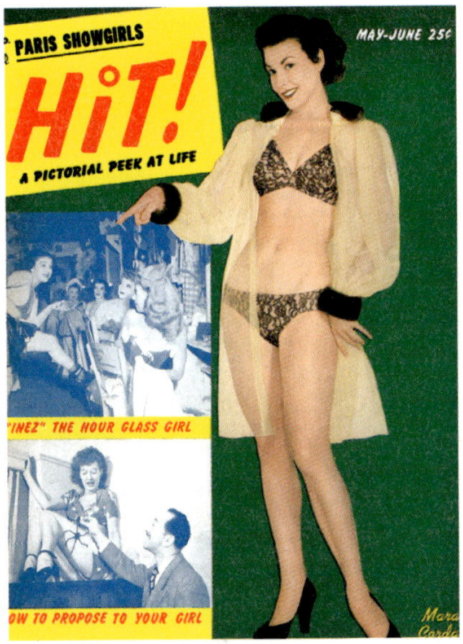

Year: **1952.** Title: **Hit!** Country: **USA.**

Hugh Hefner, apocryphally, said one of the reasons he started *Playboy* was because he was tired of seeing nothing but strippers in other men's titles. There's no denying that American magazines pre-*Playboy* relied heavily on exotic dancers, but there's also no reason to believe most men objected. Burlesque dates back to the 1840s in the US, and even earlier in parts of Europe. The word derives from the Italian word for jest; original burlesque was a variety show for the lower classes that made fun of upper-class entertainments like opera and bal-

Hugh Hefner soll einmal gesagt haben, dass er mit *Playboy* angefangen habe, weil er es leid war, immer nur Stripperinnen in Männermagazinen zu sehen. Ja, man kann kaum leugnen, dass die amerikanischen Magazine vor dem *Playboy* hauptsächlich auf „exotische Tänzerinnen" setzten, aber es deutet auch nichts darauf hin, dass sich viele Männer darüber beschwerten. Die Wurzeln des Varietés beziehungsweise der Burleske in den USA reichen zurück bis in die vierziger Jahre des 19. Jahrhunderts, und in Europa noch weiter. Das Wort „burlesk" stammt aus dem Italienischen und bedeutet Witz, Spaß; die ursprünglichen burlesken Shows richteten sich an ein proletarisches Publikum und parodierten Kulturgüter der Oberschicht wie Oper und Ballett. Hübsche Mädchen waren stets Bestandteil der Aufführungen: Oft trugen sie fleischfarbene Strumpfhosen, die in der viktorianischen Zeit als skandalös galten. Mit der Zeit spielten Frauen in den Shows eine immer größere Rolle, doch erst in den zwanziger Jahren des 20. Jahrhunderts bekam man nackte Haut zu sehen.

Um 1900 entwickelte sich aus der Burleske das familientauglichere Vaudeville und löste seine Vorläuferin in den besseren Theatern schnell ab. In den Zwanzigern musste sich die Burlesque-Show auch noch gegen die aufblühende Filmin-

Hugh Hefner aurait déclaré que l'une des raisons qui l'avaient incité à créer son célèbre magazine était qu'il en avait assez de ne voir que des strip-teaseuses dans les revues pour hommes. Il est indéniable que les magazines américains d'avant *Playboy* faisaient largement appel aux danseuses nues, mais il n'y a aucune raison de croire que la plupart des hommes s'en plaignaient. Le théâtre burlesque remonte aux années 1840 aux États-Unis et plus loin encore dans certaines parties d'Europe. Puisant son nom dans le mot

Original burlesque was a variety show for the lower classes that made fun of upper class entertainment.

italien *burla*, « plaisanterie », il s'agissait à l'origine d'un spectacle de variétés populaires se moquant des divertissements destinés aux classes supérieures comme l'opéra et le ballet. De jolies filles figuraient toujours au programme, souvent vêtues de collants couleur chair considérés scandaleux à l'époque victorienne. A

Year: **1954.** Title: **Modern Man.**
Country: **USA.**

SWAGGER
JA
25
K
EVERY MAN'S MAGAZINE
A HOUSE OF ASSIGNATION
GOING TO FLORIDA?
READ . . .
WINTER PLUNDERLAND
COMBATING
JUVENILE DELINQUENCY
IN NAPLES
CHILDBIRTH
IN A TENEMENT
A PICTURE STORY
CONTRABAN
EXCLUSIVE PICTURES
OF SMUGGLING
OVER SWISS
BORDER
"THE TUNIS DAGGER" A NEW WADE MILLER THRILLE

One of the first titles with a true fun-loving 50s look, Swagger debuted in 1951, but for all its exuberance didn't last long.

Swagger erschien erstmals 1951 und war eines der ersten Magazine, die eindeutig die Spaßgesellschaft der Fünfziger reflektierten. Trotz dieser Ausgelassenheit war ihm kein langes Dasein vergönnt.

Un des premiers titres à l'humeur rigolarde typique des années 50, Swagger parut en 1951 mais, en dépit de son exubérance, ne fit pas long feu.

During World War II strippers were downplayed as bad for morals, if good for morale.

let. Pretty girls were always part of the show, often dressed in flesh-toned tights considered scandalous to the Victorians. As burlesque evolved women played an ever-larger role, though nudity would not be part of it until the 1920s. Around 1900 the popularity of burlesque gave birth to the more family-oriented vaudeville, which quickly displaced its parent in the better theaters. By 1920 burlesque had to compete against the fledgling film industry as well, so when striptease was added a couple years later it was done as a desperate bid for survival. The ecdysiasts quickly eclipsed all other parts of the show.

It wasn't long before burlesque was creating true stars. Soon after, strippers first became a staple of men's magazines. During World War II they were downplayed as bad for morals, if good for morale, but as soon as the war ended they enjoyed a vigorous return. Robert Harrison's *Titter*, *Wink*, et al succeeded because they were burlesque shows in magazine form. Most other American men's magazines made between 1946 and 1955 concentrated on dancers and dance clubs as well. *Cavalcade of Burlesque*, from 1951, was openly devoted to the stars, as was 1952's *Wolf Bait*. With interest in dancers so strong *La Vie Parisienne* was persuaded to introduce an American edition titled *Paris Life*. Sadly, the US was not as advanced as France; bras were crudely painted onto the photos of topless cabaret stars.

Modern Man was a particularly bold magazine of this period. Started in 1951 by a leading art nude publisher, it had burlesque stars photographed in the style of art nudes: topless with neatly airbrushed crotches. This was a time when

Year: **1948.** Title: **Picture Show.** Country: **USA.**

dustrie behaupten, daher entsprang es dem verzweifelten Kampf ums Überleben, dass man den Striptease ins Programm nahm.

Die Nackttänzerinnen stellten schnell alle anderen Programmpunkte der Shows in den Schatten.

Es dauerte nicht lange, und die Burlesque-Shows brachten eigene Stars hervor. Wenig später wurden Stripperinnen erstmals zur Hauptattraktion von Männermagazinen. Während des Zweiten Weltkrieges stigmatisiert als der Moral abträglich, wenn auch gut für den Kampfgeist, kehrten sie nach Kriegsende mit Schwung zurück. Die Magazine von Robert Harrison wie *Titter* oder *Wink* waren so erfolgreich, weil sie Burlesque-Shows in Magazinform waren. Auch die meisten anderen amerikanischen Männermagazine konzentrierten sich zwischen 1946 und 1955 auf Tänzerinnen und Stripclubs. *Cavalcade of Burlesque*

mesure que le genre évolua, les femmes y jouèrent un rôle de plus en plus important, même si la nudité n'apparut pas avant les années 1920. Vers 1900, la popularité du burlesque donna naissance au genre plus familial du vaudeville, qui chassa rapidement son précurseur des meilleurs théâtres. A partir de 1920, le burlesque dut également essuyer la rude concurrence du cinématographe et, lorsque que le strip-tease fut introduit quelques années plus tard, il le fut comme une dernière tentative désespérée pour assurer sa survie. Les effeuilleuses devinrent rapidement le clou du spectacle.

Il ne fallut pas longtemps au burlesque pour produire de vraies stars. Peu après, les strip-teaseuses devinrent la matière première des magazines pour hommes. Au cours de la Seconde Guerre mondiale, on les écarta comme immorales (quoique bonnes pour le moral des troupes) mais sitôt le conflit terminé, elles revinrent en force sur le devant de la scène. Les revues de Robert Harrison *Titter*, *Wink* et autres, faisaient recette car elles n'étaient rien d'autre que des spectacles de burlesque sur papier. La plupart des autres magazines pour hommes américains réalisés entre 1946 et 1955 se concentraient également sur les danseuses et les dancings. *Cavalcade of Burlesque*, lancé en 1951, était consacré aux stars, tout comme *Wolf Bait*, apparu en 1952. Devant un tel engouement pour les danseuses, *La Vie Parisienne* lança une édition américaine intitulée *Paris Life*. Hélas, les États-Unis n'étaient pas aussi avancés que la France et des soutiens-gorge étaient grossièrement peints sur les photos des vedettes de cabaret topless.

Pour la période, *Modern Man* était un magazine particulièrement culotté.

Year: **1951.** Title: **Swagger.**
Country: **USA.**

Opposite: Tempest Storm was burlesque's biggest draw when she appeared in this Gala in the mid-50s. A couple years later she would insure her breasts for a record one million dollars with Lloyd's of London.

Rechte Seite: Die stürmische Tempest Storm war der größte Publikumsmagnet des Varietétheaters, als sie Mitte der fünfziger Jahre in dieser Gala erschien. Ein paar Jahre später ließ sie ihre Brüste bei Lloyd's of London für die Rekordsumme von einer Million Dollar versichern.

Page de droite: Tempest Storm (tempête du désert) était le meilleur atout du music-hall quand elle parut dans ce Gala du milieu des années 50. Quelques années plus tard, elle assura ses seins pour un million de dollars (un record!) auprès de la Lloyd's de Londres.

YEAR: **1954.** TITLE: **Frolic.** COUNTRY: **USA.**

YEAR: **1954.** TITLE: **Gala.** COUNTRY: **USA.**

GALA
America's Greatest Array of Glamor
Who's Who in Burly Q?
BUBBLE-BATH BEAUTIES

Burlesque was still enormously popular in 1951 when Cavalcade of Burlesque *appeared from a company pretentiously calling itself the "Burlesque Historical Society".*

Das Varietétheater war 1951 noch immer ungeheuer populär, als Cavalcade of Burlesque *von einer Gesellschaft verlegt wurde, die sich hochtrabend als „Burlesque Historical Society" bezeichnete.*

Le théâtre burlesque était encore très populaire quand parut en 1951 Cavalcade of Burlesque, *publié par une maison d'édition au nom prétentieux de « Société historique du théâtre burlesque ».*

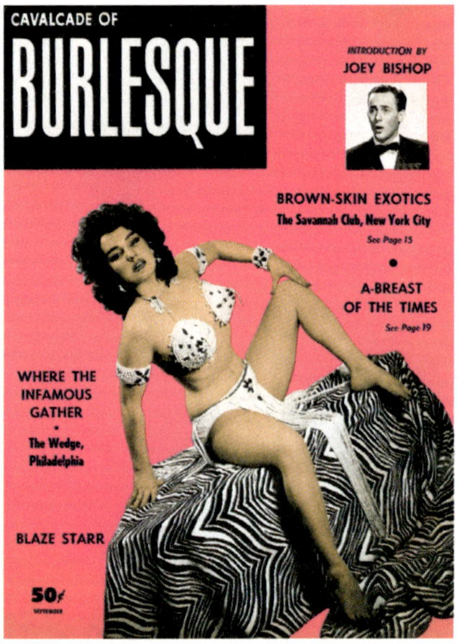

Year: **1954.** Title: **Cavalcade of Burlesque.** Country: **USA.**

most magazines still showed no nudity, but *MM* combined high production values with pages of nonsexual men's interest articles and got away with it. If Hugh Hefner hadn't come along *MM* might have been America's *Playboy*. As it was, *Modern Man* would sink to the bottom of the second division over the next two decades. American burlesque lasted into the 70s, but by the mid-50s strippers were losing their exclusive with the men's magazines. Increasingly, the bad girls had to give up pages to the Girl Next Door.

von 1951 widmete sich ebenso wie *Wolf Bait* von 1952 unverblümt diesen Stars. Da das Interesse an Tänzerinnen so groß war, fand sich *La Vie Parisienne* bereit, unter dem Titel *Paris Life* eine amerikanische Ausgabe zu produzieren. Leider waren die Staaten nicht so fortschrittlich wie Frankreich: Den Fotos barbusiger Cabaret-Stars rückte man mit unelegant darübergemalten BHs zu Leibe.

Ein besonders wagemutiges Magazin dieser Ära war *Modern Man*. 1951 von einem führenden Verleger für künstlerische Aktfotografie gestartet, zeigte es Stars der Burlesque-Shows im Stil künstlerischer Akte fotografiert: oben ohne mit hübsch retuschierter Scham. Zu dieser Zeit zeigten die meisten Magazine noch keine nackte Haut, aber *MM* kombinierte hochwertige Produktionsmaßstäbe und an ein männliches Publikum gerichtete General-Interest-Artikel und kam damit durch.

Wäre Hugh Hefner nicht auf der Bildfläche erschienen, wäre *MM* vielleicht der amerikanische *Playboy* geworden. Doch so rutschte *Modern Man* in den nächsten zwei Jahrzehnten in die Zweitklassigkeit ab. Die Burlesque-Shows überlebten in den USA bis in die Siebziger, doch schon Mitte der Fünfziger gehörten die Männermagazine nicht mehr den Stripperinnen allein. Die gefallenen Mädchen mussten zunehmend dem Mädchen von nebenan weichen.

Lancé en 1951 par un grand éditeur de nus artistiques, il montrait des stars du burlesque photographiées dans le style des nus académiques : seins nus avec les parties génitales soigneusement retouchées. À cette époque, la plupart des magazines ne montraient pas encore de nudité, mais *MM* passait entre les mailles de

Cavalcade of Burlesque, from 1951, was openly devoted to the stars, as was 1952's *Wolf Bait.*

la censure en associant un gros budget avec des articles non érotiques intéressant un public masculin. Si Hugh Hefner n'était pas arrivé, *MM* serait sans doute devenu le *Playboy* américain. En fait, la revue tomba en fin de seconde division au cours des deux décennies suivantes. Le burlesque américain perdura jusque dans les années soixante-dix mais, dès le milieu des années cinquante, les strip-teaseuses commencèrent à perdre leur exclusivité dans les pages des magazines pour hommes. De plus en plus, les « mauvaises filles » devaient laisser la place à la « fille d'à côté ».

Year: **1952.** Title: **Wolf Bait.** Country: **USA.**

WOLF
BAIT
Price
$1.00
Tempest Storm
John E. Reed
HOLLYWOOD

YEAR: **1952.** TITLE: **Hit!** COUNTRY: **USA.**

YEAR: **1954.** TITLE: **Gala.** COUNTRY: **USA.**

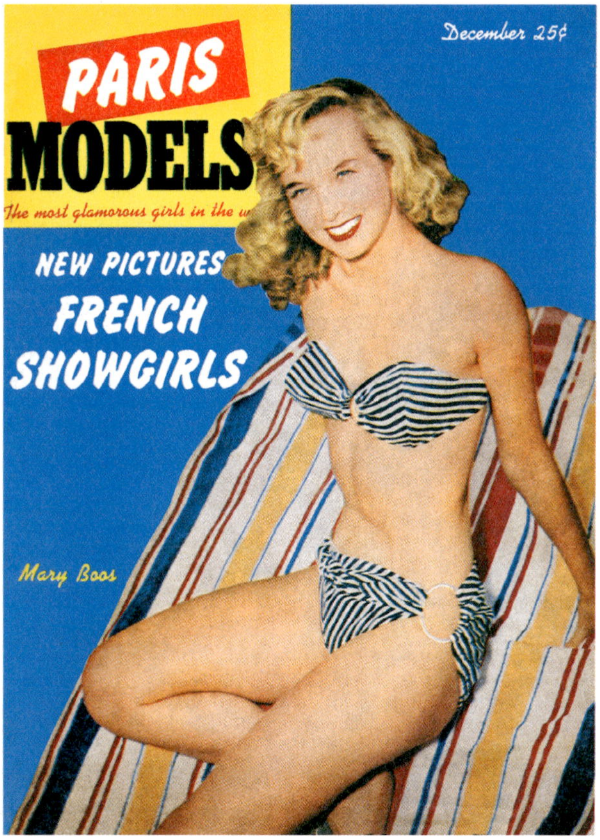

YEAR: **1952.** TITLE: **Paris Models.** COUNTRY: **USA.**

YEAR: **1949.** TITLE: **Glamorous Models.** COUNTRY: **USA.**

YEAR: **1950.** TITLE: **Peep Show.**
COUNTRY: **USA.**

PEEP SHOW
NO. 1
25c
CDC
TWO-FACED BEAUTY
THE NEXT TIME YOU SEE PARIS
ROSEMARY WILLIAMS

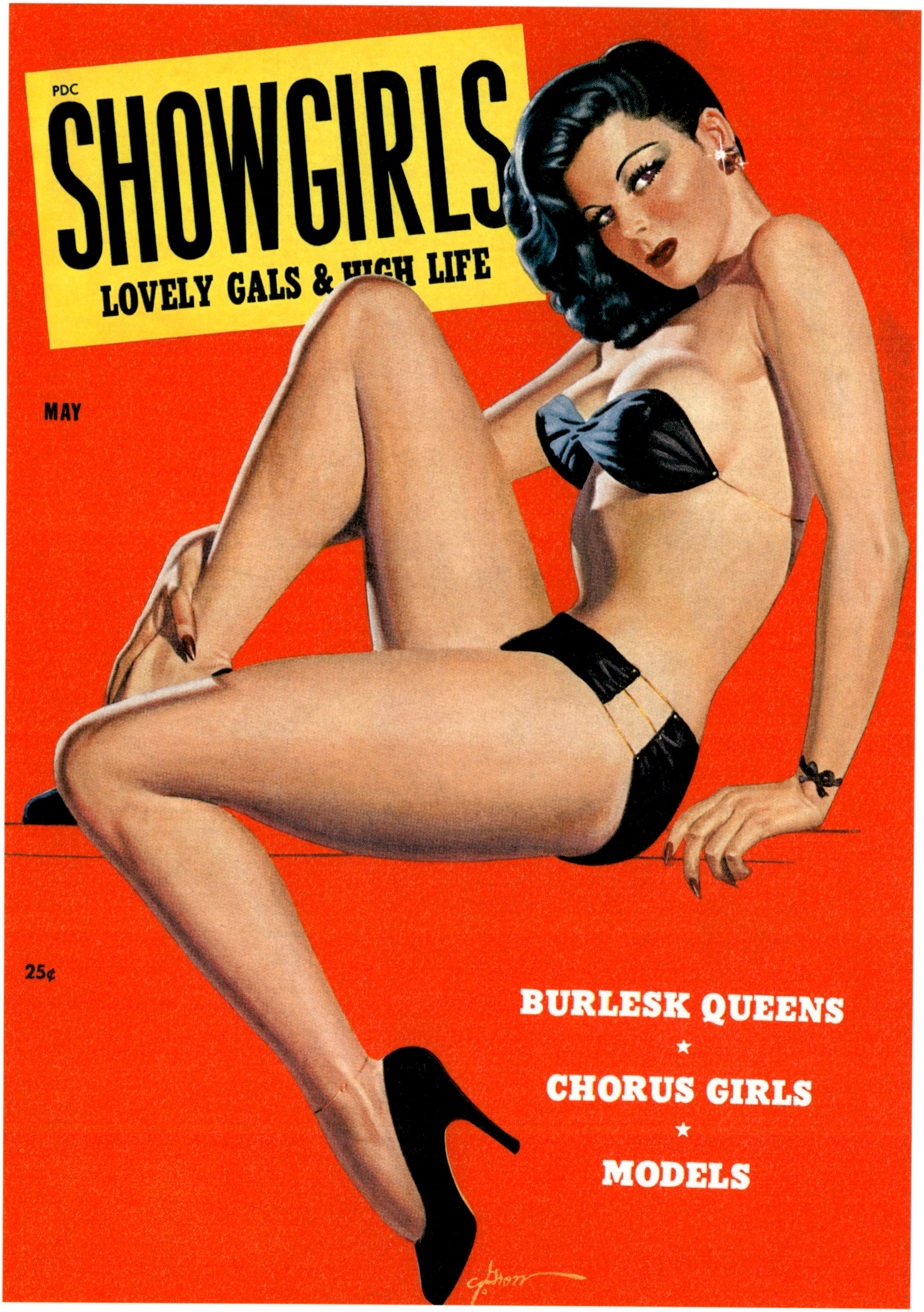

YEAR: **1947.** TITLE: **Showgirls.** ARTIST: **George Gross.** COUNTRY: **USA.**

YEAR: **1947.** TITLE: **Showgirls.** ARTIST: **George Gross.** COUNTRY: **USA.**

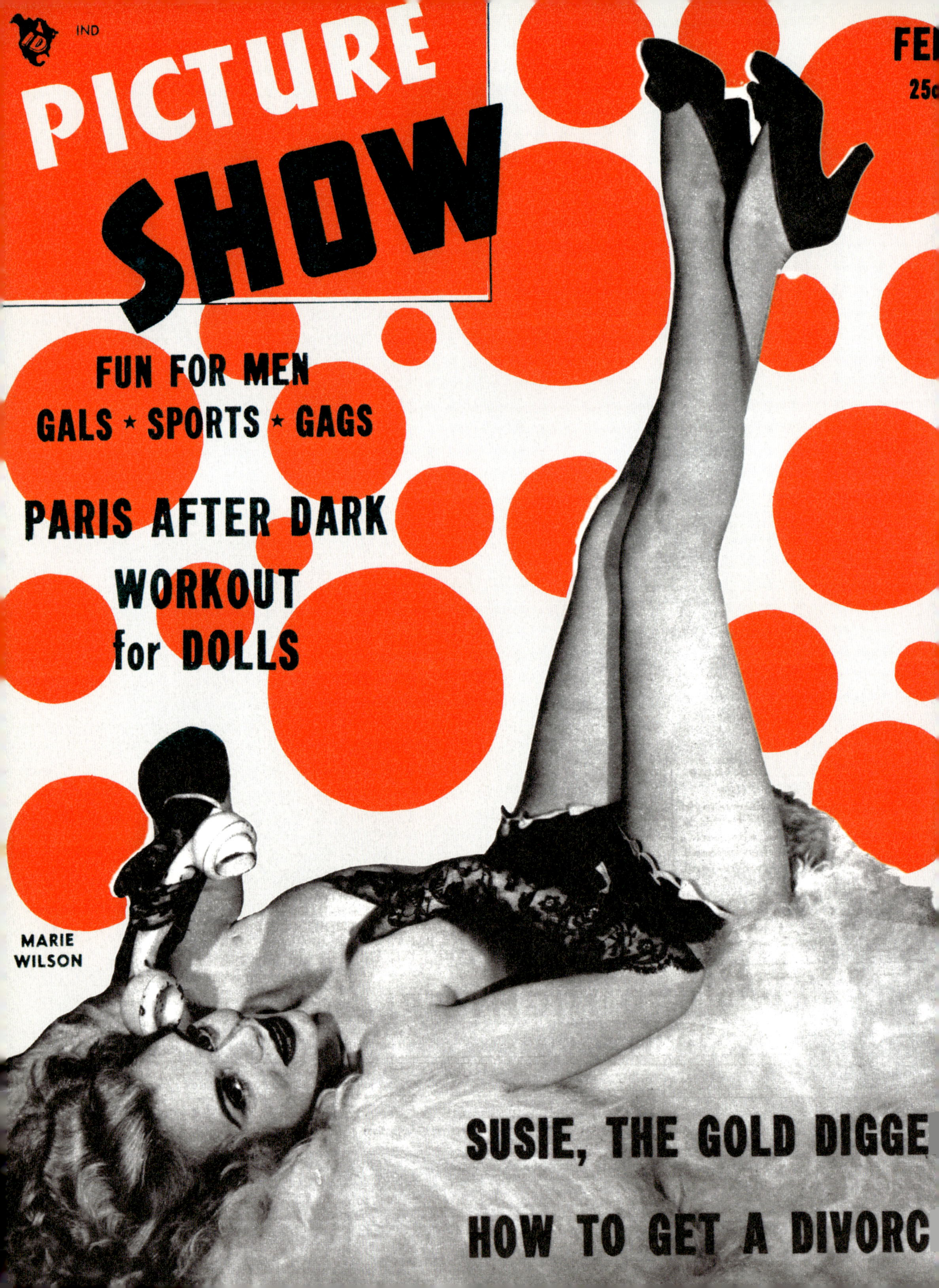
IND
PICTURE
SHOW
FE
25c
FUN FOR MEN
GALS ★ SPORTS ★ GAGS
PARIS AFTER DARK
WORKOUT
for DOLLS
MARIE
WILSON
SUSIE, THE GOLD DIGGE
HOW TO GET A DIVORC

YEAR: **1954.** TITLE: **Modern Man.** COUNTRY: **USA.**

YEAR: **1948.** TITLE: **Picture Show.**
COUNTRY: **USA.**

Though quim as a slang term for the female pudendum dates to the 19th century, the publishers of this 1951 issue of Follies clearly counted on its obscurity in the US to get them past the censors.

Obwohl das Wort quim als Slangausdruck für die weibliche Scham bereits im 19. Jahrhundert belegt ist, bauten die Herausgeber dieser Follies-Ausgabe von 1951 wohl eindeutig darauf, dass der Begriff den Zensoren in den USA nicht vertraut war.

En argot britannique « quim » désigne le sexe de la femme depuis le 19e siècle mais les éditeurs de ce numéro de Follies de 1951 espéraient bien que ce terme serait inconnu aux États-Unis afin de franchir la barrière de la censure.

YEAR: **1954.** TITLE: **Cover Girls Models.** COUNTRY: **USA.**

YEAR: **1952.** TITLE: **Paris Life.** COUNTRY: **USA.**

YEAR: **1952.** TITLE: **Paris Life.** COUNTRY: **USA.**

YEAR: **1953.** TITLE: **Paris Life.** COUNTRY: **USA.**

YEAR: **1951.** TITLE: **Follies.**
ARTIST: **Steffa.** COUNTRY: **USA.**

Follies
A GAY ALL GIRL REVUE
JAN.
25c
K
WARNING:
IS YOUR GIRL
A QUIM?
See page 36
DANGER
THIN ICE

NIGHT
AMERICA'S PICTURE MAGAZINE OF ENTERTAINMENT
and DAY
AMERICA'S PICTURE MAGAZINE OF ENTERTAINMEN
SEE PAGE
24

NIGHT *and* DAY

25 CENTS

ERICA'S PICTURE MAGAZINE OF ENTERTAINMENT

AMERICA'S PICTURE MAGAZINE OF ENTERTAINMENT

SEE PAGE 36

YEAR: **1948.** TITLE: **Peek.** COUNTRY: **USA.**

PAGE 196 + 197:
YEAR: **1955.** TITLE: **Night and Day.** COUNTRY: **USA.**
YEAR: **1954.** TITLE: **Night and Day.** COUNTRY: **USA.**

YEAR: **1948.** TITLE: **Peek.** COUNTRY: **USA.**

YEAR: **1954.** TITLE: **Frolic.** COUNTRY: **USA.**

YEAR: **1954.** TITLE: **Frolic.** COUNTRY: **USA.**

YEAR: **1953.** TITLE: **Paris Life.** COUNTRY: **USA.**

YEAR: **1951.** TITLE: **Follies.** COUNTRY: **USA.**

YEAR: **1951.** TITLE: **Cavalcade of Burlesque.** COUNTRY: **USA.**

CAVALCADE
OF
BURLESQUE
INTRODUCTION
by
ROBERT ALDA
KITTY LYNN

YEAR: **1954.** TITLE: **Cover Girls Models.** COUNTRY: **USA.**

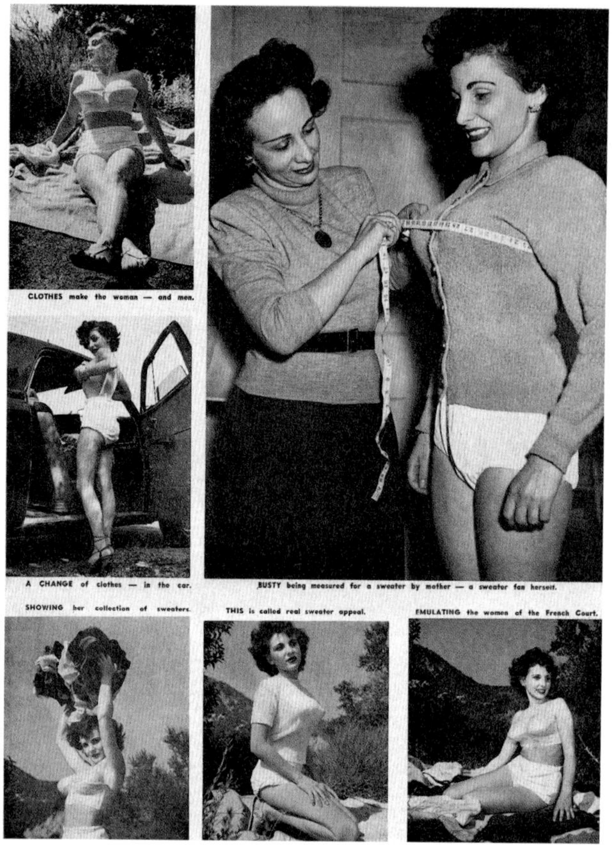

YEAR: **1950.** TITLE: **Peep Show.** COUNTRY: **USA.**

YEAR: **1954.** TITLE: **Frolic.** COUNTRY: **USA.**

YEAR: **1954.** TITLE: **Frolic.** COUNTRY: **USA.**

YEAR: **1952.** TITLE: **Paris Life.**
COUNTRY: **USA.**

CDC
PARIS LIFE
LA VIE PARISIENNE
AMERICAN EDITION
25¢
NO. 5
SECRETS OF
ARIS NIGHTS
EAUTY à la
RANCAISE

DATE

Hugh Hefner: Playboy of the Western World

Hugh Hefner: Beruf Playboy
Hugh Hefner : Playboy du monde occidental

By Richard Jaccoma and Dian Hanson

Hugh Marston Hefner launched the most influential men's magazine of the 20th century in 1953 at the age of 27 with $8,000 raised from family and friends — including several hundred dollars borrowed by using his furniture as collateral. His official biography describes young Hef as possessing "a genius IQ (152)" but being only an average student. Instead, throughout high school Hefner devoted much time to extracurricular activities such as car-

Hugh M. Hefner

Hugh Marston Hefner gründete das einflussreichste Männermagazin des 20. Jahrhunderts 1953 im Alter von 27 Jahren. Das Startkapital von 8.000 Dollar organisierte er bei Verwandten und Bekannten, hinzu kamen mehrere hundert geliehene Dollar, für die er seine eigenen Möbel verpfändet hatte. Nach seiner offiziellen Biographie verfügte der junge Hef zwar über den „IQ eines Genies (152)“, war aber nur ein mittelmäßiger Schüler. Hefner hatte seine Highschool-

One of his innovations for the campus humor magazine was a feature called "Coed of the Month" (yes, even then he knew).

Zeit lieber mit außerschulischen Aktivitäten wie dem Zeichnen von Comics und der Herausgabe einer Schülerzeitung verbracht. Nach einem kurzen Gastspiel bei der Army Ende des Zweiten Welt-

Hugh Marston Hefner, à vingt-huit ans lança en 1953 le magazine pour homme qui eut le plus d'influence sur le XXe siècle, avec 8 000 dollars empruntés à sa famille et à des amis – y compris plusieurs centaines de dollars sur la garantie de ses meubles. Nous lisons dans sa biographie officielle que le jeune Hugh avait « le QI d'un génie (152)» mais n'était qu'un étudiant moyen. Pendant ses études secondaires Hefner passait plutôt son temps à des activités extracurriculaires, comme le dessin humoristique et la publication du journal scolaire. Après avoir servi dans l'armée à la fin de la Seconde Guerre mondiale, Hefner étudia la psychologie à l'université de l'Illinois et devint le rédacteur de *Shaft*, le journal humoristique du campus. L'une de ses premières innovations fut l'introduction d'une rubrique intitulée « l'étudiante du mois » (oui, même à l'époque il savait déjà).

Après ses études Hefner exerça des tas de petits boulots pour finalement devenir rédacteur publicitaire pour *Esquire*. Lorsque *Esquire* transféra les bureaux de la rédaction de Chicago à New York, Hefner demanda une augmentation de cinq dollars. *Esquire* refusa et Hefner resta à Chicago et lança son propre magazine.

Esquire lui servit de modèle. Le distingué mensuel pour hommes, fondé en 1933

Year: **1956**. Title: **Playboy**. Country: **USA**.

Year: **1953.** Title: **Playboy.** Country: **USA.**
Reproduced by Special Permission of *Playboy* Magazine. Copyright 1953, 1981 by *Playboy*. Used with permission, all rights reserved.

The first issue of *Playboy* had something that many men most definitely wanted —Marilyn Monroe naked.

Year: **1957**. Title: **Playboy.**
Artist: **Alberto Vargas.** Country: **USA.**

tooning and publishing a school newspaper. After a stint in the Army towards the end of World War II, Hefner attended the University of Illinois where he majored in psychology and edited *Shaft*, the campus humor magazine. One of his innovations was the introduction of a feature called "Coed of the Month" (yes, even then he knew).

After college Hefner held a variety of jobs, eventually working for his favorite magazine, *Esquire*, as a copywriter. When *Esquire* moved its editorial offices from Chicago to New York Hefner asked for a five-dollar raise. *Esquire* refused and Hefner stayed in Chicago to create a men's magazine of his own.

He used *Esquire* as his template. The sophisticated men's monthly, founded in 1933 by Arnold Gingrich, garnered its fame through the thirties and forties for mixing serious literary fare

krieges besuchte Hefner die University of Illinois, an der er im Hauptfach Psychologie studierte und das humoristische Campusblatt *Shaft* herausgab. Eine seiner Neuerungen dort war die Rubrik „Studentin des Monats" (ja, schon damals wusste er, wie der Hase lief).

Nach dem College hatte er diverse Jobs und landete schließlich als Werbetexter bei *Esquire*. Als der *Esquire* seine Redaktion von Chicago nach New York verlegte, bat Hefner um eine Gehaltserhöhung von fünf Dollar. *Esquire* weigerte sich, und so blieb Hefner in Chicago, um ein eigenes Männermagazin herauszubringen. *Esquire* diente ihm als Blaupause. Das 1933 von Arnold Gingrich gegründete Monatsmagazin für den distinguierten Herrn war in den dreißiger und vierziger Jahren zu Berühmtheit gelangt, indem es seriöse literarische Beiträge zeitgenössischer Autoren mit Pettys Pin-up-Girls, Glamourphotos von George Hurrell und pikanten Cartoons anreicherte. Hefner: „In den dreißiger Jahren war *Esquire* das tollste Männermagazin der Staaten." Doch er und die anderen Veteranen des Zweiten Weltkrieges repräsentierten eine neue Generation, und mit dem Selbstvertrauen der Jugend plante er das Erfolgsrezept von *Esquire* für den Leser der Kinsey-Ära zu verbessern. Ursprünglich sollte er sein Magazin *Stag Party* (dt. etwa „Junggesellenparty") heißen, doch als die Zeitschrift *Stag* dagegen Einspruch erhob, ließ er das bereits in Auftrag gegebene Logo mit einem Hirschen als Maskottchen in das berühmte Häschen umwandeln und nannte sein Magazin *Playboy*. Die erste Nummer trug kein Erscheinungsdatum, angeblich, weil Hefner nicht wusste, wann –

par Arnold Gingrich, acquit sa notoriété dans les années 30 et 40 en combinant des textes littéraires rédigés par de grands écrivains de l'époque avec des pin-ups de Petty, des photos glamour par George Hurrel et des dessins humoristiques osés. Hefner raconte que « dans les années 30, *Esquire* était le magazine pour hommes le plus connu en Amérique ». Lui et les vétérans de la Seconde Guerre mondiale formaient la nouvelle génération, et avec un culot qui n'appartient qu'à la jeunesse, il se proposa d'améliorer la formule d'*Esquire* pour l'adapter au goût du lecteur de l'après-Kinsey. Il voulut appeler la nouvelle publication *Stag Party*, mais quand le magazine *Stag* émit une objection, il changea le cerf mascotte du logo qu'il avait déjà commandé en un lapin, et intitula son magazine *Playboy*. Le premier numéro sortit

Year: **1953.** Title: **Playboy.** Country: **USA.**
Miss December 1953, Marilyn Monroe

PLAYBOY
ENTERTAINMENT FOR MEN
50c
FIRST TIME
in any magazine
FULL COLOR
the famous
MARILYN
MONROE
NUDE
VIP ON SEX
1st
ISSUE

With a young man's brash confidence Hefner envisioned improving the *Esquire* formula for the post-Kinsey reader

from top writers of the day with Petty pin-up girls, George Hurrell glamour photos and risque cartoons. Hefner says, "In the 1930s *Esquire* was the greatest men's magazine in America." He and his fellow World War II vets represented a new generation, though, and with a young manís brash confidence he envisioned improving the *Esquire* formula for the post-Kinsey reader. He hoped to call the new publication *Stag Party*, but when *Stag* magazine objected, he changed the buck mascot logo he'd already commissioned into a rabbit, and his magazine's title became *Playboy*. The first issue bore no date on the cover, reportedly because he was unsure how long — if ever — it would be before the next issue, and Hefner's name didn't appear on the inside, supposedly to make it easier for him to find a new job in the publishing industry if the issue failed.

The anonymous editor's note in the very first issue of *Playboy* set a tone which was somewhat smug and yet paradoxically welcoming and inclusive, a tone that said we are a cut above, but happy to help you rise to our level. This tone would permeate the magazine for decades to come, and be aped by a host of imitators. An excerpt:

"If you're a man between the ages of 18 and 80, *Playboy* is meant for you. If you like your entertainment served up with humor, sophistication and spice, *Playboy* will become a very special favorite. "Within the pages of *Playboy* you will find articles, fiction, picture stories, cartoons, humor and special features culled from many sources, past and present, to form a pleasure-primer styled to the masculine taste.

wenn überhaupt – eine zweite Ausgabe an die Kioske kommen würde. Auch Hefners Name tauchte nirgendwo im Heft auf, vermutlich, um im Falle eines Misserfolges leichter wieder einen Job in der Verlagswelt zu bekommen.

Das Geleitwort des anonymen Herausgebers schlug einen Ton an, der zwar in gewisser Weise arrogant war, aber paradoxerweise zugleich auch zum Mitmachen einlud, ein Tonfall, der besagte: Wir sind zwar um einiges hipper als die anderen, aber gerne bereit, den Leser auf unser Niveau zu verhelfen. Dieser Stil sollte das Magazin für die kommenden Jahrzehnte prägen und eine Vielzahl Nachahmer auf den Plan rufen. Hier eine kleine Kostprobe:

„Wenn Sie ein Mann zwischen 18 und 80 sind, dann ist *Playboy* das Richtige für Sie. Wenn Sie sich gerne mit Humor, Finesse und dem gewissen Prickeln

YEAR: **1937.** TITLE: **Esquire.** COUNTRY: **USA.**

YEAR: **1953.** TITLE: **Esquire.** COUNTRY: **USA.**

sans date sur la couverture, parce que, d'après ce que l'on en a dit, il n'était pas sûr de la date de parution – s'il y en avait une – du prochain numéro, et le nom de Hefner n'était mentionné sur aucune des pages pour, on le suppose, lui permettre de retrouver plus facilement du travail dans l'édtion si le numéro était un flop.

La « note de l'éditeur » anonyme du premier numéro de *Playboy* donna tout de suite le ton, un ton qui dénotait une certaine suffisance mais paradoxalement accueillant avec une connotation d'appartenance, un ton qui signifiait : nous sommes élitistes, mais nous serions ravis de vous aider à vous hisser à notre niveau. Nous retrouvons le même ton dans toutes les pages du magazine au cours des décennies suivantes et il sera suivi par une foule d'imitateurs. Quelques extraits :

« Si vous êtes un homme entre 18 et 80 ans, *Playboy* est fait pour vous. Si vous

Year: **1943.** Title: **Esquire.** Country: **USA.**

Year: **1941.** Title: **Esquire.** Country: **USA.**

Year: **1941.** Title: **Esquire.** Country: **USA.**

Year: **1942.** Title: **Esquire.** Country: **USA.**

ENTERTAINMENT FOR MEN
PLAYBOY
JANUARY, 1954
MERRY CHRISTMAS
MERRY CHRISTMAS
50c
HOLIDAY
ISSU
NUDES by de DIENES

Year: **1955.** Title: **Playboy.** Country: **USA.**

Year: **1954.** Title: **Playboy.** Country: **USA.**

PLAYBOY
ENTERTAINMENT FOR MEN
MARCH 50 cents

YEAR: **1957.** TITLE: **Playboy.** COUNTRY: **USA.**

Hefner was deadly serious about delivering the high quality content he promised; and he had the taste to seek it out.

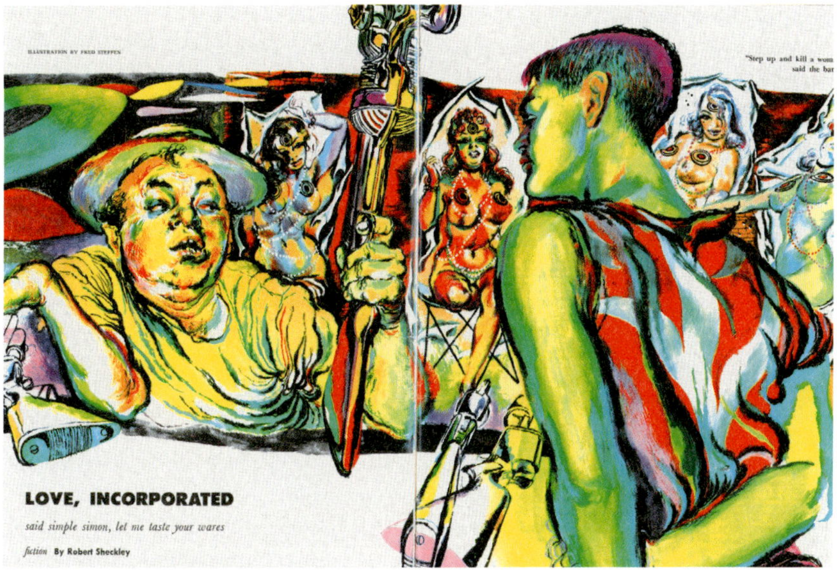

YEAR: **1956.** TITLE: **Playboy.** COUNTRY: **USA.**
Art for Love, Incorporated by Fred Steffen

Most of today's 'magazines for men' spend all their time out-of-doors — thrashing through thorny thickets or splashing about in fast-flowing streams. We'll be out there too, occasionally, but we don't mind telling you in advance — we plan on spending most of our time inside.... We enjoy mixing up cocktails and an hors d'oeuvre or two, putting a little mood music on the phonograph and inviting in a female acquaintance for a quiet discussion on Picasso, Nietzsche, jazz, sex...."

"Humor, sophistication and spice" aside, the first issue of *Playboy* had something which many men most definitely wanted — namely, that now-iconic centerfold picture of Marilyn Monroe naked, which Hefner had bought from a local calendar printer. From the very first issue, the magazine's carefully considered formula worked splendidly:

unterhalten lassen, dann wird der *Playboy* Ihr ganz spezielles Lieblingsblatt werden.

Im *Playboy* werden Sie Reportagen finden, Literatur, Bildberichte, Cartoons, Humor und Artikel aus verschiedensten Quellen, aus Vergangenheit und Gegenwart, die alle zusammen eine Vergnügungsanleitung für den maskulinen Geschmack bilden.

Die meisten der heutigen ‚Männermagazine' bewegen sich hauptsächlich in der freien Natur – durchpflügen dorniges Gestrüpp oder plantschen in reißenden Flüssen herum. Auch wir werden uns gelegentlich hinaus wagen, doch wir wollen Ihnen von Anfang an eines gestehen – die meisten Zeit möchten wir im Haus verbringen ... Wir ziehen es vor, Cocktails zu mixen und ein oder zwei Horsd'oeuvres anzurichten, etwas gedämpfte Musik aufzulegen und eine

aimez l'humour, le raffinement et la grivoiserie, *Playboy* deviendra vite votre favori très spécial. Dans les pages de *Playboy* vous trouverez des articles, de la fiction, des histoires en images, des dessins humoristiques, de l'humour et des articles de fond provenant de différentes sources d'hier et d'aujourd'hui, pour le plaisir d'une lecture adaptée au goût masculin. Dans la plupart des ‹ magazines pour homme › l'action se situe à l'extérieur – se tailler un chemin à travers des buissons épineux ou remonter des torrents impétueux. Nous les y suivront aussi, occasionnellement, mais nous vous prévenons – avec nous elle se passera aussi beaucoup à la maison. Nous aimons préparer des cocktails et un hors d'œuvre ou deux, mettre une musique d'ambiance sur le phonographe et inviter une amie pour une conversation intime sur Picasso, Nietzsche, le jazz, le sexe… »

YEAR: **1957.** TITLE: **Playboy.**
ARTIST: **Leroy Neiman.** COUNTRY: **USA.**

"We enjoy mixing up cocktails and an hors d'oeuvre or two, putting a little mood music on the phonograph and inviting in a female acquaintance for a quiet discussion on Picasso, Nietzsche, jazz, sex..."

—from editorial, Playboy issue 1, 1953

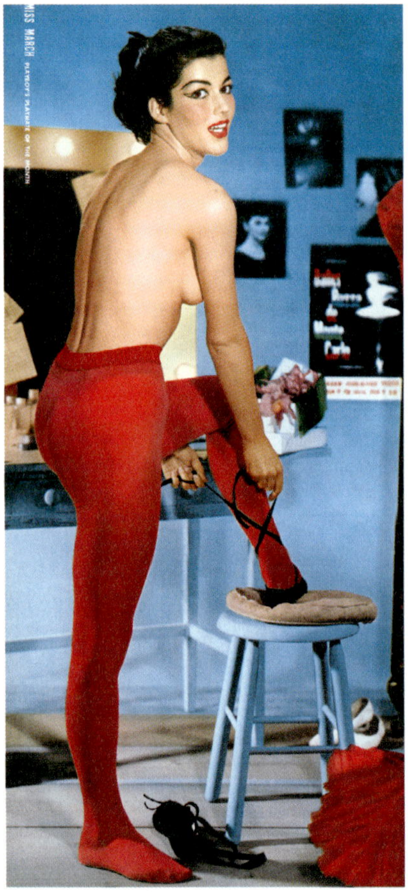

YEAR: **1957.** TITLE: **Playboy.** COUNTRY: **USA.**
Miss March 1957, Sandra Edwards

Playboy's first issue sold over 54,000 copies of its 70,000 print run, definitely enough to pay the bills and to justify producing issue number two. And three... and four....and for Hefner to proudly add his name to the masthead.

What made *Playboy*'s formula so immediately successful? That line about "spending most of our time inside" is central. With the exception of *Esquire*, all American men's magazines up to that point assumed their readership to

weibliche Bekannte zu einer gepflegten Unterhaltung über Picasso, Nietzsche, Jazz und Sex einzuladen ..."

Von „Humor, Finesse und dem gewissen Prickeln" mal abgesehen, bot die erste Ausgabe des *Playboy* etwas, das die meisten Männer garantiert sehen wollten: das zur Ikone gewordene Centerfold-Foto der nackten Marilyn Monroe, das Hefner einem ortsansässigen Kalenderverlag abgekauft hatte. Vom ersten Moment an funktionierte das sorgfältig erwogene Konzept des Magazins: das erste Heft des *Playboys* verkaufte 54.000 Exemplare seiner Auflage von 70.000, entschieden genug, um die Rechnungen zu bezahlen und sich an die zweite Nummer zu setzen. Und an die dritte ... und vierte ... und für Hefner, um nun stolz seinen Namen ins Impressum zu setzen.

Was machte den *Playboy* auf Anhieb so erfolgreich? Jene Zeile über die Aktivitäten im Haus ist von zentraler Bedeutung. Mit Ausnahme von *Esquire*

« L'humour, le raffinement et la grivoiserie » à part, le premier numéro de *Playboy* avait quand même une chose qui intéressait énormément les hommes – à savoir la page du milieu, une icône aujourd'hui, la photographie de Marilyn Monroe dans le plus simple appareil, que Hefner avait rachetée à un imprimeur de calendrier local. Dès le premier numéro, la formule soigneusement élaborée du magazine fut une éclatante réussite : le premier numéro de *Playboy* se vendit à plus de 54 000 exemplaires sur les 70 000 imprimés, ce qui était plus que suffisant pour payer les factures et justifier la sortie du deuxième. Et du troisième… et du quatrième… et pour Hefner d'ajouter fièrement son nom en haut sur la couverture. Pour quelle raison la formule connut un tel succès ? La clef réside dans l'expression « à la maison ». A l'exception d'*Esquire*, jusque là tous les magazines américains pour homme supposaient que leurs lecteurs étaient des « hommes à hommes », des chasseurs, pêcheurs, amateurs de bière, des fiers-à-bras

YEAR: **1956.** TITLE: **Playboy.** COUNTRY: **USA.**
Miss June 1956, June Walker

PLAYBOY
ENTERTAINMENT R MEN
AUGUST 50 cents

Playboy proposed a more sensual life where culture trumped brawn, where a man might actually share his leisure time with women and like it.

YEAR: **1960.** TITLE: **Playboy.** COUNTRY: **USA.**
Hefner at the launch of his television show *Playboy's Penthouse*

be "men's men", hunting, fishing, beer-drinking, bar-brawling fellows who associated with females only for sex and to have their wounds bandaged, and then rushed back to punching shoulders with their buddies. *Playboy* proposed a more sensual life where culture trumped brawn, where a man might actually share his leisure time with women and like it. In the *Playboy* world a man could wear stylish clothes (witness Hef's silk pajamas), decorate his apartment, become a gourmet cook, and in so doing become a chick magnet. That so many embraced this so eagerly revealed the lie in America's prevailing male stereotypes.

Hefner was deadly serious about delivering the high quality content he promised; and he had both the taste to seek it out and the intelligence to recognize it when he found it. As growing

richteten sich bis dato alle amerikanischen Männermagazine an „echte Kerle", Burschen, die zur Jagd gingen, angelten, Bier tranken, sich in Kneipen prügelten und sich nur zum Sex mit Frauen abgaben, oder um ihre Wunden verpflastern zu lassen, bevor es zurück zu den Jungs ging. Der *Playboy* propagierte ein kultivierteres Leben, in dem Geist Muskelkraft übertrumpft, in dem ein Mann seine Freizeit mit Frauen teilt und echtes Vergnügen daran findet. In der *Playboy*-Welt durfte ein Mann elegante Kleidung tragen (man denke nur an Hefs seidene Pyjamas), seine Wohnung ansprechend einrichten und sich zum Gourmet-Koch ausbilden, um so zum Schwarm der Frauen zu werden. Der Erfolg dieser Formel zeigt, wie verlogen das vorherrschende Männerbild in den Vereinigten Staaten war.

Hefner war es absolut ernst damit, die

de bistrots qui ne s'intéressaient aux femmes que pour le sexe et panser leurs blessures, pour ensuite retourner se mesurer à leurs copains. *Playboy* offrait une vie plus sensuelle, où la culture l'emportait sur le muscle, où un homme pouvait passer ses loisirs en compagnie des femmes et y prendre plaisir. Dans le monde de *Playboy*, un homme pouvait s'habiller avec élégance (les pyjamas de soie de Hef' sont là pour en témoigner), décorer son appartement, être un fin cuisinier, et ne rien perdre de son charme auprès des femmes. Qu'ils aient été si nombreux à s'y rallier exposa le mensonge du mâle dominant des stéréotypes américains.

Hefner était absolument sérieux lorsqu'il parlait de produire un magazine de très grande qualité comme il l'avait promis ; et il avait à la fois le goût de la rechercher et l'intelligence de la reconnaî-

Playboy Building, Chicago

YEAR: **1959.** TITLE: **Playboy.** COUNTRY: **USA.**
Through the late fifties and sixties the magazine regularly featured architects' fantasy renderings of *Playboy* pads.

YEAR: **1959.** TITLE: **Playboy.** COUNTRY: **USA.**

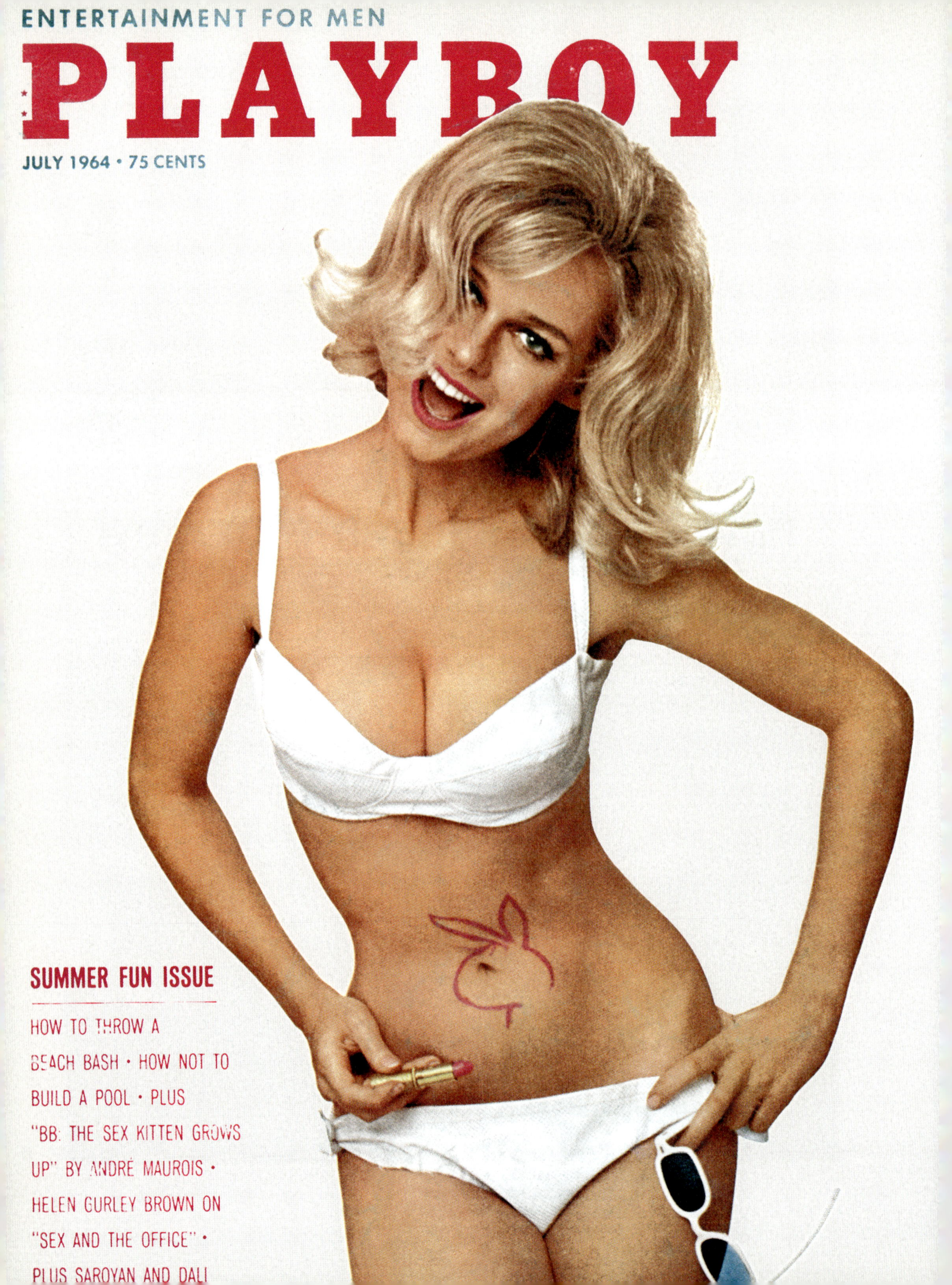
ENTERTAINMENT FOR MEN
PLAYBOY
JULY 1964 • 75 CENTS
SUMMER FUN ISSUE
HOW TO THROW A BEACH BASH • HOW NOT TO BUILD A POOL • PLUS "BB: THE SEX KITTEN GROWS UP" BY ANDRÉ MAUROIS • HELEN GURLEY BROWN ON "SEX AND THE OFFICE" • PLUS SAROYAN AND DALI

By 1960 *Playboy* was selling over a million copies a month. This was the beginning of Hefner "living large".

YEAR: **1963.** TITLE: **Playboy.** COUNTRY: **USA.**

sales allowed, he hired a skilled staff of designers, editors, photographers and illustrators; and famously paid all his contributors top dollar right from the earliest issues. The generous rates insured the magazine its choice of world-class writers, often the more controversial of their day, including Henry Miller, Vladimir Nabokov, Norman Mailer, Ray Bradbury, Philip Roth and John Updike. To complete his vision of an *Esquire* tailored to younger tastes, in 1960 Hefner contracted Alberto Vargas, a somewhat racier artist than George Petty, to paint a monthly *Playboy* pin-up.

Over the years enough jokes have been made about "buying *Playboy* for the articles" to make it impossible even to mention without stifling a yawn, but also undeniably, over the decades there have been countless times when *Playboy*'s articles have been too good

von ihm versprochene hohe inhaltliche Qualität zu gewährleisten; er verfügte sowohl über den nötigen guten Geschmack wie über die Intelligenz, sie zu erkennen, wenn er ihr begegnete. Als es die steigenden Verkaufszahlen erlaubten, heuerte er eine erfahrene Mannschaft aus Grafikern, Redakteuren, Fotografen und Illustratoren an und bezahlte von Beginn an allen Mitarbeitern ein legendär üppiges Gehalt. Die großzügigen Honorare sicherten dem Magazin seinen Stamm an erstklassigen Autoren, oft zu ihrer Zeit durchaus umstrittene Vertreter ihrer Zunft, darunter u.a. Henry Miller, Vladimir Nabokov, Norman Mailer, Ray Bradbury, Philip Roth oder John Updike. Um seiner Vorstellung von einem *Esquire* für einen jüngeren Geschmack näherzukommen, engagierte Hefner 1960 Alberto Vargas, einen etwas wagemutigeren Künstler

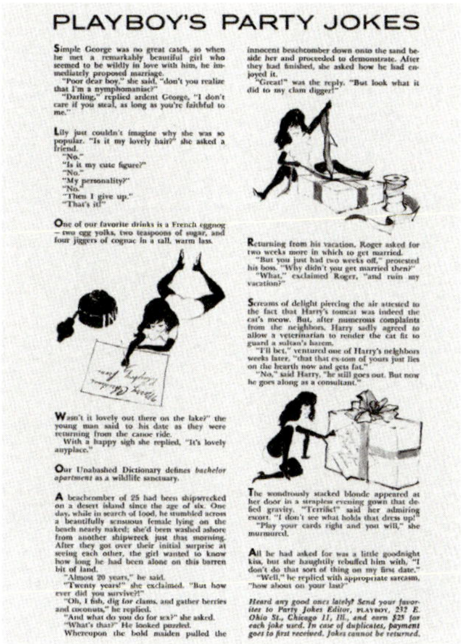

PLAYBOY'S PARTY JOKES

Simple George was no great catch, so when he met a remarkably beautiful girl who seemed to be wildly in love with him, he immediately proposed marriage.
"Poor dear boy," she said, "don't you realize that I'm a nymphomaniac?"
"Darling," replied ardent George, "I don't care if you steal, as long as you're faithful to me."

Lily just couldn't imagine why she was so popular. "Is it my lovely hair?" she asked a friend.
"No."
"Is it my cute figure?"
"No."
"My personality?"
"No."
"Then I give up."
"That's it!"

One of our favorite drinks is a French eggnog – two egg yolks, two teaspoons of sugar, and four jiggers of cognac in a tall, warm lass.

Wasn't it lovely out there on the lake?" the young man said to his date as they were returning from the canoe ride.
With a happy sigh she replied, "It's lovely anyplace."

Our Unabashed Dictionary defines *bachelor apartment* as a wildlife sanctuary.

A beachcomber of 25 had been shipwrecked on a desert island since the age of six. One day, while in search of food, he stumbled across a beautifully sensuous female lying on the beach nearly naked; she'd been washed ashore from another shipwreck just that morning. After they got over their initial surprise at seeing each other, the girl wanted to know how long he had been alone on this barren bit of land.
"Almost 20 years," he said.
"Twenty years!" she exclaimed. "But how ever did you survive?!"
"Oh, I fish, dig for clams, and gather berries and coconuts," he replied.
"And what do you do for sex?" she asked.
"What's that?" He looked puzzled.
Whereupon the bold maiden pulled the innocent beachcomber down onto the sand beside her and proceeded to demonstrate. After they had finished, she asked how he had enjoyed it.
"Great!" was the reply. "But look what it did to my clam digger!"

Returning from his vacation, Roger asked for two weeks more in which to get married.
"But you just had two weeks off," protested his boss. "Why didn't you get married then?"
"What," exclaimed Roger, "and ruin my vacation?"

Screams of delight piercing the air attested to the fact that Harry's tomcat was indeed the cat's meow. But, after numerous complaints from the neighbors, Harry sadly agreed to allow a veterinarian to render the cat fit to guard a sultan's harem.
"I'll bet," ventured one of Harry's neighbors weeks later, "that that ex-tom of yours just lies on the hearth now and gets fat."
"No," said Harry, "he still goes out. But now he goes along as a consultant."

The wondrously stacked blonde appeared at her door in a strapless evening gown that defied gravity. "Terrific!" said her admiring escort. "I don't see what holds that dress up!"
"Play your cards right and you will," she murmured.

All he had asked for was a little goodnight kiss, but she haughtily rebuffed him with, "I don't do that sort of thing on my first date."
"Well," he replied with appropriate sarcasm, "how about on your last?"

Heard any good ones lately? Send your favorites to Party Jokes Editor, PLAYBOY, 232 E. Ohio St., Chicago 11, Ill., and earn $25 for each joke used. In case of duplicates, payment goes to first received. Jokes cannot be returned.

YEAR: **1961.** TITLE: **Playboy.** COUNTRY: **USA.**

YEAR: **1961.** TITLE: **Playboy.** COUNTRY: **USA.**

tre lorsqu'il la rencontrait. Comme les ventes continuaient à augmenter, il recruta une équipe de rédacteurs, de dessinateurs, de photographes et d'illustrateurs de talent ; et il était connu pour payer tous ses collaborateurs à prix d'or dès les premiers numéros. Ces tarifs généreux lui assurèrent la collaboration d'écrivains d'une classe internationale, souvent très contestés à leur époque, comme Henry Miller, Vladimir Nabokov, Norman Mailer, Ray Bradbury, Philip Roth et John Updike. Pour parachever sa vision d'un *Esquire* pour une génération plus jeune, Hefner engagea Alberto Vargas, un artiste quelque peu plus audacieux que George Petty pour dessiner tous les mois la pin-up de *Playboy*.

Avec les années, les sempiternelles plaisanteries sur le fait « d'acheter *Playboy* pour les articles » en ont rendu impossible la simple évocation sans étouffer un baillement, mais il faut reconnaître qu'au

Year: **1956.** Title: **Playboy.** Artist: **Charles W. Miller.** Country: **USA.**

Year: **1956.** Title: **Playboy.** Artist: **Sokol.** Country: **USA.**

Year: **1976.** Title: **Playboy.** Artist: **Gahan Wilson.** Country: **USA.**

Year: **1979.** Title: **Playboy.** Artist: **Buck Brown.** Country: **USA.**

Year: **1962.** Title: **Playboy.**
Artist: **Harvey Kurtzman.** Country: **USA.**

Little Annie Fanny
By HARVEY KURTZMAN AND WILLY ELDER
ON MADISON AVENUE, WHERE THE SOAP HUCKSTER DONS A GRAY FLANNEL SUIT, OUR LITTLE ANNIE TAKES ONE OFF...
LET'S TAKE THE SHOT OVER AGAIN A COUPLE MORE TIMES, MISS FANNY.
BUT, MR. BATTBARTON, ALL THE SOAPSUDS HAVE DISSOLVED!
SOAP-SUDS!
WHO'S GOT THE SOAPSUDS?
ANYONE GOT THE SOAPSUDS?
I HAVE THE FILM AND I HAVE THE SOAPSU-AWK!
SST! GET HIM OUTTA HERE!
BEETHOV
SUDS
Elder

HI, ANNIE SWEETIE... DID I HEAR YOU TALKING TO YOURSELF AS I CAME IN?
TALKING TO MY-SELF?... DON'T BE SILLY, RUTHIE... I WAS TALKING TO MY WINSOM CIGARETTES.
MISS MANICOTTI 1962
MISS PANACEA 1962
To Anny... FROM: AF-L&CIO
MISS KNISH OF 1959
MISS CHUCK STEAK 1960
MISS ASPIC 1958

Year: **1979**. Title: **Playboy**. Country: **USA**.

Hefner had always been of the opinion that *Playboy* was liberating women from sexual repression, saying, "I was a feminist before there was such a thing as feminism".

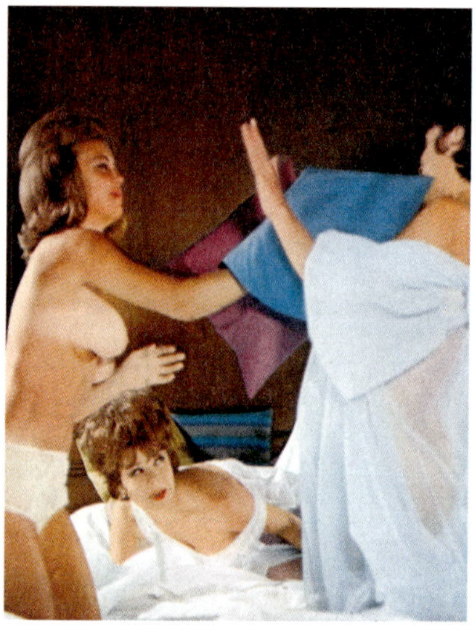

Year: **1963**. Title: **Playboy**. Country: **USA**.

to miss. The *Playboy* Interview series with the famous and infamous now amounts to an astonishing body of work. It began in 1962 with Miles Davis, interviewed by Alex Haley. Over the years numerous luminaries followed — from Ayn Rand, Malcolm X, and Dr. Albert Schweitzer, to Fidel Castro, Snoop Dogg and presidential candidate Jimmy Carter. Interviews of groups small and large have included Siskel and Ebert, Masters and Johnson, John, Paul, George and Ringo, the Nicaraguan Sandinistas and the Irish Republican Army.

By 1960 *Playboy* was selling over a million copies a month. This was the beginning of Hefner "living large" — acting out in reality the fantasy life endlessly espoused on the pages of his publication. Throughout the early 1960s, Hefner saw to it that life would imitate art in many other ways as well.

als Petty, um dem *Playboy* allmonatlich ein Pin-up zu malen. Witze darüber, dass man den *Playboy* „nur der Artikel wegen" kaufe, sind so überstrapaziert worden, dass man dabei heute kaum ein Gähnen unterdrücken kann, doch unbestreitbar hat es über die Jahrzehnte hinweg immer wieder legendäre Beiträge im *Playboy* gegeben. Die Interviews, die der *Playboy* mit den Berühmten wie den Berüchtigten führte, sind mittlerweile auf eine beeindruckende Zahl angewachsen. Es begann 1962 mit Miles Davis, der von Alex Haley interviewt wurde, ihm folgten zahllose Berühmtheiten von Ayn Rand, Malcolm X und Dr. Albert Schweitzer über Fidel Castro und Präsidentschaftskandidat Jimmy Carter bis Snoop Dogg. Gesprächsrunden, im großen wie im kleinen Rahmen, wurden u.a. mit Siskel und Ebert geführt, mit Masters und

Year: **1966**. Title: **Playboy**. Country: **USA**.
Playmate of the Year Jo Collins visiting the troupes in Viet Nam.

Year: **1967**. Title: **Playboy**. Country: **USA**.

cours de son histoire, *Playboy* a publié à maintes reprises d'excellents articles à ne pas manquer. La série des *Playboy* Interviews de gens célèbres pour le meilleur ou pour le pire, forme à l'heure actuelle une impressionnante somme de travail. Le premier fut Miles Davis, en 1962, interviewé par Alex Haley. Au cours des années suivantes, de nombreuses personnalités importantes se sont succédées, de Ayn Rand, Malcolm X, le Dr Albert Schweitzer, à Fidel Castro, Snoop Dogg et le candidat à l'élection présidentielle Jimmy Carter. Ont aussi été publiés des interviews de groupes, petits et grands, comme Siskel et Ebert, Masters et Johnson, John, Paul, George et Ringo, les sandinistes du Nicaragua et l'armée républicaine irlandaise.

En 1960 *Playboy* se vendait à plus d'un million d'exemplaires par mois. Ce fut le début de la « grande vie » pour Hefner – réalisant la vie de rêve qu'il nous présentait régulièrement dans les pages de son

PLAYBOY
NTERTAINMENT FOR MEN
MAY 1979 • $2.00
EXCLUSIVE!
THE SECRET
LIFE OF
MARILYN
MONROE
OREIGN SEX STARS · DAN RATHER · WORKING THE VICE
QUAD · SPRING FASHIONS · A SURPRISE PLAYBOY INTERVIEW

By 1971 the magazine was selling seven million copies a month, and Playboy Enterprises went public with twenty-three Playboy Clubs.

YEAR: **1963.** TITLE: **Playboy.** COUNTRY: **USA.**
Hefner at the opening of yet another *Playboy* Club.

This included the launch of his TV show *Playboy's Penthouse* in October 1959, his sponsorship of the first Playboy Jazz Festival the same year, and his purchase of the Chicago Playboy mansion in 1960. In keeping with the inclusionary part of the Playboy message — which remained key to its market success — he launched the first of the Playboy Clubs in Chicago that year.

By 1971 the magazine was selling seven million copies a month, and Playboy Enterprises went public with twenty-three Playboy Clubs, resorts and casinos worldwide, plus a book publishing house, a modeling agency, a record label, television and motion picture production companies and even a limousine service. Hefner purchased the Playboy Mansion West in 1971 and moved completely to Los Angeles in 1975 to begin living The Good Life in

Johnson, mit John, Paul, George und Ringo, den nicaraguanischen Sandinistas und der IRA.

1960 verkaufte der *Playboy* über eine Million Hefte pro Ausgabe. Zu diesem Zeitpunkt begann Hefner selbst „auf großem Fuß" die Fantasien auszuleben, die auf den Seiten seines Blattes immer wieder ausgemalt wurden. „Life imitates art", dazu passte u.a. auch der Start seiner eigenen Fernsehshow, *Playboy's Penthouse*, im Jahr 1959, seine Schirmherrschaft über das erste Playboy-Jazzfestival im selben Jahr und 1960 der Erwerb des Playboy-Mansion in Chicago. Dem Gemeinschafts-Aspekt der Playboy-Philosophie treu bleibend – der weiterhin der Schlüssel zum Erfolg war –, gründete er im selben Jahr eben dort den ersten Playboy-Club.

1971 verkaufte das Magazin schon sieben Millionen Hefte im Monat, und Playboy-Enterprises unterhielt 23 Playboy-Clubs, -Resorts und -Casinos auf der ganzen Welt. Ein Buchverlag, Merchandising und eine TV- und Filmproduktion gehörten ebenfalls dazu, ja sogar eine Mietlimousinen-Firma. 1971 erwarb Hefner das Playboy Mansion West und zog 1975 ganz nach Los Angeles um, um sich ernsthaft dem „süßen Leben" zu widmen. Seine Stellung hatte ihm schon immer die schönsten Playmates als Gespielinnen zugeführt, doch in den Siebzigern mussten sich auch diese Frauen darauf einstellen, Gemeingut zu werden: das Leben im Mansion war eine einzige große Swingerparty. Der einzige Wermutstropfen in dieser Ära war die zunehmende Kritik, der sich der *Playboy* seitens der Feministinnen ausgesetzt sah. Hefner vertrat stets die Auffassung, der *Playboy* befreie die Frauen von der

YEAR: **1963.** TITLE: **Playboy.** COUNTRY: **USA.**

magazine. Au début des années 60, Hefner s'arrangea pour que la vie imite aussi l'art dans d'autres domaines. Cela se matérialisa par le lancement du TV show *Playboy's Penthouse* en octobre 1959, le financement du premier Playboy Jazz Festival la même année et l'achat d'une luxueuse résidence à Chicago, le Playboy Mansion. Et pour rester fidèle à cette notion d'appartenance du message de Playboy – qui est la clé de son succès commercial – il ouvrit cette année là le premier des Clubs Playboy à Chicago.

En 1971 le magazine se vendait à sept millions d'exemplaires par mois et la Société Playboy fit son entrée en bourse avec vingt-trois Clubs Playboy, des villégiatures et des casinos dans le monde entier, plus une maison d'édition du livre, une agence de modèles, un label de disque, plusieurs compagnies de production de cinéma et de télévision et même un service

Year: **1963.** Title: **Playboy.** Country: **USA.**

ENTERTAINMENT FOR MEN
SEPTEMBER 1969 • ONE DOLLAR
PLAYBOY
"THE HUMAN ZOO" BY "NAKED APE" AUTHOR DESMOND MORRIS • A NEW NOVELETTE BY JOHN UPDIKE • PIGSKIN PREVIEW • CAMPUS FASHIONS • GIRLS OF AUSTRALIA
STUDENT POWER
SEX ON CAMPUS • A PLAYBOY PANEL ON STUDENT REVOLT WITH HAYAKAWA, HAYDEN OF SDS AND OTHERS • ANDY WARHOL • KEN W. PURDY • SENATOR GAYLORD NELSON

Year: **1969.** Title: **Playboy.** Country: **USA.**

To balance the feminist attacks, many women rallied in Hef's defense, claiming *Playboy* helped them gain sexual freedom.

Year: **1970.** Title: **Playboy.** Country: **USA.**

earnest. Naturally his position had always ensured him pick-of-the-litter in terms of Playmates, and over the years the list of his girlfriends could be cross-referenced to the pages of his own publication. In the seventies even those special women had to be prepared to share: life at the Mansion was one long swing party. In this golden era the only fly in the KY was the criticism *Playboy* began receiving from feminists. Hefner had always been of the opinion that *Playboy* was liberating women from sexual repression. As he explains, "I helped sponsor the lower-court cases that eventually led to Roe vs Wade. I was a feminist before there was such a thing as feminism" That anti-sexual part of feminism is very antiquated, and quite frankly was anti-revolutionary at the time." To balance the feminist attacks, many women rallied in

sexuellen Unterdrückung: „Ich half dabei, die ersten Verfahren mitzufinanzieren, die schließlich zum Prozess Roe gegen Wade führten. Ich war Feminist, bevor es überhaupt so etwas wie Feminismus gab. Dieser sexualfeindliche Aspekt des Feminismus ist sehr antiquiert und war damals ehrlich gesagt anti-revolutionär.“ Natürlich fanden sich auch zahlreiche Frauen, die sich in dieser Kontroverse auf Hefners Seite stellten.

In den achtziger Jahren, dem dunkelsten Kapitel in der Geschichte des Magazins, sah sich der *Playboy* weiteren Herausforderungen gegenüber. Der damalige Aufschwung bei sexuell zeigefreudigeren Magazinen als der *Playboy* und der Videoboom fielen mit der Wahl Ronald Reagans zum Präsidenten 1980 zusammen. Als einige Jahre später die ersten AIDS-Fälle auftraten, vollzog Amerika eine konservative moralische Wende, auf deren Höhepunkt 1984 Reagan die Meese-Kommission zur Untersuchung der sozialen Folgen der Pornografie einberief.

Die Kommission war eine seltsame Versammlung aus rechtslastigen Politikern, Laienpredigern und radikalen Feministinnen. Ihre 1986 veröffentlichten Ergebnisse beurteilten die Pornografie tatsächlich als schlimmes, schlimmes Übel, und zu Hefners Entsetzen warf man sein geliebtes Magazin mit den übrigen in einen Topf. Derartig gebrandmarkt verlor der *Playboy* viele seiner Abnehmer und Anzeigenkunden. Die Verkaufszahlen fielen auf 3,5 Millionen im Monat, wo sie auch zu Beginn des 21. Jahrhunderts noch stehen. Zu allem Übel erlitt Hefner 1985 im Alter von 59 Jahren einen leichten Schlag-

Year: **1971.** Title: **Playboy.** Country: **USA.**

de location de limousines. Hefner acheta une résidence, le Playboy Mansion West, en 1971 et s'installa définitivement à Los Angeles en 1975 pour mener la Grande Vie dans tous les sens du terme. Naturellement, sa position lui avait toujours garanti « les plus belles de la portée », je parle des Playmates, et au cours des années la liste de ses petites amies renvoyait aux pages de sa propre publication. Dans les années 70, même ces femmes particulières ont dû apprendre à partager : la vie au Mansion n'était qu'une longue fête échangiste. La seule ombre au tableau de cet Âge d'or fut que *Playboy* devint la cible des féministes. Hefner avait toujours pensé que *Playboy* libérerait la femme de la répression sexuelle. Comme il l'explique : « J'ai aidé au financement des causes au tribunal de première instance, ce qui finalement a mené au procès Roe contre Wade. J'étais un féministe avant la lettre.

Year: **1956.** Title: **Playboy.** Country: **USA.**

In the *Playboy* world a man could wear stylish clothes, decorate his apartment, become a gourmet cook, and in so doing become a chick magnet.

Year: **1957.** Title: **Playboy.** Country: **USA.**

Hef's defense, claiming *Playboy* helped them gain sexual freedom.

More attacks followed in the eighties, *Playboy*'s darkest decade. A boom in explicit magazines and video coincided with the election of president Ronald Reagan in 1980. When the first AIDS cases appeared a couple years later America took a conservative moral turn, culminating in Reagan appointing the Meese Commission to study the social effects of pornography in 1984.

The commission was a strange mix of right wing politicians, lay preachers and radical feminists. Their conclusions, published in 1986, were that pornography was very bad indeed and to Hefner's horror his upscale lifestyle magazine was lumped in with all the rest. Thus branded, *Playboy* lost considerable newsstand distribution and

anfall. Heute bezeichnet er diesen Gehirnschlag als „Glücksfall". Zeitlebens ein Workaholic und Perfektionist, der so hart zu feiern wie zu arbeiten verstand, trat Hef nun kürzer und setzte seine Tochter als Geschäftsführerin ein, während er sich selbst mit der Rolle des Editor-in-chief zufrieden gab. 1989 gab er gar seinen hedonistischen Lebenswandel auf, heiratete das Playmate des Jahres Kimberley Conrad und bekam zwei weitere Kinder, beides Jungen. Fast zehn Jahre hielt Hefner sich vom Partytreiben fern und zog seine Söhne groß. Mit der Wahl des Lebemanns Clinton zum Präsidenten endeten 1992 die Hexenjagden der Reagan-Ära. Tatsächlich gab es während beider Amtsperioden Clintons keine Pornografieprozesse vor Bundesgerichten. In diesem freundlicheren Klima erholten sich der *Playboy* wie auch Hefner. In den späten neunziger

D'ailleurs, ce côté anti-sexuel du féminisme est tombé complétement en désuétude et franchement était même anti-révolutionnaire à l'époque. » Pour contrecarrer les attaques des féministes, de nombreuses femmes se rallièrent pour prendre la défense de Hef, en déclarant que *Playboy* leur avait permis de conquérir leur liberté sexuelle.

Les attaques augmentèrent dans les années 80, la période la plus sombre de l'histoire de *Playboy*. Une reprise des ventes des magazines et des vidéos à caractère pornographique coïncida avec l'élection de Ronald Reagan à la présidence en 1980. Lorsque les premiers cas de SIDA apparurent quelques années plus tard, l'Amérique revint à une morale plus stricte qui culmina en 1984 avec la nomination par Reagan de la commission Meese pour une étude sur les retombées sociales de la pornographie.

La commission était un mélange bizar-

Year: **1974.** Title: **Playboy.** Country: **USA.**

VON LENGERKE & ANTOINE—CHICAGO

Impossible to measure the sleeve length . . . . . while he's reading PLAYBOY. Fortunately most of our readers brief themselves on the latest in fashions *before* they venture into smart emporiums like VL & A, where this fan seems to be holding up the parade. However, it's this combination of enthusiasm for the magazine and acute clothes consciousness that makes PLAYBOY a perfectly tailored medium for anyone interested in reaching the important young men who are spending their way up in the world. Want to get an accurate measure of the PLAYBOY audience (with arms at side)?

PLAYBOY ADVERTISING DEPARTMENT • 11 E. Superior St., Chicago, MI 2-1000 • 270 Park Ave., New York, PL 9-3076

Year: **1969.** Title: **Playboy.** Country: **USA.**
Barbie Benton, the brunette
who won blonde-loving Hefner's heart.

His position had always ensured him pick-of-the-litter in terms of Playmates, and over the years the list of his girlfriends could be cross-referenced to the pages of his own publication.

Year: **1977.** Title: **Playboy.** Country: **USA.**

many of its advertisers. Sales dropped to around 3.5 million a month, where they have remained through the early 21st Century. In the middle of it all, Hefner suffered a mild stroke in 1985 at age 59.

Today he chooses to call his cerebral accident a "stroke of luck".

A lifelong workaholic and perfectionist who partied as hard as he worked, Hefner reined in after the stroke, naming his daughter Christie chairman and CEO of the company, and limiting himself to his editor-in-chief's role. In 1989 he even gave up his pluralistic ways and married Playmate of the Year Kimberley Conrad, settling down monogamously in the Mansion to father two more children, both sons.

For nearly ten years Hef stayed away from the party, making his magazine and raising his sons. With the election of playboy president Clinton in 1992

Jahren meldete sich der Pyjama-Mann auf dem gesellschaftlichen Parkett zurück. Kimberley und er gaben ihre Trennung bekannt, im Playboy Mansion West herrschten schlagartig wieder die siebziger Jahre, und der Gastgeber in seinen Siebziger haute wieder wie ein Junger auf den Putz. Auch heute, 2004, ist die Party noch nicht vorbei und ganz wie in alten Tagen nimmt eine bunte Schar von Hollywood- und TV-Größen an den wüsten Junggesellenfeten teil, darunter Drew Carey, Ben Stiller oder der aus Austin Power bekannte „Mini-Me" Verne Troyer. Hefner mitsamt seinem Gefolge ist zum bewunderten Nestor und Fixstern in der Clubszene von LA geworden. Ob zuhause oder unterwegs, eine Eskorte von sieben blonden „Freundinnen" umkreist ihn ständig und macht Hefner zu einem – wenngleich betagten – Aushängeschild für den *Playboy*-Lifestyle und natürlich für

re de politiciens conservateurs, de prédicateurs laïques et de féministes radicales. Le rapport, publié en 1986, concluait que la pornographie était effectivement pernicieuse et à la grande horreur de Hefner, son magazine haut de gamme se retrouva sur la même pile que le reste. Marqué au fer rouge, *Playboy* perdit un grand nombre de points de vente sur les stands de journaux et beaucoup de ses annonceurs publicitaires. Les ventes dégringolèrent autour de 3,5 millions par mois et sont restées stables jusqu'à aujour-d'hui. En plus de toute cette affaire, en 1985 Hefner eut une légère hémorragie cérébrale, à 59 ans.

Aujourd'hui il appelle ça son « coup de chance».

Ayant été toute sa vie un archané au travail et un perfectionniste qui faisait la fête autant qu'il travaillait, Hefner fut obligé de cesser une partie de ses activités à la suite de sa maladie et désigna sa fille Christie à la présidence du conseil d'administration et au poste de PDG de son entreprise, se contentant du rôle de rédacteur en chef. En 1989, il renonça même à la pluralité pour épouser Kimberley Conrad, la Playmate de l'année, fonder un foyer monogame au Mansion et faire deux enfants de plus, deux garçons. Pendant presque dix ans Hef se maintint à l'écart de la vie mondaine, s'occupant de son magazine et élevant ses fils. L'élection du playboy Clinton à la présidence en 1992 mit fin à la chasse aux sorcières de la période Reagan. En fait, il n'y eu aucun procès fédéral pour obscénité pendant les deux mandats de Clinton. Cette période plus relaxée vit une reprise des affaires pour *Playboy* et pour Hef. A la fin des années 90, l'homme aux pyjamas refit son entrée dans la société. Lui et Kimberly an-

ENTERTAINMENT FOR MEN
JULY 1969 • ONE DOLLAR
PLAYBOY
PLAYBOY INTERVIEWS ROD STEIGER, GOES ON A FUN-BUGGY BASH, FOCUSES ON A FLOCK OF SEXY AMERICAN BIRDS, EXAMINES THE SENSUAL "LETTING GO" MOVEMENT, PLUGS INTO THE WORLD OF ROBOTS AND OFFERS FACT AND FICTION BY JUSTICE WILLIAM O. DOUGLAS, EVAN HUNTER, J. PAUL GETTY, HEINRICH BÖLL, ROGER PRICE AND DONALD E. WESTLAKE

ENTERTAINMENT FOR MEN
OCTOBER 1971 • ONE DOLLAR
PLAYBOY
BUTKUS: MR. MEAN
THE PORNO GIRLS
YOUR JAZZ AND
POP POLL BALLOT
FOUR POEMS BY
YEVTUSHENKO
FALL AND WINTER
FASHION FORECAST

YEAR: **1971.** TITLE: **Playboy.** COUNTRY: **France.**

YEAR: **1971.** TITLE: **Playboy.** COUNTRY: **France.**

YEAR: **1971.** TITLE: **Playboy.** COUNTRY: **France.**

YEAR: **1971.** TITLE: **Playboy.** COUNTRY: **France.**

YEAR: **1978.** TITLE: **Playboy.** COUNTRY: **USA.**

YEAR: **1972.** TITLE: **Playboy.** COUNTRY: **USA.**
From a feature on creative uses for *The New York Times*.

Hefner's Playboy Foundation put his money where his mind was, supporting a liberal agenda including free speech, civil rights, and humane drug law reform.

the Reagan era witch-hunts ended. In fact, there were no federal obscenity trials at all during Clinton's two terms in office. In the improved climate *Playboy*, and Hef, rallied. In the late nineties the pajamaed one reentered the social scene. He and Kimberly announced their separation and at Mansion West it was suddenly the seventies again, with the seventy-something host kicking up his heels like a young kid. As of 2004 the party hasn't stopped, and just like the old days the frenetic bachelor activities include a host of Hollywood regulars, from TV's Drew Carey to Ben Stiller to Austin Powers' Verne "Mini-Me" Troyer. With his entourage in tow, Hefner has also become an admired elder and stellar fixture in the LA club scene. Both at home and out-and-about, a revolving tag-team of seven (count 'em) blonde "girlfriends" called the Party Posse continue to make Hefner a poster boy, or more accurately a poster senior, for the *Playboy* lifestyle, and of course for Viagra. As a result of Hefner's renewed high profile the *Playboy* brand seems hotter than ever, especially with young women, who flaunt the bunny symbol in reaction against the anti-sexual rhetoric of their mother's generation. For *Playboy* the magazine, and Hefner the man, it's an amazing story of cultural staying power.

For critics it's easy to dismiss the *Playboy* image — an unlikely materialistic world of male luxury and airbrushed feminine flesh — as more than a little puerile and pompous, as well as "unabashedly" (a favorite word in the magazine's lexicon) chauvinistic. But to do so misses the point. To fully grasp how culturally subversive Hefner and his empire were and remain, consider

YEAR: **1976.** TITLE: **Playboy.** COUNTRY: **USA.**
Jimmy Carter's *Playboy* interview almost upset the election.

YEAR: **1977.** TITLE: **Playboy.** COUNTRY: **USA.**
Brother Billy Carter got equal time in *Playboy* a year later.

Viagra. Hefners erneuerte Präsenz hat das Markenzeichen *Playboy* aktueller denn je gemacht, besonders bei jungen Frauen, die das Bunny-Symbol aus Protest gegen die sexualfeindlichen Phrasen der Generation ihrer Mütter tragen. *Playboy* das Magazin und Hefner als Mann haben ein beeindruckendes kulturelles Stehvermögen bewiesen.

Kritikern fällt es nicht schwer, die *Playboy*-Vision – eine unrealistisch materialistische Welt zwischen männlichem Luxus und mit Airbrush retuschierten Frauenkörpern – als ziemlich infantil, aufgeblasen, und, nicht zu vergessen, „unverfroren" (ein Lieblingswort im *Playboy*-Lexikon) chauvinistisch abzutun. Aber das würde am Kern der Dinge vorbeizielen. Um wirklich zu begreifen, wie kulturell subversiv Hefner und sein Imperium waren und sind, muss man sich Ort und Zeit ihrer Entstehung

noncèrent leur séparation et le Mansion retrouva l'ambiance des années 70, avec un maître des lieux d'un peu plus de soixante-dix ans, fringuant comme un jeune homme. En 2004, c'est toujours la fête, et comme au bon vieux temps, ce célibataire frénétique reçoit le Tout-Hollywood, de la vedette de télévision Drew Carey à Ben Stiller et Verne Troyer, alias « Mini-moi » dans Austin Powers. Accompagné de son entourage, Hefner est aussi devenu un senior admiré et une figure proéminente des clubs de Los Angeles. Chez lui comme à la ville, Hefner est entouré d'une équipe tournante de sept blondes (j'ai compté), des « petites amies » que l'on appelle la Bande des Fêtardes, qui font de Hefner le type de l'affiche, ou plus précisement le senior de l'affiche, l'affiche de *Playboy* et bien sûr, celle du Viagra. A la suite du renouvellement de l'image de Hefner, le nom de *Playboy* est plus en vue

Year: **1970.** Title: **Playboy.** Country: **USA.**
The monthly fashion spread was as much a part of the *Playboy* formula as the centerfold.

As of 2004 the party hasn't stopped, and just like the old days the frenetic bachelor activities include a host of Hollywood regulars.

Year: **1970.** Title: **Playboy.** Country: **USA.**

the time and place from which they sprang. In 1953, just six months before *Playboy* was launched, the Korean War had ended in a stalemate and Julius and Ethel Rosenberg had been electrocuted as Russian spies; Senator Joe McCarthy was at the height of his power and a year from falling into disgrace. A chilling, poisonous ethos of bland consumerism, anti-Communist political paranoia and cultural Puritanism was in full sway. *Playboy* provided the antidote — not initially through political criticism, which would hardly have found a mass audience — but indirectly, by offering an alternative universe of eroticism and sybaritic delight.

Later, Hefner's Playboy Foundation put his money where his mind was, supporting a liberal agenda including free speech, civil rights, sex education and humane drug law reform. What has be-

vergegenwärtigen. Nur sechs Monate bevor 1953 der erste *Playboy* erschien, war der Koreakrieg mit einer Pattsituation zuende gegangen und Julius und Ethel Rosenberg waren als russische Spione auf dem elektrischen Stuhl gelandet. Senator Joe McCarthy war auf dem Höhepunkt seiner Macht und sollte erst ein ganzes Jahr später in Ungnade fallen. Im Land herrschte frostiges, fades Konsumdenken, antikommunistische Paranoia und kultureller Puritanismus. *Playboy* lieferte dazu das Gegengift – anfangs nicht durch direkte Kritik an der Politik, damit hätte man kaum ein Massenpublikum erreicht, sondern auf indirekte Weise, indem das Magazin den Blick in ein alternatives Universum der Erotik und des hedonistischen Vergnügens ermöglichte.

In späteren Jahren drückten sich Hefners politischen Sympathien auch in finanzielle Zuwendungen aus: die *Playboy*-Stiftung unterstützte eine liberale Politik, zu der Meinungsfreiheit, Bürgerrechte, Sexualaufklärung und eine Reform der Betäubungsmittelgesetze zählten. Über die Jahre hinweg ist deutlich geworden, dass Hefner diese Dinge aufrichtig am Herzen liegen. Er hat auf seinem Anwesen ein sinnenfreudiges Leben vorgelebt, zugleich aber stets sichergestellt, dass der *Playboy* die fortschrittlichen politischen Ansichten der Amerikaner ebenso widerspiegelt und unterstützt wie ihre sinnenfreudigen. Wie wurde Hefner erst kürzlich im *Esquire* zitiert? „Erst wenn du in einer Position bist, die dir erlaubt, ein schlechter Mensch zu sein, findest du heraus, wer du wirklich bist."

Hugh Marston Hefner empfand sich immer als romantischen *Playboy* mit einem ausgeprägtem sozialen Verantwor-

que jamais, spécialement auprès des jeunes femmes qui arborent le symbole du lapin en réaction contre les discours féministes sur la sexualité de la génération de leur mère. Pour le magazine *Playboy* et pour Hefner l'homme, c'est une étonnante histoire d'un pouvoir qui s'est fait sa place au sein d'une culture.

La critique n'a aucun mal à discréditer l'image de *Playboy* – le monde invraisemblable du luxe masculin et de la chair féminine à l'airbrush – plus que puéril et pompeux, et aussi « effrontément » (un favori du lexique du magazine) chauviniste. Mais le faire, c'est manquer la cible. Pour vraiment comprendre le rôle culturellement subversif de Hefner et de son empire, il faut se rappeler de l'époque et d'où ils viennent. En 1953, six mois avant le lancement de *Playboy*, la guerre de Corée s'était terminée en impasse et Julius et Ethel Rosenberg, accusés d'être

Year: **1967.** Title: **Playboy.** Country: **USA.**

Year: **1977.** Title: **Playboy.** Country: **USA.**

Year: **1980.** Title: **Playboy.** Country: **USA.**

come clear over the years is that Hugh Hefner truly is interested in all those things in equal measure. He has publicly led an indulgent personal life at the Mansions East and West, but at the same time consistently ensured that *Playboy* itself reflects and encourages Americans' politically progressive instincts as well as their sensual ones. As Hefner was quoted in *Esquire* recently, "When you are in a position to not be a nice person, that's when you find out who you really are."

Hugh Marston Hefner found he was a romantic playboy with a strong social conscience, a unique combination that has made him and *Playboy* the most enduring icons in all the history of men's magazines.

tungsgefühl, eine ungewöhnliche Kombination, die ihn und den *Playboy* zu den beständigsten Ikonen in der Geschichte der Männermagazine haben werden lassen.

Today the *Playboy* brand seems hotter than ever. For *Playboy* the magazine, and Hefner the man, it's an amazing story of cultural staying power.

des espions russes, avaient été électrocutés ; le sénateur Joe McCarthy était à l'apogée de son pouvoir avant sa disgrâce, un an plus tard. Une culture effrayante et pernicieuse, un mélange de consumérisme aveugle, de paranoïa anticommuniste et de puritanisme affiché se répandait. *Playboy* offrait l'antidote – non pas en se mettant à critiquer la politique, ce qui n'aurait pas intéressé grand monde – mais indirectement, en offrant l'alternative d'un univers d'érotisme et de délices sybarites.

Plus tard, la Fondation Playboy de Hefner investira dans plusieurs projets, supportant financièrement la défense de la liberté de parole, les droits du citoyen, l'éducation sexuelle et une réforme plus humaine de la législation sur la drogue. Ce qui ressort de toutes ces années c'est que Hugh Hefner fait preuve d'un véritable intérêt pour toutes ces choses dans une égale mesure. Il a mené publiquement une vie personnelle dorée aux Mansions Est et Ouest, mais en même temps s'est toujours assuré que *Playboy* reflète et encourage les instincts de progression de la politique américaine autant que ceux de la sensualité. Comme nous l'indique une citation récente de Hefner dans *Esquire:* « Quand vous êtes dans une position où vous pouvez vous permettre de ne pas être gentil, c'est là que vous découvrez vraiment qui vous êtes. »

Hugh Marston Hefner a découvert qu'il était un playboy romantique à la conscience sociale très développée, un mélange unique qui a fait de lui et de *Playboy* les symboles les plus constants de toute l'histoire des magazines pour hommes.

FORM 1040
Deductions
THE DUDE
WILLIAM FAULKNER
BUDD SCHULBERG
PAUL BOWLES
WILLARD MARSH
Taxpayer sign here

"FOR THE ARTICLES":

Men's Magazines and Literature

„… nur wegen der Artikel": Männermagazine und Literatur

« Pour les articles »: Les magazines pour hommes et la littérature

By Geoff Nicholson

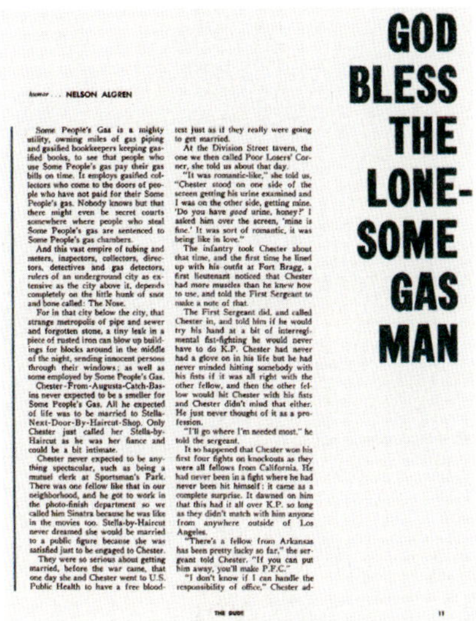

GOD BLESS THE LONESOME GAS MAN

humor … NELSON ALGREN

Some People's Gas is a mighty utility, owning miles of gas piping and gasified bookkeepers keeping gasified books, to see that people who use Some People's gas pay their gas bills on time. It employs gasified collectors who come to the doors of people who have not paid for their Some People's gas. Nobody knows but that there might even be secret courts somewhere where people who steal Some People's gas are sentenced to Some People's gas chambers.

And this vast empire of tubing and meters, inspectors, collectors, directors, detectives and gas detectors, rulers of an underground city as extensive as the city above it, depends completely on the little hunk of snot and bone called: The Nose.

For in that city below the city, that strange metropolis of pipe and sewer and forgotten stone, a tiny leak in a piece of rusted iron can blow up buildings for blocks around in the middle of the night, sending innocent persons through their windows; as well as some employed by Some People's Gas.

Chester-From-Augusta-Catch-Basins never expected to be a smeller for Some People's Gas. All he expected of life was to be married to Stella-Next-Door-By-Haircut-Shop. Only Chester just called her Stella-by-Haircut as he was her fiance and could be a bit intimate.

Chester never expected to be anything spectacular, such as being a mutuel clerk at Sportsman's Park. There was one fellow like that in our neighborhood, and he got to work in the photo-finish department so we called him Sinatra because he was like in the movies too. Stella-by-Haircut never dreamed she would be married to a public figure because she was satisfied just to be engaged to Chester.

They were so serious about getting married, before the war came, that one day she and Chester went to U.S. Public Health to have a free blood-test just as if they really were going to get married.

At the Division Street tavern, the one we then called Poor Losers' Corner, she told us about that day.

"It was romantic-like," she told us. "Chester stood on one side of the screen getting his urine examined and I was on the other side, getting mine. 'Do you have *good* urine, honey?' I asked him over the screen, 'mine is fine.' It was sort of romantic, it was being like in love."

The infantry took Chester about that time, and the first time he lined up with his outfit at Fort Bragg, a first lieutenant noticed that Chester had more muscles than he knew how to use, and told the First Sergeant to make a note of that.

The First Sergeant did, and called Chester in, and told him if he would try his hand at a bit of interregimental fist-fighting he would never have to do K.P. Chester had never had a glove on in his life but he had never minded hitting somebody with his fists if it was all right with the other fellow, and then the other fellow would hit Chester with his fists and Chester didn't mind that either. He just never thought of it as a profession.

"I'll go where I'm needed most," he told the sergeant.

It so happened that Chester won his first four fights on knockouts as they were all fellows from California. He had never been in a fight where he had never been hit himself: it came as a complete surprise. It dawned on him that this had it all over K.P. so long as they didn't match with him anyone from anywhere outside of Los Angeles.

"There's a fellow from Arkansas has been pretty lucky so far," the sergeant told Chester. "If you can put him away, you'll make P.F.C."

"I don't know if I can handle the responsibility of office," Chester ad-

THE DUDE

YEAR: **1962.** TITLE: **The Dude.** COUNTRY: **USA.**

Here's a question to test your literary friends: who, in 1971, in *Suck* magazine (the European sex paper), wrote "Why not send us a photograph of your own cunt, with your name labeled on it?"

The answer is Germaine Greer, author of the massively influential, proto-feminist *The Female Eunuch*, and to be fair, she was writing in the name of liberation as much as titillation. I also suspect she had to write an editorial in a hurry and was trying to fill up space.

Which perhaps raises the question of why men's magazines need writers at all. Publishers might point to the historical

YEAR: **1957.** TITLE: **The Dude.** COUNTRY: **USA.**

Hier eine Testfrage für Ihre belesenen Freunde: Wer schrieb 1975 in dem europäischen Sexheft *Suck* folgenden Satz: „Warum schicken Sie uns nicht ein Foto Ihrer eigenen Fotze mit Ihrem Namensschild?"

Die Lösung lautete: Germaine Greer, die Autorin des bahnbrechenden, protofeministischen Buches *Der weibliche Eunuch*. Um der Wahrheit Genüge zu tun, sie wird es nicht nur im Namen der Befreiung, sondern auch der Provokation

Voici une question pour tester nos amis érudits: Qui, en 1971, dans le magazine *Suck* (le journal érotique européen) a écrit: « Pourquoi ne pas nous envoyer une photographie de votre con avec une étiquette portant votre nom? »

Réponse: Germaine Greer, auteur de l'ouvrage proto-féministe immensément influent *La Femme eunuque*. Il faut dire qu'elle s'exprimait autant au nom de la libération qu'à celui de la provocation. Je soupçonne également qu'elle était en

YEAR: **1961.** TITLE: **Cavalcade.** COUNTRY: **USA.**

JUNE, 1957
Fifty Cents
NUGGET
THE UNIQUE MONIQUE: an interview
CAPRI: ISLE OF IDYLLS AND ECCENTRICITIES
MOVIES YOU'LL NEVER SEE

Year: **1957.** Title: **Nugget.**
Country: **USA.**

At the bottom end there was much less edifying stuff; exposés of beatniks, hippies, wife-swappers and on-campus shenanigans.

test for obscenity introduced in 1934 by Judge Hand in the case of United States vs. One Book Called Ulysses, that a work taken as a whole must have libidinous effect to be found obscene. Writing is widely considered to provide the redeeming social value that guards against obscenity convictions, but my intuition is that the presence of "proper" writing in a magazine serves psychological purposes as well, asserting that it's not just porn. And for certain editors as well as certain readers, this is very important.

Hugh Hefner, of course, is the prime mover behind all this, claiming he had a mission to educate as well as entertain. The old line about people buying *Playboy* for the articles may be widely regarded as a joke, but by the mid-1960s it was very much a text-led magazine. Hefner's "Playboy philosophy" purported to encompass the best of everything – women, cars, highballs – so why not the best writ-

wegen geschrieben haben. Außerdem habe ich den Verdacht, dass sie ganz schnell einen Artikel schreiben musste und nur Zeilen schinden wollte.

Was vielleicht die Frage aufwirft, wieso Männermagazine überhaupt Schriftsteller brauchen. Die Verleger können auf die 1934 von Richter Hand im Prozess Vereinigte Staaten gegen das Buch *Ulysses* gewählte Definition verweisen, dass ein Werk als obszön einzustufen ist, wenn es im Ganzen einen sexuellen Reiz ausübt. Literatur gilt allgemein als der erforderliche mildernde Umstand, um sich eine Verurteilung wegen Verbreitung obszönen Materials zu ersparen, aber ich vermute, dass die Präsenz „echter" Literatur in Männermagazinen auch einen psychologischen Zweck erfüllt: Sie ist die Bestätigung dafür, dass man es nicht bloß mit blanker Pornografie zu tun hat. Und das ist für gewisse Verleger wie für gewisse Leser von entscheidener Bedeutung.

Year: **1962.** Title: **Nugget.** Country: **USA.**

retard dans la rédaction de son éditorial et cherchait à noircir du papier.

Ce qui soulève peut-être la question de savoir pourquoi les magazines pour hommes ont besoin d'auteurs. Les éditeurs nous rappelleront sans doute la définition de l'obscénité introduite par le juge Hand lors du procès contre « l'ouvrage intitulé *Ulysse* »: une œuvre doit être considérée comme ayant un effet libidineux dans son ensemble pour être jugée obscène. L'écriture est généralement considérée comme apportant une valeur sociale rédemptrice protégeant contre les accusations d'obscénité mais j'ai comme l'impression que la présence d'un texte « digne de ce nom » dans les magazines répond également à une fonction psychologique, gage qu'il ne s'agit pas simplement de pornographie. Or, pour certains éditeurs, comme pour certains lecteurs, c'est une distinction primordiale.

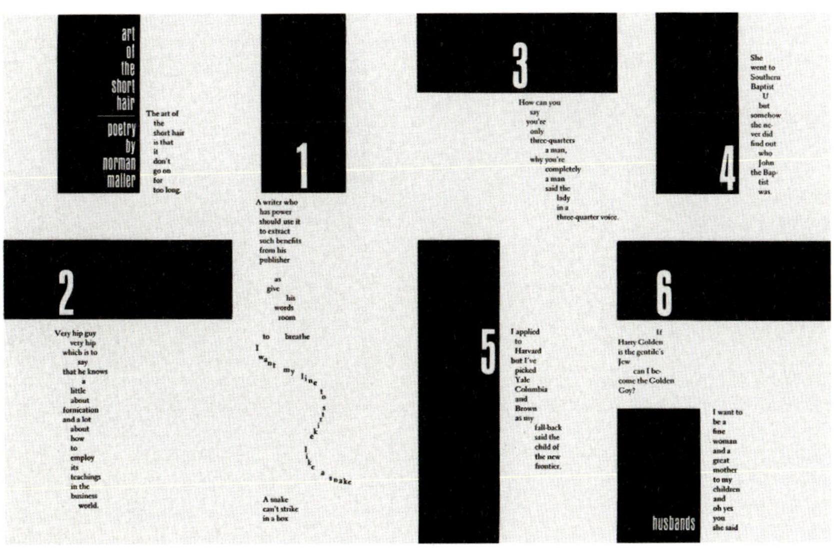

Year: **1962.** Title: **Nugget.** Country: **USA.**

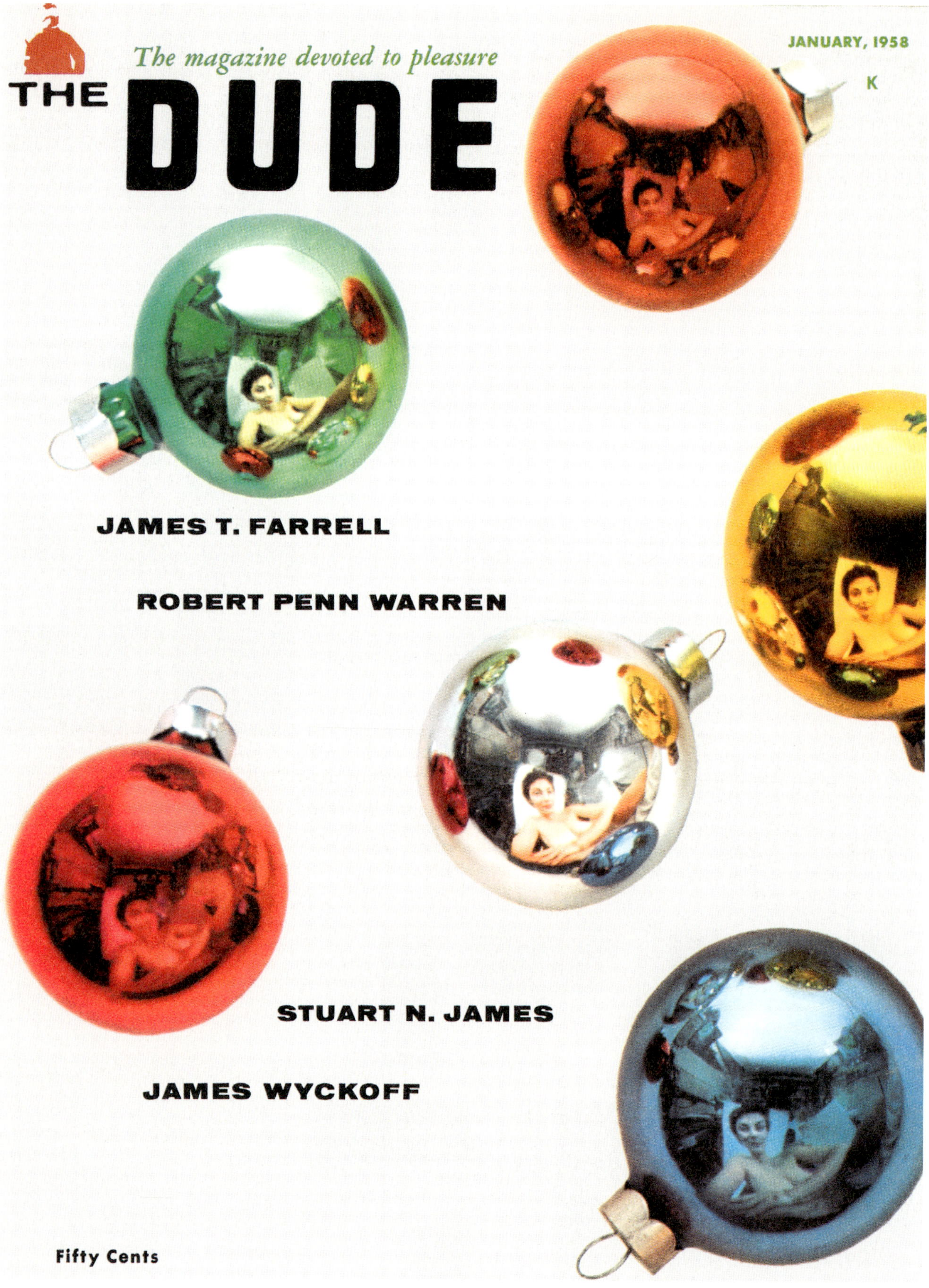

YEAR: **1958.** TITLE: **The Dude.** COUNTRY: **USA.**

YEAR: **1957.** TITLE: **The Dude.** COUNTRY: **USA.**

Year: **1961.** Title: **Bachelor.** Country: **USA.**

Hugh Hefner claimed he had a mission to educate as well as entertain.

Year: **1959.** Title: **Cavalier.** Country: **USA.**

Year: **1961.** Title: **Cavalcade.** Country: **USA.**

ers? The would-be *Playboy* imitators followed suit.

So you would have found John Clellon Holmes writing about Lee Harvey Oswald in *Playboy* (November 1965), Gore Vidal on Richard Nixon in *Penthouse* (September 1972). You could have found LSD guru Timothy Leary expounding the joys of the psychedelic revolution just about anywhere.

At the bottom end there was much less edifying stuff; exposés of beatniks, hippies, wife-swappers and on-campus shenanigans, along with any number of "how to" articles, from "How to Buy a Used Car" in *Caper* June 1966, down to "How to Beat a Paternity Rap" in *Rugged* February 1957. This might be the sort of information men needed from time to time, yet it's hard to believe they relied on men's magazines to provide it.

So, if men didn't buy these magazines

Die treibende Kraft hinter all dem war natürlich Hugh Hefner, der für sich in Anspruch nahm, ebenso zu bilden wie zu unterhalten. Der bekannte Spruch, dass jemand den *Playboy* wegen der Artikel kauft, mag vielen als Witz erscheinen, doch bis Mitte der Sechziger war der *Playboy* ein äußerst textlastiges Magazin. Hefners *Playboy*-Philosophie umfasste unter anderem, von allem nur das Beste zu bieten, seien es Frauen, Autos oder Highballs – warum dann nicht auch die besten Autoren? Die zahllosen *Playboy*-Imitatoren taten es ihm gleich.

So schrieb etwa John Clellon Holmes über Lee Harvey Oswald im *Playboy* (November 1965), Gore Vidal über Richard Nixon in *Penthouse* (September 1972), und LSD-Guru Timothy Leary praktisch überall über die Freuden der psychedelischen Revolution.

Am unteren Ende der Skala fand man

Naturellement, Hugh Hefner est le principal instigateur de cette tendance, affirmant qu'il avait pour mission d'éduquer autant que de divertir. La vieille rengaine selon laquelle les gens achètent *Playboy* pour les articles peut faire sourire mais, vers le milieu des années soixante, le magazine était effectivement dominé par ses textes. La « philosophie *Playboy* » d'Hefner visait à rechercher le mieux en tout – en femmes, en voitures, en cocktails. Pourquoi pas les meilleurs auteurs? Les émules de *Playboy* l'ont vite compris aussi.

C'est ainsi que l'on trouve John Clellon Holmes écrivant sur Lee Harvey Oswald dans *Playboy* (novembre 1965), ou Gore Vidal sur Richard Nixon dans *Penthouse* (septembre 1972). Quant au gourou du LSD, Timothy Leary, il s'épanchait sur les joies de la révolution psychédélique à peu près n'importe où.

Dans le bas de gamme, les textes étaient nettement moins édifiants: témoignages de beatniks, d'hippies, d'échangistes, comptes rendus de bacchanales universitaires, aux côtés d'articles « comment faire », de « comment acheter une voiture d'occasion » dans le numéro de juin 1966 de *Caper*, à « comment échapper à un procès en reconnaissance de paternité », dans le numéro de février 1957 de *Rugged*. Certes, ce genre d'information peut s'avérer utile mais on a du mal à croire que les hommes la cherchaient dans ce genre de revue.

Donc, si les hommes n'achetaient pas ces magazines pour les articles, peut-être était-ce pour la fiction? C'était là un domaine où un texte pouvait émoustiller sans prétendre être éducatif. Pourtant, les auteurs choisis par certains magazines étaient étonnamment littéraires.

BACHELOR

THE MAGAZINE FOR THE YOUNG AT HEART

SEPTEMBER
FIFTY CENTS
B

IN THIS ISSUE:

JAMES T. FARRELL
MORTON GOLDING
CHARLES V. NEMO
TED MARK

OVER 30 STORIES ARTICLES FEATURES

NEW! EIGHT PAGES OF FULL COLOR

APRIL 50 CENTS CDC
ESCAPADE
PLEASURE FOR EVERY MAN
A VISIT TO
OHIO STATE UNIVERSITY
WINTER PLAYGROUND
FOR BACHELORS
PHOTOGRAPHING
AN ESCAPADE
MODEL
HOCKEY'S KING
OF BRAWLS
PLUS: KEROUAC

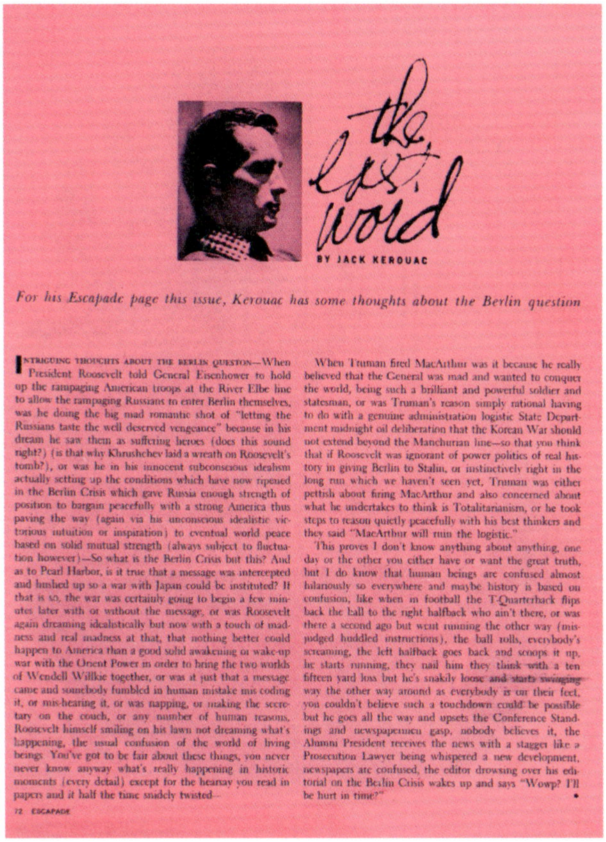

the last word

BY JACK KEROUAC

For his Escapade page this issue, Kerouac has some thoughts about the Berlin question

INTRIGUING THOUGHTS ABOUT THE BERLIN QUESTION—When President Roosevelt told General Eisenhower to hold up the rampaging American troops at the River Elbe line to allow the rampaging Russians to enter Berlin themselves, was he doing the big mad romantic shot of "letting the Russians taste the well deserved vengeance" because in his dream he saw them as suffering heroes (does this sound right?) (is that why Khrushchev laid a wreath on Roosevelt's tomb?), or was he in his innocent subconscious idealism actually setting up the conditions which have now ripened in the Berlin Crisis which gave Russia enough strength of position to bargain peacefully with a strong America thus paving the way (again via his unconscious idealistic victorious intuition or inspiration) to eventual world peace based on solid mutual strength (always subject to fluctuation however)—So what is the Berlin Crisis but this? And as to Pearl Harbor, is it true that a message was intercepted and hushed up so a war with Japan could be instituted? If that is so, the war was certainly going to begin a few minutes later with or without the message, or was Roosevelt again dreaming idealistically but now with a touch of madness and real madness at that, that nothing better could happen to America than a good solid awakening or wake-up war with the Orient Power in order to bring the two worlds of Wendell Willkie together, or was it just that a message came and somebody fumbled in human mistake mis coding it, or mis-hearing it, or was napping, or making the secretary on the couch, or any number of human reasons, Roosevelt himself smiling on his lawn not dreaming what's happening, the usual confusion of the world of living beings. You've got to be fair about these things, you never never know anyway what's really happening in historic moments (every detail) except for the hearsay you read in papers and it half the time snidely twisted—

When Truman fired MacArthur was it because he really believed that the General was mad and wanted to conquer the world, being such a brilliant and powerful soldier and statesman, or was Truman's reason simply rational having to do with a genuine administration logistic State Department midnight oil deliberation that the Korean War should not extend beyond the Manchurian line—so that you think that if Roosevelt was ignorant of power politics of real history in giving Berlin to Stalin, or instinctively right in the long run which we haven't seen yet, Truman was either pettish about firing MacArthur and also concerned about what he undertakes to think is Totalitarianism, or he took steps to reason quietly peacefully with his best thinkers and they said "MacArthur will ruin the logistic."

This proves I don't know anything about anything, one day or the other you either have or want the great truth, but I do know that human beings are confused almost hilariously so everywhere and maybe history is based on confusion, like when in football the T-Quarterback flips back the ball to the right halfback who ain't there, or was there a second ago but went running the other way (misjudged huddled instructions), the ball rolls, everybody's screaming, the left halfback goes back and scoops it up, he starts running, they nail him they think with a ten fifteen yard loss but he's snakily loose and starts swinging way the other way around as everybody is on their feet, you couldn't believe such a touchdown could be possible but he goes all the way and upsets the Conference Standings and newspapermen gasp, nobody believes it, the Alumni President receives the news with a stagger like a Prosecution Lawyer being whispered a new development, newspapers are confused, the editor drowsing over his editorial on the Berlin Crisis wakes up and says "Wowp? I'll be hurt in time?" •

72 ESCAPADE

YEAR: **1960.** TITLE: **Escapade.** COUNTRY: **USA.**

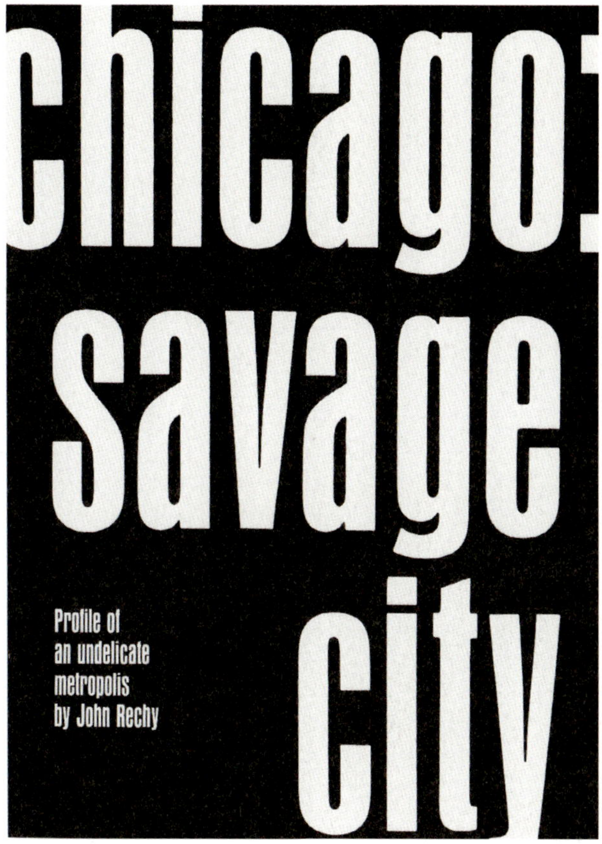

YEAR: **1962.** TITLE: **Nugget.** COUNTRY: **USA.**

YEAR: **1961.** TITLE: **Rogue.** COUNTRY: **USA.**

CAVALIER welcomes back MICKEY SPILLANE who here introduces Ryan, his toughest character yet

ME, HOOD!

By Mickey Spillane

They picked me up in a bar on Second Avenue and waited for the supper crowd to flow out before they made their tap, two tall smiling lads with late model narrow-brim Kellys that helped them blend into the background of young junior executives.

But both of them had that almost imperceptible cock to their arms that comes from wearing a gun too long on one side, and that made them something else again.

When they came in, they pulled out stools on either side of me and began the routine, but I saved them all the trouble they had planned to go to. I finished my drink, pocketed my change and stood up. "We go now?"

Without changing the size of his smile the one with the pale blue eyes said, "We go now."

I grinned, nodded toward the bartender and walked to the door. On the street a gentle nudge edged me north, then another turned me at the corner to where the car was parked. One got behind the wheel and one was on my right. I didn't feel any gun rubbing against my hip where it should have so I knew the guy on my right had it in his hand.

At the door, the squat little man stood with his legs spraddled and hands in his pockets, looking at nothing, yet watching everything. The other one sat on the window ledge at my shoulder without saying anything.

Across the city the clock on the square boomed nine. Behind me the door to the inside office opened and a voice said, "Bring him in."

Smiling Boy let me go ahead of him, followed me in and closed the door.

Then, for the first time, I was wishing I hadn't played the wise guy. I felt like an idiot for being so damn dumb and while I was

Illustrated by Norman Baer

NB

YEAR: **1959.** TITLE: **Cavalier.** COUNTRY: **USA.**

YEAR: **1960.** TITLE: **Escapade.**
COUNTRY: **USA.**

YEAR: **1961.** TITLE: **Swank.** COUNTRY: **USA.**

It's easy to forget how exciting and daring fiction seemed in the late 50s and 60s.

YEAR: **1963.** TITLE: **Caper.** COUNTRY: **USA.**

for the articles, did they perhaps buy them for the fiction? This was an area where the writing could be titillating without any pretense at education. Yet the fiction authors chosen by some men's magazines were surprisingly literary. The first issue of *Nugget* (November 1955) simply had a list of its contributors on the cover: Erskine Caldwell, John Steinbeck and James Joyce, a roster that swelled to include Noel Coward, Graham Greene, Chekhov and Balzac. In some cases these were obviously just reprints of extant material (Balzac had been dead for over a century), but it's still amazing that these authors were there at all, especially when you consider the current style of *Nugget* which is likely to have shout lines such as "Sniffs and Stain" (February '99) or "Big Boob Bondage" (August '99).

Gent magazine could boast Jean Paul Sartre (December '56), William Faulkner

deutlich weniger erbauliche Sachen; Enthüllungen über Beatniks, Hippies, Partnertausch und das zügellose Treiben auf dem Campus, dazu jede Menge Ratgeber-Artikel, von „Wie kaufe ich einen Gebrauchtwagen?" in *Caper* (Juni 1966) bis „Wie wehre ich eine Vaterschaftsklage ab?" in *Rugged* (Februar 1957). Möglich, dass der Mann solche Informationen gelegentlich braucht, doch dann wird er sich kaum auf ein Männermagazin verlassen.

Wenn Männer diese Magazine schon nicht wegen der Artikel kauften, dann vielleicht wegen der Erzählungen? Das war ein Feld, auf dem man durchaus ohne Anspruch auf erzieherischen Wert unanständig sein konnte. Dennoch waren die Schriftsteller, die einige dieser Magazine abdruckten, überraschend intellektuell.

Den Titel der ersten Nummer von *Nugget* (November 1955) zierte schlicht eine Liste der Autoren: Erskine Caldwell, John Steinbeck und James Joyce, zu denen sich bald auch Noel Coward, Graham Greene, Tschechow und Balzac gesellten. Heute wundert man sich über diese erlesene Auswahl, vor allem, wenn man sich den aktuellen Stil von *Nugget* ansieht, der schrille Aufmacher wie „Sniffs and Stain" (Februar '99) oder „Big Boob Bondage" (August '99) bevorzugt.

Das Magazin *Gent* konnte sich mit den Namen von Jean Paul Sartre (Dezember '56), William Faulkner (Juni '57) und P.G. Wodehouse, dem wohl unschuldigsten und asexuellsten englischen Autor, schmücken (August '59). *Escapade* wartete mit Maugham, Caldwell und wiederum P.G. Wodehouse auf, *Hi-Life* mit Paul Bowles, Faulkner und Maupassant. Manchmal nahm das geradezu lächerliche Formen an. 1963 druckte das

La couverture du premier numéro de *Nugget* (nov. 1955) citait simplement la liste de ses contributeurs: Erskine Caldwell, John Steinbeck et James Joyce, un annuaire qui s'allongea bientôt pour inclure Noel Coward, Graham Greene, Tchekhov et Balzac. Certes, certains textes n'étaient que des rééditions de classiques (Balzac était mort depuis plus d'un siècle) mais il n'en est pas moins incroyable que ces auteurs figurent dans le magazine, surtout quand on considère le style actuel de *Nugget*, plutôt du genre à afficher des manchettes telles que « Vive les petites odeurs » (février '99) ou « Gros lolos ligotés » (août '99).

Gent pouvait se targuer de publier Jean-Paul Sartre (déc. '56), William Faulkner (juin '57) et le plus innocent et le moins sexuel des auteurs anglais P. G. Wodehouse (avril '59). *Escapade* avait également S. Maugham, Calwell et P. G. Wodehouse; *Hi-Life*, Paul Bowles, Faulkner et Maupassant. Parfois, cela frisait le ridicule. En 1963, *Pix* publia le poème « To His Coy Mistress » (« à sa maîtresse faussement timide ») d'Andrew Marvell, composé trois siècles plus tôt.

On peut se demander si les lecteurs de ces magazines attendaient vraiment des documents aussi intellectuels mais ils les acceptaient volontiers. La littérature faisait partie intégrante de ces magazines d'une manière qui paraît inconcevable aujourd'hui.

Cependant, l'histoire était de leur côté. On oublie facilement à quel point la fiction était excitante et audacieuse à la fin des années cinquante et pendant les années soixante. Au cours de la première moitié du siècle, de grands romans tels qu'*Ulysse* de James Joyce, *L'amant de lady Chatterley* de D. H. Lawrence ou *Le*

Dual Feature by JAMES T. FARRELL and ALLEN GINSBERG

swank

JAN 50c PDC

SPECIAL!
PLUSH
PAD
FOR MOBILE
ROMEOS

* * * *

BIG
BUSINESS
TAKES
A
SEX
BREAK

* * * *

LARDNER
SHECKLEY
SLESAR

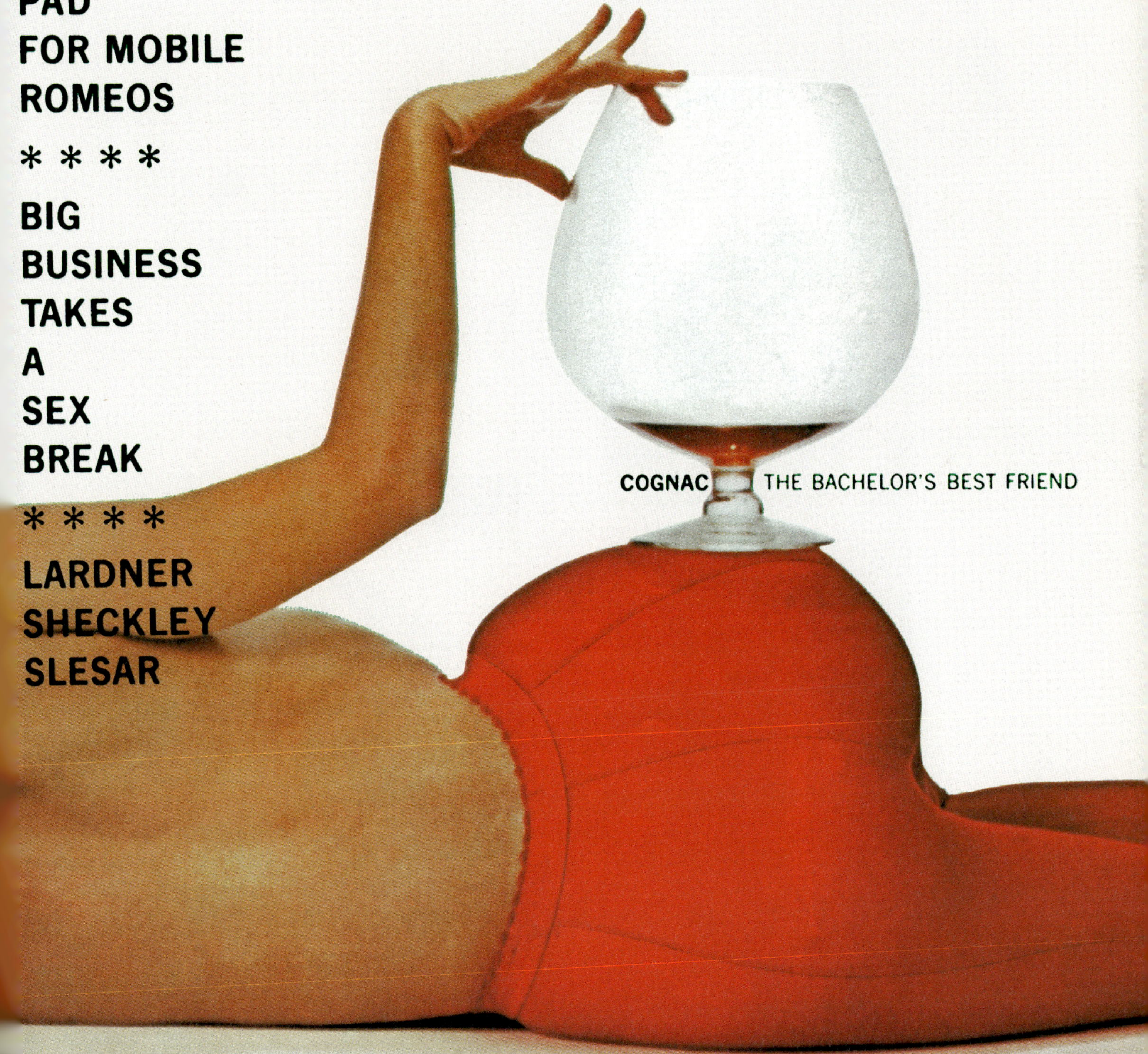

the swinging moderns

BILL MANVILLE * LEROI JONES * RAY BREMSER * and others

The magazine devoted to pleasure
THE DUDE
SEPTEMBER, 1959
PHONE
NEW: the CONCENTRIC
FEMALE
R.V. CASSILL
LOUIS-CHARLES ROYE
MARGARET ST. CLAIR
GUY DANIELS
FIFTY CENT

YEAR: **1959.** TITLE: **The Dude.**
COUNTRY: **USA.**

Serious writers were in demand and were happy to be published in men's magazines. This was a state of affairs that didn't last long.

(June '57) and that most innocent and least sexual of English writers, P.G. Wodehouse (April '59). *Escapade* also had Maugham, Caldwell and P.G Wodehouse. *Hi-Life* had Paul Bowles, Faulkner and Maupassant. Sometimes this could get downright silly. *Pix* magazine in 1963 reprinted Andrew Marvell's "To His Coy Mistress" which had first seen the light of day some three hundred years previously.

You may wonder whether the readers of these magazines really wanted any of this high-brow stuff, but they certainly accepted it. Fiction, indeed literature, seemed to be part of men's magazines in a way that seems unthinkable today. History, however, was on their side. It's easy to forget how exciting and daring fiction seemed in the late 50s and 60s. Serious literary novels like Joyce's *Ulysses*, Lawrence's *Lady Chatterley's Lover*, and

Magazin *Pix* Andrew Marvells „To His Coy Mistress" ab, einen Text, der gut dreihundert Jahre auf dem Buckel hatte.

Man mag sich fragen, ob die Leser dieser Magazine wirklich irgendwas von diesem intellektuellen Zeug lesen wollten, auf jeden Fall akzeptierten sie es. Erzählerische Texte, ja, anspruchsvolle Literatur, waren auf eine heute undenkbare Weise fester Bestandteil von Männermagazinen.

Aber das lag auch an der Zeit. Man vergisst leicht, wie aufregend und kühn Literatur in den späten Fünfzigern und Sechzigern wirkte. Bücher wie *Ulysses* von Joyce, *Lady Chatterley* von Lawrence oder Henry Millers *Wendekreis des Krebses* waren in der ersten Hälfte des Jahrhunderts Zensur und Indizierung unterworfen gewesen, ein Zustand, der den Appetit auf gewagte Literatur angeregt hatte.

In den Sechzigern schien der Kampf um literarische Freiheit gewonnen zu sein, und die Literatur war freizügiger denn je. Joyce und Lawrence waren da längst tot, aber Henry Miller war quicklebendig. Viele Jahre seiner Karriere war er entweder völlig ignoriert oder bestenfalls von obskuren Literaturzeitschriften veröffentlicht worden. Der Chance, ein breiteres Publikum zu erreichen, konnte er nicht widerstehen. In den Sechzigern und Siebzigern erschienen Texte von ihm in *Swank*, *Gallery*, *Cavalier* und *Lui*, wie auch in *Playboy* und *Penthouse*. 1971 veröffentlichte *Playboy* sogar sein Buch *My Life and Times* mitsamt Fotografien, die zeigten, wie Miller mit nackten Models Tischtennis spielte.

Miller zählte bereits zu einer älteren Generation, aber die Sechziger brachten auch eigene Schriftstellergrößen hervor;

Tropique du cancer d'Henry Miller avaient été interdits dans de nombreux pays, ce qui ne pouvait manquer d'aiguiser les appétits pour les écrits émoustillants.

Dans les années soixante, la bataille pour la liberté littéraire sembla avoir été gagnée et la fiction s'exprima de manière plus explicite que jamais. Joyce et Lawrence étaient morts depuis longtemps mais Henry Miller était encore très guilleret. Il avait passé une grande partie de sa carrière dans une indifférence totale ou, au mieux, en étant publié dans d'obscurs magazines littéraires. L'occasion de toucher un public plus large était irrésistible. Dans les années soixante et soixante-dix, il publia dans *Swank*, *Gallery*, *Cavalier*, *Lui* ainsi que dans *Penthouse* et *Playboy*. En 1971, *Playboy* édita même son livre *My Life and Times*, qui incluait des photos du romancier jouant au ping-pong avec des

YEAR: **1960.** TITLE: **The Gent.** COUNTRY: **USA.**

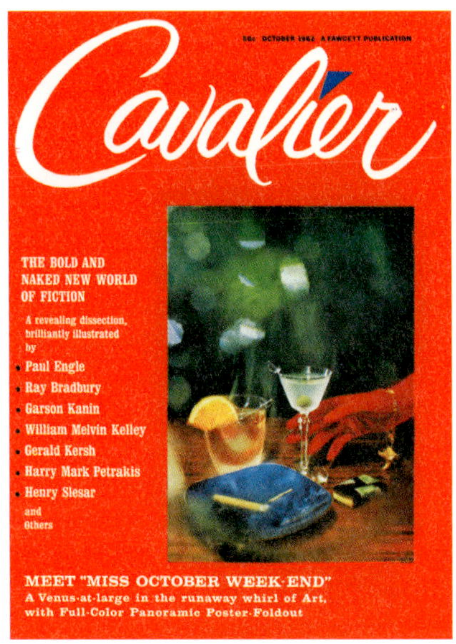

YEAR: **1962.** TITLE: **Cavalier.** COUNTRY: **USA.**

Erotography means erotic writing. In Webster's dictionary erotography is not listed. The substitute term is pornography, which means harlot writing. Erotic writing, in other words, is equated with writing about whores.

–Lovemaps, John Money, 1986

Henry Miller's *Tropic of Cancer* had been subject to international bans and censorship in the first half of the century; a state of affairs that was likely to whet the appetite for the naughty written word.

By the 1960s the battle for literary freedom seemed to have been won and fiction was speaking more explicitly than ever before. Joyce and Lawrence were long dead by then, but Henry Miller was still very much alive. He had spent a large part of his career either being neglected completely or at best being published by obscure literary magazines. The chance to speak to a wider public was irresistible. In the 60s and 70s he was published by *Swank*, *Gallery*, *Cavalier*, *Lui*, as well as *Penthouse* and *Playboy*. In 1971 *Playboy* even published his book *My Life and Times* which featured a pictorial of Miller playing ping pong with nude models.

If Miller belonged to an earlier generation, the 60s were perfectly able to produce their own literary heroes; Vladimir Nabokov's *Lolita* (actually pubished in 1959) was a crucial book at this time, while novels such as John Updike's *Couples*, Norman Mailer's *The American Dream*, Philip Roth's *Portnoy's Complaint* proved that fiction could be sexy as well as serious. Serious writers were in demand and were happy to be published in men's magazines. This was a state of affairs that didn't last long.

We know that in the early 70s the young Stephen King was living in Maine, and struggling to support a wife and kids by working in a laundry. "The only edge we had," he recalls in *On Writing*, "came courtesy of magazines like *Dude*, *Cavalier*, *Adam* and *Swank* – what my uncle

Vladimir Nabokovs *Lolita* (1959) war damals ein vieldiskutiertes Buch, während Romane wie John Updikes *Ehepaare*, Norman Mailers *The American Dream* oder Philip Roths *Portnoys Beschwerden* bewiesen, dass Literatur zugleich sexy und seriös sein konnte. Ernsthafte Schriftsteller waren gefragt und glücklich, in Männermagazinen veröffentlichen zu können. Aber diese Verhältnisse sollten nicht lange währen.

In den frühen Siebzigern mühte sich der junge Stephen King in Maine, seine Familie mit Arbeit in einer Wäscherei durchzubringen. „Das Einzige, was uns über die Runden brachte", erinnert er sich in *On Writing*, „verdankten wir Magazinen wie *Dude*, *Cavalier*, *Adam* und *Swank* – was mein Onkel Oren immer ‚Tittenhefte' nannte". Seine Storys erschienen noch bis 1981 in *Cavalier*.

Wie King einräumt, zeigten die Hefte schon damals wesentlich mehr als nur „Titten", und der Markt für Literatur schrumpfte. Er sagt, er habe gerade noch auf den letzten Zug aufspringen können.

Der schleichende Tod hochwertiger Literatur in Männermagazinen fällt zusammen mit dem Aufkommen des Feminismus, und das erklärt einiges. In den Sechzigern hatte es eine Art Symbiose gegeben. Alles, was mit Sex zu tun hatte, galt als hip. Die Präsenz ernsthafter Autoren in Männermagazinen verstärkte den Hipfaktor auf beiden Seiten. Aber als der Feminismus sich auf breiter Front durchsetzte, waren Männermagazine bestenfalls noch ein Vergnügen, dessen man sich schämte, und schlimmstenfalls ein Instrument der Unterdrückung; und Schriftsteller sehen es nicht gerne, wenn man sie für Unterdrücker hält. Die

YEAR: **1958.** TITLE: **The Dude.** COUNTRY: **USA.**

modèles nues. Si Miller appartenait à une génération antérieure, les années soixante étaient parfaitement capables de produire leurs propres héros littéraires. *Lolita* de Vladimir Nabokov (en fait publié en 1959) fut un livre crucial pour son temps, tandis que des romans tels que *Couples* de John Updike, *Un rêve américain* de Norman Mailer ou *Portnoy et son complexe* de Philip Roth démontrèrent que la littérature pouvait être à la fois sérieuse et érotique. Les auteurs sérieux étaient en vogue et ravis d'être publiés dans des magazines pour hommes. Ce phénomène ne dura pas longtemps.

Au début des années soixante-dix, le jeune Stephen King vivait dans le Maine, se démenant pour subvenir aux besoins de sa femme et de leurs enfants en travaillant dans une blanchisserie. Dans *Ecriture*, mémoire d'un métier, il se souvient: « Notre seul ouverture sur la

YEAR: **1957.** TITLE: **Swank.**
COUNTRY: **USA.**

Swank
ATLAS
35c
FEB.
GIRL APPRECIATION ISSUE:
Those Slippery Convention Girls
A New One About The Farmer's Daughter
Diary Of A What-The-Hell Girl
Dramatic New Stories by
WILLIAM SAROYAN · LEONARD BISHOP
CROSWELL BOWEN · HENRY KANE

THE

GENT

JUNE, 195

AN APPROACH TO RELAXATION

FIFTY CEN

GEORGE MOORSE
ROGER ALLAN

CARL H. WINSTON
CARLTON BROWN

YEAR: **1959.** TITLE: **The Gent.**
COUNTRY: **USA.**

By the 1960s the battle for literary freedom seemed to have been won and fiction was speaking more explicitly than ever before.

Oren used to call 'the titty books'." He was being published in *Cavalier* as late as 1981.

As King acknowledges, the magazines were showing a lot more than "titties" by then, and the market for fiction was shrinking. He says that he was just about able to "ride the last wave". The slow death of quality fiction in men's magazines coincided with the rise of mainstream feminism, and this explains a great deal. In the 60s there was a symbiosis at work. Anything to do with sex was considered hip. The presence of good writers in men's magazines therefore increased the hip credentials of both sides. But with the broad acceptance of feminism, men's magazines became at best a guilty pleasure, at worst an instrument of oppression, and writers are reluctant to be seen as oppressors. The fact that magazines tended to become increasingly explicit only created more difficulties.

This is surely why any young contemporary writer with a reputation to consider steers well clear of men's magazines today. You won't find Jonathan Franzen and Dave Eggers in *Hustler* or *Nugget*, not even in conservative *Playboy*. They don't want women to perceive them as the enemy. Neither do they want their words seen rubbing up against explicit images.

Germaine Greer now writes a gardening column for the English *Daily Telegraph*.

YEAR: **1962.** TITLE: **The Gent.** COUNTRY: **USA.**

Tatsache, dass die Magazine sexuell immer freizügiger wurden, vergrößerte diese Schwierigkeiten noch.

Aus diesem Grund machen heute junge Autoren, die auf ihren Ruf achten müssen, einen Bogen um Männermagazine. Jonathan Franzen oder Dave Eggers würde man kaum im *Hustler* oder in *Nugget* finden, nicht einmal im konservativen *Playboy*. Sie wollen von Frauen nicht als Feind betrachtet werden. Und sie wollen ihre Texte nicht in unmittelbarer Nachbarschaft von expliziten Fotos sehen.

Germaine Greer schreibt übrigens heute eine Gartenkolumne für den englischen *Daily Telegraph*.

modernité nous était fournie par des magazines comme *The Dude*, *Cavalier*, *Adam* ou *Swank*, que mon oncle Oren appelait des ‹bouquins à roberts›». Lui-même fut publié dans *Cavalier* jusqu'en 1981.

La lente agonie de la fiction de qualité dans les magazines pour hommes coïncida avec l'avènement du féminisme grand public, ce qui explique beaucoup de choses. Dans les années soixante s'opérait une symbiose: tout ce qui avait trait à la sexualité était dans le vent. La présence de bons auteurs dans les magazines de charme conférait aux deux parties une aura branchée. Mais, à mesure que le féminisme se propageait, les revues pour hommes devinrent, au mieux, un plaisir coupable, au pire, un instrument de l'oppression. Or, les auteurs ne tenaient pas à passer pour des oppresseurs. Le fait que les magazines devenaient de plus en plus crus ne fit qu'accélérer leur désistement.

Voici probablement pourquoi les jeunes auteurs d'aujourd'hui qui soignent leur réputation gardent leurs distances avec les magazines pour hommes. On ne lira pas Jonathan Franzen ou Dave Eggers dans *Hustler* ou *Nuggets*, pas même dans *Playboy*. Ils ne veulent pas être perçus par les femmes comme l'ennemi. Ils ne tiennent pas non plus à ce que leurs mots se frottent à des images explicites.

Germaine Greer tient désormais une rubrique jardinage dans le quotidien britannique *The Daily Telegraph*.

YEAR: **1961.** TITLE: **Rogue.** COUNTRY: **USA.**

YEAR: **1961.** TITLE: **Rogue.** COUNTRY: **USA.**

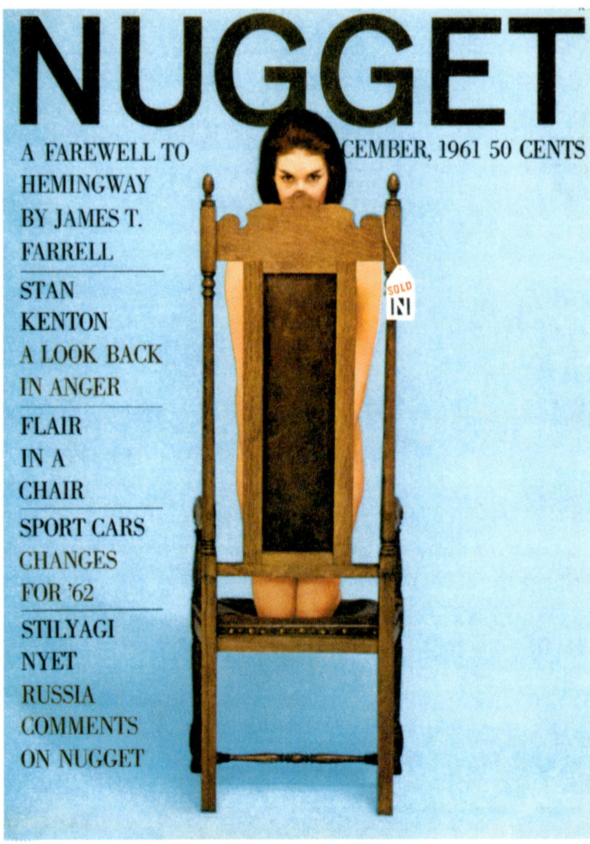

YEAR: **1961.** TITLE: **Nugget.** COUNTRY: **USA.**

YEAR: **1963.** TITLE: **Nugget.** COUNTRY: **USA.**

YEAR: **1961.** TITLE: **Rogue.**
COUNTRY: **USA.**

DESIGNED FOR MEN
Rogue
JULY 1961 • 50c
fiction and fact by:
NELSON ALGREN • ROBERT BLOCH
BEN HECHT • BORDEN DEAL
GAUGUIN GIRL ANN VILA:
Your Favorite Rogue Girl Revisited

YEAR: **1956.** TITLE: **Nugget.** COUNTRY: **USA.**

YEAR: **1959.** TITLE: **Rogue.** COUNTRY: **USA.**

YEAR: **1959.** TITLE: **Nugget.** COUNTRY: **USA.**

YEAR: **1962.** TITLE: **The Dude.** COUNTRY: **USA.**

YEAR: **1960.** TITLE: **Nugget.** COUNTRY: **USA.**

THE

GENT

DECEMBER, 1956

AN APPROACH TO RELAXATION

NELSON ALGREN

JEAN-PAUL SARTRE

CALDER WILLINGHAM

EARLE W. THOMPSON

Fifty Cents

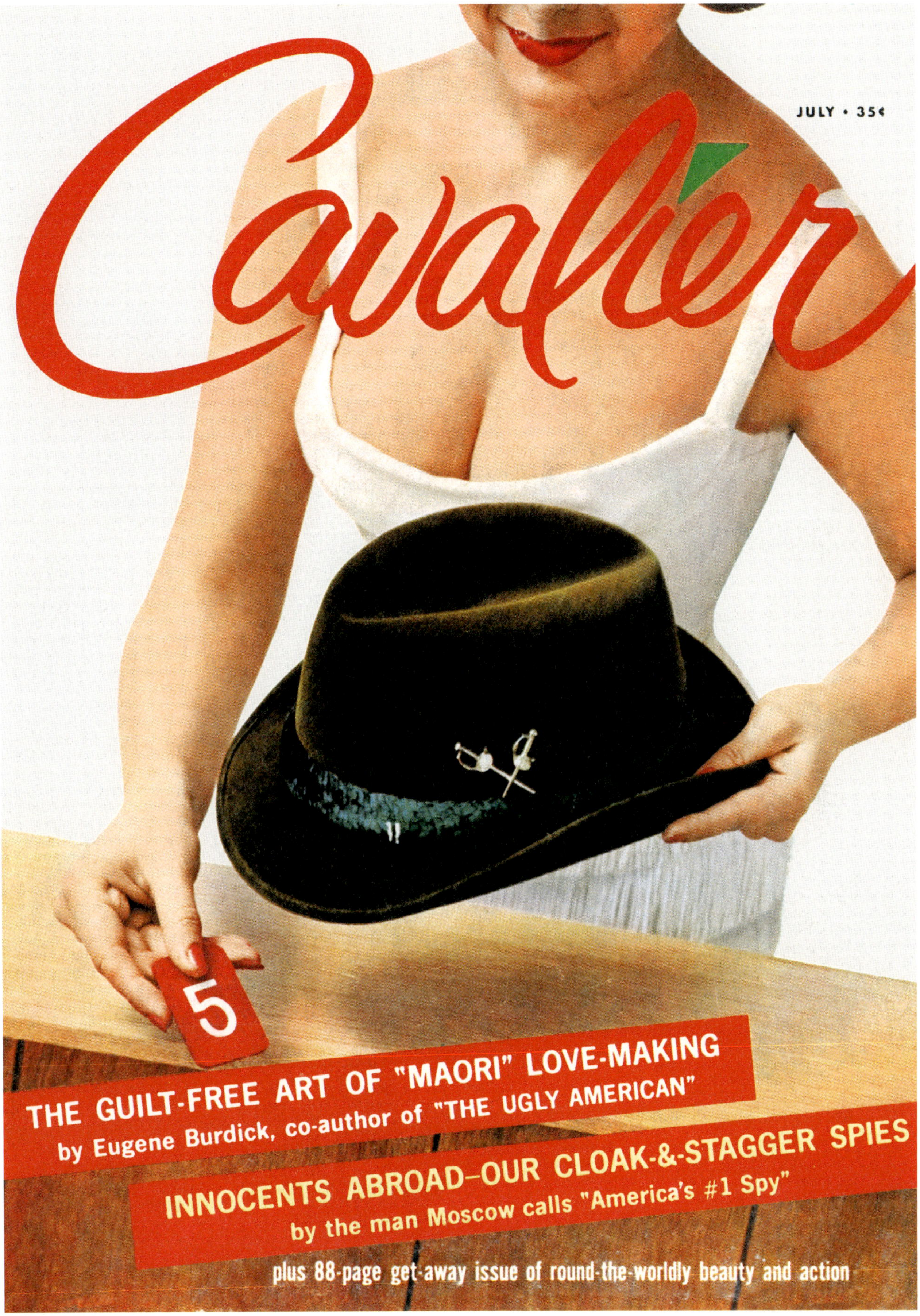

YEAR: **1960.** TITLE: **Cavalier.** COUNTRY: **USA.**

YEAR: **1956.** TITLE: **The Gent.**
COUNTRY: **USA.**

NEWS AND NUDES:

The Sleazy Pulp Digests

News und Nackte: Schlüpfrige Pulp-Magazine
Du cru et du nu : Les « pulp » bas de gamme

A curiosity of the 1950s was a number of American men's lifestyle digests that foretold the "lad magazines" of today. Imagine a *Reader's Digest* that combined all the elements of the era's men's magazines, including sports, pin-ups, scandal, men's adventure, detective stories, human oddities and slapstick photo stories in a pocket-sized package costing less than a quarter. They were the best deal going and offered amazing variety. For example, an issue of *Picture Digest* combined photos of Yugoslavian dictator Marshal Tito's stripper girlfriend with Caribbean voodoo, Jayne Mansfield's stage act, and African tree-dwelling goats. *Rave* mixed the scandal of Ernest Hemingway's alcoholism with Shelley Winters' lingerie shots and Bugsy Siegal's post-mortem photos. *Scoop!* had horrendous photos of African women executed for adultery, a stripper bathing with her dog, female contortionists and more voodoo.

The cheapest were only a dime, and only the sexually blatant went up to thirty-five cents.

Year: **1956.** Title: **Picture Digest.** Country: **USA.**

Year: **1954.** Title: **Tell.** Country: **USA.**

Eine Kuriosität der Fünfziger waren die amerikanischen Lifestyle-Magazine für Männer im Digest-Format, Vorläufer der heutigen „Lad"-Magazine. Man stelle sich eine Art *Reader's Digest* vor, der alle Ingredienzen der Männermagazine jener Jahre in sich vereinte: Sport, Pin-ups, Skandale, Abenteuer, Detektivgeschichten, menschliche Kuriositäten und Slapstick-Fotos im Taschenbuchformat, das alles für weniger als einen Vierteldollar. Preiswerter ging es nicht, und sie boten eine erstaunliche Bandbreite. Eine Ausgabe des *Picture Digest* kombinierte Fotos einer Stripperin, der Freundin des jugoslawischen Diktators Marschall Tito,

Les années cinquante produisirent une curiosité sous la forme de digests généralistes pour hommes qui annonçaient les magazines de charme d'aujourd'hui. Imaginez un *Reader's Digest* qui associerait tous les éléments des magazines pour hommes de l'époque, y compris les sports, les pin-up, les scandales, les aventures, les histoires policières, les bizarreries humaines et les farces en séquence photo, le tout sous format de poche et coûtant moins de 25 cents. On ne pouvait faire mieux et offrir une telle variété. Un numéro de *Picture Digest*, par exemple, conjuguait des photos de la petite amie strip-teaseuse du maréchal Tito, le dictateur yougoslave, avec du vaudou antillais, le numéro de scène de Jayne Mansfield et des chèvres arboricoles africaines. *Rave* mêlait des ragots sur les beuveries d'Ernest Hemingway avec des photos de Shelley Winters en petite tenue et des clichés post-mortem de Bugsy Siegal. *Scoop !* présentait des images atroces d'Africaines exécutées pour adultère aux côtés d'une strip-teaseuse se baignant avec son chien, de femmes contorsionnistes et encore de vaudou.

Tell montrait des strip-teaseuses, un chimpanzé élevé comme un enfant, encore des strip-teaseuses et un manchot qui mangeait avec ses pieds. Sur chaque couverture de *He* un gros titre promettait quelque nouvelle étrange permutation

YEAR: **1953.** TITLE: **Rave.** COUNTRY: **USA.**

YEAR: **1959.** TITLE: **Foto-rama.**
COUNTRY: **USA.**

Year: **1954.** Title: **Rave.**
Country: **USA.**

Picture Digest combined photos of Yugoslavian dictator Marshal Tito's stripper girlfriend with Caribbean voodoo.

Tell featured strippers, a chimp who was raised as a boy, more strippers and an armless man who ate with his feet. Every cover of *He* was emblazoned with a banner promising some strange new permutation on sex ("Sex and Hypnosis!") that was almost as amusing as the "He-Man Pinups" inside. *Tempo* pretended to appeal to both sexes with fashion and Hollywood features, but cheesecake was still the main course. *Foto-rama* also promoted itself as a cinema magazine, but with stripper Candy Barr on the cover and a semi-nude centerfold it offered more sin than cinema. There were many, many more. *Bold*, *Brief*, *Behind the Scene*, *People Today*, *Sensation* all offered the same lurid coverlines and laddish content. The cheapest were only a dime, and only the sexually blatant *Foto-rama* went up to thirty-five cents. All but

Year: **1956.** Title: **Picture Digest.** Country: **USA.**

mit Voodoo aus der Karibik, Jayne Mansfields Bühnennummer und in Bäumen lebenden Ziegen in Afrika. *Rave* kombinierte den Skandal um Ernest Hemingways Alkoholismus mit Bildern von Shelley Winters in Unterwäsche und Fotos des toten Bugsy Siegel. *Scoop*! zeigte entsetzliche Fotos von Afrikanerinnen, die wegen Ehebruchs hingerichtet wurden, eine Stripperin mit ihrem Hund beim Baden, weibliche Schlangenmenschen und noch mehr Voodoo.

In *Tell* sah man Stripperinnen, einen Schimpansen, der wie ein Junge großgezogen wurde, noch mehr Stripperinnen und einen Mann ohne Arme, der mit den Füßen aß. Jede neue Nummer von *He* zierte eine Schlagzeile, die eine neue seltsame sexuelle Permutation versprach (Sex und Hypnose!) und fast so amüsant war, wie die Pin-ups im Heft. *Tempo* gab sich mit Beiträgen über Mode und Film den Anschein, beide Geschlechter anzusprechen, doch Cheesecake war weiterhin der Hauptgang. Auch *Foto-rama* warb für sich als Filmzeitung, doch mit den Fotos von der Stripperin Candy Barr und einem halbnackten Centerfold bot es mehr Sünde als Sündenbabel Hollywood. Es gab noch zahllose andere. *Bold*, *Brief*, *Behind the Scene*, *People Today* oder *Sensation* lieferten alle die gleichen lockenden Schlagzeilen und Themen für große Jungen. Die billigsten kosteten nur zehn Cent, und nur das unverhohlen sexlastige *Foto-rama* wagte es, fünfunddreißig Cent zu verlangen. Mit Ausnahme von *Tempo*, dem harmlosesten dieser Magazine, waren sie alle Nebenprodukte der New Yorker Pulpfabriken, Resteverwertung der Bilder, die bei den großformatigen Magazinen der Verleger abgefallen waren. Als es mit den Pulps in den Sechzi-

sur le sexe (Sexualité et hypnose !) qui était aussi amusante que les « pin-up He-Man » du digest. *Tempo* prétendait s'adresser aux deux sexes avec des rubriques mode et potins d'Hollywood mais le plat de résistance restait les images de jolies filles. *Foto-rama* se présentait également comme un magazine de cinéma mais, avec la strip-teaseuse Candy Barr en couverture et un poster central semi-nu, il était plus centré sur le sexe que sur le grand écran. Il y en avait beaucoup, beaucoup d'autres. *Bold*, *Brief*, *Behind the Scene*, *People Today*, *Sensation*, tous offraient les mêmes manchettes sensationnelles et les mêmes contenus machos. Les moins chers ne coûtaient que dix cents. Seul le plus ouvertement érotique, *Foto-rama*, grimpa jusqu'à trente-cinq cents. A l'exception de *Tempo*, le plus soft, tous étaient des produits dérivés des

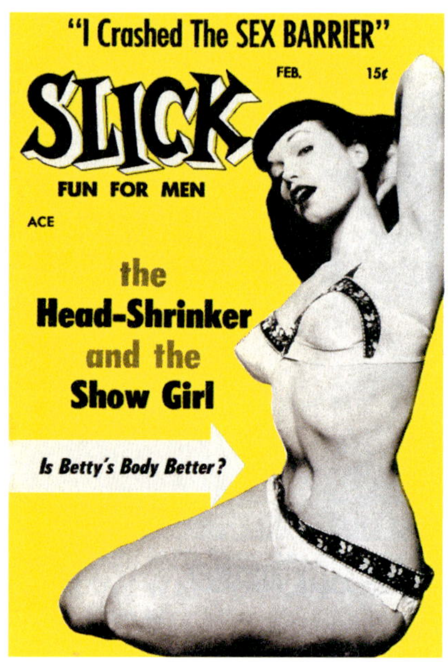

Year: **1957.** Title: **Slick.** Country: **USA.**

ARTHUR GODFREY: TV'S BIGGEST PHONY?

RAVE

APRIL

25c

THE GIRLS OF HOLLYWOOD

PDC

YEAR: **1955.** TITLE: **Rave.** COUNTRY: **USA.**

Murder and celebrity bosoms were the winning formula behind Rave's early 50s success.

Mord, Totschlag und Promi-Busen waren das Erfolgsrezept für Rave in den frühen fünfziger Jahren.

Rave dut son succès au début des années 50 à sa formule conjuguant les meurtres et les seins de célébrités.

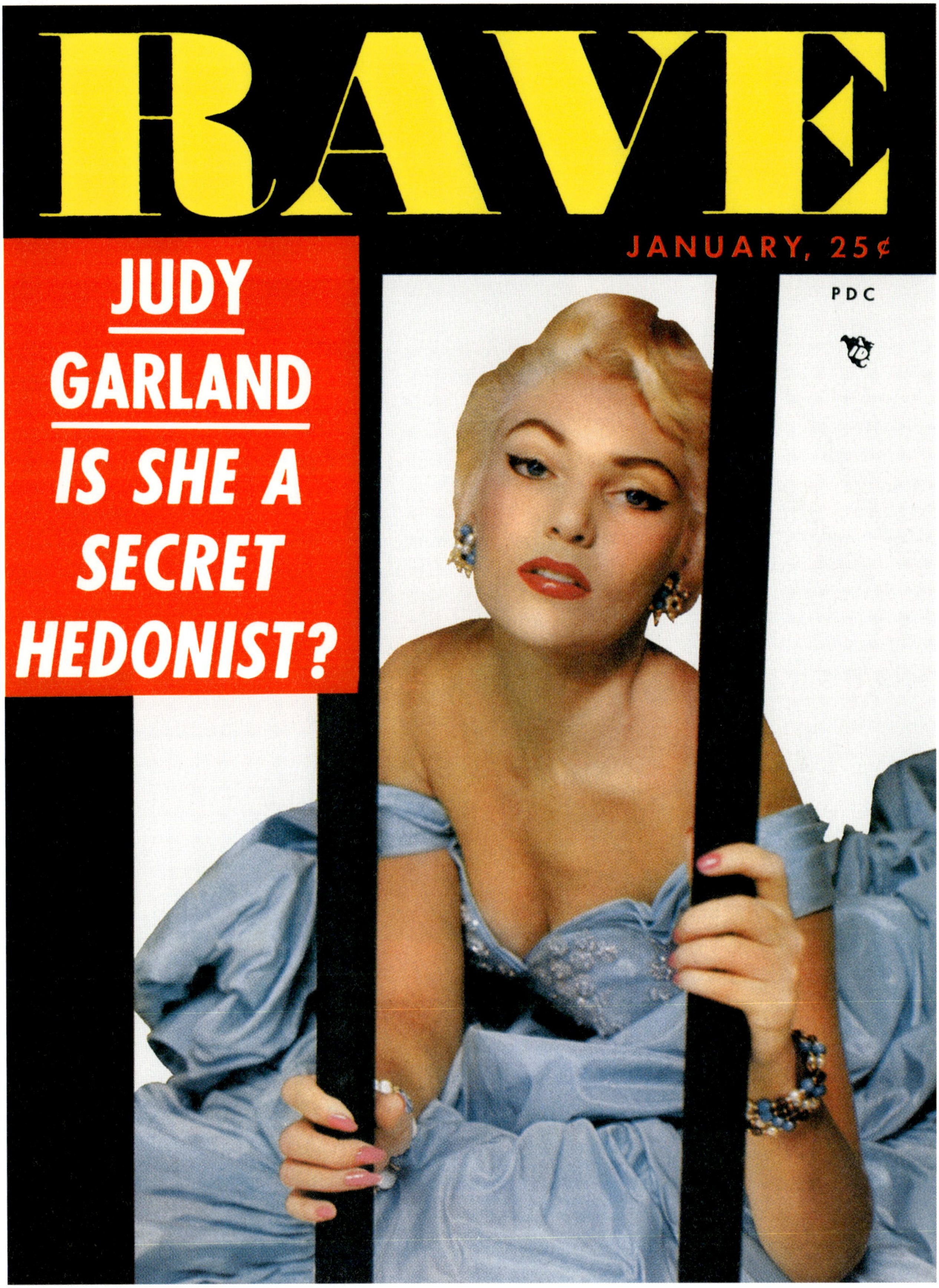

YEAR: **1955.** TITLE: **Rave.** COUNTRY: **USA.**

THE MOST!
NO. 1
25¢
ANC
WHAT'S HE MEAN, "THE MOST"?
HE MEANS THE MOST GAGS, GIGGLES, GUFFAWS AND GORGEOUS GALS IN ANY MAG-AZINE, DAD!
2 BITS

Photos such as this were customarily staged using magazine staffers, so that no actual Pig Town residents would have to be imported—or paid—for this December 1954 Sensation *expose.*

Fotos wie dieses für eine Enthüllungsgeschichte im Sensation*-Heft vom Dezember 1954 wurden üblicherweise von Redakteuren nachgestellt, damit man keine wirklichen Einwohner von Pig Town (auf Kosten des Hauses) einfliegen musste.*

Ce genre de photos était généralement mis en scène avec des membres de la rédaction, si bien qu'aucun vrai habitant de Pig Town (ville du cochon) ne dut être importé (ni payé) pour ce reportage paru dans le numéro de décembre 1954 de Sensation.

All were by-products of the New York pulp mills, casseroles concocted of images left over from full size magazines.

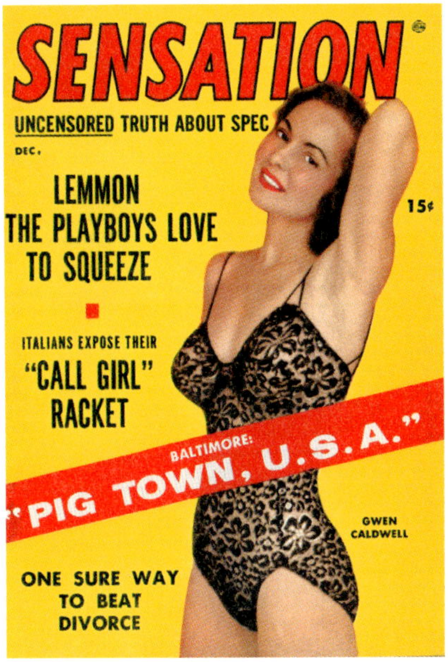

Year: **1954.** Title: **Sensation.** Country: **USA.**

BALTIMORE:

"PIG TOWN, U.S.A."

▶ Just a senator's throw from virginal Washington, D. C., bleak, fish-smelling Baltimore must take top honors when the roll of America's slob-towns is called. Famous for its sea food, Baltimore is infamous for dirty MORE

PIG ALLEY

Photos by Paul Schutzer

34

35

Year: **1954.** Title: **Sensation.** Country: **USA.**

Tempo, the mildest, were by-products of the New York pulp mills, casseroles concocted of images left over from their publisher's full-size magazines. As by-products, the digests disappeared when pulp declined in the 60s. There was a weak attempt to resurrect them in the 70s in the form of blatantly sexual digests like *Pic*, but by then men were used to full-sized magazines with glossy color pages. It would take the English to reinvent the genre with the high quality 90s lad titles like *Maxim*, *FHM* and *Bizarre*, now the bestselling men's magazines in the western world.

gern bergab ging, verschwanden auch diese Magazine. In den Siebzigern gab es mit sexuell freizügigen Magazinen wie *Pic* einen halbherzigen Versuch, sie wiederzubeleben, doch die Männerwelt war mittlerweile an großformatige und farbige Hochglanzmagazine gewöhnt. Erst die Engländer sollten in den Neunzigern mit erstklassigen Titeln wie *Maxim*, *FHM* oder *Bizarre*, die heute zu den meistverkauften Männermagazinen in der westlichen Welt gehören, dieses Genre neu erfinden.

éditeurs new-yorkais, des sauces concoctées avec les images rejetées par leurs magazines grand format. Ils disparurent lorsque les pulps entamèrent leur déclin dans les années soixante. Dans les années soixante-dix, il y eut une faible tentative pour les faire revivre sous la forme de digests ouvertement sexuels tels que *Pic* mais, entre-temps, les hommes s'étaient habitués aux grands magazines avec des photos en couleur sur papier glacé. Il n'y avait que les Anglais pour savoir réinventer le genre dans les années quatre-vingt-dix avec des titres de qualité tels que *Maxim*, *FHM* et *Bizarre*, aujourd'hui les magazines pour hommes les plus vendus en Occident.

Year: **1955.** Title: **The Most!**
Country: **USA.**

DANGER GLAND!

MEDICS CLAIM HEAVY PETTING CAN CAUSE PROSTATE TROUBLE LATER.

YEAR: **1954.** TITLE: **Tempo.** COUNTRY: **USA.**

YEAR: **1954.** TITLE: **Tempo.** COUNTRY: **USA.**

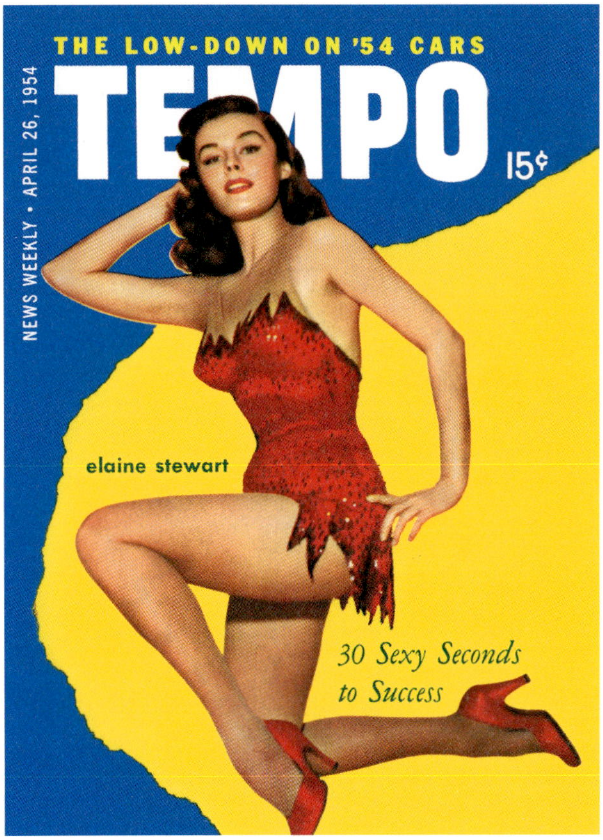

YEAR: **1954.** TITLE: **Tempo.** COUNTRY: **USA.**

YEAR: **1954.** TITLE: **Tempo.** COUNTRY: **USA.**

YEAR: **1954.** TITLE: **He.**
COUNTRY: **USA.**

SLAUGHTER
ON THE HIGHWAY!
ON WATCH FOR A SUCKER.

YEAR: **1954.** TITLE: **He.** COUNTRY: **USA.**

YEAR: **1954.** TITLE: **He.**
COUNTRY: **USA.**

K
HE
10c
SEPT. 1954
FOR GUYS WITH GUTS
CAFE SOCIETY'S TOP LOVER
SEX WAR IN RUSSIA
HE-MAN PIN-UPS
JEANNE O'CONNOR

This 1954 digest bannered a different sexual hot topic on every issue.

Dieser Digest von 1954 stellte jede Ausgabe unter ein anderes heißes Sex-Motto.

Chaque couverture de ce digest de 1954 annonçait un nouveau sujet très chaud sur la sexualité.

LEFT + ABOVE: YEAR: **1954.** TITLE: **He.** COUNTRY: **USA.**

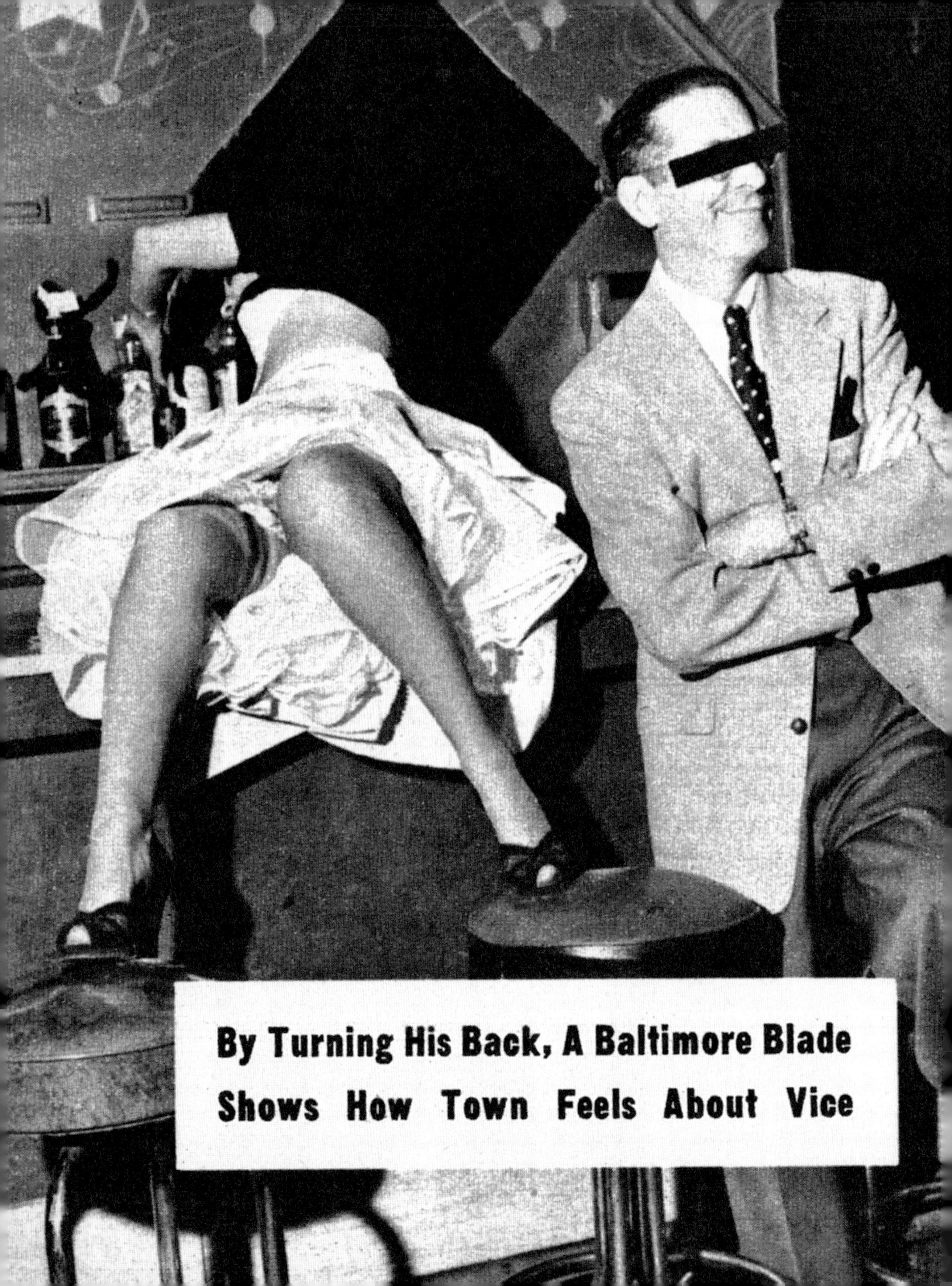

By Turning His Back, A Baltimore Blade Shows How Town Feels About Vice

Year: **1954.** Title: **Bold.** Country: **USA.**

Year: **1953.** Title: **People Today.** Country: **USA.**

Year: **1953.** Title: **People Today.** Country: **USA.**

Year: **1953.** Title: **People Today.** Country: **USA.**

Year: **1954.** Title: **Sensation.**
Country: **USA.**

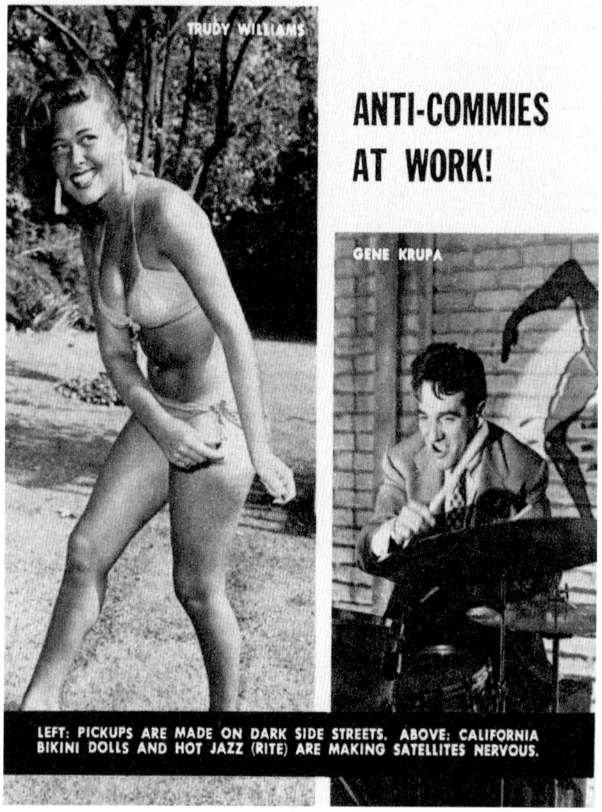

YEAR: **1954.** TITLE: **He.** COUNTRY: **USA.**

YEAR: **1954.** TITLE: **Scoop!** COUNTRY: **USA.**

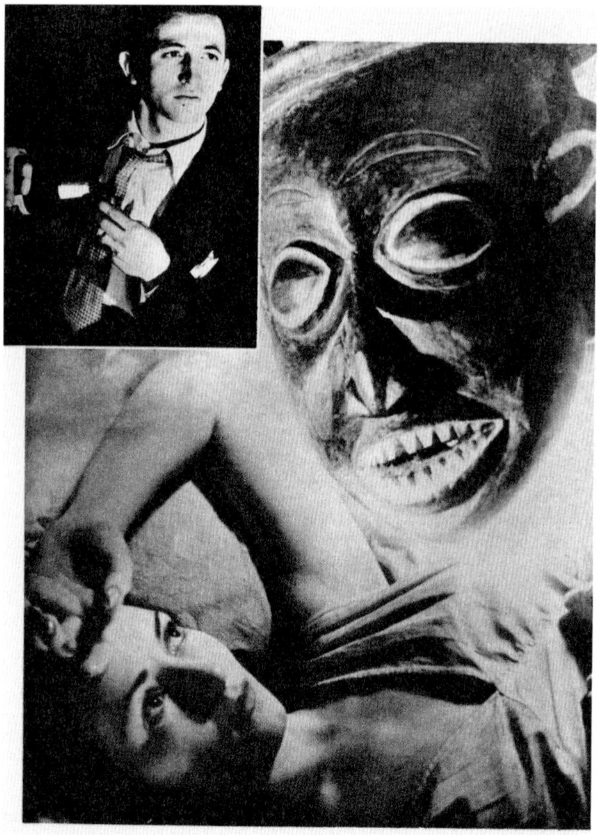

YEAR: **1954.** TITLE: **Scoop!** COUNTRY: **USA.**

YEAR: **1955.** TITLE: **Rave.** COUNTRY: **USA.**

YEAR: **1954.** TITLE: **Scoop!** COUNTRY: **USA.**

YEAR: **1956.** TITLE: **Brief.** COUNTRY: **USA.**

YEAR: **1956.** TITLE: **Picture Digest.**
COUNTRY: **USA.**

WOMAN No. 5

"What has Lili St. Cyr got that I haven't got?"

YEAR: **1959.** TITLE: **Foto-rama.** COUNTRY: **USA.**

YEAR: **1953.** TITLE: **Show.** COUNTRY: **USA.**

YEAR: **1960.** TITLE: **Photo Life.** COUNTRY: **USA.**

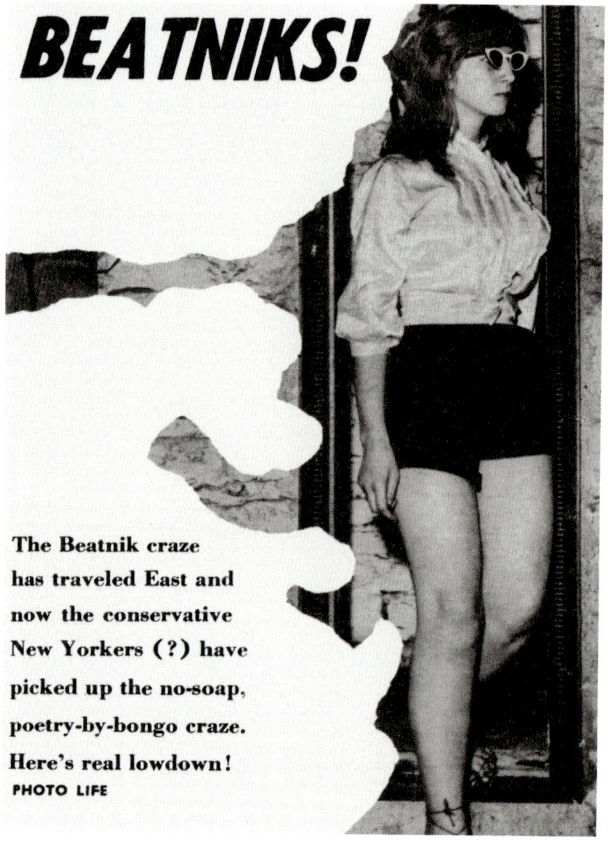

YEAR: **1959.** TITLE: **Foto-rama.** COUNTRY: **USA.**

Foto-rama *and* Photo Life *were the only news and nudes titles from an established men's magazine publisher. Myron Fass also produced the sexy humor title* Ogle.

Foto-rama *und* Photo Life *waren die einzigen Zeitschriften, die Nacktes mit Nachrichten vermischten und in einem etablierten Verlag für Männermagazine erschienen. Myron Fass produzierte auch das Sex-Witzblatt* Ogle.

Foto-rama *et* Photo Life *étaient les seuls titres d'information et de nu publiés par un éditeur établi de magazines pour hommes. Myron Fass produisit également le titre d'humour grivois* Ogle.

YEAR: **1959.** TITLE: **Foto-rama.** COUNTRY: **USA.**

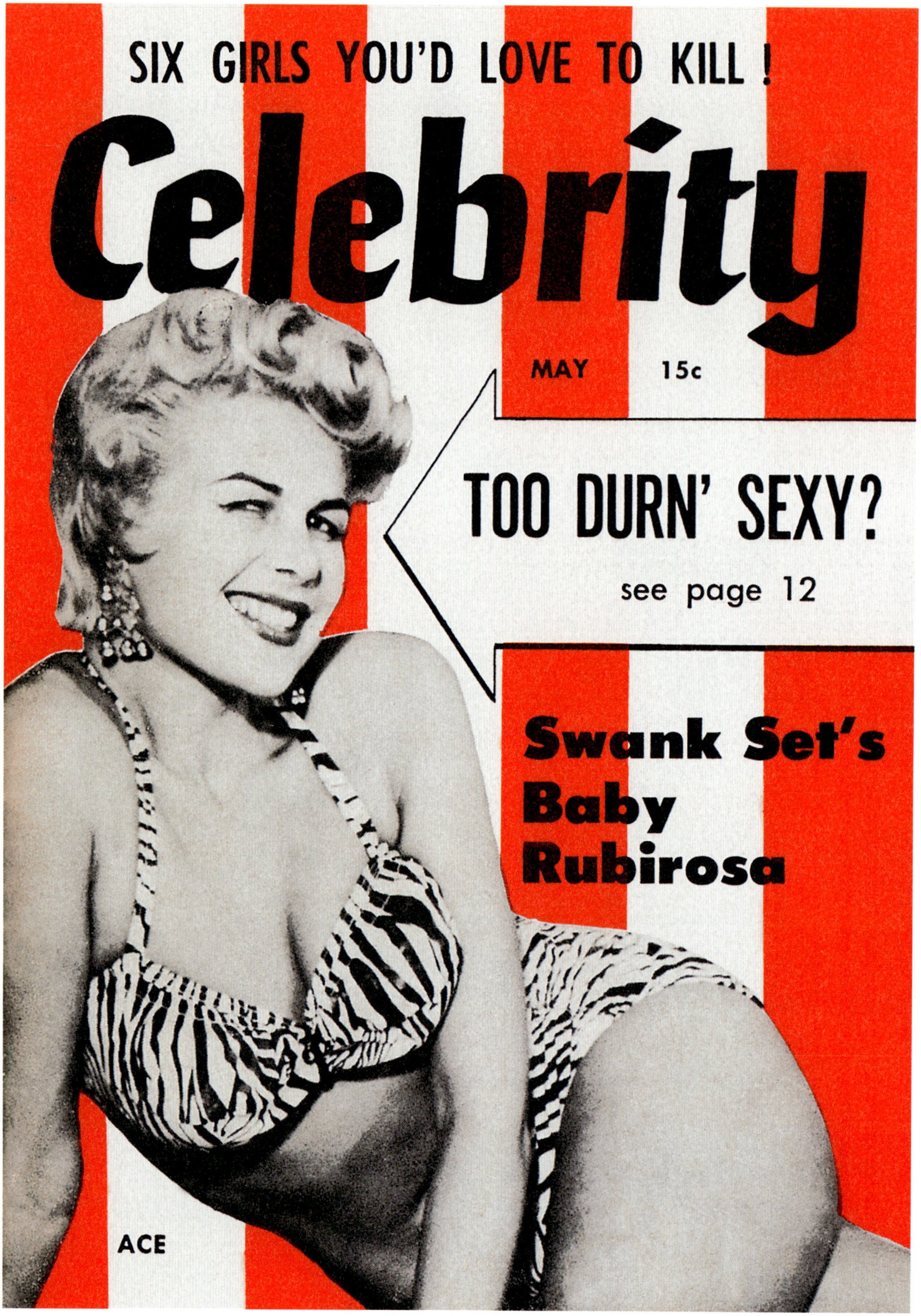

YEAR: **1955.** TITLE: **Celebrity.** COUNTRY: **USA.**

YEAR: **1955.** TITLE: **Male Life.** COUNTRY: **USA.**

YEAR: **1956.** TITLE: **Male Life.** COUNTRY: **USA.**

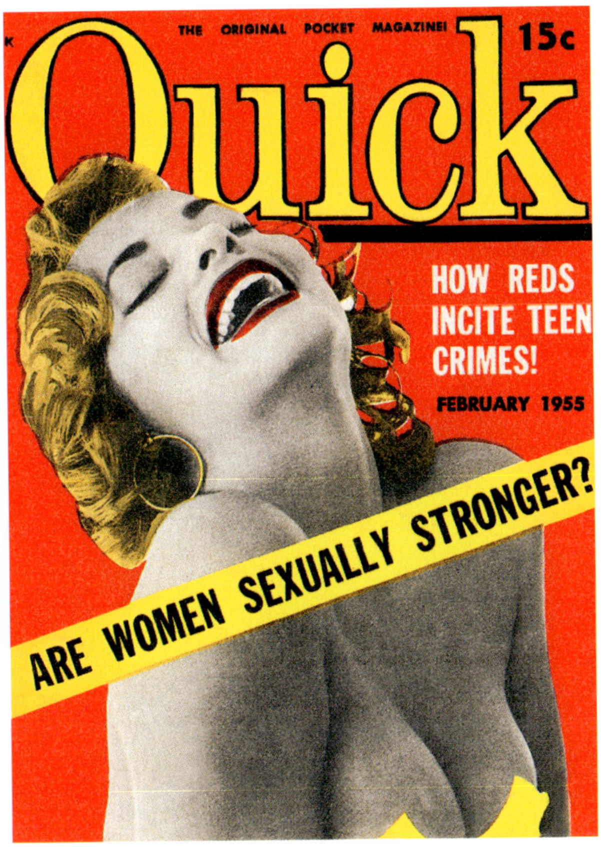

YEAR: **1955.** TITLE: **Quick.** COUNTRY: **USA.**

YEAR: **1958.** TITLE: **She.** COUNTRY: **USA.**

34

Height: 5′7″

Hair: Chestnut red

Eyes: Brown

Bust: 36″

Waist: 25″

Hips: 36″

Weight: 123 lbs.

On a sunny day in Italy, perfection appears like this

Groping for adjectives Hollywood blurb writers have produced such inanities as 'cosmic beauty' and 'somnolent contrast in moods' to describe Elsa. Movie-goers, using plainer, but more accurate phrases, will flock to theatres.

35

YEAR: **1956.** TITLE: **Brief.** COUNTRY: **USA.**

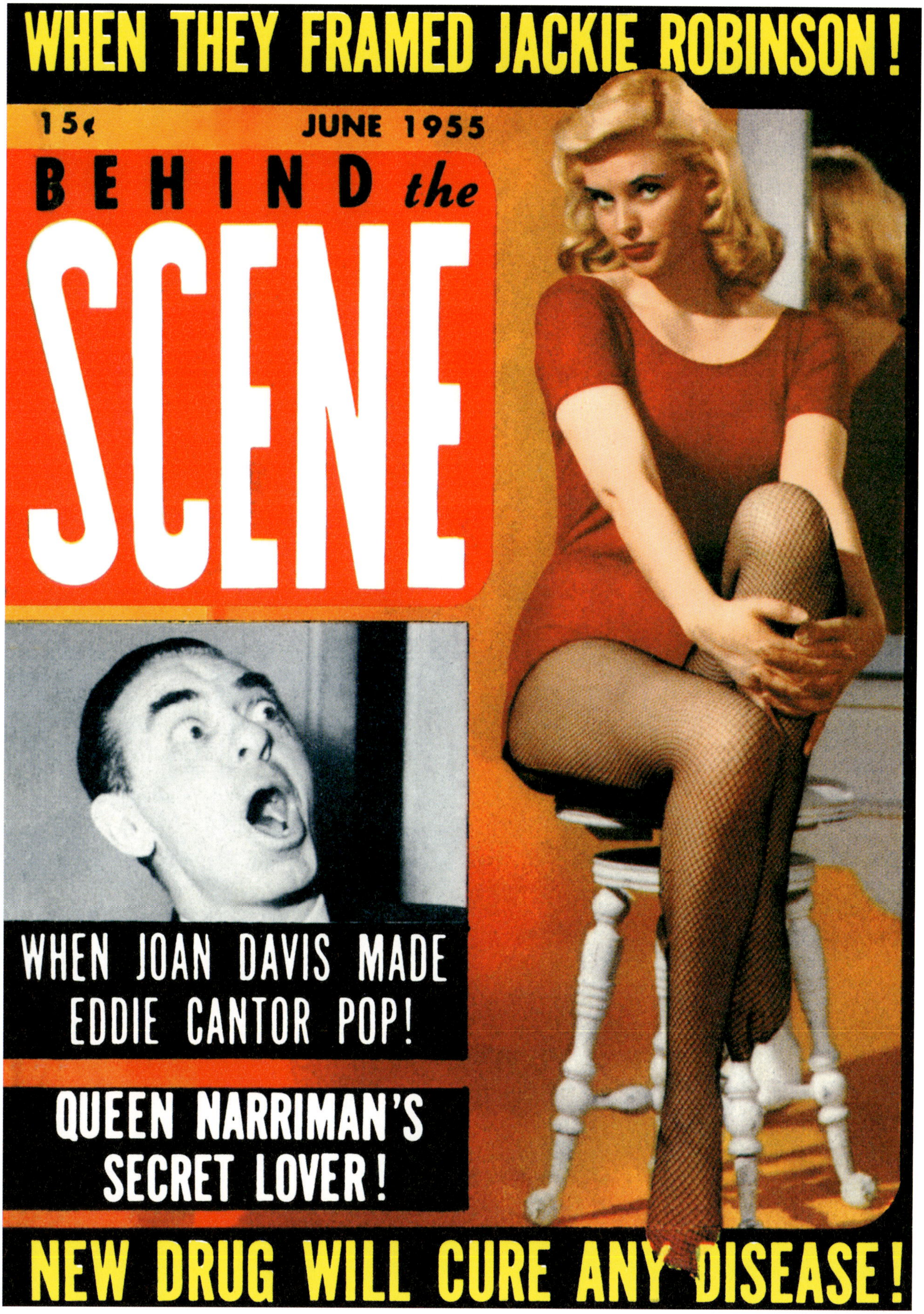

YEAR: **1955.** TITLE: **Behind the Scene.** COUNTRY: **USA.**

YEAR: **1954.** TITLE: **Bold.** COUNTRY: **USA.**

YEAR: **1954.** TITLE: **Tell.** COUNTRY: **USA.**

YEAR: **1954.** TITLE: **Scoop!** COUNTRY: **USA.**

YEAR: **1954.** TITLE: **Rave.** COUNTRY: **USA.**

YEAR: **1954.** TITLE: **Tell.**
COUNTRY: **USA.**

WHAT ITALY'S "MISS KINSEY" FOUND OUT
TELL
JULY 25¢
Confessions
OF A
THORNTON
MODEL

Take Me Home Daddy!
just pay the
nice newsdealer
fifty cents and
put me in your pocket

RABBIT AND STRIPPERS NECK AND NECK:

The Race to the 60s

Häschen und Stripperin Kopf an Kopf: Der Wettlauf in die Sechziger
Le lapin contre les effeuilleuses : Dernière ligne droite vers les années soixante

It was youth against age, white collar against blue collar, Madonna against whore, Cro-Magnon against Neandertal.

The second half of the 1950s saw a battle waged between the new and the old for dominance of America's newsstands. Hugh Hefner, *Playboy* publisher, led one army and George E. von Rosen, publisher of *Modern Man* led the other. On Hefner's side, the Girl Next Door, cocktails, jazz and journalism; on von Rosen's, strippers, cars, guns and fishing features. It was youth against age, white collar against blue collar, Madonna against whore, Cro-Magnon against Neandertal. I don't know how old von Rosen was in 1955, but everything in his magazines except the nudity was stubbornly old guard, a slicked-up version of the previous generation's fantasies. While Hef was dissing strippers in '55, von Rosen launched *Cabaret*, a top-of-the-line burlesque title filled with photos by Russ

Year: **1959.** Title: **Girl Watcher.**
Country: **USA.**

In der zweiten Hälfte der fünfziger Jahre konnte man einen verbissenen Kampf um die Vorherrschaft an amerikanischen Zeitungskiosken verfolgen. Hugh Hefner, der Verleger des *Playboy*, kommandierte die eine Armee, und George E. von Rosen, der Verleger von *Modern Man*, die andere. Hefner führte das Mädchen von nebenan, Cocktails, Jazz und Journalismus ins Feld, auf der Seite von Rosen kämpften Stripperinnen, Autos, Waffen und Angelabenteuer. Es war der Kampf zwischen Jung und Alt, zwischen Angestelltenkultur und dem Malocher, Madonna gegen Hure, Cro-Magnon gegen Neandertaler. Ich weiß nicht, wie alt Rosen 1955 war, doch bis auf die nackte Haut war in seinen Magazinen alles Schnee von gestern, eine runderneuerte Version der Fantasien der vorangegangenen Generation. Während Hef 1955 Stripper längst disste, startete Rosen *Cabaret*, ein Burlesque-Titel voller Fotos von Russ Meyer, Keith Bernard und Bernard of Hollywood. 1956 druckten *Modern Man* wie auch *Cabaret* Centerfolds in hochwertigem Vierfarbdruck auf dem allerfeinsten Papier und zeigten mehr nackte Haut als der *Playboy*. Sie brachten Artikel über echte Prominente (*Cabaret* feierte im März 1957 den 40. Geburtstag von Lena Horne und fragte: „Wie lange hält sich ein Glamourgirl?"), und trotzdem fehlte das gewisse Etwas. „Der

Year: **1959.** Title: **Pose!** Country: **USA.**

La seconde moitié des années cinquante fut marquée par la bataille entre le nouveau et l'ancien pour la domination des kiosques américains. Hugh Hefner, l'éditeur de *Playboy*, menait une armée, et George E. von Rosen, éditeur de *Modern Man*, était à la tête de l'autre. Dans le camp d'Hefner on trouvait la fille d'à côté, les cocktails, le jazz et le journalisme ; dans celui de von Rosen, les stripteaseuses, les voitures, les armes et la pêche. C'était la jeunesse contre l'âge

Year: **1956.** Title: **Caper.**
Country: **USA.**

Meyer, Keith Bernard and Bruno of Hollywood. By '56 both *Modern Man* and *Cabaret* were printing high-quality color centerfolds on the best paper and showing more nudity than *Playboy*. They ran top celebrity features too (March '57 *Cabaret* celebrated Lena Horne's 40th birthday, asking "How Long Can A Glamour Girl Last?"), but still lacked cutting edge. "*Modern Man* goes to a Beatnik Party" was the lead article in the October

The legalization of pubic hair in nudist magazines in 1958 hinted at a liberal trend.

'59 issue, but a line like "'Chicks' and 'cats' beer it up in Village 'pad' where Buddha is boss and 'beat' is the byword" sounds like a suburban Dad smirking at hip hop. *Playboy* understood it was far better to *be* Beat than report Beat, as did many of its new competitors. *Escapade* went so far as to give Jack Kerouac a column for six months in 1959 (and yes, he did use it to promote Zen Buddhism). *Escapade* publisher David Zentner was not completely confident of the new style in men's magazines, though; while *Escapade* was a convincing *Playboy* imitation, his *Caper* title copied *Modern Man*.

As the 50s wore on, Hefner and von Rosen continued to vie for the hearts of America's men while secondary publishers watched their sales and mimicked ac-

Year: **1957.** Title: **Dazzle.** Country: **USA.**

Modern Man geht auf eine Beatnik-Party" hieß die Titelstory im Heft vom Oktober 1959, aber ein Satz wie „'Chicks' and ‚cats' beer it up in Village ‚pad' where Buddha is boss and ‚beat' is the byword", hört sich an, als würde ein spießiger Vorstadtvater sich über Hip-Hop lustig machen. Wie viele der anderen neuen Magazine verstand es auch der *Playboy* viel besser, „Beat" zu sein, anstatt bloß über „Beat" zu schreiben. *Escapade* ging sogar so weit, Jack Kerouac 1959 für sechs Monate eine eigene Kolumne zu geben (genau in der warb er dann für Zen-Buddhismus). Ganz so viel Vertrauen in den neuen Stil bei Männermagazinen hatte David Zentner, der Verleger von *Escapade*, dann doch nicht: Während *Escapade* den *Playboy* kopierte, kopierte sein Magazin *Caper* den *Modern Man*.

mûr, les cadres contre les ouvriers, la Madone contre la putain, l'homme de Cro-Magnon contre l'homme de Neandertal. J'ignore quel âge avait von Rosen en 1955 mais tout dans ses magazines, à l'exception de la nudité, appartenait résolument à la veille garde, une version améliorée des fantasmes de la génération antérieure. Pendant qu'Hefner dénigrait les strip-teaseuses, von Rosen lançait *Cabaret*, un titre burlesque haut de gamme, rempli de photos de Russ Meyer, Keith Bernard et Bruno of Hollywood. En 1956, *Cabaret* et *Modern Man* publiaient de superbes posters centraux en couleur sur du meilleur papier et montrant plus de nudité que *Playboy*. Ils contenaient des articles sur les plus grandes célébrités (le *Cabaret* de mars 1957 célébrait le 40e anniversaire de Lena Horne en demandant « Combien de temps une beauté peut-elle tenir le haut du pavé ? ») mais sans parvenir à être modernes. Le numéro d'octobre 59 avait pour dossier principal « *Modern Man* assiste à une fête beatnik » mais le ton restait celui d'un bon père de famille dépassé observant les mœurs des jeunes avec une moue ironique. *Playboy* avait compris qu'il valait mieux *être* beatnik plutôt que d'en parler comme le faisaient bon nombre de ses concurrents. En 1959, *Escapade* alla jusqu'à confier une chronique pendant six mois à Jack Kerouac. Son éditeur, David Zentner, n'était pas totalement convaincu par ce nouveau style des magazines pour hommes et si *Escapade* était un émule convaincant de *Playboy*, son autre titre, *Caper*, copiait *Modern Man*.

Jusqu'à la fin des années cinquante, Hefner et von Rosen continuèrent à se disputer le cœur des hommes américains, tandis que des éditeurs secondai-

CAPER
DECEMBER 1956
50 CENTS
HOLIDAY BONUS:
CAPER'S PARTY GAL-LERY IN FULL COLOR
HOW TO TAME RELUCTANT FEMALES

cordingly. With World War II ten years past, the soldiers who'd returned home and rushed into marriage and fatherhood were eager for some fantasy escape from 50s domesticity. At the same time censorship laws were loosening; publishers could freely print topless photos and were finding it easier to distribute their magazines on the newsstand. The legalization of pubic hair in nudist magazines didn't directly help the men's magazines, but the precedent hinted at a liberal trend. Accordingly, between 1957 and 1959 there was a huge increase in new men's titles on America's newsstands, including *Adam, Best for Men, Cavalcade, Cavalier, Dude, Frolic, Gay Blade, Gent, Girl Watcher, High, Hi-Life, Knave, Mr., Nugget, Play, Plush, Pose!, Rascal, Rogue, Rugged, Satan, Sir Knight, Tiger* and *Venus*. Of these roughly half followed Hefner, including *Cavalier, Hi-Life, Nugget* and *Venus*, and half trailed von Rosen and the strippers. In the next decade this balance would shift sharply.

By 1956 both *Modern Man* and *Cabaret* were showing more nudity than *Playboy*.

Während Hefner und Rosen in den Fünfzigern weiter um den amerikanischen Mann wetteiferten, beobachteten andere Verleger aus der zweiten Reihe deren Verkaufszahlen und eiferten ihnen entsprechend nach. Zehn Jahre nach Ende des Zweiten Weltkrieges sehnten sich die heimgekehrten Soldaten, die sich in Ehe und Vaterrolle gestürzt hatten, nach etwas Ablenkung vom häuslichen Alltag. Zur gleichen Zeit lockerten sich die Zensurbestimmungen; die Verleger durften Oben-ohne-Fotos abdrucken und ihre Magazine problemloser an den Zeitungsständen verkaufen. Die Legalisierung von Schamhaar in den Nudistenmagazinen half den Männermagazinen nicht direkt, doch dieser Präzedenzfall verriet einen Trend zu mehr Liberalität. Dementsprechend stieg die Zahl der Männermagazine an amerikanischen Kiosken zwischen 1957 und 1959 enorm an, darunter Titel wie *Adam, Best for Men, Cavalcade, Cavalier, Dude, Frolic, Gay Blade, Gent, Girl Watcher, High, Hi-Life, Knave, Mr., Nugget, Play, Plush, Pose!, Rascal, Rogue, Rugged, Satan, Sir Knight, Tiger* und *Venus*. Während etwa die Hälfte, darunter *Cavalier, Hi-Life, Nugget* und *Venus*, Hefner folgte, orientierte sich die andere an Rosen und den Strippern. Im nächsten Jahrzehnt sollte sich das Verhältnis deutlich verschieben.

res observaient attentivement leurs ventes et les imitaient. Dix ans après la Seconde Guerre mondiale, les anciens soldats rentrés au bercail pour se marier à la hâte et fonder une famille recherchaient avant tout une échappatoire à l'atmosphère casanière des années cinquante. Parallèlement, les lois de la censure se relâchaient ; les éditeurs pouvaient publier librement des photos topless et avaient plus de facilités pour distribuer leurs magazines dans les kiosques. La légalisation des poils pubiens dans les magazines nudistes n'aida pas directement les revues de charme mais créa un précédent, signe d'une ouverture. De fait, entre 1957 et 1959, on observa une très forte augmentation du nombre de titres pour hommes dans les kiosques américains dont *Adam*, *Best for Men*, *Cavalcade*, *Cavalier*, *Dude*, *Frolic*, *Gay Blade*, *Gent*, *Girl Watcher*, *High*, *Hi-Life*, *Knave*, *Mr.*, *Nugget*, *Play*, *Plush*, *Pose !*, *Rascal*, *Rogue*, *Satan*, *Sir Knight*, *Tiger* et *Venus*. Parmi ces derniers, la moitié environ étaient des émules d'Hefner, dont *Cavalier*, *Hi-Life*, *Nugget* et *Venus*, les autres suivant von Rosen et ses strip-teaseuses. Au cours de la décennie suivante, cet équilibre allait rapidement changer.

Year: **1956.** Title: **Nugget.** Country: **USA.**

NUGGET
ENTERTAINMENT
IN A LIGHTER MOOD
FEBRUARY, 1956
Fifty Cents
THE MERMAIDS' ISLAND
SULTRY "SIZZLE"
SOPHIA LOREN
SOMERSET MAUGHAM - ERSKINE CALDWELL

NOW
MAKE YOUR OWN SEX SURVEY!
MARCH
MR.
Only 25¢
WHY
HOMOS
HATE
Elvis

YEAR: **1958.** TITLE: **Mr.** COUNTRY: **USA.**

YEAR: **1957.** TITLE: **Mr.** COUNTRY: **USA.**

YEAR: **1957.** TITLE: **Modern Man.** COUNTRY: **USA.**

YEAR: **1958.** TITLE: **Adam.**
COUNTRY: **USA.**

S^N
50
Adam
VOL. 2 NO. 2
The Man's Space Companion!
ADULTS ONLY!

YEAR: **1958.** TITLE: **Hi-Life.** COUNTRY: **USA.**

YEAR: **1958.** TITLE: **The Dude.** COUNTRY: **USA.**

The magazine devoted to pleasure
THE DUDE
MAY, 1958
K
CHANDLER BROSSARD
W. L. GRESHAM
CARLTON BROWN
R. V. CASSILL
Fifty Cents

Year: **1957.** Title: **Escapade.** Country: **USA.**

Year: **1957.** Title: **Modern Man.**
Country: **USA.**

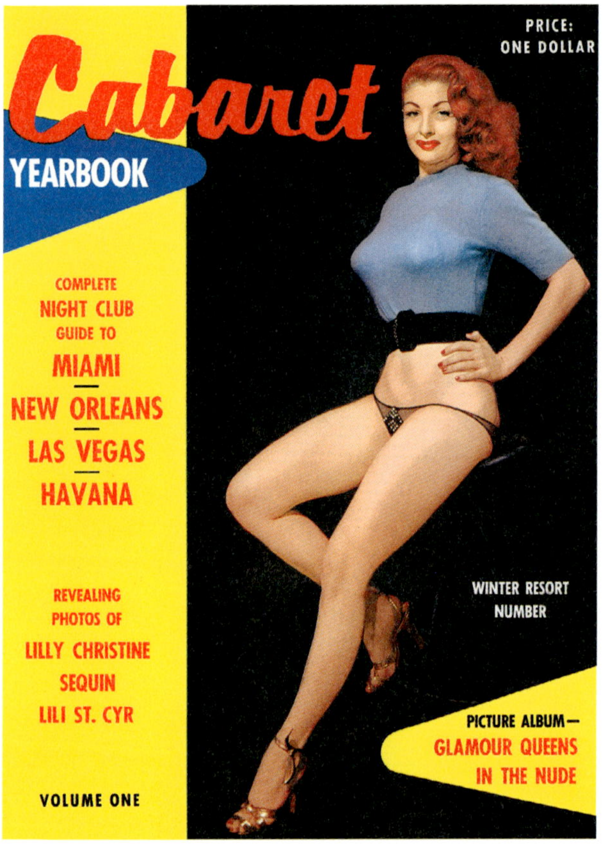

Year: **1950s.** Title: **Cabaret Yearbook.** Country: **USA.**

Year: **1956.** Title: **Cabaret.** Country: **USA.**

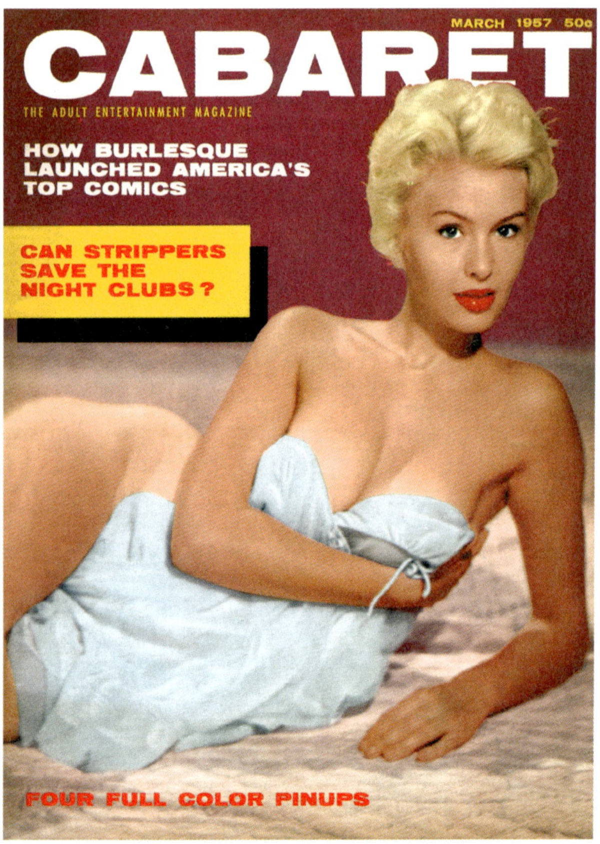

Year: **1957.** Title: **Cabaret.** Country: **USA.**

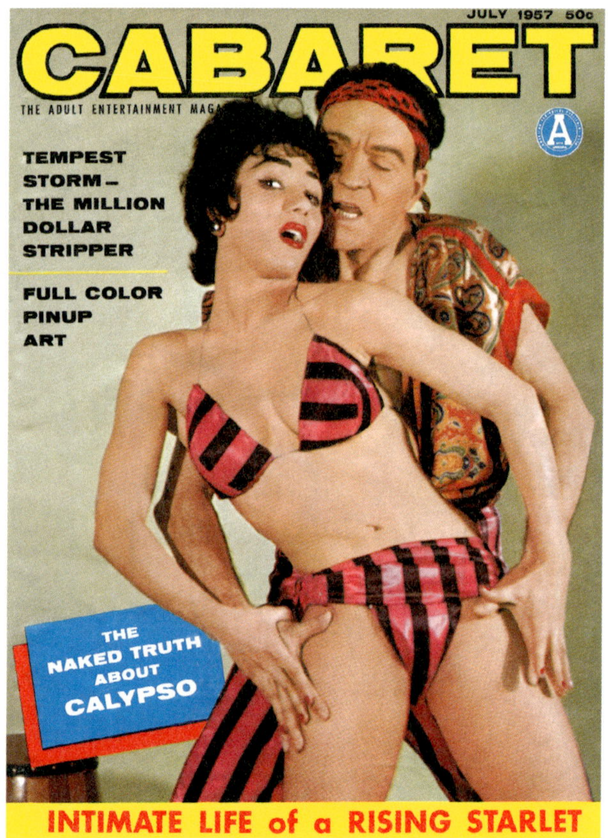

Year: **1957.** Title: **Cabaret.** Country: **USA.**

Year: **1959.** Title: **Pose!**
Country: **USA.**

Pose!
THE PICTURE MAGAZINE
Special GIANT ISSUE
over 120 photos!
FEBRUARY • 35¢
WORLD'S SEXIEST GIRLS
80 PAGES OF PHOTOS
SHOWGIRLS
MODELS
BEAUTY QUEENS
EXOTICS
MOVIE STARS
BURLESQUE

GOOD HUMOR for men
A Charlton Publication
OCTOBER
35c
Cinderella issue
• a sorority house after dark
• dinah washington-the greatest

YEAR: **1957.** TITLE: **Caper.** COUNTRY: **USA.**

YEAR: **1958.** TITLE: **Good Humor.**
COUNTRY: **USA.**

Year: **1959.** Title: **Play.** Country: **USA.**

Year: **1957.** Title: **21.**
Country: **USA.**

Amorous Adventures of Female Spies

Year: **1957.** Title: **Cabaret.** Country: **USA.**

Evelyn West

Ray Barrett

Year: **1959.** Title: **High Wide Handsome.** Country: **USA.**

FEEL FENCED IN? LIKE TO BREAK OUT OF THE OLD CORRAL? THEN READ

High FOR THAT WIDE AND HANDSOME FEELING

FICTION • ARTICLES • PICTURE STORIES • CARTOONS • GLAMOUR ALBUM • HUMOR

YEAR: **1957.** TITLE: **Europe's Top Pin-ups.** COUNTRY: **USA.**

RIGHT:
YEAR: **1957.** TITLE: **Europe's Top Pin-ups.** COUNTRY: **USA.**
PAGE 318 + 319:
YEAR: **1957.** TITLE: **Cabaret.** COUNTRY: **USA.**
PAGE 320 + 321:
YEAR: **1959.** TITLE: **High.** COUNTRY: **USA.**

EUROPE'S TOP PIN-UPS

NO. 3

100 GLAMOROUS PHOTOS

25¢

GINA LOLLOBRIGIDA

A DAZZLING PICTURE ROUNDUP OF THE CONTINENT'S MOST BEAUTIFUL GLAMOUR QUEENS

JUL
195
50
ACE
High
THE MAN'S HOME COMPANION
PARIS: A GUIDED TOUR THROUGH ITS EROTIC ZONES
BY COLIN ROSS
HOW ARE YOU FIXED FOR GIRLS?
BY RICHARD L. GROSSMAN
BOTTLE PARTY
BY
JOHN COLLIER

MISS WENDY HOLIDAY

YEAR: **1959.** TITLE: **High.** COUNTRY: **USA.**

YEAR: **1959.** TITLE: **High.**
COUNTRY: **USA.**

YEAR: **1950s.** TITLE: **After Dark.** COUNTRY: **USA.**

YEAR: **1959.** TITLE: **High.**
COUNTRY: **USA.**

High
THE MAN'S HOME COMPANION
SEPTEMBER 1959 • 50¢
ACE
ANOTHER LOOK AT
LADY GODIVA
WILL CUPPY
THE MONOTONY OF MONOGAMY
COLIN ROSS
SLEEPING BEAUTY
JOHN COLLIER
WEEPING IN THE CHINESE WINDOW
JAMES LEO HERLIHY
EXCLUSIVE
WHAT THE WELL-DRESSED MAN WILL WEAR THIS SUMMER

YEAR: **1957.** TITLE: **Cabaret.** COUNTRY: **USA.**

YEAR: **1957.** TITLE: **Caper.** COUNTRY: **USA.**

YEAR: **1956.** TITLE: **Caper.** COUNTRY: **USA.**

YEAR: **1959.** TITLE: **Modern Man.**
COUNTRY: **USA.**

YEAR: **1956.** TITLE: **Escapade's Choicest.** COUNTRY: **USA.**

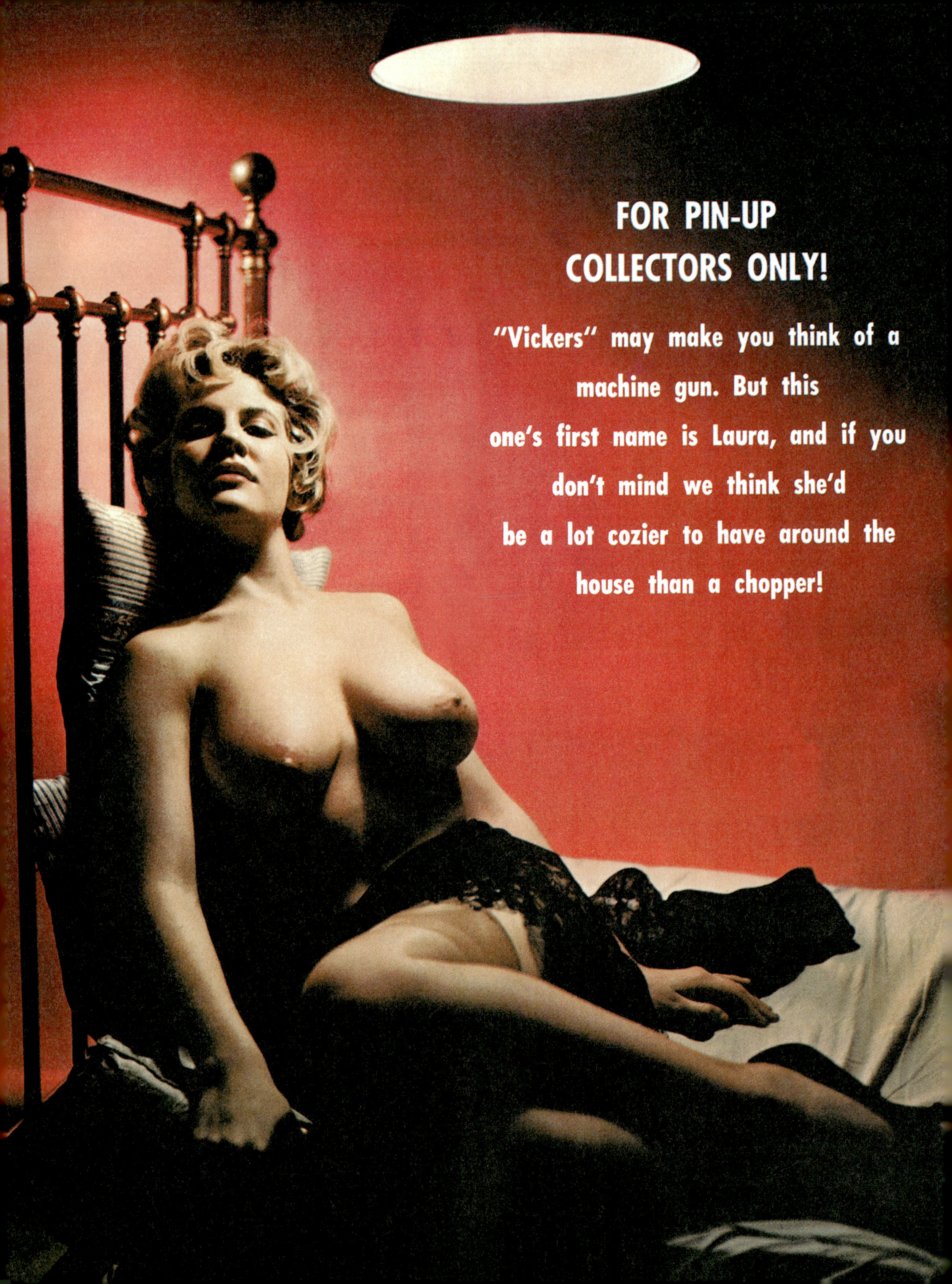

FOR PIN-UP COLLECTORS ONLY!

"Vickers" may make you think of a machine gun. But this one's first name is Laura, and if you don't mind we think she'd be a lot cozier to have around the house than a chopper!

YEAR: **1959.** TITLE: **Plush.** COUNTRY: **USA.**

LEFT: YEAR: **1959.** TITLE: **Hi-Life.** COUNTRY: **USA.**
PAGE 330 + 331: YEAR: **1958.** TITLE: **The Dude.** COUNTRY: **USA.**
YEAR: **1957.** TITLE: **Jackpot.** COUNTRY: **USA.**

JAN. 50 CENTS

JACKPOT

The Cad's Home Companion

Playboy vs Plowboy
See Page 16

Absolutely Nothing of Value
by Max Ruark

Up at Payton's Place
By Maxine Metallious

Jackpot's Consumers Report
on 1958's Girls all models

Didi Doll
By West Virginia Williams

The Funniest Magazine of the Year

P.D.C.

CASANOVA

FOR LOVERS OF LIFE

May · 50¢

HILARIOUS TAKE-OFF ON FRANCOISE SAGAN

BLACK MADONNA IN GREENWICH VILLAGE

PERVERSE INGENUE OF MONTPARNASSE
by Gary Pascal

MARIO SOLDATI
RICHARD ARMOUR
MAXWELL BODENHEIM

YEAR: **1957.** TITLE: **Relax.** COUNTRY: **USA.**

YEAR: **1957.** TITLE: **Casanova.**
COUNTRY: **USA.**

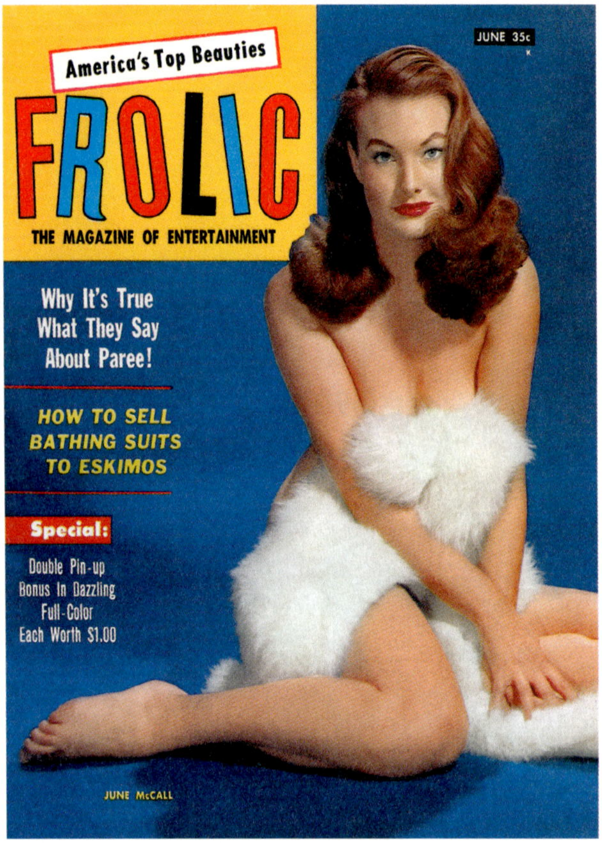

Year: **1958.** Title: **Frolic.** Country: **USA.**

Year: **1959.** Title: **21.** Country: **USA.**

Year: **1958.** Title: **Venus.** Country: **USA.**

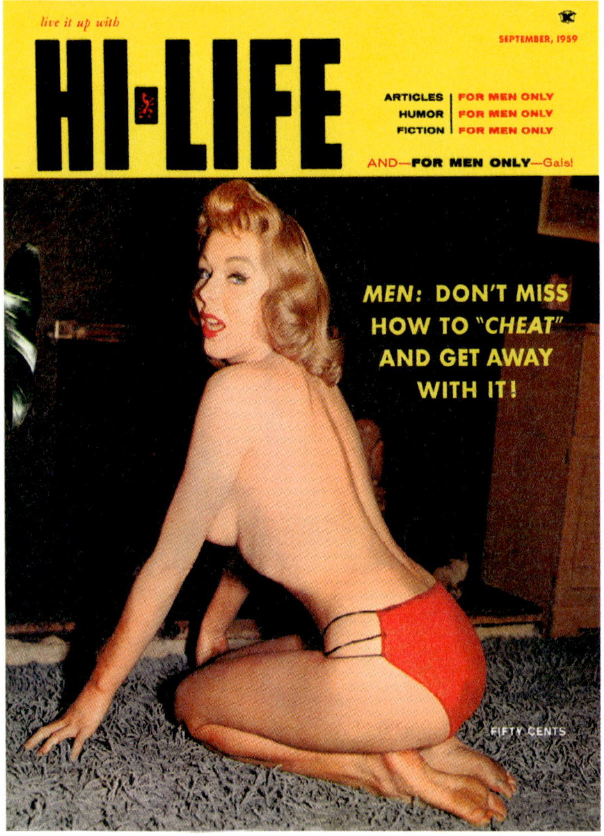

Year: **1959.** Title: **Hi-Life.** Country: **USA.**

Year: **1957.**
Title: **Rex.** Country: **USA.**

REX
FOR THE MAN ABOUT TOWN
DECEMBER • FIFTY CENTS
THE NEW JULIE NEWMAR
The One and Only 52nd Street
PLUS
Basil
WHO MADE OUT LIKE MAD

Year: **1957.** Title: **21.** Country: **USA.**

Year: **1957.** Title: **21.**
Country: **USA.**

21

JANUARY, 1957 • 50¢

JAYNE MANSFIELD IN COLOR

EARLY GIRLY DRAWINGS

THE BOGUS BRIDE

A NIGHT WITH HOLLY DAYE

OBSCENE What Does It Mean?

YEAR: **1957.** TITLE: **Europe's Top Pin-ups.** COUNTRY: **USA.**

YEAR: **1959.** TITLE: **Escort.** COUNTRY: **USA.**

YEAR: **1957.** TITLE: **Cabaret.** COUNTRY: **USA.**

YEAR: **1957.** TITLE: **Mr.** COUNTRY: **USA.**

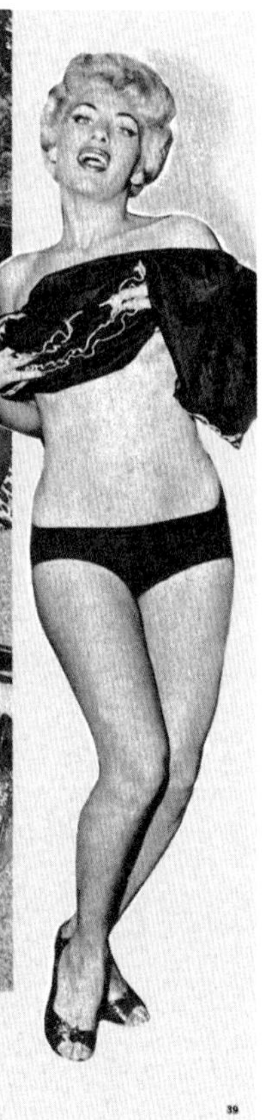

YEAR: **1957.** TITLE: **Modern Man.** COUNTRY: **USA.**

YEAR: **1957.** TITLE: **Hi.** COUNTRY: **USA.**

YEAR: **1957.** TITLE: **Ho!** COUNTRY: **USA.**

YEAR: **1957.** TITLE: **Night and Day.** COUNTRY: **USA.**

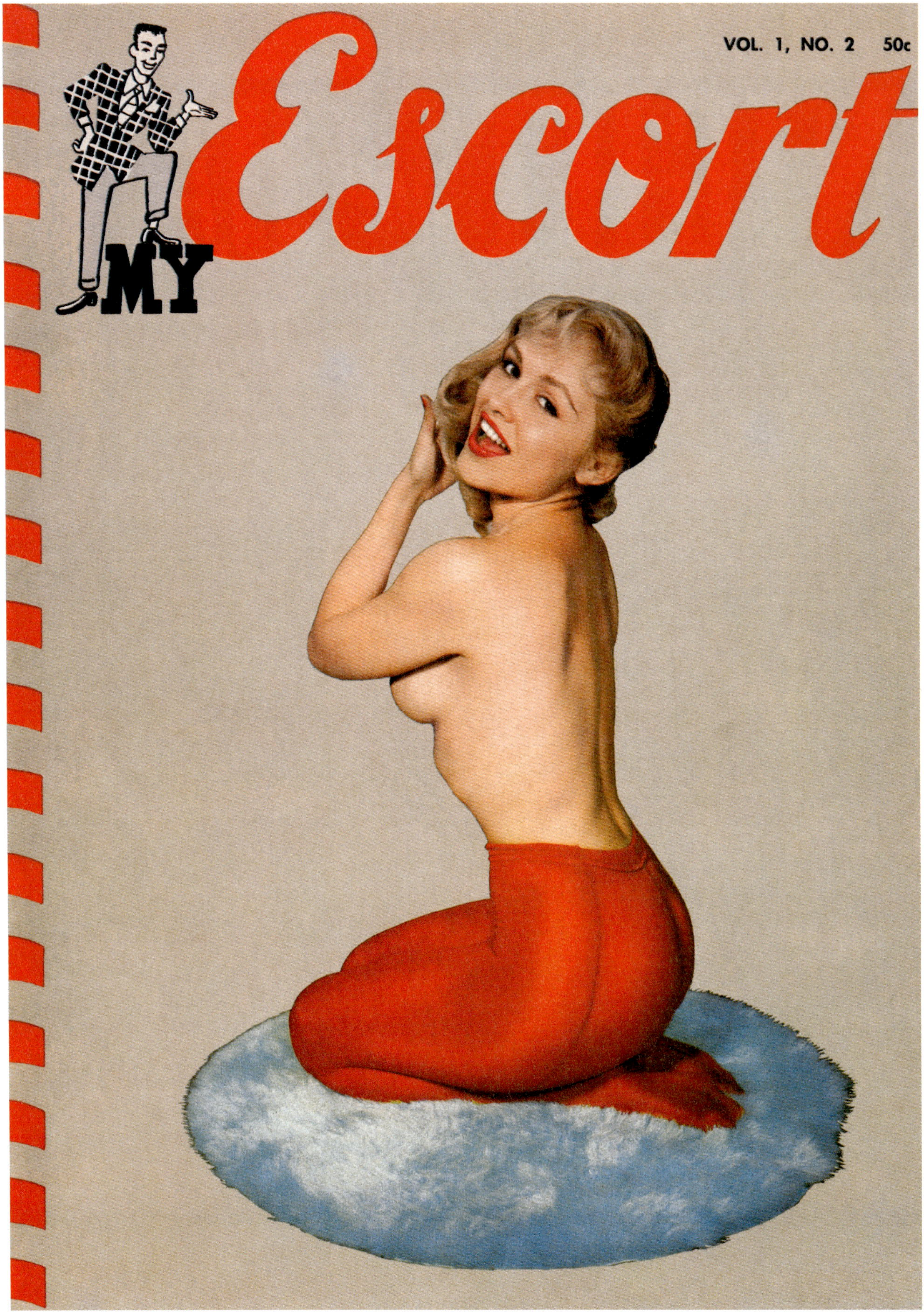

Year: **1959.** Title: **My Escort.** Country: **USA.**

Year: **1959.** Title: **My Escort.**
Country: **USA.**

Year: **1959.** Title: **Frolic.** Country: **USA.**

Right:
Year: **1959.** Title: **The Girl Watcher.** Country: **USA.**
Page 346 + 347:
Year: **1956.** Title: **Escapade.** Country: **USA.**
Year: **1956.** Title: **Escapade's Choicest.** Country: **USA.**

THE

girl watcher

A GUIDE TO GIRL WATCHING

MARCH 1959

PRICE 50¢

Tired of Collecting Bottle Tops, Race Horses

Start a Girl Collection

Escapade
MAY 1956 50 CENTS
IN THIS ISSUE
SEMINAR ON VIRGINITY
PHOTOGRAPHER'S
PRIVATE FILE

Escapade's CHOICEST

FALL, 1956
ONE DOLLAR

A READERS' SELECTION

JOE WEIDER:

Of Beef and Betty

Joe Weider: Bizeps und Betty
Joe Weider : Betty et les beaux mâles

By Richard Jaccoma

Joe Weider was a Canadian bodybuilder who, as a teenager in the 1940s, resolved with wonderfully single-minded focus to build an empire based on beefcake. Weider founded such well-known bodybuilding and fitness titles as *Your Physique*, *Muscle Builder*, *Muscle and Fitness*, *Shape*, *Flex* and *Men's Fitness*. And the far less known *Adonis*, *Jem* and *Monsieur*.

Bodybuilding can often be an all-involving narcissistic pursuit; and homoeroticism has been linked to it from the start. In the early 1950s, Weider directly targeted the still-closeted gay market with digest-size "mini-mags", including *Body Beautiful*, *The Young Physique*, *Demi-Gods* and *Muscle Teens*, as well as *Adonis*. Cover photos of Weider's *Adonis* featured strapping young lads in classical Greek settings; while paintings by such gay genre masters as George Quaintance welcomed readers to *Body Beautiful (Studies in Masculine Art)*.

Why Weider chose to jeopardize his status in the body building market – a market he was already dominating by

The linking of cheesecake to Weider's beefcake-based business enhanced its acceptability as a heterosexual pursuit.

Joe Weider war ein kanadischer Bodybuilder, der sich als Teenager in den vierziger Jahren mit wunderbarer Zielstrebigkeit daran machte, ein Imperium des Beefcake zu errichten. Weider gründete so bekannte Bodybuilding- und Fitnesszeitschriften wie *Your Physique, Muscle Builder, Muscle and Fitness, Shape, Flex* und *Men's Fitness*, aber auch deutlich weniger bekannte Titel wie *Adonis, Jem* und *Monsieur*. Bodybuilding kann eine narzistische Freizeitbeschäftigung sein, die einen ganz vereinnahmt, und von Anfang an spielte auch immer Homosexualität mit hinein. In den frühen Fünfzigern richtete sich Weider mit „Mini-Mags" im Taschenbuchformat, darunter Titel wie *Body Beautiful, The Young Physique, Demi-Gods* und eben *Adonis*, direkt an ein damals noch ganz ungeoutet lebendes, schwules Publikum. Auf den Covern von *Adonis* sah man stramme Jungs in klassisch-griechischer Kulisse, während den Leser von *Body Beautiful (Studies in Masculine Art)* Bilder von George Quaintance, dem Meister der Gay-Genremale-

Joe Weider

Joe Weider était un culturiste canadien qui, adolescent dans les années quarante, avait décidé avec une admirable opiniâtreté de bâtir un empire sur des muscles. Il fut le père des célèbres magazines de culturisme et de fitness *Your Physique*, *Muscle Builder*, *Muscle and Fitness*, *Shape*, *Flex* et *Men's Fitness* ... Et d'autres beaucoup moins connus comme *Adonis*, *Jem* et *Monsieur*. Le culturisme est souvent perçu comme une discipline obsessionnelle et narcissique. On lui a toujours tissé des liens avec l'érotisme homosexuel. Au début des années cinquante, Weider cibla directement le mar-

YEAR: **1957.** TITLE: **Monsieur.**
COUNTRY: **USA.**

YEAR: **1958.** TITLE: **Jem.** COUNTRY: **USA.**

YEAR: **1958.** TITLE: **Jem.** COUNTRY: **USA.**

1954 – by producing gay titles isn't clear, but at first glance a bodybuilding guru seems an even less likely choice as publisher of spicy heterosexual men's magazines. That's exactly what Joe became during the late1950s, however, with *Jem* and *Monsieur* and *Beauty and Figure*. Today these magazines have little more than a naive charm – and quite a bit of misogynistic humor. Many men's magazines of the period traded on dumb-broad jokes, but only Joe devoted an entire issue to training your wife as a domestic slave.

If Weider's magazines lacked the polish of *Playboy*, at least they had plenty of Betty. Betty Brosmer, the woman who would become Joe Weider's bride and lifelong partner, began as a magazine model, eventually appearing on cover after cover of *Jem* and *Monsieur* – and in ads for his bodybuilding products. Arguably the linking of cheesecake to Wei-

Joe devoted an entire issue to training your wife as a domestic slave.

rei, erwarteten. Warum Weider seinen Status in der Bodybuilding-Szene – einen Markt, den er 1954 bereits beherrschte, – dadurch gefährdete, dass er schwule Titel publizierte, ist nicht ganz klar, andererseits erwartet man von einem Bodybuilding-Guru auch nicht unbedingt, dass er heterosexuelle Männermagazine herausbringt. Aber genau das tat Joe mit *Jem*, *Monsieur* und *Beauty and Figure* in den späten Fünfzigern. Heute haben diese Magazine bestenfalls noch einen naiven Charme – und einen ziemlich frauenfeindlichen Humor. Viele Männermagazine jener Jahre setzten auf Witze über naive Frauen, aber nur Joe widmete ein ganzes Heft dem Thema, wie man aus der eigenen Frau einen Haushaltssklaven macht.

Wenn Weiders Magazinen auch der Glanz des *Playboy* fehlte, so boten sie doch jede Menge Betty. Betty Brosmer, die Frau, die Joe Weiders Ehefrau und lebenslange Geschäftspartnerin werden sollte, begann als Modell für Männermagazine und erschien dann auf Cover um Cover von *Jem* und *Monsieur* – und in den Anzeigen für Weiders Bodybuilding-Produkte. Die Verbindung von Cheesecake mit Weiders auf Beefcake basierendem Geschäft dürfte wohl darauf abgezielt haben, die Akzeptanz von Bodybuilding als heterosexuellem Hobby zu verstärken. In den Fünfzigern reiste Betty als Fotomodell durchs Land. Der offiziellen Version ihrer Geschichte nach traf sie Joe

ché encore caché des homosexuels avec ses « mini-mags » sous format digest dont *Beautiful Body*, *The Young Physique*, *Demi-Gods*, *Muscle Teens* et *Adonis*. Les photos en couverture d'*Adonis* montraient de beaux gaillards dans un décor inspiré de la Grèce antique. *Body Beautiful (« Etudes en art masculin »)*, lui, accueillait ses lecteurs avec des peintures, entre autres, d'un des maîtres de l'art homo-érotique, George Quaintance. On peut se demander pourquoi Weider choisit de mettre en danger son statut sur le marché du culturisme (qu'il dominait déjà en 1954) en publiant des revues

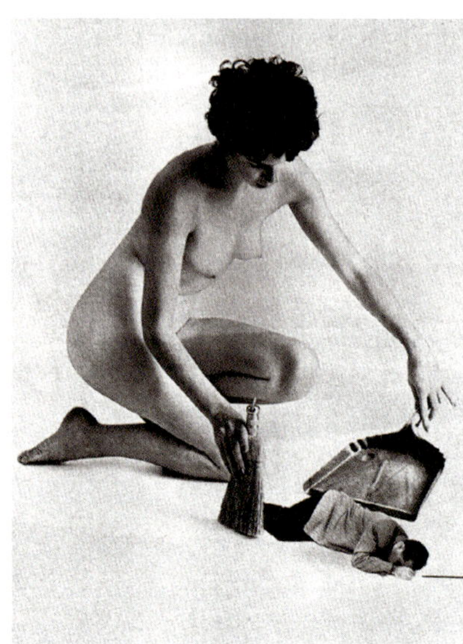

YEAR: **1958.** TITLE: **Jem.** COUNTRY: **USA.**

HOW TO BE A PLAYBOY ON $50 A WEEK!
K
Jem
THE MAGAZINE FOR MASTERFUL MEN
MARCH/50c
WOMEN OVERRATE SEX
SWEETHEARTS FOR RENT
PICKING UP A DAME—LATEST STYLE

YEAR: **1961.** TITLE: **Jem.** COUNTRY: **USA.**

YEAR: **1959.** TITLE: **Jem.**
COUNTRY: **USA.**

TEXANS ARE LOUSY LOVERS

K

Jem

THE MAGAZINE FOR MASTERFUL MEN

JUNE / 50¢

How to make your wife—

DO WHAT YOU WANT HER TO!

K
FICTION
HUMOR
GIRLS
ARTICLES
A TREASURE CHEST OF RARE SPICE
Jem
APRIL /50¢
Handsome Men
Make
Lousy Lovers!
The Truth
About
Call Girls
What Sexy Type
Dame Do You
Go For ?
New Techniques
For Winning
The Fair Sex
COVER GIRL: BETTY BROSMER

Year: **1959.** Title: **Jem.**
Country: **USA.**

Brosmer was a lovely woman in the voluptuous 50s style, with blonde hair, big breasts and an amazingly tiny wasp-waist.

der's beefcake-based business was aimed at enhancing its acceptability as a heterosexual pursuit.

Betty was traveling around the country doing photographic modeling during the 1950s. According to the official story, she met Joe in New York at a photo shoot for *Beauty and Figure*, charming him with her understanding of "the art layout of the magazine". Weider contracted for a dozen covers and they dated after each shoot. In 1961, at the age of 26, she became his second wife. "It wasn't love at first sight," Betty has observed about their relationship. "I became his psychiatrist, and he fell in love with me."

However, Dan Lurie, another bodybuilding/fitness expert who for a time worked with Weider supplying weightlifting gear for his enterprise, but then parted company in a bitter legal battle, has a less charitable explanation of exactly how the Weiders met, courted and wed. "My understanding is that Betty was a well-known prostitute," Lurie said. "Joe saw her picture in a magazine and made a bet with somebody he'd find her and, you know, date her."

Regardless of the details of their courtship, Betty Brosmer made an immensely valuable contribution to the Weider bottom line. She was a lovely woman in the voluptuous 50s style, with blonde hair, big breasts and an amazingly tiny wasp-waist. In the muscle magazines Betty instantly validated pumped and sculpted muscle mass as a male trait attractive to gorgeous women, giving bulked-up boys her ultra-feminine stamp of approval.

In the men's magazines, Betty's constant appearances as a covergirl validat-

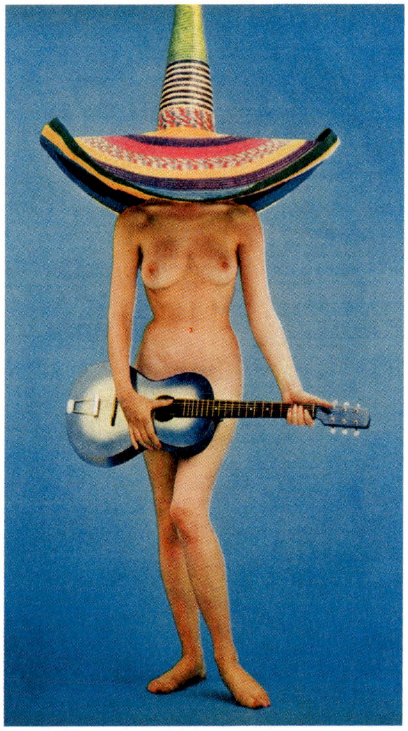

Year: **1959.** Title: **Jem.** Country: **USA.**

bei Aufnahmen für *Beauty and Figure* in New York und becirete ihn mit ihrem Gespür für „die Gestaltung des Magazins". Weider buchte sie für ein Dutzend Cover und ging nach jedem Fototermin mit ihr aus. Im Alter von 26 Jahren wurde Betty 1961 seine zweite Ehefrau. „Es war nicht die Liebe auf den ersten Blick", erzählte Betty über ihre Beziehung. „Ich wurde zu seiner Psychiaterin, und er verliebte sich in mich." Dan Lurie, ein weiterer Bodybuilding-Experte und bis zu einem erbitterten Rechtsstreit Weiders Lieferant für Hanteln und anderen Gewichtheberbedarf, hat allerdings eine weniger freundliche Erinnerung daran, wie sich die Weiders begegneten, verliebten und

homosexuelles. D'un autre côté, il est encore plus étrange qu'un gourou du bodybuilding ait décidé d'éditer des magazines de charme hétérosexuels. C'est pourtant ce qu'il fit à la fin des années cinquante avec *Jem*, *Monsieur* et *Beauty and Figure*. Aujourd'hui, ces magazines dégagent un charme naïf … et un humour franchement misogyne. Un grand nombre de publications de l'époque recouraient abondamment aux blagues mettant en scène de ravissantes idiotes, mais Joe fut le seul à consacrer un numéro entier sur la manière de dresser sa femme pour en faire une esclave domestique.

Si les magazines de Weider n'avaient pas le lustre de *Playboy*, ils étaient néanmoins pleins de Betty. Betty Brosner, future épouse de Joe Weider qu'elle accompagnerait jusqu'à la fin de sa vie, commença comme simple modèle avant

Year: **1957.** Title: **Jem.** Country: **USA.**

Year: **1957.** Title: **Jem.**
Country: **USA.**

Why Weider chose to jeopardize his status in the body building market by producing gay titles isn't clear.

ed her as an erotic icon. Supporters and detractors alike agree Weider seldom left any avenue unexplored in the effort to turn a profit. He flogged glossy cheesecake pictures and 8 and 16mm movies of the sex symbol he'd created via mail order. A *Jem* ad from January 1961 (yes, Betty's on the cover) exclaims: "See this blonde bombshell the way you've always wanted to see her – in breathtaking studio stills and action movies!... Never has there been a woman with such exquisite perfection of face... such a tiny-waisted, voluptuous figure!" Even after some of the blush left the rose, and Weider folded

Year: **1957.** Title: **Body Beautiful.**
Country: **USA.**

heirateten. „Soviel ich weiß, war Betty eine stadtbekannte Prostituierte", berichtete Lurie. „Joe sah ihr Bild in einem Magazin und wettete mit irgendwem, dass er sie aufspüren und sich mit ihr verabreden würde."

Wie auch immer, Betty Brosmer leistete einen unschätzbaren Beitrag zu Weiders Profiten. Sie war eine hübsche Blondine im üppigen Stil der Fünfziger, mit ansehnlicher Oberweite und verblüffend schmaler Wespen-Taille. In den Bodybuilding-Magazinen fungierte sie als lebender Beweis dafür, dass aufgepumpte und definierte Muskeln ein männliches Attribut waren, das tolle Frauen anzieht, und gab den kernigen Jungs so ihr ultrafeminines Okay.

Ihre ständige Präsenz in den Männermagazinen machte Betty zu einer erotischen Ikone. Anhänger wie Kritiker Weiders stimmen darin überein, dass er kaum einen Weg ausließ, Geld zu machen. Via Mailorder verscherbelte er Hochglanz-Cheesecakefotos und 8- und 16mm-Filme von Betty, diesem von ihm erschaffenen Sexsymbol. In einer Anzeige in der *Jem*-Ausgabe vom Januar 1961 (ja, Betty ist das Covergirl) heißt es: „Erleben Sie diese atemberaubende blonde Sexgöttin so, wie Sie sie schon immer erleben wollten: in atemberaubenden Studioaufnahmen und Filmen! … Noch nie gab es eine Frau mit derart makellosem Gesicht … derart schmaler Taille und sinnlicher Figur!" Auch als die Rose schon etwas verblüht war und Weider

de faire pratiquement toutes les couvertures de *Jem* et de *Monsieur* et de figurer dans les publicités pour les produits de culturisme de Weider. Apparemment, cette branche « cheesecake » (les jolies filles montrant leurs jambes) issue de son entreprise basée sur le « beefcake » (les beaux mâles musclés) visait surtout à faire accepter Weider dans le monde hétérosexuel. Dans les années cinquante, Betty sillonnait le pays en posant pour des photos. Selon son histoire officielle, elle rencontra Joe Weider à New York lors d'une séance de prises de vue pour *Beauty and Figure*, le séduisant par « sa compréhension de la maquette artistique du magazine ». Weider l'engagea pour poser pour une douzaine de couvertures et, après chaque séance, ils dînèrent ensemble. En 1961, à l'âge de 26 ans, elle devint sa seconde épouse. Sur leur relation, elle a expliqué elle-même : « Ce ne fut pas un coup de foudre. Je suis devenu son psychiatre et il est tombé amoureux de moi ».

Dan Lurie, un autre expert en culturisme et fitness qui travailla un temps avec Weider en lui fournissant des appareils de musculation avant de se brouiller avec lui lors d'une âpre bataille juridique, présente une version moins idyllique de la manière dont le couple Weider se rencontra, se courtisa et se maria. « Je crois savoir que Betty était une prostituée notoire. Joe a vu sa photo dans un magazine et a parié qu'il la trouverait et … lui ferait la cour, si vous voyez ce que je veux dire. »

Indépendamment des détails de leur rencontre, Betty Brosmer fut une affaire en or pour l'entreprise Weider. C'était une femme ravissante dans le pur style voluptueux des années cinquante, blonde

A TREASURE CHEST OF RARE SPICE

anc

jem

Aug. / 50¢

FICTION

HUMOR

PIN-UPS

YEAR: **1959.** TITLE: **Monsieur.** COUNTRY: **USA.**

YEAR: **1957.** TITLE: **Monsieur.** COUNTRY: **USA.**

his men's magazines, Betty continued posing with the muscleboy stars Joe created. She remains an attractive and fit woman somewhere in the vicinity of 70 years of age.

No doubt as bodybuilding and fitness moved towards mainstream acceptance, and Weider's fortunes grew, his overtly erotic publications, of either stripe, became more of an embarrassment than they were worth. But during the critical empire-building decades of the 50s and 60s Joe so thoroughly exploited both homoerotic interest in hardbody hunks, and hetero-male interest in Betty's delectable face and form, that in significant part his fitness empire can fairly be described as a solid-brick building built by beautiful boys and Betty Brosmer's bosom.

Betty has observed about their relationship, "I became his psychiatrist, and he fell in love with me."

seine Magazine eingestellt hatte, posierte Betty weiter mit Bodybuildinghelden, die Joe aufgebaut hatte. Auch heute, im Alter von rund 70 Jahren, ist Betty noch eine attraktive und sportliche Frau. Als Bodybuilding und Fitness breitere Akzeptanz fanden und Weiders Vermögen wuchs, wurden die unverblümt erotischen Magazine beider Couleur zweifellos zu einem Klotz am Bein. Doch in den

avec de gros seins et une incroyable taille de guêpe. Dans les magazines de musculation, elle valida instantanément les gros muscles sculptés comme un atout masculin qui faisait craquer les femmes superbes, confortant les garçons gonflés à bloc par son approbation hyper-féminine.

Les apparitions constantes de Betty sur les couvertures des magazines pour hommes l'érigèrent en idole érotique. Les détracteurs comme les défenseurs de Weider concordent à dire que, quand il s'agissait de gagner de l'argent, il était prêt à tout essayer. Il inondait ses revues d'annonces de vente par correspondance de portfolios et de films en 8 et 16mm du sex-symbol qu'il avait créé. Une annonce parue dans *Jem* en janvier 1961 (vous l'aurez deviné, Betty est en couverture) s'exclame : « Contemplez cette bombe blonde comme vous avez toujours rêvé de

YEAR: **1957.** TITLE: **Monsieur.** COUNTRY: **USA.**

ENTERTAINMENT FOR SOPHISTICATED MEN

Monsieur

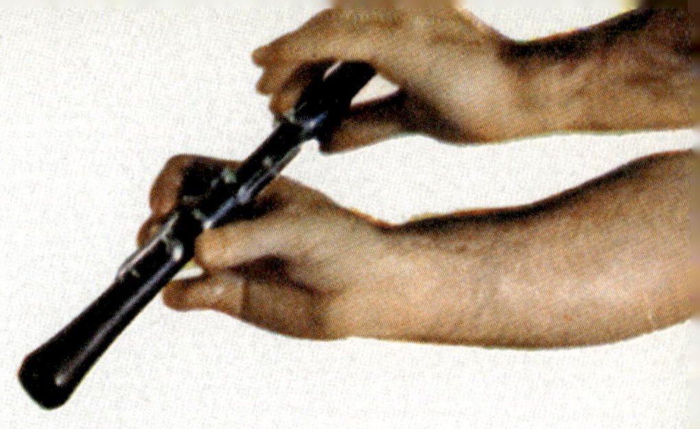

MUSIC: THE AGE OLD SEDUCER!

LOWDOWN ON HIGH SOCIETY THE PLAYBOY AND THE PLAYGIRL

DUBRONYI: THE SCULPTOR AND HIS NUDE PRINCESS!

JULY/50c

EXCLUSIVE PHOTOS OF PARIS NIGHTLIFE– BACKSTAGE, ON STAGE AND OFF STAGE!

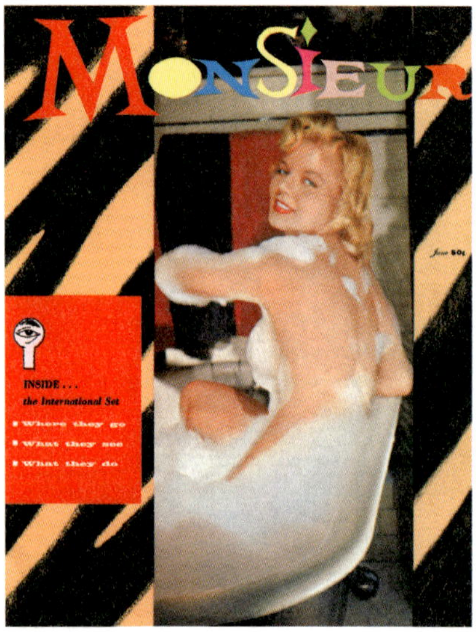

YEAR: **1957.** TITLE: **Monsieur.** COUNTRY: **USA.**

YEAR: **1957.** TITLE: **Monsieur.** COUNTRY: **USA.**

The church, the home, and the school are the chief sources of the sexual inhibitions, the distaste for all aspects of sex...

–Sexual Behavior in the Human Female, Alfred C. Kinsey, 1953

entscheidenden Jahrzehnten, in denen er sein Imperium aufbaute, in den Fünfzigern und Sechzigern, beutete Joe so gründlich sowohl homoerotische Interessen an durchtrainierten männlichen Körpern wie das Interesse von Hetero-Männern an Bettys reizender Erscheinung aus, dass man durchaus sagen darf, dass sein Imperium zum guten Teil auf hübschen Jungs und Betty Brosmers Busen aufbaute.

la contempler ... dans des photos de studio et des films époustouflants ! ... Jamais encore on n'avait vu une femme au visage d'une perfection aussi exquise ... une silhouette aussi voluptueuse, une taille aussi menue !» Même après que la rose eut perdu un peu de sa fraîcheur et que Weider eut fermé ses magazines de charme, Betty continua à poser aux côtés des stars de la gonflette façonnés par son mari.

Aujourd'hui, elle reste une séduisante septuagénaire et garde toujours la ligne. Naturellement, à mesure que le culturisme et la musculation entrèrent dans la culture populaire et que la fortune de Weider augmenta, ses publications ouvertement érotiques, d'un bord comme de l'autre, devinrent plus gênantes qu'autre chose. Toutefois, au cours des années critiques 1950 et 60, alors qu'il bâtissait son empire, Joe Weider exploita tant le goût homosexuel pour les éphèbes au corps d'acier et celui des hétérosexuels pour le visage et les formes délectables de Betty, qu'on peut raisonnablement décrire son univers de la culture physique comme un bâtiment solidement construit brique après brique par de beaux garçons et la poitrine de Betty Brosmer.

YEAR: **1957.** TITLE: **Jem.**
COUNTRY: **USA.**

SAY UNCLE

WHY WOMEN MUST BE UNFAITHFUL!
MONSIEUR
FEB./50c
K
ENTERTAINMENT FOR SOPHISTICATED MEN
LOVE—
A LA PARIS
MAKING A DAME ON A PLANE
THE LEWD, THE VIEWED AND THE PRUDE

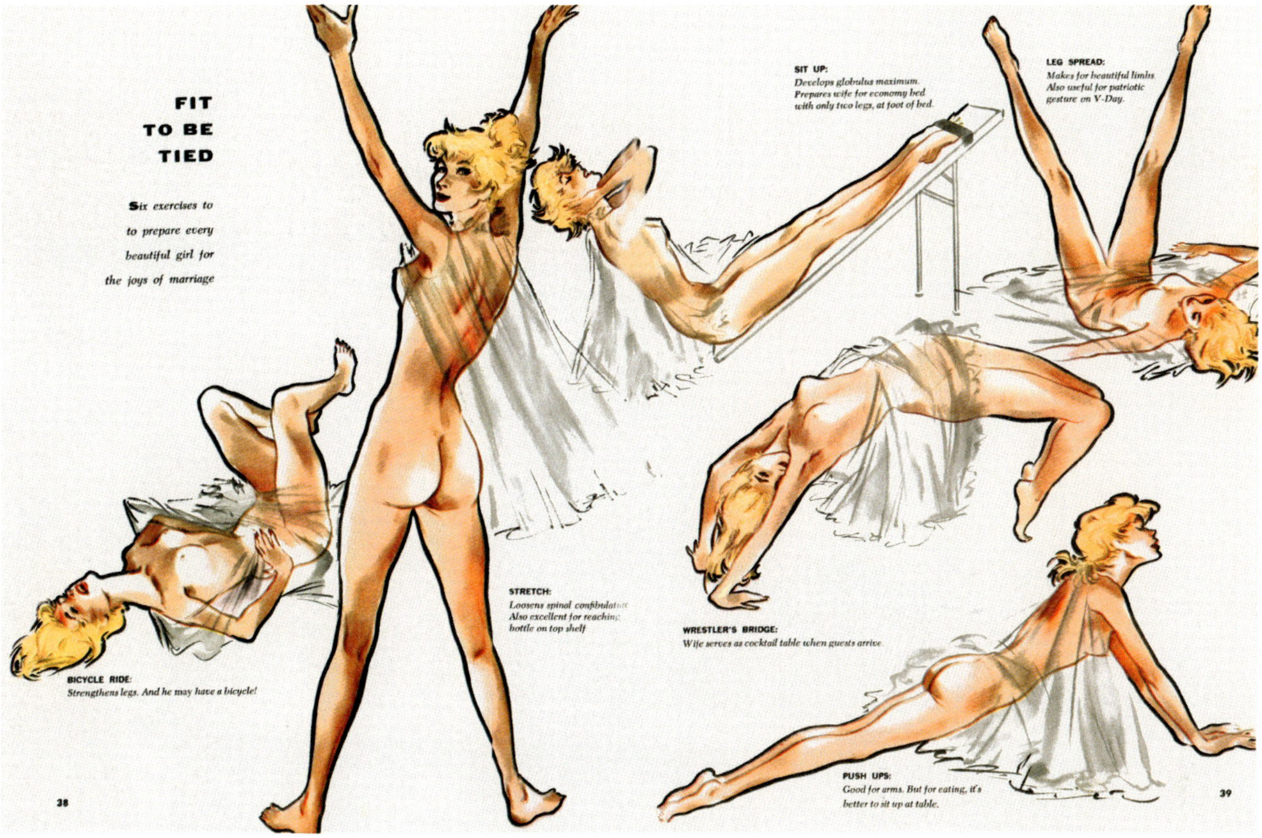

YEAR: **1959.** TITLE: **Monsieur.** COUNTRY: **USA.**

YEAR: **1957.** TITLE: **Monsieur.** COUNTRY: **USA.**

YEAR: **1961.** TITLE: **Jem.** COUNTRY: **USA.**

YEAR: **1957.** TITLE: **Monsieur.**
COUNTRY: **USA.**

SPAWN OF THE BUNNY:

Playboy Competitors' Cartoon Mascots

Die Saat des Häschens: Die Maskottchen der *Playboy*-Konkurrenz
Le lapin fait des petits : Les mascottes des concurrents de *Playboy*

Playboy's bunny was seen as a magic talisman by some publishers as they tried to analyze and profit from the magazine's mystique. At the same time they scrutinized what their real competitors – other secondary girlie magazines – were up to and copied them as well, all leading to the Great Cartoon Mascot Fad of 1956/57.

Rogue's wolf was clearly the frontrunner in this competition, but low-rent *Tiger*'s eponymous mascot also boasted a certain crude charm. Even upscale *Swank* tried out a leering hound for a while, a replacement for their original mustachioed old gent. In a reversal of *Swank*'s logic, *Rugged* thought the ticket to increased sales would be a grubby old tramp. *Mate!* took the human mascot route as well, with a lovable swabby to represent them. Both miscalculated; their runs were short. *Satan* should have been a sure winner, given the eternal allure of sin and their cleverly positioned mascot whose hooves and horns placed him squarely astride both human and animal kingdoms. Sadly, *Satan*'s sin quotient was slim; even the powers of almighty Lucifer couldn't make men buy it.

In the mid-60s *Jaguar* tried to revive the cartoon mascot with its Secret Agent 69. The crude cat tried hard to tie the popularity of James Bond to the magic of the bunny. The character appeared on

Year: **1958.** Title: **Man About Town.** Country: **USA.**

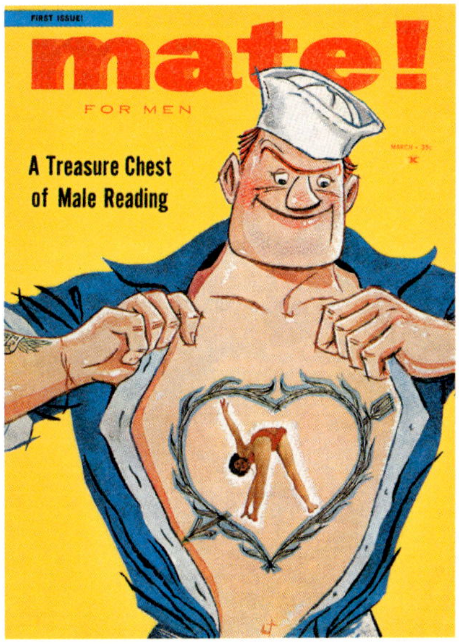

Year: **1961.** Title: **Mate!** Country: **USA.**

Einige Verleger, die versuchten, das Erfolgsgeheimnis des *Playboy* zu ergründen und zu übernehmen, sahen im *Playboy*-Bunny einen magischen Talisman. Gleichzeitig behielten sie das Treiben ihrer eigentlichen Konkurrenten – andere zweitklassige Männermagazine – im Auge und kopierten diese ebenfalls, was zum großen Maskottchen-Tick der Jahre '56/57 führte.

Der Wolf von *Rogue* war zweifellos der Spitzenreiter in diesem Wettbewerb, aber auch die Raubkatze des Billig-Magazins *Tiger* verfügte über einen gewissen plumpen Charme. Selbst das gediegene-

Le petit lapin de *Playboy* était considéré comme un talisman magique par certains éditeurs qui tentaient d'analyser et de s'inspirer de l'esprit du magazine. Parallèlement, ils passaient au crible ce que faisaient leurs vrais rivaux – les autres revues de charme de moindre importance – et les copiaient aussi, ce qui déboucha autour de 1956/57 sur la grande mode des mascottes inspirées des dessins animés.

Dans cette compétition, le loup de *Rogue* était de loin en tête, mais le tigre du bas de gamme *Tiger* n'était pas dénué non plus d'un certain charme canaille. Même *Swank*, plus classe, adopta un

Most mammals, both female and male, engage in coitus or try to engage in coitus as soon as they are able to make the necessary physical coordinations.

–Sexual Behavior in the Human Female, Alfred C. Kinsey, 1953

RUGGED
Entertainment for Real Men
APRIL 35¢ PDC
Why your girl friends are nuts about ELVIS PRESLEY, JIMMY DEAN, PAT BOONE and BILL HALEY by Frank Kane
BAGDAD U.

YEAR: **1957.** TITLE: **Satan.** COUNTRY: **USA.**

YEAR: **1957.** TITLE: **Rugged.**
COUNTRY: **USA.**

YEAR: **1957.** TITLE: **Satan.**
COUNTRY: **USA.**

YEAR: **1957.** TITLE: **Satan.** COUNTRY: **USA.**

every cover for months, often overshadowing the cover model, and starred in a multi-page comic strip inside. It's one of life's tough lessons that hard work is not always rewarded; Jaguar Bond was dead as *Rogue*'s wolf by the 1970.

Satan's sin quotient was slim; even the powers of almighty Lucifer couldn't make men buy it.

re *Swank* versuchte es eine Weile mit einem anzüglich grinsenden Köter als Ersatz für den ursprünglichen schnurrbärtigen alten Ritter. *Rugged* machte es genau anders herum und meinte, dass der Verkauf sich mit einem schmuddeligen alten Tramp ankurbeln ließe. Auch *Mate!* setzte auf ein menschliches Maskottchen und machte einen reizenden Leichtmatrosen zu seinem Repräsentanten. Beide verkalkulierten sich, die Umsätze blieben bescheiden. *Satan* hätte eigentlich groß rauskommen müssen, bedenkt man den unvergänglichen Reiz der Sünde und ein geschickt postiertes Maskottchen, dem mit seinen Hufen und Hörnern ein Spagat zwischen Mensch und Tier gelang. Leider war der Sündenquotient von *Satan* mager, selbst der allmächtige Luzifer konnte die Männer nicht bewegen, das Magazin zu kaufen.

Mitte der Sechziger versuchte *Jaguar*, das Cartoon-Maskottchen mit seinem Secret Agent 69 wiederzubeleben. Die Raubkatze mühte sich redlich, die Popularität eines James Bond mit der Zauberkraft des Bunnys zu verbinden. Die Figur tauchte monatelang auf allen Titelbildern auf, überdeckte oft gar das Covermodell und erschien im Heft in mehrseitigen Comicgeschichten. Jedoch: Jaguar Bond war 1970 genauso Geschichte wie der Wolf von *Rogue*.

temps un limier lubrique à la place de son vieux moustachu.

Prenant le contre-pied de la logique de *Swank*, *Rugged* opta lui, pour un clochard dépenaillé. *Mate !* choisit lui aussi une mascotte humaine sous la forme d'un matelot goguenard. Tous deux firent un mauvais calcul, ils abandonnèrent en cours de route. *Satan* aurait dû l'emporter haut la main compte tenu du charme éternel du péché et de sa mascotte dont les cornes et les sabots la situait astucieusement à cheval entre le monde humain et le monde animal.

Malheureusement, la revue péchait surtout par manque de salacité, même les pouvoirs du tout-puissant Lucifer ne purent convaincre les hommes de l'acheter.

Vers le milieu des années soixante, *Jaguar* tenta de réhabiliter la mascotte dessinée avec son Agent Secret 69. Le félin coquin s'efforçait de marier la popularité de James Bond à la magie du petit lapin. Le personnage apparut sur la couverture pendant des mois, projetant souvent son ombre sur le modèle, et tenait le premier rôle dans une bande dessinée de plusieurs pages à l'intérieur du magazine. Hélas, la vie nous a souvent appris que le dur labeur ne paye pas toujours : Jaguar Bond et le loup de *Rogue* ne survécurent pas au-delà de 1970.

satan
devilish
entertainment
for men
AUG.
50¢
PDC
fiction, photography,
articles, ribaldry

Year: **1956.** Title: **Rogue**. Artist: **George Pollard.** Country: **USA.**

Year: **1957.** Title: **Rogue.** Country: **USA.**

Year: **1957.** Title: **Rogue.** Country: **USA.**

Year: **1957.** Title: **Rogue.** Country: **USA.**

Year: **1957.** Title: **Rogue.**
Artist: **L. N. Rognan.** Country: **USA.**

MAY 1957 - 35¢
Rogue
FOR MEN
The BED and..
.. the BEAUTIFUL
KING of the COUNTERFEITERS
L.N. Rognan

YEAR: **1957.** TITLE: **Gay Blade.** COUNTRY: **USA.**

YEAR: **1957.** TITLE: **Rugged.** COUNTRY: **USA.**

FEB 35¢
PDC
RUGGED
Entertainment for Real Men
A GUIDE BOOK FOR
UNMARRIED FATHERS
OR . . . . HOW TO
BEAT A PATERNITY RAP

FEB.

THE NEW MAN'S MAGAZINE

Swank

35¢

AN IMPERTINENT SURVEY:

WHY NICE GIRLS SPURN UNDERWEAR

New Stories by James T. Farrell Erskine Caldwell and Helen Lawrenson

YEAR: **1956.** TITLE: **Tiger.** COUNTRY: **USA.**

YEAR: **1956.** TITLE: **Swank.**
COUNTRY: **USA.**

YEAR: **1956.** TITLE: **Tiger.** COUNTRY: **USA.**

YEAR: **1956.** TITLE: **Rogue.**
COUNTRY: **USA.**

Rogue's GALLERY

It's summer, at long last, and Rogue's camera visits the sea shore—with lovely results that include Vera Darling (left) and friends.

YEAR: **1969.** TITLE: **Jaguar.** COUNTRY: **USA.**

YEAR: **1967.** TITLE: **Jaguar.** COUNTRY: **USA.**

YEAR: **1970.** TITLE: **Duke.** COUNTRY: **USA.**

YEAR: **1970.** TITLE: **Buccaneer.** COUNTRY: **USA.**

YEAR: **1968.**
TITLE: **Jaguar.** COUNTRY: **USA.**

75¢
pdc
Jaguar
JUNE 1968
THAT'S JAGUAR BOND 0069 THE MAN FROM ORGY. HE'S ALWAYS TRYING TO GET INTO MY DRAWS..ER..I MEAN, –TO MAKE ME DRAW!
GIRLS WHO SWING IN ALL DIRECTIONS
BANNED UNTIL NOW SIX NEW EROTIC CLASSICS
COLDFINGER— IN THE VALLEY OF THE MOLLS
THE ACTION STARTS AT 3 A.M. LONDON'S AFTER-HOUR CLUBS

YEAR: **1966.** TITLE: **Debonair.** COUNTRY: **USA.**

YEAR: **1966.** TITLE: **Debonair.**
COUNTRY: **USA.**

THE MAGAZINE FOR THE MAN ABOUT TOWN
JULY • 75¢ • PDC
DEBONAIR
Articles • Fiction
Cartoons • Photography

YEAR: **1965.** TITLE: **Jaguar.** COUNTRY: **USA.**

YEAR: **1965.** TITLE: **Jaguar.** COUNTRY: **USA.**

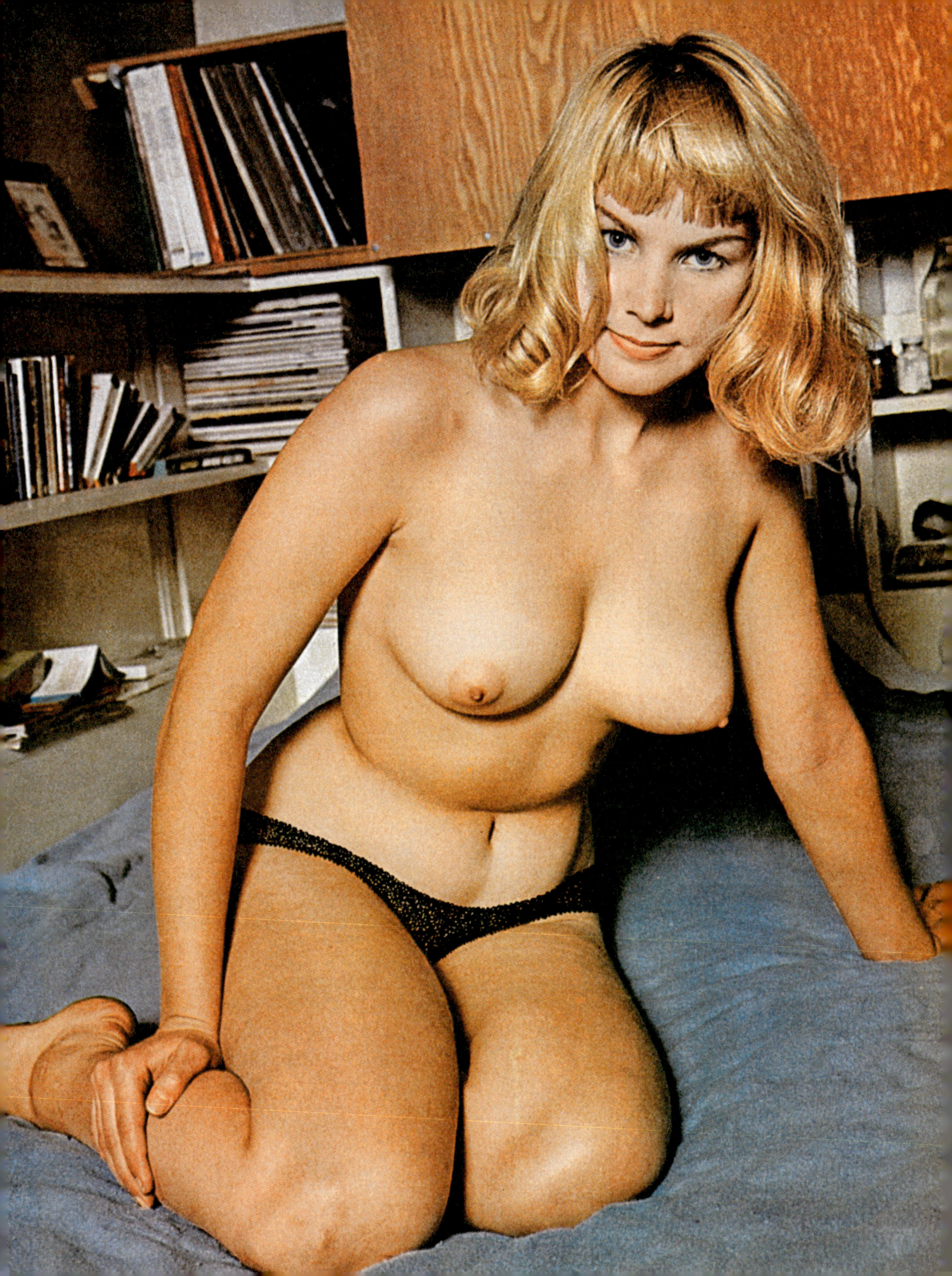

DUKE MAGAZINE:

The Great Black Hope

Duke: Die große schwarze Hoffnung
Duke : Le grand espoir noir

A fascinating look at black men's fantasies and frustrations when much of America was still segregated.

What to make of *Duke* and its disturbing button-eyed mascot? Coming out of Chicago in 1957, *Duke* was the first – and last – attempt at a *Playboy* magazine for and by black men. It lasted only six issues, but featured the top African-American writers and entertainers of the day. Chester Himes and James Baldwin were regular contributors, while Sammy Davis Jr. and Harry Belafonte made multiple modeling appearances displaying their wardrobes. *Duke* had a minor obsession with personal clothing collections. A feature in issue no 5, headlined *America's Most Dressed Negro,* adds up the number of cummerbunds, shoes and tuxedos owned by a country club maître d', who, states the text, may not be the best dressed, but, since he has more clothes than any other man they know, qualifies as the *most* dressed, an accomplishment in its own right. *Duke* had money behind it; Russ Meyer shot

YEAR: **1957.** TITLE: **Duke.**
COUNTRY: **USA.**

Was soll man von *Duke* und seinem verwirrenden, im wahrsten Wortsinne knopfäugigen Maskottchen halten? 1957 in Chicago begründet, war *Duke* der erste – und letzte – Versuch, einen *Playboy* von und für schwarze Männer zu machen. Er sollte nur sechs Nummern alt werden, doch darin fanden sich die größten afroamerikanischen Autoren und Entertainer der damaligen Zeit. Chester Himes und James Baldwin schrieben regelmäßig für das Magazin, und Sammy Davis Jr. und Harry Bellafonte führten wiederholt vor,

Comment doit-on prendre *Duke* et sa troublante mascotte aux yeux en boutons ? Lancée à Chicago en 1957, *Duke* fut la première (et dernière) tentative pour créer un *Playboy* pour et par des hommes noirs. Il ne dura que six numéros mais fit appel aux meilleurs auteurs et artistes noirs américains du jour. Chester Himes et James Baldwin y contribuèrent régulièrement, tandis que Sammy Davis Jr. et Harry Bellafonte y firent plusieurs apparitions en mannequins présentant leur garde-robe. *Duke* faisait une

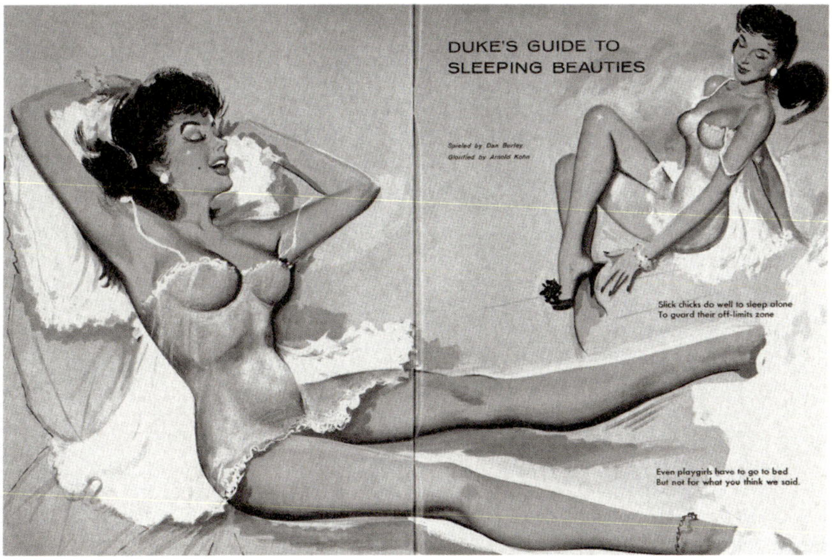

YEAR: **1957.** TITLE: **Duke.** COUNTRY: **USA.**

DUKE
JUNE 1957
50c
FICTION BY
CHESTER HIMES
RAY BRADBURY
LANGSTON HUGHES
ERSKINE CALDWELL

"Sure, I feel the same way, baby. But we're only two miles off the coast of South Carolina."

„Natürlich fühle ich genauso wie du, Liebling. Aber wir sind nur zwei Meilen von der Küste von South Carolina entfernt!"
« Bien sûr, j'éprouve la même chose, chérie. Mais nous sommes seulement à deux miles de la côte de la Caroline du Sud. »

YEAR: **1957.** TITLE: **Duke.** COUNTRY: **USA.**

YEAR: **1957.** TITLE: **Duke.**
COUNTRY: **USA.**

The first US magazine made by and for African-American males was launched in 1957, and folded after only 6 issues.

Die erste US-amerikanische Zeitschrift von und für männliche Afro-Amerikaner erschien 1957 und wurde nach nur sechs Ausgaben eingestellt.

Le premier magazine américain conçu par et pour les hommes afro-américains fut lancé en 1957 et cessa de paraître après 6 numéros.

Censorship is a typical expression of the authoritarian point of view. The censor has no faith in the intelligence or decency of ordinary people.

–Aldous Huxley

centerfolds of not-quite-nude, lightly tanned "Duchesses" for the magazine; Bill Ward did sultry brunette versions of his cartoon goddesses for them, and even Ray Bradbury contributed racially specific fiction.

Today *Duke* is a fascinating look at black men's fantasies and frustrations at a time when much of America was still segregated and most blacks struggled for minimum wage. Men's magazines have always reflected yearning rather than reality; for many black men in Chicago in the 1950s that meant big wardrobes, flashy cars and a girlfriend who was "damn near white", as editor Dan Burley described in a personally penned poem. *Duke* was far from politically correct by today's standards, but it was brave and bold for its time, and I

Year: **1957.** Title: **Duke.** Country: **USA.**

was ihr Kleiderschrank hergab. Private Garderobe war eine kleine Obsession von *Duke*. In Heft 5 fand sich ein Beitrag, der mit „America's Most Dressed Negro" übertitelt war und aufzählte, wieviele Kummerbunde, Schuhe und Smokings ein schwarzer Oberkellner eines Country Clubs besaß, was ihn – so der Text – vielleicht nicht zum bestgekleideten Mann, aber da er mehr Garderobe besaß als sonst jemand, immerhin zum „most dressed" Mann machte, was ja auch eine Leistung ist. *Duke* hatte Geld im Rücken; Russ Meyer fotografierte Centerfolds mit gerade noch bekleideten, sehr hellbraunen „Duchesses" für das Heft, Bill Ward zeichnete temperamentvolle brünette Versionen seiner Cartoongöttinnen, und selbst Ray Bradbury lieferte eigens auf ein schwarzes Publikum zugeschnittene Beiträge.

Betrachtet man sich den *Duke* heute, bietet er faszinierende Einblicke in die Sehnsüchte und Ängste afro-amerikanischer Männer einer Ära, in der in den Vereinigten Staaten immer noch Rassentrennung herrschte und die meisten Schwarzen für einen Hungerlohn arbeiteten. Männermagazine spiegelten schon immer eher die Sehnsüchte denn die Realität wieder; für viele Schwarze im Chicago der Fünfziger war das gleichbedeutend mit einer umfangreichen Garderobe, schicken Autos und einer Freundin, die „verdammt nah an weiß" war, wie Chefredakteur Dan Burley in einem Gedicht schrieb.

Aus heutiger Sicht ist *Duke* alles andere als politisch korrekt, aber für seine Zeit war es mutig, und ich wüsste zu gerne, was aus Chefredakteur Burley geworden ist. Auch wüsste ich gerne, wer ihn finanziert hat. Hat womöglich Hugh

légère fixation sur les collections particulières de vêtements. Dans le numéro 5, un article intitulé « Le nègre le plus habillé d'Amérique » dressait l'inventaire des ceintures en satin, souliers et smokings d'un maître d'hôtel de country club qui, précisait le texte, n'était peut-être pas le mieux habillé mais, dans la mesure où il possédait plus de tenues que n'importe quel autre homme connu de la rédaction, méritait le qualificatif de « plus habillé », ce qui était un accomplissement en soi. *Duke* ne manquait pas de moyens. Russ Meyer réalisa pour lui des posters centraux de « duchesses » pas tout à fait nues et légèrement hâlées. Bill Ward lui dessina des versions brunes sensuelles de ses déesses et même Ray Bradbury contribua avec des nouvelles adaptées pour le magazine.

Aujourd'hui, *Duke* offre une vision fascinante des fantasmes et des frustrations des hommes noirs à une époque où la ségrégation régnait presque partout aux États-Unis et où la plupart des Noirs se battaient pour obtenir le salaire minimum. Les magazines pour hommes ont toujours reflété les aspirations humaines plutôt que la réalité. Pour de nombreux hommes noirs dans le Chicago des années cinquante, cela signifiait une vaste garde-robe, une voiture tape-à-l'œil et une petite amie « presque blanche », comme le décrivit son rédacteur en chef Dan Burley. *Duke* était loin d'être politiquement correct selon les normes actuelles mais, pour son époque, c'était une tentative courageuse et pleine d'audace. J'aimerais bien savoir ce que Burley a fait ensuite. Je serais également curieuse de savoir d'où venait son financement. Se pourrait-il qu'Hugh Hefner, également basé à Chicago, ait été secrètement der-

Year: **1957.** Title: **Duke.** Country: **USA.**

DUKE
AUGUST 1957
50c
NEGROES DON'T KNOW ANYTHING ABOUT JAZZ
By Billy Taylor

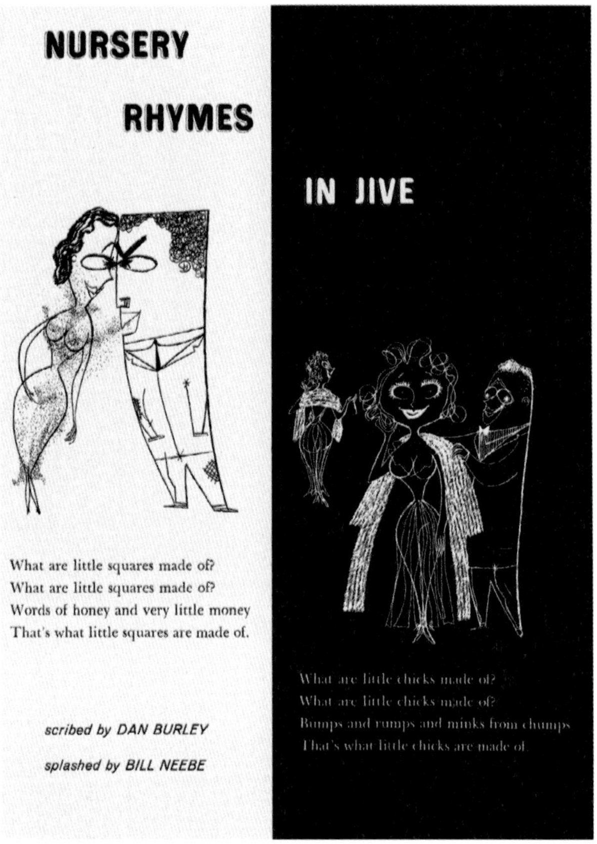

NURSERY RHYMES IN JIVE

What are little squares made of?
What are little squares made of?
Words of honey and very little money
That's what little squares are made of.

What are little chicks made of?
What are little chicks made of?
Bumps and rumps and minks from chumps
That's what little chicks are made of.

scribed by DAN BURLEY

splashed by BILL NEEBE

Year: **1957.** Title: **Duke.** Country: **USA.**

LET'S LOOK AT CARS IN THE YEAR 2000

McKinley Thompson is the first and only Negro designer in the automotive field. He is a staff member of the Ford Motor Company's Styling Center. In this article he looks into the future and predicts the shape of cars to come in the year of 2,000. Here, Thompson is off duty and his predictions of things to come are his own and do not reflect the thinking of his employer. All the illustrations are the work of Thompson.

Solarplane (above) will be commuter's special in year 2,000 with patches on nose and foils storing sun's energy and converting it to power. Ducted fan (left) will be in common use, able to hover or rise vertically with blades in saucer-like fuselage.

Only Negro stylist in auto industry predicts shape of cars to come

by McKINLEY THOMPSON

THE YEAR 2000 is closer than you think—especially in autos.

Already some of the things imagined in science fiction are a reality today, but many more are going to come true before the turn of this century. And from all signs the days of man's most useful tool, the wheel, are numbered.

Looking ahead to 50 years from now when the 21st Century turns up on the calendar, the sky no doubt will be the highroad and there will be three cars in every garage. If the evolution of transit keeps pace with the last half century,

62 DUKE / JULY

Year: **1957.** Title: **Duke.** Country: **USA.**

Year: **1957.** Title: **Duke.** Country: **USA.**

Year: **1957.** Title: **Duke.** Country: **USA.**

DUKE
JULY 1957
50c
THE MYTH OF
OUR VIRILITY
By George S. Schuyler

Year: **1957.** Title: **Duke.**
Country: **USA.**

Year: **1957.** Title: **Duke.** Country: **USA.**

would love to know what editor Burley moved on to. I would also like to know where his funding came from. Could Hugh Hefner, also Chicago-based, have secretly bankrolled the project? The next mainstream sex magazine aimed specifically at black men was *Players*, showing up in November 1973. It came from the white publishers of *Adam* magazine and has never had the passion seen in the curious artifact that was *Duke*.

Note: A second magazine called *Duke* was published in the 60s. It had no connection with the original.

Hefner, der auch in Chicago saß, das Projekt insgeheim finanziert? Das nächste Mainstream-Männermagazin, das sich an ein schwarzes Publikum richtete, war *Players*, das erstmals im November 1973 erschien. Es stammte von den weißen Verlegern von *Adam* und legte nie die Leidenschaft des kuriosen Zeitzeugnisses *Duke* an den Tag.

Achtung: In den Sechzigern erschien noch eine Zeitschrift mit dem Titel *Duke*, die aber nichts mit dem Original zu tun hatte.

The establishment of democracy on the American continent was scarcely as radical a break with the past as was the necessity ... of broadening this concept to include black men.

—James Baldwin

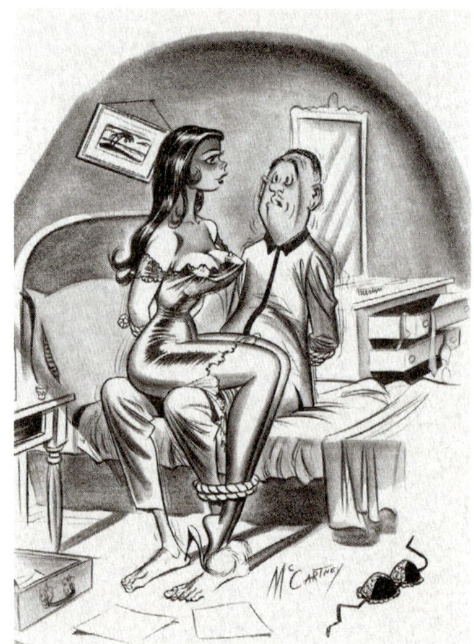

Year: **1957.** Title: **Duke.** Country: **USA.**

rière ce projet ? Il fallut attendre novembre 1973 pour que paraisse un autre magazine de charme s'adressant spécifiquement aux hommes noirs. Initiative des éditeurs blancs du magazine *Adam*, il n'a jamais été habité par la passion que l'on pouvait trouver dans ce curieux ovni que fut *Duke*.

Note : un second magazine baptisé *Duke* parut dans les années soixante, sans lien avec l'original.

DUKE
DUKE ELLINGTON'S
ALL-TIME
DREAM BAND
NOVEMBER
50¢

Did Lord Byron Seduce His Sister?
Inter-Views Number One
Rita Hayworth
Japanese Love
Sex In Space
Letters From Abroad
and Other Exciting
Pictures & Stories

SAMUEL ROTH VS. UNITED STATES OF AMERICA:

How *Good Times* Defined Obscenity

Samuel Roth gegen die Vereinigten Staaten: Wie *Good Times* die Obszönität definierte

Samuel Roth vs. les Etats-Unis d'Amérique : Comment *Good Times* redéfinit l'obscénité

The name Samuel Roth means nothing now, but in 1957 he was responsible for defining obscenity in America and for opening the door to the publishing freedom we enjoy today.

Roth was an Austrian Jewish immigrant who with his brother set up a publishing house in New York City in the 1920s. During that libertine time he began printing erotic books, including D. H. Lawrence's *Lady Chatterley's Lover* and James Joyce's *Ulysses*, albeit without Joyce's permission. His first arrest and conviction was for this, and he served three years in prison. When Roth got out of prison he went back to his chosen profession, printing his books and distributing them through mail order. This was in violation of the Comstock Law that forbade using the US mails to disseminate obscenity, but at that time there were few other avenues available to

Senator Estes Kefauver declared *Good Times* "slime" with the power to corrupt America's youth.

Year: **1953.** Title: **Good Times.** Country: **USA.**

Heute ist der Name Samuel Roth vergessen, doch 1957 sorgte Roth dafür, dass der Begriff Obszönität definiert wurde und stieß die Tür zu den verlegerischen Freiheiten auf, die wir heute genießen.

Roth war ein jüdischer Immigrant aus Österreich, der in New York gemeinsam mit seinem Bruder in den zwanziger Jahren einen Verlag gründete. Während dieser freizügigen Jahre begann er, erotische und kontroverse Bücher zu verlegen, darunter *Lady Chatterley* und *Ulys-*

Year: **1954.** Title: **Good Times.** Country: **USA.**

Aujourd'hui le nom de Samuel Roth ne nous dit plus rien, pourtant, en 1957, il fut responsable de la redéfinition de l'obscénité aux États-Unis et a ouvert la porte à la liberté éditoriale dont nous profitons désormais.

Immigrant juif autrichien, Roth monta sa maison d'édition avec son frère à New York dans les années vingt. Au cours de cette époque libertine, il publia des livres érotiques dont *L'amant de lady Chatterley* et *Ulysse* de James Joyce (sans demander la permission de ce dernier). Cela lui valut sa première arrestation. Il fut condamné à trois ans de prison ferme. Une fois libéré, il reprit sa profession, éditant ses livres et les distribuant par correspondance. C'était violer la loi Comstock qui interdisait la diffusion de matériel obscène par la poste mais, à l'époque, il n'avait pas beaucoup d'autres possibilités pour acheminer ses textes érotiques. Sa méthode était simple : il achetait des listes d'adresses, envoyait des prospectus décrivant ses publications puis envoyait les articles commandés. Ce système fonctionna sans incident jusqu'en 1951 quand il eut l'idée d'ajouter des magazines à son catalogue. Son premier, coédité par son ami Hal Zucker, s'appelait *American Aphrodite*. Ce trimestriel de 200 pages vendu cinq dollars contenait beaucoup de littérature érotique et quelques images d'art.

The Isle of Lesbos. The isles of Greece, the isles of Greece, where burning Sappho loved and sung! ... Byron

Die Insel Lesbos. Die Inselland' in Aegeus See, Wo Sappho sang ihr glühend Weh! ... Byron

L'île de Lesbos. Les îles grecques, les îles grecques, où l'ardente Sappho aima et chanta ! ... Byron

YEAR: **1953.** TITLE: **Good Times.** COUNTRY: **USA.**

distribute his erotic materials. Roth's method was simple: he sent flyers describing his books to names on purchased mailing lists, then fulfilled the orders that resulted. The system worked without incident until 1951, when he got the idea to add magazines to his creative efforts. His first, co-edited by friend Hal Zucker, was *American Aphrodite*. This five-dollar, 200-page quarterly featured lots of erotic literature and a few pieces of art. In his brochures Roth described it as produced "in collaboration with a group of writers, painters and photogra-

Roth vs. the US meant a person could no longer be convicted on the basis of a single photo in a magazine.

ses von James Joyce, allerdings ohne dessen Erlaubnis. Das brachte ihm sein erstes Verfahren und eine dreijährige Gefängnisstrafe ein. Nach seiner Haftentlassung wandte Roth sich wieder seinem Beruf zu, verlegte Bücher und vertrieb sie per Mailorder. Damit verstieß er gegen das Comstock Law, das die Verbreitung obszöner Bücher auf dem Postweg untersagte, aber damals gab es für ihn nur wenige andere Möglichkeiten, seine erotischen Schriften zu vertreiben. Roth ging denkbar einfach vor: Er verschickte Flyer, in denen er seine Bücher potenziellen Kunden von gekauften Adressenlisten vorstellte, und erfüllte dann die eingehenden Bestellungen. Dieses System funktionierte problemlos bis 1951, als er auf die Idee kam, seine Kreativität auch auf Männermagazine auszuweiten. Das erste, das er mit seinem Freund Hal Zucker herausgab, hieß *American Aphrodite*. Dieses vierteljährlich erscheinende, 200 Seiten dicke und vier Dollar teure Heft brachte viel erotischen Lesestoff und einige wenige Illustrationen. In seinen Werbebroschüren erklärte Roth, es sei „in Zusammenarbeit mit einer Gruppe von Autoren, Malern und Fotografen entstanden, die sich gegen die Beschränkungen im kommerziellen Verlagswesen zur Wehr setzen." Heute wirkt das unglaublich zahm und ein wenig prätentiös, aber in seiner Zeit kam es literarischer Anarchie gleich, doppelt gefährlich, weil es sich an ein in-

Dans ses prospectus, Roth le décrivait « réalisé en collaboration avec un groupe d'auteurs, de peintres et de photographes en rébellion contre les entraves à l'édition ». Aujourd'hui la revue paraît incroyablement sage et un tantinet prétentieuse mais, pour l'époque, c'était véritablement de l'anarchie littéraire, doublement dangereuse car elle s'adressait à un public d'intellectuels. Comme on pouvait s'y attendre, elle se vendit bien, et donc, début 1953, plusieurs mois avant la parution de *Playboy*, Roth lança *Good Times*, un petit digest mensuel dont le contenu était légèrement plus leste que celui d'*American Aphrodite*. Ce fut ce magazine qui attira l'attention du sénateur Estes Kefauver, ardent défenseur de la morale, qui déclara qu'une telle « vase » avait le pou-

YEAR: **1953.** TITLE: **Good Times.** COUNTRY: **USA.**

YEAR: **1953.** TITLE: **Good Times.** COUNTRY: **USA.**

For its time it amounted to literary anarchy, doubly dangerous because it targeted a highbrow audience.

phers in rebellion against the restraints of commercial publishing." Today it seems unimaginably tame and a bit pretentious, but for its time it amounted to literary anarchy, doubly dangerous because it targeted a highbrow audience. Sales were understandably good, so in early 1953, several months before *Playboy*'s debut, Roth added *Good Times*, a small monthly digest with a content slightly racier than *Aphrodite*'s. It was this magazine that came to the attention of morals czar Senator Estes Kefauver, who declared it "slime" with the power to corrupt America's youth. Kefauver was head of the committee for the Investigation of Juvenile Delinquency at the time and when he subpoenaed Roth to appear before the committee he found experts to claim *Good Times* and *American Aphrodite* caused sexual perversion in adolescents. Roth was ultimately convicted under the Comstock Law of mailing obscene materials through the US mail. He fought his conviction on grounds of the material's artistic merit, and kept fighting all the way to the Supreme Court. The trial dragged on for years. By the time the Supreme Court handed down its decision in 1957, magazines with more nudity than Roth's were everywhere. Still, the justices found liberal Roth particularly odious for publishing Aubrey Beardsley's homoerotic writing in *Aphrodite*, and for his method of blind mailing his brochures, which, in their opinion, could too easily fall into the hands of adolescents or mental defectives, groups thought to be particularly vulnerable to perversion. The Supreme Court upheld Roth's conviction and ordered him to serve his five-year prison sentence.

tellektuelles Publikum wandte. Der Absatz war verständlicherweise gut, so dass Roth 1953, einige Monate vor der ersten Ausgabe des *Playboy*, auch noch *Good Times* aus der Taufe hob, ein kleinformatiges, monatliches Heft mit einem unwesentlich schärferen Inhalt als *Aphrodite*. Genau dieses Magazin kam dem Moralapostel und Senator Estes Kefauver unter die Augen, der es zu „Schmutz" erklärte, der dazu angetan sei, Amerikas Jugend zu verderben. Kefauver stand einem Komitee vor, das die Jugendkriminalität untersuchte, und als er Roth zu einer Anhörung vorlud, hatte er Experten zur Hand, die behaupteten, dass *Good Times* und *American Aphrodite* bei Jugendlichen sexuelle Perversionen hervorrufen könnten. Roth wurde schließlich nach dem Comstock Law wegen des Versands von obszönem Material durch die Post verurteilt. Mit Verweis auf die künstlerische Qualität seines Materials ging er in Berufung und schließlich bis vor den Supreme Court. Der Prozess zog sich Jahre hin. Als das Gericht 1957 endlich sein Urteil fällte, waren längst überall Magazine erhältlich, die mehr nackte Haut zeigten als die von Roth. Dennoch befanden die Richter den liberalen Roth für besonders verabscheuungswürdig, weil er in *Aphrodite* homoerotische Texte von Aubrey Beardsley abgedruckt hatte und weil er seine Broschüren verschickte, ohne die Adressaten zu kennen, wodurch sie ihrer Meinung nach leicht in die Hände von Heranwachsenden oder seelisch gestörten Menschen geraten konnten, die besonders anfällig für sozialethische Desorientierung seien. Der Supreme Court bestätigte das Urteil gegen Roth und schickte ihn für fünf Jahre ins Gefängnis. Wie Roth dann die Rechts-

YEAR: **1953.** TITLE: **Good Times.** COUNTRY: **USA.**

voir de corrompre la jeunesse américaine. A l'époque, Kefauver était à la tête du comité d'enquête sur la délinquance juvénile. Il cita Roth à comparaître devant le comité et fit venir des experts pour expliquer que *Good Times* et *American Aphrodite* engendraient des perversions sexuelles chez les adolescents. En vertu de la loi Comstock, Roth fut condamné à cinq ans de prison pour avoir diffusé du matériel obscène par la poste. Il fit appel en se basant sur les qualités artistiques de ses revues et continua de se battre jusqu'à ce que son cas soit porté devant la Cour suprême. Le procès dura des années. Lorsque la Cour suprême rendit enfin sa décision en 1957, il y avait partout des magazines montrant plus de nudité que ceux de Roth. Toutefois, les juges critiquèrent violemment Roth pour avoir publié des textes homo-érotiques d'Aubrey Beardsley dans *Aphrodite* et

“I have the same confidence in the ability of our people to reject noxious literature as I have in their capacity to sort out the true from the false in theology, economics, politics or any other field.”

–Justice William O. Douglas commenting on Samuel Roth vs. the United States, 1958

Year: **1951.** Title: **American Aphrodite.**
Country: **USA.**

Year: **1950s.** Title: **Hum.**
Country: **USA.**

So how did this change the law? In their deliberation the justices were forced to define obscenity and to distinguish it from art. To do this they proposed the following test: “Whether the average person, applying contemporary community standards, finds the dominant theme of the material taken as a whole appeals to prurient interest.” On these grounds they condemned Roth and his *Good Times* and *American Aphrodite*, but in the years to follow this test would be used over and over to the advantage of publishers. Roth vs. the US meant a person could no longer be convicted on the basis of a single passage in a book or a single photo in a magazine. It meant if there was some bit of art or redeeming value in a work it could not be judged obscene. It established that something

sprechung verändert hat? Nun, das tat er, indem er die Richter nötigte, den Unterschied zwischen Kunst und Obszönität zu definieren. Die Definition, die sie vorschlugen, war: obszön sei etwas, „wenn ein Durchschnittsbürger, an gegenwärtigen gesellschaftlichen Maßstäben gemessen, ein Werk in seiner Gesamtheit als sexuell stimulierend betrachtet.“ Mit dieser Begründung verurteilten sie Roth und *Good Times* und *American Aphrodite*, aber in den folgenden Jahren sollte dieses Kriterium immer wieder zum Vorteil der Verleger herangezogen werden. Das Urteil im Fall Roth gegen die Vereinigten Staaten bedeutete, dass ein Mensch nicht länger aufgrund einer einzelnen Passage in einem Buch oder eines einzelnen Fotos in einem Magazin verurteilt werden konnte. Es bedeutete, dass

pour sa méthode de mailing aveugle, estimant que ses prospectus pouvaient facilement tomber entre les mains d'adolescents ou d'attardés mentaux, deux catégories jugées particulièrement vulnérables aux perversions. La Cour suprême confirma la condamnation de Roth et lui ordonna se servir sa peine.

En quoi cela changea-t-il la loi ? Au cours de leurs délibérations, les juges furent contraints de formuler une définition l'obscénité et de la distinguer de l'art. Ils conclurent alors qu'un document était obscène quand : « en appliquant les critères contemporains de la communauté, l'individu moyen trouve que le thème dominant dans son ensemble satisfait un intérêt lubrique ». Ce fut sur cette base que Roth fut condamné pour *Good Times* et *American Aprodite*. Toutefois, au cours des années suivantes, cette même définition fut reprise par les éditeurs à leur avantage. Le précédent de l'affaire Roth signifiait qu'un individu ne pouvait plus être condamné pour un simple passage ou une photo isolée dans un magazine. A partir du moment où il y avait un peu d'art ou une quelconque qualité compensant le caractère lubrique, l'ouvrage ne pouvait plus être jugé obscène. Cela signifiait aussi qu'un magazine pouvait être légal à New York et interdit dans le Mississippi. Bref, cela constitua la base sur laquelle tous les procès pour obscénité ont été perdus depuis lors. Malheureusement, Samuel Roth ne profita pas de sa contribution historique, contrairement à son ami Hal Zucker qui put publier son étrange magazine *Hum*.

American Aphrodite est aujourd'hui considéré avec respect comme le premier trimestriel érotique américain.

YEAR: **1954.** TITLE: **Good Times.** COUNTRY: **USA.**

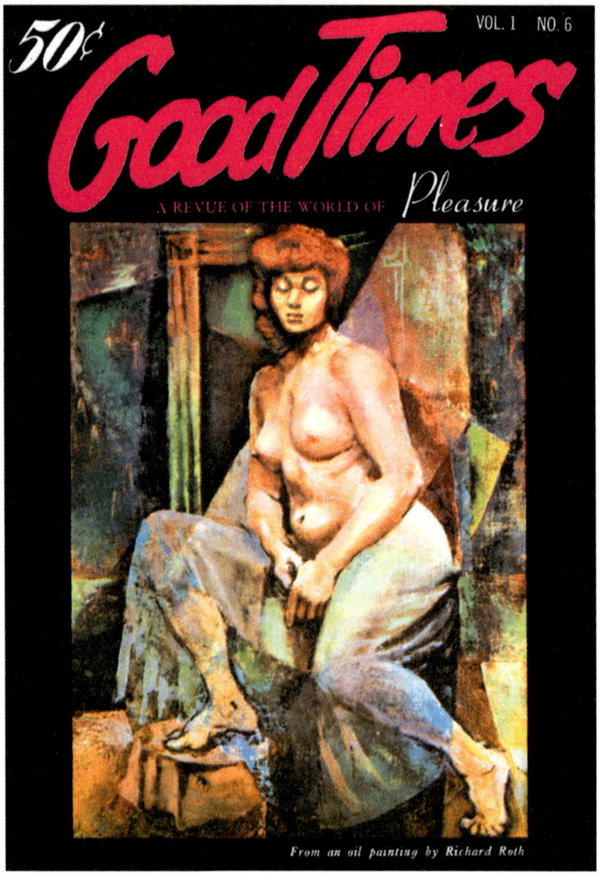

YEAR: **1953.** TITLE: **Good Times.** COUNTRY: **USA.**

YEAR: **1953.** TITLE: **Good Times.** COUNTRY: **USA.**

YEAR: **1953.** TITLE: **Good Times.** COUNTRY: **USA.**

YEAR: **1953.** TITLE: **Good Times.** COUNTRY: **USA.**

YEAR: **1953.**
TITLE: **Good Times.** COUNTRY: **USA.**

GOOD TIMES
50
A Revue of the World of
PLEASURE

Roth's friend Hal Zucker went on to publish his strange magazine *Hum* under protection of The Roth Test.

YEAR: **1953.** TITLE: **Good Times.** COUNTRY: **USA.**

YEAR: **1954.** TITLE: **Good Times.** COUNTRY: **USA.**

YEAR: **1954.** TITLE: **Good Times.** COUNTRY: **USA.**

could be legal in New York that would be banned in Mississippi. In short, it formed the basis on which all obscenity trials in the US would be won from that time to the present. Sadly, Samuel Roth wasn't able to benefit from his contribution to history, but his friend Hal Zucker did, going on to publish his strange magazine *Hum* under protection of The Roth Test.

American Aphrodite is today respected as America's first erotic quarterly.

ein Werk nicht mehr als obszön eingestuft werden konnte, wenn es darin irgendein künstlerisches Gegengewicht gab. Außerdem war damit festgestellt, dass etwas in New York legal sein konnte, was in Mississippi noch illegal war. Kurz gesagt, es bildete die Grundlage, auf der alle Verfahren wegen Obszönität in den USA bis zum heutigen Tag gewonnen werden. Bedauerlicherweise profitierte Samuel Roth nicht mehr von seinem Beitrag zur Geschichte, wohl aber sein Freund Hal Zucker, der sein seltsames Magazin *Hum* geschützt durch das Urteil im Falle Roth herausbringen konnte.

Heute wird *American Aphrodite* als erstes vierteljährliches Sexmagazin der Vereinigten Staaten gewürdigt.

The justices found liberal Roth particularly odious for publishing Aubrey Beardsley's homoerotic writing.

YEAR: **1950s.** TITLE: **Hum.**
ARTIST: **Gene Bilbrew.** COUNTRY: **USA.**

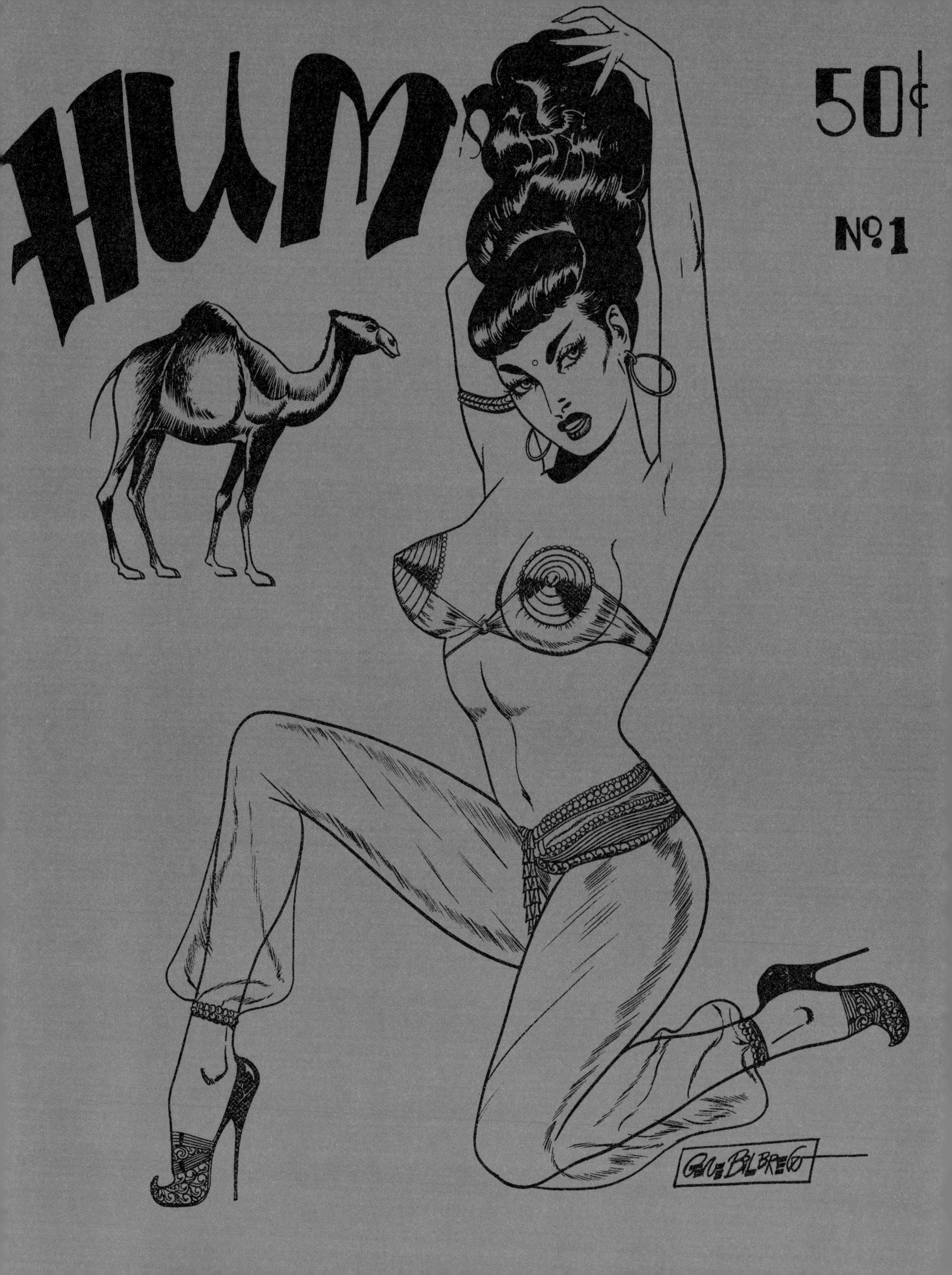
HUM
50¢
№1
GENE BILBREW

Jayne Mansfield
"... we got married—and nine months and ten seconds later I had a baby!"

Top 5 American Covergirls:

Top 5 American Covergirls:
Les 5 plus grandes cover-girls des Etats-Unis :

Year: **1959.** Title: **Tonight.** Country: **USA.**

Life is neither fair nor equal. Certain models always had more power to move product, that combination of beauty and charisma that made them especially desirable as covergirls. By the 1950s the American men's magazine market was so established that real stars were emerging. While many quickly faded, some are as popular now as they were then. To compile this list of the five 50s covergirls with the most iconic staying power I queried several dealers in vintage erotica on the Ebay Internet auction site. Everyone had a personal favorite who didn't

Das Leben ist ungerecht: Manche Modelle verkaufen sich einfach besser als andere. Sie verfügen über diese Kombination aus Schönheit und Charisma, die sie zu besonders beliebten Covergirls macht. In den fünfziger Jahren des 20. Jahrhunderts brachten die Männermagazine in den USA echte Stars hervor. Einige von ihnen verschwanden bald wieder in der Versenkung, andere sind noch heute so populär wie damals. Um die fünf Covergirls der Fünfziger auszuwählen, die sich am nachhaltigsten ins Gedächtnis eingeschrieben haben und zu Ikonen geworden sind, habe ich Händler befragt, die über Ebay Erotika von damals anbieten. Jeder von ihnen hatte unter seinen Top 5 eine persönliche Favoritin, die es nicht auf meine Liste geschafft hat, aber alle waren sich einig darin, dass die aus-gewählten fünf auf die vorderen Plätze gehören.

War es Diane Webbers coole, klassische Schönheit, ihr üppiges, rotes Haar und ihr Kurvenreichtum oder der Umstand, dass sie eine echte Nudistin war, der ihr Mitte der Fünfziger eine derartige Popularität einbrachte? Wohl von allem etwas. Diane wurde 1932 geboren und in den frühen Fünfzigern von dem Fotografen Andre de Dienes entdeckt. Sie wurde zu einem bevorzugten Modell von Russ Meyer, Peter Gowland und Bunny Yeager und war unter dem Namen Marguerite Empey zweimal im *Playboy* zu sehen (Mai 1955

La vie n'est pas juste et on ne naît pas tous égaux. Certains modèles ont plus d'impact que d'autres pour promouvoir un produit, un mélange de beauté et de charisme qui les rend particulièrement désirables sur une couverture de magazine. Dans les années cinquante, le marché des revues pour hommes était déjà si établi que de vraies étoiles commencèrent à poindre. Si beaucoup d'entre elles s'éteignirent rapidement, d'autres brillent toujours autant. Pour établir cette liste des plus grandes cinq cover-girls érigées

Year: **1957.** Title: **Tiger.** Country: **USA.**

Year: **1950s.** Title: **Earl Wilson's Showgirls.** Country: **USA.**

NO. 5:

Diane Webber

Classy Diane Webber was a bonafide nudist!

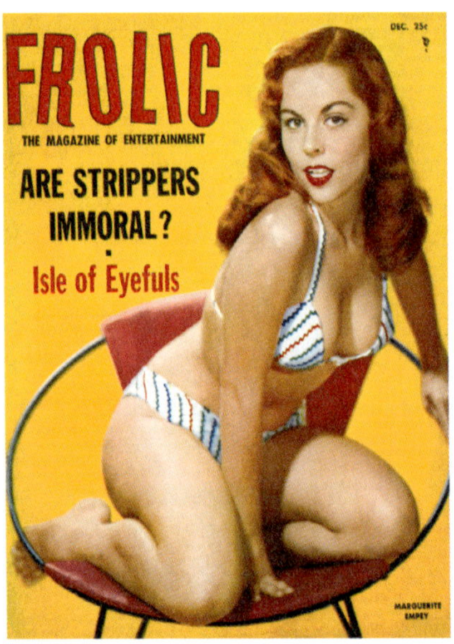

YEAR: **1955.** TITLE: **Frolic.** COUNTRY: **USA.**

make the list, but all agreed these five have gone the distance.

Was it Diane Webber's cool, classic beauty, her lush red hair, her curvy figure or the fact that she was a bona fide nudist that made her such a popular model in the mid-50s? The answer, of course, is all these things. Diane was born in 1932 and discovered by photographer Andre de Dienes in the early 50s. Through the 50s she was a favorite model of Russ Meyer, Peter Gowland and Bunny Yeager. She appeared twice in *Playboy* (May 1955 and February 1956) under the name

und Februar 1956), doch ihr wirklicher Ruhm begann mit ihrem Bekenntnis zum Nudismus. Auch Bettie Page und Marilyn Monroe waren auf den Covern von Nudistenmagazinen abgebildet worden, doch allein Diane zeigte sich auch innen im Heft. Als die Nudistenmagazine 1958 das Recht erstritten, auch Schamhaar zu zeigen, wurde Diane Webber das einzige berühmte Pin-up-Girl ihrer Zeit, das seinen dankbaren Fans wirklich alles zeigte.

June Wilkinson kam 1940 in Essex in England zur Welt. Mit fünfzehn trat sie im berüchtigten Windmill Theatre in London auf, und als Siebzehnjährige war sie bereits eine bekannte Tänzerin. Darüber, wie sie in den *Playboy* kam, gehen die Meinungen auseinander. Die einen sagen, Hugh Hefner habe sie entdeckt, die anderen, sie selbst habe ihn angerufen. Begleitet von ihrer Mutter als Anstandsdame, wurde sie jedenfalls schon mit siebzehn für das Magazin fotogra-fiert, dann wartete man mit der Veröffent-lichung, bis sie achtzehn war. Die Foto-strecke erschien unter dem Titel „The Bosom", und dies sollte zu ihrem Spitz-namen werden. Zwar wurde sie nie ein Playmate, doch sie erschien immerhin siebenmal im *Playboy* und in zahllosen Konkurrenzblättern. Russ Meyer schätzte „The Bosom" und gab ihr in seinem ersten kommerziellen Film, *The Immoral Mr. Teas*, die Rolle der

YEAR: **1950s.** TITLE: **Blush.** COUNTRY: **USA.**

en idoles durables, j'ai questionné plusieurs marchands spécialisés dans les anciennes publications érotiques sur le site Internet de vente aux enchères Ebay. Chacun avait sa favorite qui n'entrait pas dans la liste mais tous convinrent que ces cinq-là tenaient toujours la route.

Diane Webber: Etait-ce sa beauté froide et glacée, sa luxuriante chevelure rousse, sa silhouette toute en courbes, ou le fait qu'elle soit une nudiste impénitente qui la rendit si populaire au milieu des années cinquante? Naturellement, c'est tout à la fois. Née en 1932, Diane fut dé-

YEAR: **1961.** TITLE: **The Vagabond.** COUNTRY: **USA.**

MAN OF THE WORLD
THE VAGABOND
Vol.3 $1
A VISIT WITH TV'S ALEXANDER KING • NASSAU'S FANCY RACING LADIES

Escapade
DECEMBER 1955
50 CENTS

YEAR: **1955.** TITLE: **Escapade.**
COUNTRY: **USA.**

Though Bettie Page and even Marilyn Monroe appeared on nudist magazine covers, only Diane backed them up with interior spreads.

YEAR: **1961.** TITLE: **Modern Sunbathing.**
COUNTRY: **USA.**

YEAR: **1961.** TITLE: **Modern Sunbathing.**
COUNTRY: **USA.**

Marguerite Empey, but her real fame began when she embraced nudism. Though Bettie Page and even Marilyn Monroe appeared on nudist magazine covers, only Diane backed them up with interior spreads. And when the nudist magazines won the right to show pubic hair in 1958 Diane Webber became the only top 50s pin-up girl to bare it all to her grateful fans.

June Wilkinson was born in 1940 in Essex, England. She began appearing at London's notorious Windmill Theatre at age fifteen, becoming a feature dancer

Torso. Heute, in ihren Sechzigern, sieht June immer noch umwerfend aus und findet bei „Glamour Conventions" ein begeistertes Publikum.

Jayne Mansfield, die Marilyn für Arme, wurde am 19. April 1933 in Texas geboren. Von Kind auf wollte Vera Jayne Palmer ein Star werden. Eine Heirat in jungen Jahren behinderte ihre Ambitionen etwas, aber 1952 machte sie sich mit ihrem Gatten Paul Mansfield und ihrem ersten Kind im Schlepptau auf nach Hollywood. Paul kehrte vier Monate später nach Texas zurück, doch Jayne

couverte par le photographe André de Dienes au début des années cinquante. Tout au long de la décennie, elle fut l'un des modèles de prédilection de Russ Meyer, de Peter Gowland et de Bunny Yeager. Elle apparut deux fois dans *Playboy* sous le pseudonyme Marguerite Empey mais devint vraiment célèbre quand elle épousa le nudisme. Bien que Bettie Page et Marilyn Monroe soient également apparues en couvertures de magazines nudistes, Diane, elle, ornait les pages intérieures. Quand, en 1958, les revues nudistes gagnèrent le droit de monter des poils pubiens, Diane Webber fut la seule grande pin-up des années cinquante à tout montrer à ses fans reconnaissants.

June Wilkinson est née en 1940 dans l'Essex, en Angleterre. Elle a fait ses débuts à Londres à l'âge de 15 ans sur les planches du sulfureux Windmill Theatre, devenant danseuse vedette à 17 ans. Les récits sur la manière dont elle en vint à poser pour *Playboy* diffèrent, certains disent qu'Hefner la dénicha tout seul, d'autres affirment que c'est elle qui l'a appelé. Quoi qu'il en soit, elle n'avait que 17 ans lors de sa première séance de pose, chaperonnée par sa mère, et les photos ne furent publiées qu'un an plus tard quand elle eut l'âge légal. Le reportage s'appelait « La poitrine », un surnom qui lui resta. Bien que n'ayant jamais été play-

NO. 4:

June Wilkinson

June made seven separate appearances in *Playboy* and posed for countless spreads in its competitors.

by seventeen. Reports differ on how she came to pose for *Playboy*, some saying Hefner tracked her down, others that she called him herself. Whatever, she was first photographed for the magazine at age seventeen, with her mother as chaperone, and the photos held until she turned eighteen. The feature was titled "The Bosom", and so she would be known ever after. Never a Playmate, June still made seven separate appearances in *Playboy* and posed for countless spreads in its competitors. A Russ Meyer favorite, The Bosom played a character named Torso in Russ's first commercial film, *The Immoral Mr. Teas*.

Still gorgeous in her 60s, June Wilkinson draws big crowds at glamour conventions.

Jayne Mansfield, the poor man's Marilyn, was born in Texas on April 19th, 1933. From earliest childhood Vera Jayne Palmer wanted to be a star. An early marriage slowed her plans, but in 1952, with her husband Paul Mansfield and first child in tow, Jayne set out for Hollywood. Paul returned to Texas four months later, but Jayne stayed on and started modeling. Her blonde hair and big bust were too sexy for some clients, but outrageous Jayne knew where to draw the line. She appeared on the cover of nearly every American men's magazine, as well as German, Mexican, Eng-

Year: **1960.** Title: **Hit Show.** Country: **USA.**

blieb und begann als Modell zu arbeiten. Ihr blondes Haar und ihre üppige Oberweite waren für manche einfach zu verführerisch, doch selbst die schamlose Mansfield wusste, wo die Grenzen lagen. Sie war fast auf jedem amerikanischen Männermagazin zu sehen, daneben auch noch auf deutschen, mexikanischen, englischen und selbst türkischen Blättern, doch das einzige Magazin, das sie nackt zeigen durfte, war der *Playboy* (Juni 1963). Jayne verkündete, sie wolle noch als Hundertjährige Pin-up-Fotos machen,

Year: **1960s.** Title: **Adam.** Country: **USA.**

mate, June posa plusieurs fois pour *Playboy*, ainsi que pour d'innombrables concurrents. Très appréciée par Russ Meyer, elle joua un personnage baptisé Torso dans le premier long métrage de celui-ci, The Immoral Mr. Teas. Aujourd'hui somptueuse sexagénaire, elle attire toujours les foules lors de congrès glamour.

Jayne Mansfield, la Marilyn du pauvre, naquit au Texas le 19 avril 1933. Dès sa plus tendre enfance, Vera Jayne Palmer voulut être star. Un mariage précoce ra-

Year: **1959.** Title: **Girl Watcher.** Country: **USA.**

girl watcher

A GUIDE TO GIRL WATCHING

JUNE 1959

PRICE 50c

Bonnie Logan and June Wilkinson

Love Goddess Issue

Year: **1961.**
Title: **June Wilkinson.** Country: **USA.**

June, dubbed "The Bosom", played a character named Torso in Russ Meyer's first commercial film, *The Immoral Mr. Teas.*

Year: **1959.** Title: **Caper.** Country: **USA.**

Year: **1950s.** Title: **My Escort.** Country: **USA.**

lish and even Turkish covers, but the only magazine to get her nude was *Playboy* (June 1963). Jayne famously declared, "When I'm 100 I'll still be doing pin-ups," and no doubt she would have if not for a fatal car accident in 1967.

For all her bright smiles Bettie Page has had no easy life. Born in Tennessee in 1923 she was placed in an orphanage at age ten when her divorced mother could no longer care for six children. Even so, Bettie graduated at the top of her class with dreams of becoming a Hollywood

und zweifellos würde sie Wort halten, wäre sie nicht 1967 bei einem Autounfall ums Leben gekommen.

Trotz strahlendem Lächeln hatte es Bettie Page in ihrem Leben nicht leicht. 1923 in Tennessee geboren, wurde sie mit zehn in ein Waisenhaus gegeben, da ihrer geschiedenen Mutter die Versorgung von sechs Kindern über den Kopf gewachsen war. Dennoch schaffte Bettie ihren Schulabschluss als Klassenbeste und träumte von einer Karriere in Hollywood. Doch stattdessen zog sie

lentit ses projets mais, en 1952, traînant dans son sillage son mari Paul Mansfield et leur premier enfant, elle mit le cap sur Hollywood. Paul rentra au Texas quatre mois plus tard mais Jayne resta et commença une carrière de mannequin. Sa blondeur et son impressionnante poitrine étaient trop provocantes pour certains annonceurs mais l'extravagante Jayne connaissait ses limites. Elle fit la couverture de pratiquement tous les magazines masculins américains, ainsi qu'allemands, mexicains, anglais et même turcs. Toutefois, le seul qui parvint à la déshabiller fut *Playboy* (juin 1963). Jayne déclara «Je poserai encore en pin-up quand j'aurais 100 ans». Cela serait sans doute arrivé sans un accident de voiture tragique en 1967.

En dépit de ses sourires éclatants, Bettie Page n'a pas eu une vie toute rose. Née en 1923 dans le Tennessee, elle fut placée en orphelinat à l'âge de 10 quand sa mère divorcée ne fut plus en mesure de subvenir aux besoins de ses six enfants. Cela n'empêcha pas Bettie de finir première de sa classe avec le rêve de devenir actrice à Hollywood. Au lieu de cela, elle s'installa à New York en 1950 et devint modèle dans un club de photo, posant sur la plage de Coney Island pour un groupe de photographes amateurs. Elle se fit enfin connaître grâce à Robert Harrison et ses revues *Wink*, *Titter* et *Eyeful*. *Playboy* la

A PICTORIAL BIOGRAPHY OF

June Wilkinson

ADULTS ONLY $1.00

NO. 3:

Jayne Mansfield

Jayne Mansfield is rumored to have loved attention so much she would pose for anyone who asked.

YEAR: **1958.** TITLE: **Eeran.**
COUNTRY: **Chile.**

actress. Instead, she moved to New York in 1950 and became a camera club model, posing on the beach at Coney Island for groups of amateur photographers. Her professional break-through came with Robert Harrison's *Wink*, *Titter*, *Eyeful Empire*. *Playboy* poached her from Harrison for its January 1955 centerfold, but it was her fetish work for bondage master Irving Klaw that won her an enduring legacy.

Today Ms. Page is celebrated as the quintessential 50s pin-up girl, and has

YEAR: **1950s.** TITLE: **Cabaret Quarterly.**
COUNTRY: **USA.**

1950 nach New York und stand im Auftrag von Fotovereinen am Strand von Coney Island Fotoamateuren Modell. Den Durchbruch schaffte sie in Robert Harrisons Magazinen *Wink*, *Titter* und *Eyeful*. Der *Playboy* luchste sie Harrison als Centerfold für das Januarheft 1955 ab, aber erst die Fetischfotos für Irving Klaw, den König des Bondage, sicherten ihr ewigen Ruhm.

Heute gilt Ms. Page als Inbegriff des Pin-ups der fünfziger Jahre und ist so allgegenwärtig, dass man ihre tat-

piqua à Harrison pour son poster central du numéro de janvier 1955 mais ce sont surtout ses photos fétichistes pour le maître du bondage Irving Klaw qui assurèrent sa notoriété. Aujourd'hui, Mlle. Page est célébrée comme la quintessence de la pin-up des années cinquante et on la voit partout au point qu'on a du mal à différentier sa valeur en tant qu'objet de collection de son véritable sex-appeal.

Née Norma Jeane Baker en 1926, Marilyn Monroe fut la plus populaire cover-girl des années cinquante. Comme Bettie Page, elle passa une partie de son en-

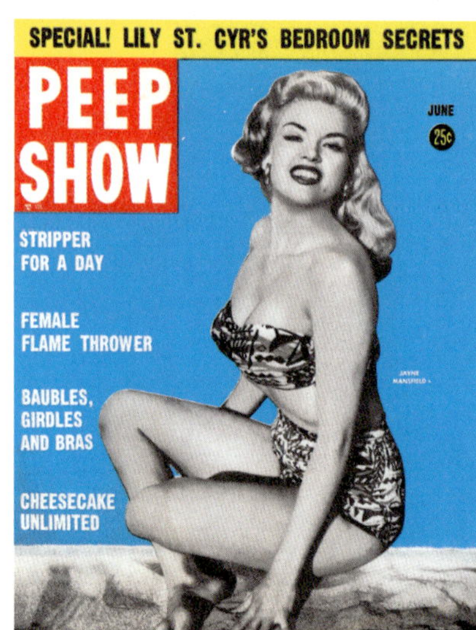

YEAR: **1956.** TITLE: **Peep Show.** COUNTRY: **USA.**

YEAR: **1956.** TITLE: **Ogle.**
COUNTRY: **USA.**

OGLE

GIRLS WITH A GIGGLE

ACE
MAR. NO. 1 25¢

IT TAKES
TWO
TO MAKE
MANSFIELD
★
1957
FATTY GIRL
CALENDAR
★
ANE RUSSELL
GETS A LOAD
FF HER CHEST

YEAR: **1950s.** TITLE: **Jayne.** COUNTRY: **USA.**

YEAR: **1958.** TITLE: **Modern Man.** COUNTRY: **USA.**

JANUARY 1958 50c
MODERN
MAN
THE ADULT PICTURE MAGAZINE
MANSFIELD SPEAKS!
— PAGE 8
TANIA VELIA—
THE SEXIEST
ONE YET
The TOUGHEST GUNFIGHTER OF 'EM ALL

NO. 2:

Bettie Page

Ms. Page has become such a commodity it's hard to separate her collectability from her actual desirability.

become such a commodity it's hard to separate her collectability from her actual desirability.

Born Norma Jeane Baker in 1926 Marilyn Monroe was our oldest and most popular 50s covergirl. Like Bettie Page, she spent part of her childhood in an orphanage, which resulted in a strong need for attention. Even so, Marilyn posed nude only twice, first for the famous calendar shots that appeared in the December 1953 *Playboy*, and second for fashion

YEAR: **1950s.** TITLE: **Meet the Girls.**
COUNTRY: **USA.**

sächliche Attraktivität kaum noch von ihrer Popularität in Sammlerkreisen unterscheiden kann.

Marilyn Monroe, 1926 als Norma Jeane Baker geboren, ist unter unseren Covergirls der Fünfziger das älteste und berühmteste. Wie Bettie Page verbrachte sie einen Teil ihrer Kindheit im Heim, was in ihr ein ausgeprägtes Bedürfnis weckte, im Mittelpunkt zu stehen. Dennoch ließ sie sich nur zweimal nackt fotografieren, das erste Mal für die legendären Kalenderfotos, die 1953 im *Playboy* erschienen, das zweite Mal für den Modefotografen Burt Stern in den Wochen vor ihrem Tod durch eine Überdosis Medikamente. Trotzdem zierte Marilyn so manches Männermagazincover. Wenn ein Chefredakteur meinte, er müsse im Heft noch etwas nachlegen, so griff er gewöhnlich zu den alten *Playboy*-Centerfolds. Die meisten wussten jedoch, dass Marilyns Gesicht schon genügte, um ihre Fans zum Kauf zu bewegen.

Und so ist es auch heute noch. Ihre ungebrochene Anziehungskraft auf Männer wie Frauen auf der ganzen Welt macht sie zum größten Covergirl aller Zeiten. Versuchen Sie nur mal, das Dezemberheft 1953 des *Playboys* für weniger als 6000 Dollar aufzutreiben.

YEAR: **1950s.** TITLE: **Fantastique.**
COUNTRY: **USA.**

fance en orphelinat, d'où sans doute son grand besoin d'attention. En fait, elle ne posa nue que deux fois, pour les célèbres images de calendrier parues dans le numéro de décembre 1953 de *Playboy* et pour le photographe de mode Burt Stern quelques semaines avant sa mort par overdose. En revanche, elle a orné la couverture de bien des magazines pour hommes. Quand les éditeurs avaient besoin de justifier sa photo en couverture, ils re-

YEAR: **1953.** TITLE: **Eyeful.**
COUNTRY: **USA.**

EYEFUL

Glorifying the American Girl

AUGUST

25¢

ARE YOU BROAD-MINDED?

See page 24

BETTIE PAGE

YEAR: **1963.** TITLE: **Focus on Bettie Page.** COUNTRY: **USA.**

YEAR: **1950s.** TITLE: **Figure Quarterly.**
COUNTRY: **USA.**

Figure
QUARTERLY
ONE DOLLAR
PHOTOGRAPHY
SCULPTURE
PAINTING
PETER GOWLAND'S
EIGHT WAYS TO LIGHT THE FIGURE
PETER BASCH:
HOW TO POSE THE NUDE
DORA GORDINE—
ENGLAND'S FOREMOST SCULPTRESS
THE GLAMOUR GIRLS of K. O. MUNSON
VOLUME THIRTEEN

Sunbathing Review
FALL, 1958
ONE DOLLAR
NUDITY
CENSORED
ON FILM

NO. 1:

Marilyn Monroe

If publishers felt any need to back up a cover photo they'd rerun the 1953 *Playboy* centerfold, but most knew that Marilyn's face was enough.

YEAR: **1950s.** TITLE: **Paris Frou Frou.** COUNTRY: **France.**

YEAR: **1956.** TITLE: **Sir!** COUNTRY: **USA.**

YEAR: **1954.** TITLE: **Night and Day.** COUNTRY: **USA.**

photographer Burt Stern in the weeks before her death from a drug overdose. Marilyn did grace the covers of many men's magazines, though. If publishers felt any need to back up the cover photo they'd rerun her *Playboy* centerfold, but most knew that Marilyn's face was enough to pull in the fans. As it still is today, Marilyn Monroe's undiminished appeal to men and women the world over makes her the number one covergirl of all time. Just try touching a December '53 issue of *Playboy* for under $6000.

Marilyn's undiminished appeal makes her the #1 covergirl of all time.

publiaient son fameux poster central de *Playboy*, mais la plupart savaient que son visage suffisait à faire vendre le numéro. Cela n'a pas changé aujourd'hui: son pouvoir de séduction sur les hommes et les femmes dans le monde entier en font la plus grande cover-girl de tous les temps. Essayez seulement de mettre la main sur un exemplaire du *Playboy* de décembre 53 pour moins de 6 000 dollars!

YEAR: **1958.** TITLE: **Sunbathing Review.** PHOTO: **Andre de Dienes.** COUNTRY: **USA.**

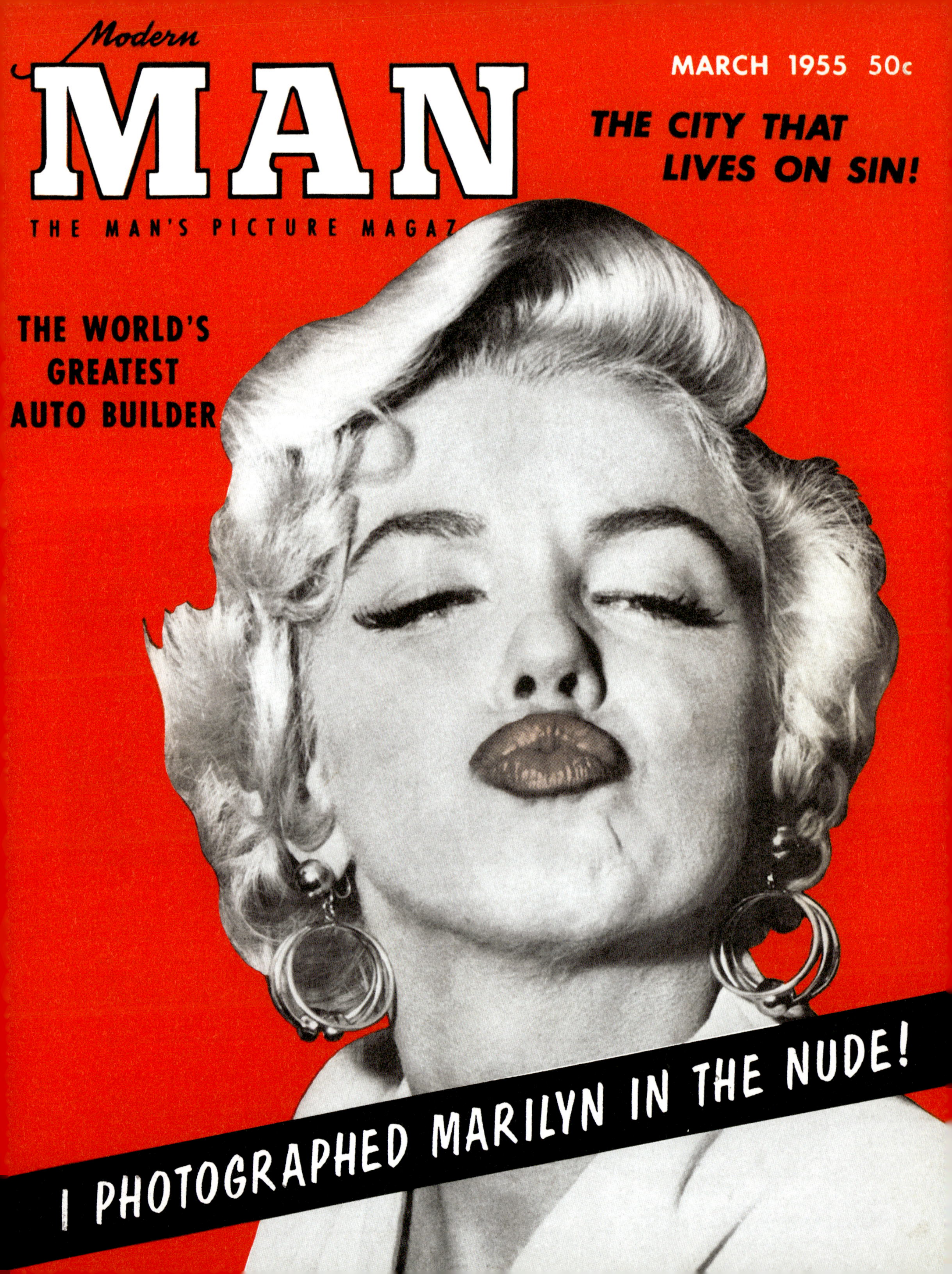
Modern
MAN
THE MAN'S PICTURE MAGAZ
MARCH 1955 50c
THE CITY THAT LIVES ON SIN!
THE WORLD'S GREATEST AUTO BUILDER
I PHOTOGRAPHED MARILYN IN THE NUDE!

YEAR: **1953.** TITLE: **Eye.** COUNTRY: **USA.**

YEAR: **1954.** TITLE: **3-D Hollywood pin-ups.** COUNTRY: **USA.**

YEAR: **1950s.** TITLE: **Marilyn Monroe Pin-ups.** COUNTRY: **USA.**

YEAR: **1953.** TITLE: **Photoplay Pinups.** COUNTRY: **USA.**

YEAR: **1955.** TITLE: **Modern Man.**
COUNTRY: **USA.**

Anything a Man Could Want

Was der Mann braucht
Tout ce qu'un homme pourrait désirer

As interesting as the covers and contents of the magazines are, the real information about a decade and the people inhabiting it is found in the back pages, where the ads reside. What did men really want in 1930, or '40 or '50?
A good truss for starters…

So interessant die Titel und Features in den Männermagazinen auch sein mögen, die aufschlussreichsten Informationen über eine Epoche und ihre Menschen finden sich auf den letzten Seiten der Hefte im Anzeigenteil. Woran waren die Männer in den dreißiger, vierziger oder fünfziger Jahren wirklich interessiert?
Nun ja, zuerst einmal an einem zuverlässigen Bruchband …

Aussi intéressants que soient les contenus et les couvertures de ces magazines, la vraie information sur la décennie et ceux qui l'ont vécue se trouve dans les dernières pages, là où paraissaient les publicités. Que désiraient vraiment les hommes en 1930, 40 ou 50?
Avant tout, un bon bandage herniaire …

"Sex! What is that but life, after all? We're all of us selling sex, because we're all selling life."

– Alvin Chereskin, president of AC&R Advertising Agency

KILL THESE HAIR-DESTROYING GERMS
WITH WARD'S FORMULA
PITYROSPORUM OVALE
MOROCOCCUS
STAPHYLOCOCCUS ALBUS
MICROBACILLUS
NOTHING, Absolutely nothing known to Science can do more to
SAVE YOUR HAIR
SCALP ITCH
FALLING HAIR
DANDRUFF
HEAD ODORS
Proof!
We get letters like these every day from grateful men and women all over the world..
Beware of your itchy scalp, hair loss, dandruff, head scales, unpleasant head odors! Nature may be warning you of approaching baldness. Heed Nature's warning! Treat your scalp to scientifically prepared Ward's Formula.
Millions of trouble-breeding bacteria, living on your sick scalp (see above) are killed on contact. Ward's Formula kills not one, but all four types of these destructive scalp germs now recognized by many medical authorities as a significant cause of baldness. Kill these germs—don't risk letting them kill your hair growth.
ENJOY THESE 5 BENEFITS IMMEDIATELY
1. Kills these 4 types of germs that retard normal hair growth—on contact
2. Removes ugly infectious dandruff—fast
3. Brings hair-nourishing blood to scalp—quickly
4. Stops annoying scalp itch and burn—instantly
5. Starts wonderful self-massaging action—within 3 seconds
Once you're bald, that's it, friends! There's nothing you can do. Your hair is gone forever. So are your chances of getting it back. But Ward's Formula, used as directed, keeps your sick scalp free of itchy dandruff, seborrhea, and stops the hair loss they cause. Almost at once your hair looks thicker, more attractive and alive.
We don't ask you to believe us. Thousands of men and women—first skeptical just as you are—have proved what we say. Read their grateful letters. Study the guarantee—it's better than a free trial! Then try Ward's Formula at our risk. Use it for only 10 short days. You must enjoy all the benefits we claim—or we return not only the price you pay—but DOUBLE YOUR MONEY BACK. You be the judge! Ward Laboratories, Inc., 320 E. 49th St., New York 17, N. Y.
I must admit I didn't have much faith in it, but I hadn't been using Ward's one week before I could see it was helping me. I could feel my hair getting thicker. E. K., Cleveland, Ohio
Out of all the Hair Experts I went to, I've gotten the most help from one bottle of Ward's Formula. C. La M., Philadelphia, Pa.
After using Ward's for only 12 days, my hair has stopped falling out. R. W. C., Cicero, Ill.
I am tickled to death with the results. In just two weeks' time—no dandruff! W. T. W., Portola, Cal.
I feel encouraged to say that the infuriating scalp itch which has bothered me for 5 years is now gone. J. M. K., Columbus, Ohio
Guarantee
This written guarantee entitles you not only to return of price paid for Ward's Formula, but Double Your Money Back unless you actually SEE, FEEL and ENJOY all benefits herein claimed in only ten days. The test is at our risk. All you do is return unused portion or the empty bottle unless completely satisfied.
SEAL
Ward Laboratories, Inc.
TO SAVE YOUR HAIR ACT NOW
Send coupon today for 10-day offer. Send No Money
© 1949
ACT TODAY or YOU MAY BE TOO LATE!
Ward Laboratories, Inc.,
320 E. 49 St., Dept. 6-S, New York 17, N. Y.
Rush Ward's Formula to me at once. I will pay postman two dollars plus postage. I must be completely satisfied within 10 days, or you GUARANTEE refund of DOUBLE MY MONEY BACK upon return of bottle and unused portion.
Name
Address
City
Zone
State
Check here if you enclose $2.00 with order, and we will pay postage. Same refund offer holds, of course.
APO, FPO, Canada & Foreign add 25c; no CODs.
DOUBLE YOUR MONEY BACK GUARANTEE

WARNING! BEWARE NATURE'S DANGER SIGNAL!

STOP BELLY BLOATED with GAS

TERRIFIC TRIUMPH OF SCIENCE
Awarded NATURE'S PATH
SEAL OF APPROVAL
by America's pioneer health magazine

Startling X-Ray View

You stomach sufferers can now throw away all those dangerous drugs and worthless remedies you have tried with little or no success. Study the revealing X-Ray picture above. See why Magay gives you DOUBLE-ACTION tablets to work in those entire 32 feet of your digestive tract, to bring really fast, thorough relief. Nothing like them! Contain a special combination of 9 medically proven ingredients. Fast-acting. Safe. Gentle. Easy to take. No dope or harsh drugs. Anti-constipating!

Now read the actual letters of grateful users, once sufferers like yourself. Check our offer and guarantee. Then try Magay for 5 full days. You must get results or we GUARANTEE YOUR MONEY BACK. You can't lose. Fill out and mail valuable coupon.

DOUBLE-ACTION FORMULA GUARANTEES YOU MONEY BACK UNLESS YOU GET SENSATIONAL DOUBLE BENEFITS!!

You get rid of even Old Gas Bloat

You Eat What You Like and Like What You Eat

Success or Your Money-Back Guaranteed

Do you feel so bloated, stuffed, puffed out, you must loosen clothing just to breathe? Stomach stretched, swollen, blown up like a balloon from awful gas? In misery with heartburn, belching, gas-pains, headaches, sour stomach, bad breath? Feel nervous, grouchy; lack appetite; sleep badly? Now you can rid yourself of these warnings of danger, due to gastric hyperacidity, to need for stimulated natural gastro-intestinal juices and carminative action.

Your physician will tell you to rid both your stomach and intestines of bloat and gas, you must use a DOUBLE ACTION remedy: one for your stomach, and one for your bowel. Not just one kind of tablet, powder or liquid. That is why new Magay Gold & White Tablets give you real results. You take a Gold Tablet BEFORE MEALS—a White Tablet AFTER MEALS—and brother, you're on easy street. You say good-bye to gas, bloat and other non-organic symptoms.

Settle your stomach worry right now! Our square-deal no-risk offer says: "Neighbor, we know how you suffer—how disappointed you are with all those useless remedies that have failed you." You need send no money, just write your name on the coupon. Magay double-action tablets must do everything stated on this page, to your satisfaction, or return the unused portion and get YOUR MONEY BACK—NO QUESTIONS ASKED! You know we couldn't make such an offer unless Magay is all we say—so order with confidence today. Big 300 tablet supply only $6.00. FREE discount coupon saves you $1.00 on first order. That makes it less than 2c per tablet for all these benefits. Don't delay relief. Mail no-risk coupon now. YOU HAVE NOTHING TO LOSE BUT A BELLY FULL OF GAS!

© Magay Corp., Box 74, Bayside 60, N. Y.

LETTERS PROVE RESULTS

"Took Magay pills for 4 days. Got relief from stomach trouble, embarrassing and painful gas I had 5 years." *K.R.*

"I suffered extreme discomfort during the day and spent countless sleepless nights due to gas and stomach upsetment. Nothing relieved this feeling until I tried Magay. Now I never suffer any more." *N.C.D.*

"Results are almost miraculous. For first time in months I can enjoy a meal without fear of suffering distress afterwards." *A.B.*

"Kept getting less and less dates. Didn't know why friends started avoiding me. Then I tried Gold & White tablets. Now getting back into circulation." *L.B.*

FREE COUPON WORTH **$1.00**
on first purchase Magay Gold & White Tablets

Magay Corporation, Box 74, Bayside 60, N. Y.

Rush big 300 tablet supply of Magay Gold & White Tablets in plain wrapper. I must be delighted with results or you Guarantee My Money Back on return of unused portion within 5 days.

☐ $5.00 enclosed. Send postpaid.
☐ Send C.O.D. plus charges.

Regular price	$6.00
Less coupon	1.00
YOU PAY ONLY	$5.00

Name ____________________

Address ____________________

City ______________ Zone ______ State ______

Canada & Foreign—no C.O.D.'s

28-G

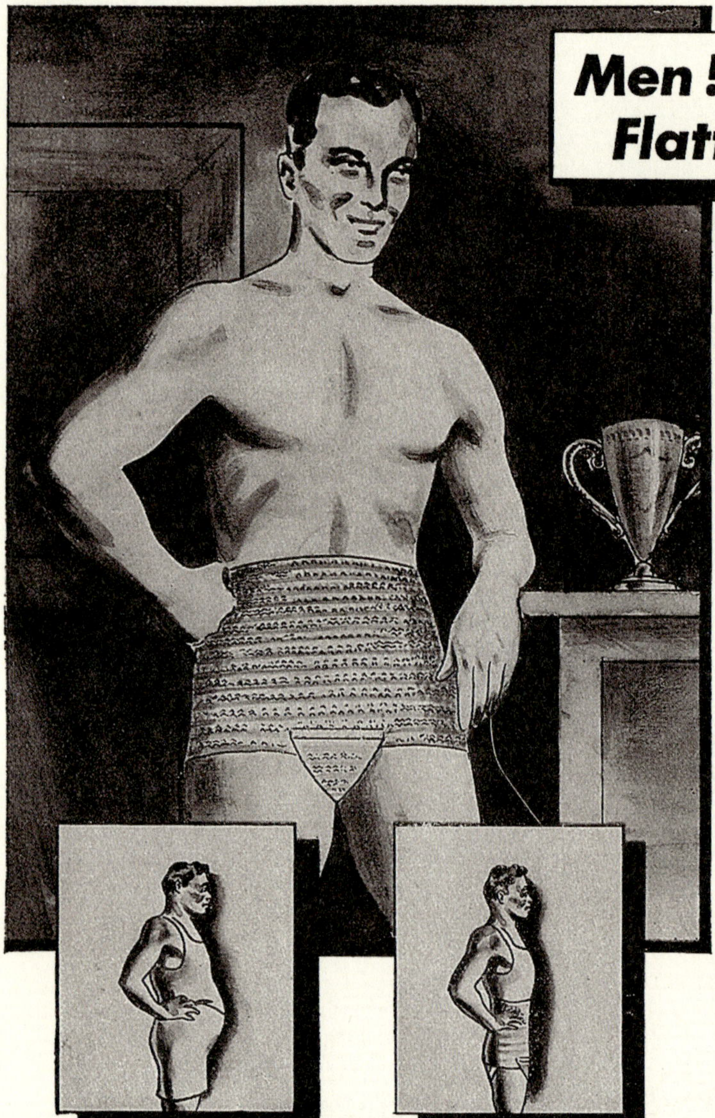

Men! Bulging Waistlines Flattened in Seconds!

WITHOUT DIET OR EXERCISE

with

THE "MANLY"

THE NEW 2-WAY ABDOMINAL SUPPORTER

Now, at once, you no longer need feel embarrassed about being "pot bellied." A trimmer, more athletic-looking appearance can be yours INSTANTLY . . . look inches slimmer, without strenuous exercise, dangerous dieting or harmful drugs . . . with MANLY, the revolutionary new abdominal supporter for MEN!

You Look Streamlined—Clothes Fit Better—You Feel More Alive

The MANLY abdominal supporter is exclusively designed to support sagging abdomens . . . give that flat, muscled, athletic appearance to "bay windows". Your suits fit better, look better, and your whole appearance seems more fit and well-proportioned. Friends will be amazed when they notice the startling improvement!

SCIENTIFIC PRINCIPLES GIVE CONTROL AND PROTECTION

MANLY is a scientifically designed men's two-in-one garment. Provides real stomach support and safeguards vital areas that all athletes know need special protection. MANLY contains NO STEEL RIBS, STRAPS, BUCKLES OR LACES! Made of specially woven elastic cotton-rayon that permits the body to move naturally, easily and comfortably. You'll hardly know you're wearing it . . . yet the streamlined appearance will be amazingly evident.

LET YOUR MIRROR BE THE JUDGE!

This special FREE EXAMINATION offer below tells you how you can examine this amazing abdominal supporter at home, without risk. When your MANLY arrives, make this simple test. Stand sideways before your mirror and note the outline your "corporation" makes. Then put on your MANLY belt. See the difference; If MANLY does not make you appear slimmer by INCHES, then it costs you ABSOLUTELY NOTHING! Order today and see for yourself!

SPECIAL MANLY FEATURES

MANLY gives you these special features: The DETACHABLE jock-type crotch, made of soft cotton and rayon mesh . . . quickly snaps into place . . . easily removed for washing. MANLY provides real protection for athletics, swimming, etc., helps make street clothes look tailored.

FREE

WEAR FOR 10 DAYS
SEND NO MONEY

Wear the MANLY for 10 days. If you are not amazed and delighted by the immediate improvement in the way you feel and look, return it and your purchase price will be immediately refunded.

SIZES 28 to 45

ONLY

$2.98

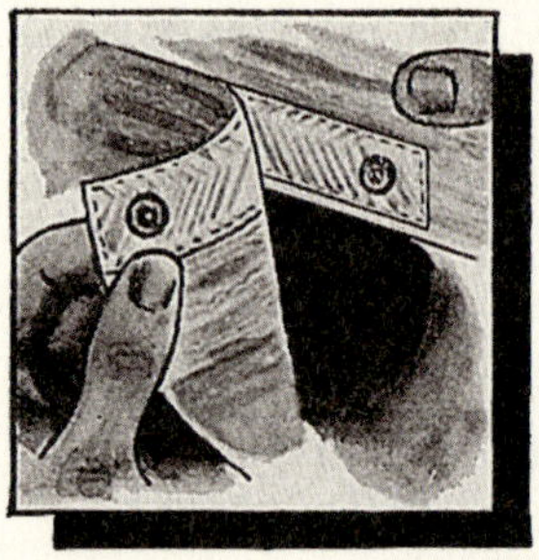

Special Large Sizes, 46 to 60—$3.98. Extra snap-button crotches — only 98c each. Makes your MANLY belt last practically twice as long.

Order *two* or *three.*

—FREE EXAMINATION COUPON—

THE MANLY CO., Dept. CJ-10
45 East 17th St., New York 3, N. Y.

( ) Send me the MANLY, complete with snap-button crotch, for no-risk 10 day trial. On arrival, I will pay postman $2.98 plus postage. ( ) Send ....extra crotches at 98c each, C.O.D. Plus postage. If not amazed and delighted, I may return within 10 days for full purchase price refund.

My waist measures..
(Send string of waist size if measure is not known)

NAME ....

ADDRESS ....

CITY.................................... STATE...........

( ) I am enclosing $2.98. Send MANLY postpaid. I enclose 98c each for.........extra crotches. Send postpaid. Same refund guarantee.

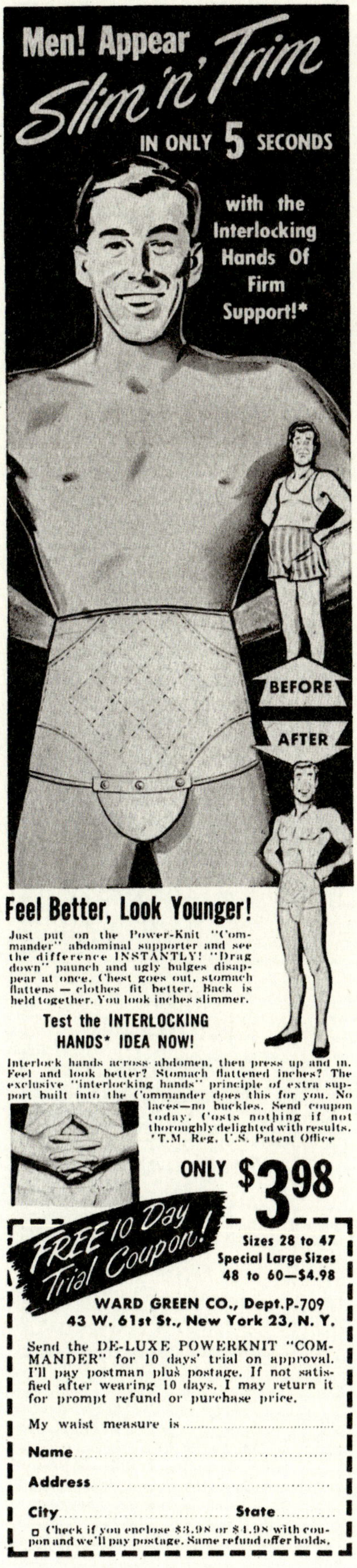

Men! Appear
Slim 'n' Trim
IN ONLY 5 SECONDS
with the Interlocking Hands Of Firm Support!*
BEFORE
AFTER
Feel Better, Look Younger!
Just put on the Power-Knit "Commander" abdominal supporter and see the difference INSTANTLY! "Drag down" paunch and ugly bulges disappear at once. Chest goes out, stomach flattens — clothes fit better. Back is held together. You look inches slimmer.
Test the INTERLOCKING HANDS* IDEA NOW!
Interlock hands across abdomen, then press up and in. Feel and look better? Stomach flattened inches? The exclusive "interlocking hands" principle of extra support built into the Commander does this for you. No laces—no buckles. Send coupon today. Costs nothing if not thoroughly delighted with results.
*T.M. Reg. U.S. Patent Office
ONLY $3.98
FREE 10 Day Trial Coupon!
Sizes 28 to 47
Special Large Sizes 48 to 60—$4.98
WARD GREEN CO., Dept.P-709
43 W. 61st St., New York 23, N. Y.
Send the DE-LUXE POWERKNIT "COMMANDER" for 10 days' trial on approval. I'll pay postman plus postage. If not satisfied after wearing 10 days, I may return it for prompt refund or purchase price.
My waist measure is
Name
Address
City State
Check if you enclose $3.98 or $4.98 with coupon and we'll pay postage. Same refund offer holds.

ONLY Truss In The World For
ONLY 3-Legged Man In The World
READ THIS!
"Brooks is the ONLY Appliance I can wear comfortably." Frank A. Lentini
ULETA, FLORIDA
THIS IS NO "GAG"
If an unfortunate man with three legs can wear a Brooks comfortably, why not you? Clip Coupon below NOW for Free Booklet on Rupture and Proof of Results. Every Brooks is made to order and Sold on Trial. Amazing Air-Cushion invention is simple, sanitary, and satisfying.
Made to Measure - Sent on Trial!
Where Is Your Rupture?
If you have reducible rupture, check this diagram and mail immediately. You will receive in reply the most welcome news you ever had.
Name
Street
City State
H. C. BROOKS
312-G State Street Marshall, Mich.
10

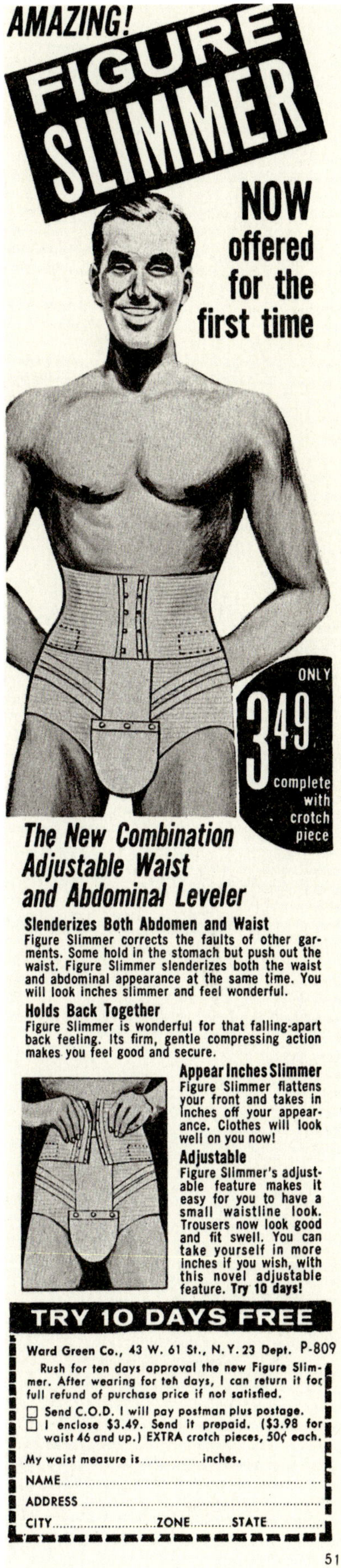

AMAZING!
FIGURE SLIMMER
NOW offered for the first time
ONLY 3.49 complete with crotch piece
The New Combination Adjustable Waist and Abdominal Leveler
Slenderizes Both Abdomen and Waist
Figure Slimmer corrects the faults of other garments. Some hold in the stomach but push out the waist. Figure Slimmer slenderizes both the waist and abdominal appearance at the same time. You will look inches slimmer and feel wonderful.
Holds Back Together
Figure Slimmer is wonderful for that falling-apart back feeling. Its firm, gentle compressing action makes you feel good and secure.
Appear Inches Slimmer
Figure Slimmer flattens your front and takes in inches off your appearance. Clothes will look well on you now!
Adjustable
Figure Slimmer's adjustable feature makes it easy for you to have a small waistline look. Trousers now look good and fit swell. You can take yourself in more inches if you wish, with this novel adjustable feature. Try 10 days!
TRY 10 DAYS FREE
Ward Green Co., 43 W. 61 St., N.Y. 23 Dept. P-809
Rush for ten days approval the new Figure Slimmer. After wearing for teh days, I can return it for full refund of purchase price if not satisfied.
Send C.O.D. I will pay postman plus postage.
I enclose $3.49. Send it prepaid. ($3.98 for waist 46 and up.) EXTRA crotch pieces, 50¢ each.
My waist measure is inches.
NAME
ADDRESS
CITY ZONE STATE
51

WHAT MEN DON'T LIKE ABOUT WOMEN

ILLUSTRATED

ONLY A BRAVE MAN WOULD DARE TO EXPOSE WOMEN LIKE THIS!

Never has the veil of secrecy been so thoroughly removed from women! Here is plain English — plain courage. For, men, in his new book WHAT MEN DON'T LIKE ABOUT WOMEN Thomas D. Horton really goes after that claim that the female is innately finer than the coarse and lusty male — and he dares to say and to prove, with experience after experience, that it *just ain't so!*

Yes, this is blunt talk your wife or sweetheart will surely hate to see you read . . . but, brother, this is talk you'll love! When you've gasped — and laughed — your way through this amusing book, you will feel that now, AT LAST, you really know women as they are!

ONLY A BRAVE WOMAN WOULD NOT BE SHOCKED!

There's dynamite in every page— in every paragraph! A woman would cry "How does he dare!" This book tells what men really think but never say about women —in every situation—at the office, at night clubs, as sweethearts, as flirts, as other men's wives. Their greediness, shamelessness, jealousy, unfaithfulness are covered daringly by the author.

BUT YOU AND EVERY MAN WILL LOVE IT!

You will hail WHAT MEN DON'T LIKE ABOUT WOMEN. You will delight in the many and often unusual types of women you will meet in this book. You will say, "Here is an experience no man should miss!" Enjoy this book as soon as you can. Get it while it's printed just as the author wrote it — NOW!

READ AND GASP ABOUT—WOMEN
AS ENGAGED ANIMALS . . . WOMEN AND MONEY . . . WOMEN AND THEIR DREAMS . . . WOMEN AS REJECTED LOVERS . . . WOMEN AND THEIR OTHER MEN . . . WOMEN AS DRINKERS . . . AND MUCH MORE!

"It is unquestionable that . . . the remarks made by Thomas D. Horton are of the shock variety, but then the truth has always been so." *Bethlehem Bulletin*

DON'T READ IT TO A WOMAN!

"There is not the slightest likelihood of any male ever reviewing this book before a woman's club. The insurance premium would be prohibitive. Turn to any chapter, any paragraph and read it aloud in the presence of a female, and you'll have fury with its claws out." *Columbus News*

SEND NO MONEY

Simply mail coupon and on delivery of WHAT MEN DON'T LIKE ABOUT WOMEN pay postman $2.00 plus postage—or enclose $2.00 with coupon, saving postage. Enjoy the most rib-tickling treat you've ever had or return in 5 days — for refund. Don't delay. A unique hilarious experience is yours! Send this coupon—TODAY!

RONOCO PUBLISHING CO., Dept. F-412
45 E. 17th St., New York 3, N. Y.

Rush my copy of "What Men Don't Like About Women" at once. On arrival I will pay the postman only $2.00 plus postage. I must be delighted or will return book within 5 days for full purchase price refund.

☐ I enclose $2.00. Send postpaid. Same refund guarantee.

NAME..

ADDRESS..

CITY & ZONE.................. STATE.......... AGE.......

BROTHER, SHE'S
ALL WOMAN
Attention all bachelors and bedroom buckaroos. Here's something new and sensational for every lusty red-blooded male. It's a miniature female torso—only more so—with all the classic curves of a Greek goddess, and every little detail of nature included. Her stunning figure (just 1½ inches high) is hand sculpted in lustrous gold plate, with heavy-duty gold chain attaching it to strong metal key-ring. But this is a key-ring with a difference: a pants-pocket companion who'll inspire you, tantalize you and rouse you to action!
Send $3.00 check or money order right now to.
HARGEM MART
P.O. Box 17
Dept. MR-19
Fort George Station
New York 40, N. Y.
FREE: Illustrated catalog featuring gorgeous pin-up models in the exciting poses which inspired our designers to create the exotic jewelry shown. Send 25c for postage & handling to address above.

AMATEUR GIRL WRESTLERS IN ACTION
Special set of Gorgeous Grapplers showing lovely young blondes and brunettes testing their strength on the wrestling mat. 16 Glossy 4 x 5's sent for only $1.00 in plain wrapper. No COD's.
RUFNEX
522-P NW 45th St.
Miami. Fla.
$1

!FROGGIRLS!
THE SECOND SERIES OF FROGGIRLS IS NOW AVAILABLE! ORDER NOW!
AMAZONS OF THE TROPICAL DEPTHS!
RUBBER-CLAD BEAUTIES AND THEIR BEAUTIFUL CAPTIVE JEANNE
8 X 10
75¢ EACH 6 EPISODES 4.00
ALL 15 EPISODES 10.00
STUDIO
BOX 414 GRAYSLAKE, ILL.

HOW TO HYPNOTIZE
IT'S EASY TO HYPNOTIZE... when you know how!
WANT the thrill of imposing your will over someone? Of making someone do exactly what you order? Try hypnotism! This amazing technique gives full personal satisfaction. You'll find it entertaining and gratifying.
The Master KEY TO HYPNOTISM shows all you need to know. It is put so simply, anyone can follow it. And there are 24 revealing photographs for your guidance.
SEND NO MONEY
FREE ten days' examination of this system is offered to you if you send the coupon today. We will ship you our copy by return mail, in plain wrapper. If not delighted with results, return it in 10 days and your money will be refunded. Stravon Publishers, Dept. H 113 West 57th Street, New York 19, N. Y.
Mail Coupon Today
STRAVON PUBLISHERS, Dept. H8711
113 West 57th St., N. Y. 19, N. Y.
Send MASTER KEY TO HYPNOTISM in plain wrapper.
Send C.O.D. I will pay postman $1.98 plus postage.
I enclose $1.98. Send postpaid.
If not delighted, I may return it in 10 days and get my money back.
Name
Address
City State
Canada & Foreign—$2.50 with order.

ART ITEMS AS YOU LIKE 'EM!
Tired of buying photos & films, that sound "out of this world"—but aren't suitable for a beginning collector? Let me send you exactly what you want. I have West's largest neg films of Hollywood's best-looking, best built, most uninhibited models. Check your choice. I'll deliver. Send $1.00 for trial photo assortment; $3.00 for complete set of 12, $3.00 for 8mm 50 ft. film, $5.00 for 16mm 100 ft. film. (No C.O.D.) Money back if I'm not your man!
Blond Brunette Red
Long Hair Short Hair
Tall Short Large Bust
Special?
CUSTOM ART, DEPT. 3
BOX 75863, LOS ANGELES 5, CALIF.

"Only a Physician Could Tell You the
Real LOW DOWN on HITLER!"
with a special introduction by
UPTON SINCLAIR who
says:
I take the liberty of telling the critics and book-readers of my
country that this volume is one of great importance to our times.
I WAS
HITLER'S
DOCTOR
His Intimate Life
by DR. KURT KRUEGER
Hitler's personal Physician for 15 years
Introduction by OTTO STRASSER
I WAS HITLER'S DOCTOR
$1.98
320 Pages
Illustrated
The Book that Bares the Shocking
Truth about the Personal Life of
EUROPE'S MADMAN
Dr. Kurt Krueger was Hitler's physician for fifteen years. He certainly knows better than anyone else the shocking truth about Hitler's unnatural and demented mind—his queer behavior—his complicated neuroses—his well-known perversions—his eroticism and hysteria—his phobias and primitivism!
HITLER'S WEAKNESS EXPOSED!
After studying Hitler intimately, Dr. Krueger tells, as only a physician could tell you, the real "low down" on Europe's eccentric madman—how Hitler's hallucinations led him into war—how Hitler duped his own fellow countrymen—how Hitler disguised his own personal weaknesses—how Hitler surrounded himself with a neurotic gang of the most amazingly ruthless criminals in history—how Hitler convinced his intimate followers that they would enslave and rule the whole world of decent men and women.
You can't know all the sensational and intimate truth about Hitler until you read this startling medical account—as disturbing as Hitler's inhuman war against humanity!
10-DAY TRIAL OFFER!
Thousands who have read Dr. Krueger's book agree that it bares the most astounding facts about Hitler's personal life. And now, you can read it on our Trial Offer—if not convinced that you want to own it and show it to your friends, return the book in 10 days and your money will be promptly refunded.
Biltmore Publishing Co., 233 Fourth Ave., H-101, New York 3, N. Y.
CONTAINS SCORES
OF SENSATIONAL REVELATIONS!
HITLER AND HIS SECRET DISEASE
LAUGHTER IN A VOID
HITLER AND WOMEN
THE PATIENT'S CONFESSION
HITLER'S BESTIALISM
OEDIPUS COMPLEX
CAMPAIGN AGAINST JEWS
CHORUS GIRL FANTASY
FRUSTRATED ARTIST
VIENNA NIGHTS
HITLER'S PRISON DAYS
BLOODY FARCE AND PURGE
TRAGEDY OF RENATE MUELLER
BLITZ-DREAMS AND NIGHTMARES
ATTEMPTED ASSASSINATION
THE SUICIDE COMPLEX
HITLER'S ODYSSEY OF TORTURE
MURDER COMPLEX
NARCISSISM
INSANITY
MANY OTHER DRAMATIC FEATURES
UPTON SINCLAIR
World Famous Author says:
"This volume is one of great importance to our times. It deserves to be read and studied carefully by all who have to fight Hitler . . . and that includes just about every adult man and woman in the Western Hemisphere!"
OTTO STRASSER
Ex-aide of Hitler
wrote an amazing introduction for this book. Strasser escaped the purge and became a violent enemy of Hitler. He knew Hitler, probably better than any living man. Strasser adds his own shocking revelations to the startling facts revealed by Dr. Krueger.
MAIL COUPON TODAY
Biltmore Publishing Co., 233 Fourth Ave., H-101, New York 3, N. Y.
Send me a copy of "I Was Hitler's Doctor." If not convinced that I wish to own this book, I may return it in 10 days and my money will be refunded.
☐ Mail C.O.D. I will pay postman $1.98 plus few cents postage.
☐ I enclose $1.98—mail postpaid.
Name
(PRINT NAME)
Address

INTERNAL BATHS END YEARS OF DISTRESS

Baffled at 47—Feels Like a Young Man at 77

Imagine how thrilling it must be for a man, feeling half-sick, half-alive for years, suddenly to find himself restored to new happiness and vitality. How wonderful he must feel to realize at last he may be able to say good-bye to the headaches, biliousness, sluggishness, that all-in feeling, due to chronic constipation suffered through many years. But such a man was Leopold Aul and as explained in his own words, "One day when I was feeling especially bad and as nervous as a cat, I met an old friend of mine. He noticed how fagged out I looked and how rapidly I seemed to be aging. 'Why don't you take Internal Baths?', he asked, 'they did wonders for me.' "

WHAT IS AN INTERNAL BATH?

Thereupon Mr. Aul began investigating Internal Baths. He found that a bonafide Internal Bath to be the administration into the lower intestine of pure warm water—Nature's greatest cleansing agent—to which is added J. B. L. Powder. Through the use of J. B. L. Cascade five quarts of the cleansing solution is sent gently swirling throughout the entire length of the colon. In fifteen minutes your impacted colon is thoroughly cleansed of its whole foul mass; the delayed waste is loosened and washed away. Often the relief is immense—often a new sense of vigor and well-being sweeps over you. Naturally, Mr. Aul did buy a J. B. L. Cascade. It proved a turning point in his life. Gone, according to his testimony, was the worry and distress that had hitherto overshadowed his whole life, sapped his ambition.

Read Mr. Aul's Astounding Letter

"I am now 77 years young, have owned a Cascade for over thirty years. When I first started using the J.B.L. Cascade I was a victim of constipation and at my wits' end as to what to do about it. Tried most everything that was recommended and prescribed for me for years without results. I now feel that Internal Bathing was responsible for bringing back my health and for keeping it ever since. I use the Cascade occasionally now, but I would not part with it for $1,000. Have sincerely recommended it to everyone suffering from the ill effects of constipation."

(Signed) Leopold Aul

SEND FOR THIS *FREE* BOOKLET

Investigate yourself the merits of Internal Bathing. Simply fill in and mail coupon below and receive, absolutely FREE your copy of "Why We Should Bathe Internally." This instructive 24-page booklet may open your eyes to many surprising facts about constipation and its many attributed ills; reveals, too, how many thousands of Internal Bathers have gained new health and vigor through this drugless treatment. MAIL YOUR COUPON TODAY.

Don't <u>stay</u> SKINNY

Amazing New Easy Way Quickly Puts Pounds and Inches of Firm Solid Flesh on Scrawny Figures

NOT A MEDICINE! NOT MERELY VITAMINS! INSTEAD A BRAND NEW CONCENTRATED FOOD WITH EASIER TO DIGEST WONDER CALORIES

You, too, can start putting weight on the first day with the amazing POUNDS PLUS plan! Thousands now gain who never thought they could with this latest discovery of medical science . . . You gain 2, 4, as much as 7 pounds in a week . . . so quickly, it's a cinch. Scrawny figures gain pounds and inches of firm, attractive flesh on body, chest, arms, legs, thighs, ankles . . . cheeks and neck fill out . . . wherever you need it.

POUNDS PLUS is entirely safe, no drugs, no fish oils . . . is not merely vitamins . . . Instead it's a delicious pleasant-tasting tablet jam-packed with wonder calories . . . a secret new concentrated food formula that also aids digestion, starts putting weight on the very first day. POUNDS PLUS plan also stimulates the appetite, supplies quick pep and energy, the magic glow of health . . . for men, women, children, convalescents. Don't be skinny, underweight or pepless. Mail the coupon today!

Easy Weight Gains of 7 Pounds in 7 Days Reported

FAMILY DOCTORS—
Your recommendation is welcome.
Write for professional samples.

SEND NO MONEY
TEST AT OUR RISK

MAIL THIS NO-RISK COUPON TODAY!

POUNDS PLUS COMPANY, Dept. 127-D, Box 820, New York 17

Send one Package of POUNDS PLUS. I'll pay $2.98 plus C.O.D. postage on arrival on guarantee that if I am not satisfied with weight gained, I may return the empty package for a full refund. (Cash orders mailed postage prepaid.)

☐ Put X here if you want 3 for $6.00
☐ I enclose payment. You stand charges
☐ Send C.O.D., I will pay postal charges

NAME. . . . .

ADDRESS. . . . .

CITY. . . . . **ZONE**. . . . . **STATE**. . . . .

(Enclose payment with APO, FPO, Canadian and foreign orders)

DID YOU EVER SEE A BALDHEADED SHEEP?

Men and women who have abused and tortured hair and scalp for years with excessive washing, alcohol tonics, permanents, dyes, rinses, bleaches. and now must pay the penalty because you've dried up or washed away the natural scalp oils that keep hair growing thick, luxurious, soft, flexible, strong, shiny and handsome . . . folks who comb hair with one hand and throw it away with the other . . . if you are alarmed at the receding hair line, the spreading bald spots, the thinning and falling hair because the scalp is shrunk tight, flaky with dandruff, itching all from dryness . . . replace the natural oils gone from hair and scalp with LANOLIN from the lowly sheep . . . the sheep whose problem isn't growing hair but getting rid of it. It's simple, easy and astonishingly successful. All you do is ask for NIL-O-NAL (spells lanolin backwards) . . . use NIL-O-NAL as directed daily on scalp and hair. In only 30 days see NIL-O-NAL repair the damage of dryness, see longer, thicker, more luxurious, shiny, wavy hair, or money back. Order today. $3.00 jar, only $2.00 plus tax and C.O.D. postage.

MAIL THIS COUPON TODAY!
SEND NO MONEY

NIL-O-NAL Company, Dept. 22P
242 East Ohio St., Chicago 11, Ill.

Rush me the 240 day supply of NIL-O-NAL. If everything you've said isn't 100% true, and I'm not entirely delighted, I can return unused portion after 30 days and receive full refund. (Economy Offer . . . THREE $2.00 Jars only $5.00 plus tax, same guarantee.)

NAME..
(Print Plainly)

ADDRESS..

CITY.......................................**ZONE**......

STATE..

☐ **Send C.O.D. I'll pay postman only $2.00 per jar plus 20% Fed. tax and C.O.D. Postage.**
☐ **THREE $2.00 Jars only $5.00 plus 20% Fed. tax and C.O.D. Postage.**
☐ **Enclosed is cash, check or money order for $2.40, ☐ $6.00 for Economy Offer.**
☐ **Send Prepaid.**

Prostatitis?

Many are finding welcome relief through the gentle vibration, **adjustable** soothing heat, and dilation provided by the DILA-THERM. A modern, **scientifically designed** instrument for easy, economical home use. **Liberal terms.** Write today for full details and 30-day trial offer. **Interesting booklet on Prostatitis FREE**

THE DILA-THERM CO., INC.
1260 E. Colfax Ave., South Bend 24, Ind.

DILA-THERM

New Bondage Story Serial!

"BOUND IN LEATHER"

This new Bondage serial is called "Bound In Leather" and tells what happens when a young man makes a casual pick-up of a high heeled booted woman in a theatre and the bizarre and thrilling events and circumstances which followed when they both found out they were bondage enthusiasts. When Ted visits Vicki's home which has been dedicated to various bondage gadgets and apparatus and is introduced to Vicki's daughter Nicki and their French maid Fifi, his adventure reaches a new high. Artist Stanton has put several illustrations on one side of each chapter to illustrate the story material typewritten alongside.

Illustrations from "Bound in Leather" drawn by Stanton — *This serial is a must for all collectors of "Damsels In Distress" material.*

Only the first 30 chapters of Bound in Leather are available at present at 50c each 8 x 10 chapter.

SEND YOUR ORDER NOW TO **IRVING KLAW,** Dept. AA-5 212 East 14th St., New York City 3, N. Y.

BETTY PAGE DANCE MOVIE! *"Joyful Dance by Betty"*

Once again beautiful model Betty Page gives a sterling dance performance in her latest 16mm movie called "Joyful Dance by Betty". In this new movie Betty dances with abandon and you will enjoy Betty's motions and facial expressions while dancing. The movie runs 100 feet in length and is well lighted with several close-ups of Betty.

The price is $12.00 for the complete movie and Betty is attired in Bra and Pantie outfit and rolled stockings and wearing 6 inch High Heel Shoes of Patent Leather

Scenes from Movie — "Joyful Dance by Betty" starring Betty Page. There are 11 different photos of Betty taken to illustrate movie at 25c each. All 11 photos for $2.20

IRVING KLAW Dept. AA-6
212 East 14th St., New York 3, N. Y.

NEW FIGHTING GIRL MOVIE!

I can now supply you with an excellent fighting and wrestling girl 16mm silent movie called "GIRLS ROUGH AND TUMBLE FIGHT". This movie features gorgeous blonde model Joan (Eve) Rydell fighting, wrestling and roughing up model Cocoa Brown in an action-packed rough and tumble fight that will keep you thrilled from start to finish. The movie comes in 2 parts of approx. 100 feet each part and sells for $15.00 each part or $28.00 for the complete movie of approx. 200 feet. The action is terrific throughout this m o v i e which never stops until the end and is one of the best fight movies you have seen in a long while. "Girls Rough and Tumble Fight" comes only in 16mm silent size, and you can order either part at $15.00 or c o m p l e t e movie for $28.00. Send orders to

'GIRLS ROUGH AND TUMBLE FIGHT'

IRVING KLAW Dept. AA-7
212 East 14th St., N Y 3, N.Y.

NEW BONDAGE CARTOON 'DUTCHESS OF THE BASTILLE'

We can now supply you with the first sixteen episodes of a new bondage cartoon serial drawn by Stanton called "Dutchess of the Bastille." This is a costume drama of the early French Revolution days, when the Baroness Lorraine kidnaps some of the rich people for ransom to pay off the heavy taxes laid on the poor people of France, by an unpopular Queen and her cohorts.

The first sixteen episodes are available now

at 50 cents each episode

ALL 16 EPISODES FOR $7.00 POSTPAID

more episodes will be added each month

IRVING KLAW

Dept AA-8

212 E. 14 St., N. Y. 3, N. Y.

How 'BLACK BEAUTY' TURNS AN ALSO-RAN into "VIDEO VIC!"
HEY, MARGE, HOW'S THIS?
OH, PULEEZE, VIC, STOP ACTING LIKE A KID!
SAY, BOSS, I'M SLATED FOR PROMOTION. HOW'S ABOUT ME HEADING UP THAT NEW CRUSHER GANG?
NO SOAP, VIC! SORRY, BUT THAT JOB TAKES TOP MUSCLE POWER!
LOOKS LIKE I'M ALWAYS AN ALSO-RAN. I MIGHT AS WELL PUNCH OUT OF THIS JOB FOR GOOD!
AW, DON'T QUIT NOW, VIC. HONEST, ALL YOU NEED IS A DAILY WORK-OUT WITH THE 'BLACK BEAUTY' PROGRESSIVE EXERCISER AND JOE BONOMO'S SPECIAL COURSE.
HECK, NO WONDER I DIDN'T MAKE THE GRADE BEFORE, TIM. IT TOOK 'BLACK BEAUTY' AND BONOMO'S COURSE TO SHOW ME REAL TRAINING. WHAT TERRIFIC ROUTINES!
GREAT, BUT CLIMB INTO YOUR CLOTHES, KID. CASEY OVER AT THE ARENA WANTS TO LOOK YOU OVER.
A FEW WEEKS LATER...
NOW, LADIES AND GENTLEMEN, THE WINNAH AT THE ARENA TONITE ...THE NEW STAR... VIDEO VIC!
GEE WHIZ, VIDEO VIC IS VIC -- MY VIC!! GANGWAY, FOLKS, I'M GETTING HIM ON THE PHONE RIGHT NOW!
OH, MARGE, DO YOU REALLY KNOW VIDEO VIC? YOU LUCKY GIRL, YOU!
I'M PROUD TO KNOW YOU, VIDEO VIC. MY WIFE AND I SAW YOU WIN LAST NIGHT. I'VE GOT BIG PLANS FOR YOU HERE.
SURE, VIC, THAT CRUSHER JOB IS YOURS IF YOU STILL WANT IT.
THANKS MR. BURKE --OKAY MORAN, I KNOW I CAN LICK ANY JOB NOW!
FREE 3 CABLE 'BLACK BEAUTY' EXERCISER
(Worth 3.95 alone)
DEVELOP REAL POWER
INCREASE YOUR STRENGTH • BUILD YOUR BODY
JOE BONOMO
World's Strongman, Hercules of the Screen, International Authority on Health & Strength.
BECOME AN ALL-AROUND WINNER
WIN FRIENDS • GAIN POPULARITY • BE A SUCCESS
Discover Your Muscles
YOUR MONEY BACK IF NOT SATISFIED
Uses Photo-Instructor Method
Contains Over 300 Illustrations
SENT WITH EVERY COURSE FREE
LOOK AT WHAT YOU GET!
This big action-packed 3-CABLE COURSE is literally packed with dynamite . . . every word batted out for you by Joe Bonomo himself. Many of today's strongmen paid $25.00 for these same instructions as a personalized mail order course. You get it now for only $2.95 . . . . including Joe Bonomo's famous 'Black Beauty' 3-CABLE EXERCISER as a FREE gift to you. Don't wait! Act RIGHT AWAY!
A FEW MINUTES A DAY
STRONGMAN'S COURSE
Free SMCA Membership Card
FREE membership in the Strongmen's Club of America also included to those who act right away!
STRONGMEN'S CLUB OF AMERICA
1841 Broadway, New York 23, N. Y.
JOE BONOMO SHOWS YOU HOW!
Why grope in the dark always wishing? Why let other guys run off with the best of everything? Specially when you CAN be the most popular fellow in your class. Just let mighty Joe Bonomo and Black Beauty show you how easy it is. Think of it! You may become a LEADER-WINNER-ATHLETE . . . "tops" in popularity.
Scientific? And how! Just wait and see!
Joe Bonomo's big action-packed Cable Course is loaded with dynamite : . . 96 complete pages that tell you how . . . hundreds of photos, diagrams and charts that show you how. Your "Black Beauty" 3-Cable Exerciser (given to you FREE) is designed by Joe Bonomo himself . . . the world's strongman and "hercules-of-the-screen." You can be sure of the best. But, don't wait! Act right away!
Bernarr Macfadden says:
"As an instructor in muscle building, you should stand at the head of the list. Many of your pupils already attest to your ability in building better bodies. I can recommend you most highly. Here's wishing you all possible success!"
Jack Dempsey says:
"I consider your Course tops for all-around physical development—power, strength—endurance. The secrets and short cuts you reveal with your system of body development are miraculous and I cannot endorse your course too highly."
COMPLETE CABLE COURSE
$2.95
including BLACK BEAUTY' 3 CABLE EXERCISER FREE!
(Worth 3.95 alone)
CUT OUT THE DREAMING!
Strongmen think fast . . . act fast! Now that you've made up your mind . . . do something about it quickly! Get going! Send your order in right away!
ACT NOW FOR FREE OFFER
STRONGMEN'S CLUB OF AMERICA
Joe Bonomo, Director
1841 Broadway, Dept. RM-1
New York 23, N. Y.
MAIL THIS SPECIAL ORDER
Okay, Joe! Rush me your famous 96 page Cable Course and include FREE your "Black Beauty" 3-Cable Exerciser plus membership in the SMCA—no dues, no fees. If I am not 100% satisfied, in any way, I can return within 30 days for full refund.
☐ I enclose $2.95 in full. Ship prepaid.
☐ Ship C. O. D. for $2.95 plus postage.
PLEASE PRINT PLAINLY
Name______ Age______
Address______ Weight______
City______ Zone____ State______ Height______
Foreign & APO's (Except Canada) $3.95 with payment in full.

SEXUAL HISTORY OF THE WORLD WAR ILLUSTRATED
LAWLESS WOMEN -a spreading menace during WAR!
Partial Contents of These Explosive Pages!
• War's Sexual Atrocities!
• Sexual Restraints Released!
• Nurse's Sex Life!
• Original Photographs!
• Today's "Camp Prostitute"!
• Immoral War Wives!
• Conquered Girls Exploited!
• Prostitution Behind the Lines!
• Russian Female Soldiers!
• Sex Diseases from War Prostitutes!
• Regulation of Army "public houses"!
• Lawless sex life of civilians back home!
• Sex life of war prisoners!
• Sex methods of female war spies!
• Sex lies for propaganda in war!
• Lower standard of soldiers' morals!
• Sex life after the Armistice!
EYE-WITNESS REPORTS!
True events, seemingly fantastic, parade before your eyes! Vividly told by men and women participants! Reckless sex passions in the face of death! Every page portrays the lawless spread of flagrant intimacies and lust murders, riotous sex life in concentration camps, trenches, hospitals, cafes, participated by soldiers, nurses, civilians, prostitutes, spies, etc., in England, France, Germany, Russia, Italy. This book was burned by Hitler—it revealed too much!
Today's "Camp Prostitute"
Up-to-date as this very minute—book includes realistic reports now taking place near our own draftee camps—chippy wagons, juke joints and loose women preying upon our boys —a difficult problem for the government to solve!
Authorities Acclaim Book
". . . none of the chapters are dull . . . work of such broad scope."—DR. NORMAN E. HIMES. "These books were burnt and are not permitted to be read in their native land."—DR. VICTOR ROBINSON. "Dr. Hirschfeld's Institute of Sexual Science, source of book material—an event in the development of human knowledge and practice." —HAVELOCK ELLIS.
You can't afford to be without this book right now! An excellent, beautiful cloth-bound De Luxe book of 350 pages—limited copies at the lowest price ever offered—$1.98. (Originally $5.00) Cadillac Publishing Co., Dept. S-60, 220 Fifth Ave., N.Y.C.
READ WITHOUT BUYING
Cadillac Publishing Co., Dept. S-60
220 Fifth Ave., N. Y. C.
Send me "Sexual History of World War" (originally $5), in plain wrapper marked "Personal." I will pay postman $1.98 plus postage on delivery. If not satisfied within 5 days, I can return book and money will be refunded. I am over 21. Mail Coupon Today.
Name
Address
City State
Canada or Foreign—No C. O. D. Send $2.50.
N. Y. C. add 1% Sales Tax.
☐ Check here if you desire to save delivery costs by enclosing only $1.98 with coupon under same money-back guarantee.

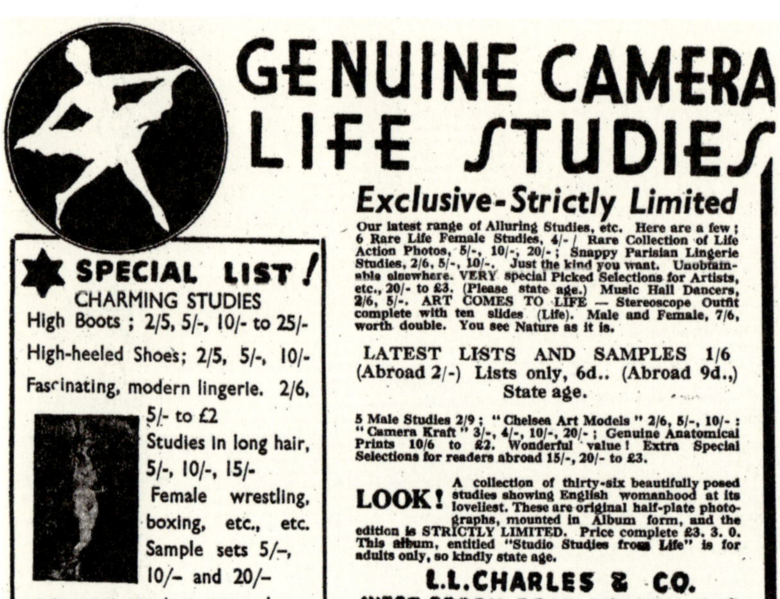
GENUINE CAMERA LIFE STUDIES
Exclusive-Strictly Limited
Our latest range of Alluring Studies, etc. Here are a few; 6 Rare Life Female Studies, 4/- / Rare Collection of Life Action Photos, 5/-, 10/-, 20/-; Snappy Parisian Lingerie Studies, 2/6, 5/-, 10/-. Just the kind you want. Unobtainable elsewhere. VERY special Picked Selections for Artists, etc., 20/- to £3. (Please state age.) Music Hall Dancers, 2/6, 5/-. ART COMES TO LIFE — Stereoscope Outfit complete with ten slides (Life). Male and Female, 7/6, worth double. You see Nature as it is.
SPECIAL LIST!
CHARMING STUDIES
High Boots; 2/5, 5/-, 10/- to 25/-
High-heeled Shoes; 2/5, 5/-, 10/-
Fascinating, modern lingerie. 2/6, 5/- to £2
Studies in long hair, 5/-, 10/-, 15/-
Female wrestling, boxing, etc., etc.
Sample sets 5/-, 10/- and 20/-
State exact requirements and age.
LATEST LISTS AND SAMPLES 1/6 (Abroad 2/-) Lists only, 6d.. (Abroad 9d.,) State age.
5 Male Studies 2/9; "Chelsea Art Models" 2/6, 5/-, 10/-: "Camera Kraft" 3/-, 4/-, 10/-, 20/-; Genuine Anatomical Prints 10/6 to £2. Wonderful value! Extra Special Selections for readers abroad 15/-, 20/- to £3.
LOOK! A collection of thirty-six beautifully posed studies showing English womanhood at its loveliest. These are original half-plate photographs, mounted in Album form, and the edition is STRICTLY LIMITED. Price complete £3. 3. 0. This album, entitled "Studio Studies from Life" is for adults only, so kindly state age.
L.L. CHARLES & CO.
WEST GREEN ROAD, LONDON, N.15

"Taboo" . . . forbidden dreams come true
Inspired by the EXCITEMENT of the FRENCH RIVIERA
BLACK as a moonless night
All the allure of GAY "PAREE"
Taboo THE FORBIDDEN NIGHTIE . . .
Imagine her in this picture perfect Parisian creation that reveals all her alluring charms. Daringly styled with a vanishing back and cut-away midrif above the hugging waistband. She'll thrill to the luxury of this wispy film of oh-so-sheer "silken" rayon with a curve-clinging top of window pane lace. It's black as a bottomless pit . . . bewitching as a starlit night. Bring that vision to life as you win her fervent love with this gift she'll treasure for years.
$7.95

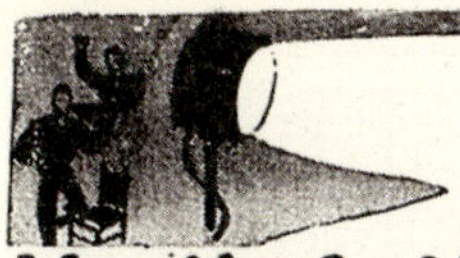

New! Saucy! Tantalizing!

Mystic Action HOLLYWOOD Pin-Up GLASSES

6 for $1.98 POST PAID

ALL GORGEOUS GALS NO TWO ALIKE

BEVY OF BEAUTIES SHED THEIR CLOTHES BEFORE YOUR VERY EYES

You've heard about "slick chicks" who looked as though they were poured into their clothes. But up 'til now you've never heard of a gal being poured out of her clothes . . . and yet that's just what happens when you fill these amazing glasses with water . . . The pin-up cuties' dresses mysteriously vanish, leaving them standing before you in all their natural beauty . . . and as you empty the glasses the girls' clothes mysteriously reappear. Order your set today. They'll add spice and zest to your parties, and guests will gasp with delight.

WATCH GUESTS' EYES POP WITH ENVY AND DELIGHT!

HOW THEY WORK! An ice cold drink causes moisture to form on outside of glass. As it does the action starts and the girls' clothes begin to fall away magically. Then as the glass dries again, their clothes reappear. A complete transformation is assured each time the glass is filled. No need to turn the glass around. All the fun and action occurs on the outside of the glass. "Fun" satisfaction guaranteed. Rush the coupon!

BRIAR STRATFORD—Dept. Z-46 118 S. Clinton St., Chicago 6, Ill.

YOU'LL BE *The Life of The Party!* with this SPICY HOME BARTENDER'S APRON

$1 POST PAID

★ *Protects Clothes* ★ *Provides Laughs*

Imagine! Only One Dollar Will Insure Your Next Party of Howling Success! When the gang comes to call, assume the role of Jolly Host, and slip into this *spicy* home bartender's apron. It's not only colorful and hilarious, but it also protects your clothes from the inevitable alcohol stains that go with mixing drinks. Send $1.00 for yours today.

★ *Has THREE Handy Pockets* ★ *Washable in Soap and Water*

BRIAR STRATFORD, Dept. Z-46, 118 S. Clinton St., Chicago 6, Ill.

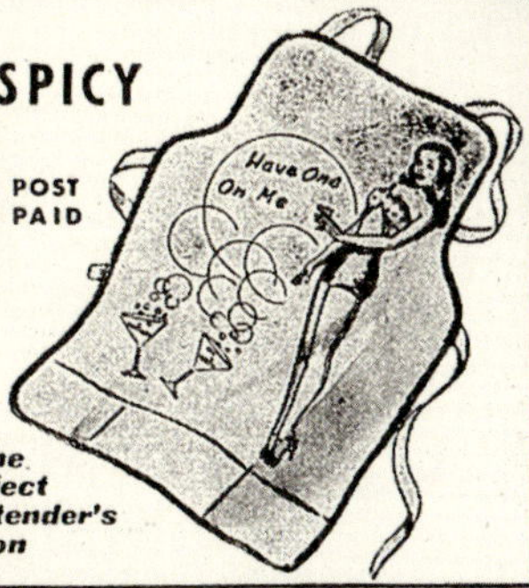

★ *The Perfect Bartender's Apron*

Roll Out The Barrel You'll Have a Barrel of Fun

Ye Olde Fashioned LIQUOR KEG

Only $3.98

Complete with SIX crystal-clear wine glasses

Leads a DOUBLE Life

1 *As a Lovely, Decorative Piece of Furniture*

2 *As a Clever, Useful Drink Dispenser*

Here's the cleverest idea to come along in years. Serves *double* duty as a smartly decorative piece of furniture for your table or mantle and also as a handy "ever-ready" drink dispenser. Keep it filled with liquor and when guests arrive, merely take a glass from the handy rack, turn the spigot, and your drink is delivered swiftly, automatically, and without the unsightly mess caused by a bottle. Order yours *today* at our low price of only $3.98.

BRIAR STRATFORD—Dept. Z-46 118 S. Clinton St., Chicago 6, Ill.

Here's the NEW SENSATIONAL LIGHTER Everyone's Talking About!

TARCO *Electric* CIGARETTE LIGHTER

Personalized With Your Name in 23-Kt. GOLD

For Only $3.98 POST PAID TAX FREE

It's Electric
No Flame
No Flint
No Fluid
No Wick
Just Press the Button
...It Does the Trick

IT'S DECORATIVE...IT'S DESIGNED FOR *Extra* CONVENIENCE

At last, here's a *new* electric post-war flameless lighter for your home and office. It gives you more than the convenience of a flint and wick lighter—much more! You just press the button, touch the cigarette tip to the contact screen—and instantly your favorite smoke is puffing. And when you lift the lid, a fresh supply of cigarettes automatically raises up for easy reach. TARCO is safe, remember! It is flameless. Material cannot ignite unless placed directly on contact screen at same time button is pressed. And TARCO'S handsome walnut-toned plastic case matches your finest furniture. Personalized with your name in gold letters it adds true distinction to your office or to any room. Order one today for home and office.

LOOK AT THESE FEATURES

- ★ Automatic
- ★ Holds Full Pack of Cigarettes
- ★ Lights in a Jiffy
- ★ Lift Lid and Cigarettes Rise Up
- ★ Completely Safe for Home and Office
- ★ Handsome Walnut Plastic Case
- ★ 6 Ft. Cord and Plug
- ★ Works on AC or DC Current

BRIAR STRATFORD—Dept. Z-46, 118 S. Clinton St., Chicago 6, Ill.

MAIL HANDY COUPON NOW

BRIAR STRATFORD, Dept. Z-46, 114-118 S. Clinton Street, Chicago 6, Illinois

Please rush my order for the following items listed below.
If not satisfied I may return them for a complete refund.

Mystic Glasses: **CHECK ITEMS WANTED**

☐ 1 set for $1.98	☐ Bar Apron... ...$1.00
☐ 2 sets for....... 3.95	☐ Tarco Lighter 3.98
☐ 4 sets for....... 7.75	☐ Wine Keg 3.98

Prices in Canada add 50c a set for Glasses—25c ea. for all other items. No C.O.D.'s.

Total Amount of Order $________

CHECK ONE

☐ I am enclosing $________ Send my order POSTPAID.

☐ Send C.O.D. I will pay postman $________ plus postage.

Name________
Please Print Clearly

Address________

City________ Zone____ State________

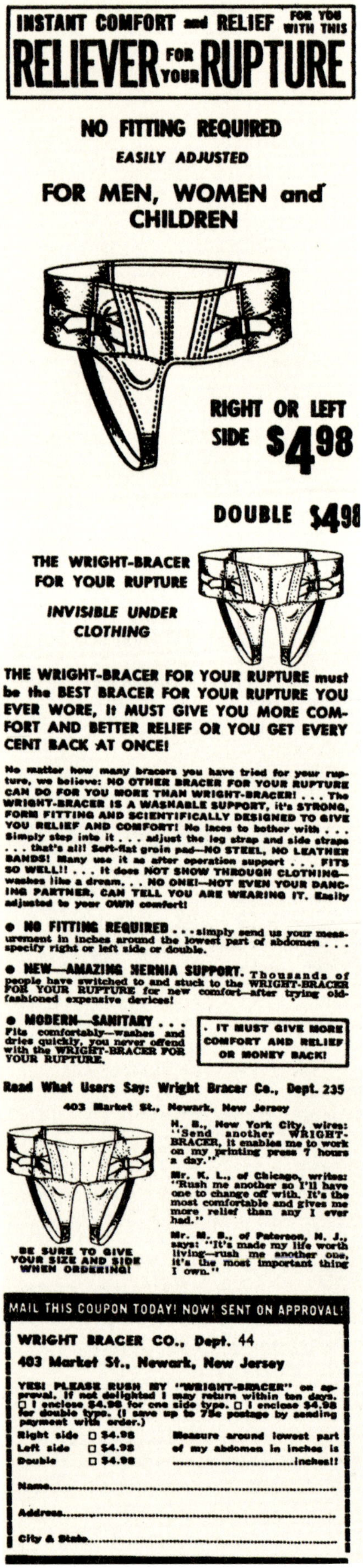
INSTANT COMFORT and RELIEF FOR YOU WITH THIS
RELIEVER FOR YOUR RUPTURE
NO FITTING REQUIRED
EASILY ADJUSTED
FOR MEN, WOMEN and CHILDREN
RIGHT OR LEFT SIDE $4.98
DOUBLE $4.98
THE WRIGHT-BRACER FOR YOUR RUPTURE
INVISIBLE UNDER CLOTHING
THE WRIGHT-BRACER FOR YOUR RUPTURE must be the BEST BRACER FOR YOUR RUPTURE YOU EVER WORE, it MUST GIVE YOU MORE COMFORT AND BETTER RELIEF OR YOU GET EVERY CENT BACK AT ONCE!
No matter how many bracers you have tried for your rupture, we believe: NO OTHER BRACER FOR YOUR RUPTURE CAN DO FOR YOU MORE THAN WRIGHT-BRACER! . . . The WRIGHT-BRACER IS A WASHABLE SUPPORT, it's STRONG, FORM FITTING AND SCIENTIFICALLY DESIGNED TO GIVE YOU RELIEF AND COMFORT! No laces to bother with . . . Simply step into it . . . adjust the leg strap and side straps . . . that's all! Soft-flat groin pad—NO STEEL, NO LEATHER BANDS! Many use it as after operation support . . . FITS SO WELL!! . . . it does NOT SHOW THROUGH CLOTHING—washes like a dream. . . NO ONE!—NOT EVEN YOUR DANCING PARTNER, CAN TELL YOU ARE WEARING IT. Easily adjusted to your OWN comfort!
● NO FITTING REQUIRED . . . simply send us your measurement in inches around the lowest part of abdomen . . . specify right or left side or double.
● NEW—AMAZING HERNIA SUPPORT. Thousands of people have switched to and stuck to the WRIGHT-BRACER FOR YOUR RUPTURE for new comfort—after trying old-fashioned expensive devices!
● MODERN—SANITARY . . . Fits comfortably—washes and dries quickly, you never offend with the WRIGHT-BRACER FOR YOUR RUPTURE.
. IT MUST GIVE MORE COMFORT AND RELIEF OR MONEY BACK!
Read What Users Say: Wright Bracer Co., Dept. 235
403 Market St., Newark, New Jersey
H. B., New York City, wires: "Send another WRIGHT-BRACER, it enables me to work on my printing press 7 hours a day."
Mr. K. L., of Chicago, writes: "Rush me another so I'll have one to change off with. It's the most comfortable and gives me more relief than any I ever had."
Mr. M. S., of Paterson, N. J., says: "It's made my life worth living—rush me another one, it's the most important thing I own."
BE SURE TO GIVE YOUR SIZE AND SIDE WHEN ORDERING!
MAIL THIS COUPON TODAY! NOW! SENT ON APPROVAL!
WRIGHT BRACER CO., Dept. 44
403 Market St., Newark, New Jersey
YES! PLEASE RUSH MY "WRIGHT-BRACER" on approval. If not delighted I may return within ten days. □ I enclose $4.98 for one side type. □ I enclose $4.98 for double type. (I save up to 75c postage by sending payment with order.)
Right side □ $4.98
Left side □ $4.98
Double □ $4.98
Measure around lowest part of my abdomen in inches is ....inches!!
Name
Address
City & State

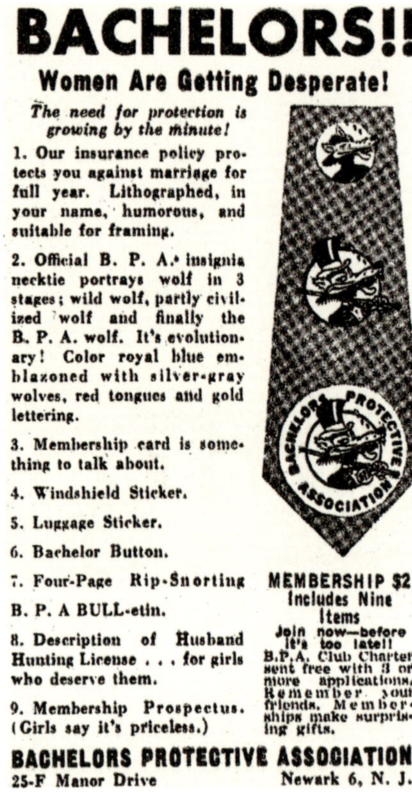
BACHELORS!!
Women Are Getting Desperate!
The need for protection is growing by the minute!
1. Our insurance policy protects you against marriage for full year. Lithographed, in your name, humorous, and suitable for framing.
2. Official B. P. A. insignia necktie portrays wolf in 3 stages; wild wolf, partly civilized wolf and finally the B. P. A. wolf. It's evolutionary! Color royal blue emblazoned with silver-gray wolves, red tongues and gold lettering.
3. Membership card is something to talk about.
4. Windshield Sticker.
5. Luggage Sticker.
6. Bachelor Button.
7. Four-Page Rip-Snorting B. P. A BULL-etin.
8. Description of Husband Hunting License . . . for girls who deserve them.
9. Membership Prospectus. (Girls say it's priceless.)
BACHELORS PROTECTIVE ASSOCIATION
MEMBERSHIP $2
Includes Nine Items
Join now—before it's too late!! B.P.A. Club Charter sent free with 3 or more applications. Remember your friends. Memberships make surprising gifts.
BACHELORS PROTECTIVE ASSOCIATION
25-F Manor Drive
Newark 6, N. J.

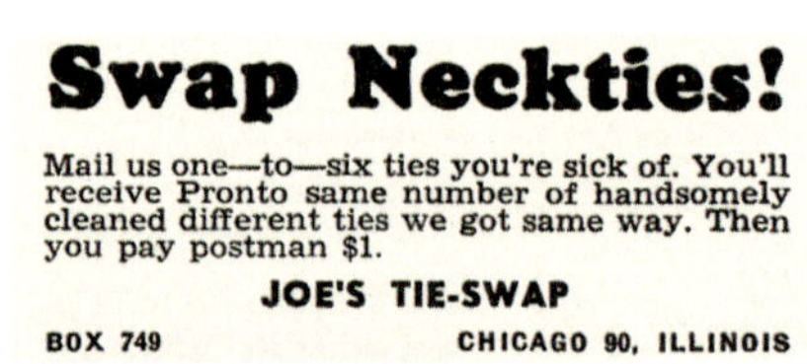
Swap Neckties!
Mail us one—to—six ties you're sick of. You'll receive Pronto same number of handsomely cleaned different ties we got same way. Then you pay postman $1.
JOE'S TIE-SWAP
BOX 749
CHICAGO 90, ILLINOIS

PERSONALIZED HOME BAR
ONLY $5.98
Personally Initialed
It's Portable
For Parties, Gatherings
Basement
This handsome portable Home Bar, personalized with your initials in a striking 3-dimensional contrast, makes it easy to serve guests in style. Made for both indoor and outdoor use. Its handsome contrast of wood grain and gold finish makes for a sparkling setting in the home. Adds class to any party or gathering, and points up the cleverness of its proud owner. And, for relaxing at home, in the parlor, den or basement it's certainly a convenient, handsome addition. Only $5.98. Comparable in satisfaction and utility to bars selling for $30. A perfect gift for any occasion.
10 DAY FREE TRIAL
Order today! If not delighted return for refund. Because of its large size we are forced to ask for 63¢ shipping charges.
FEATURES
• Personalized With Your Initials
• It's Portable—Sets Up Indoors Or Out
• Built-in Shelf Holds Full Party Supplies
• Stain Resistant Bar Top
It's Big—39" wide, 38" high, 13" deep
Sturdily built of aluminum laminated and wood grain finished Multi Flute Fibreboard, this handsome personalized Home Bar is resistant to alcohol and soda stains. Handy built-in shelf holds full supply of bottles, glasses and napkins. Full size bar top holds drinks, pretzels, chips, etc. Sets up in a jiffy and folds compact for easy storage. A beauty for your home, and a novel gift. State initials desired with each order.
MONEY BACK GUARANTEE
S. J. Wegman Co., Dept. BR-6
LYNBROOK, NEW YORK
Rush my new personalized portable Home Bar at once. If I am not delighted I may return it after ten days Free Trial for prompt refund of full purchase price.
□ Send C.O.D. I will pay postman on delivery plus C.O.D. shipping charges.
□ I enclose $5.98 plus shipping charges.
NAME
ADDRESS
MY INITIALS ARE

GENUINE STUFFED ALLIGATOR
ONLY $1.98
2 FT. LONG — BEAUTIFULLY PRESERVED
MONEY BACK GUARANTEE

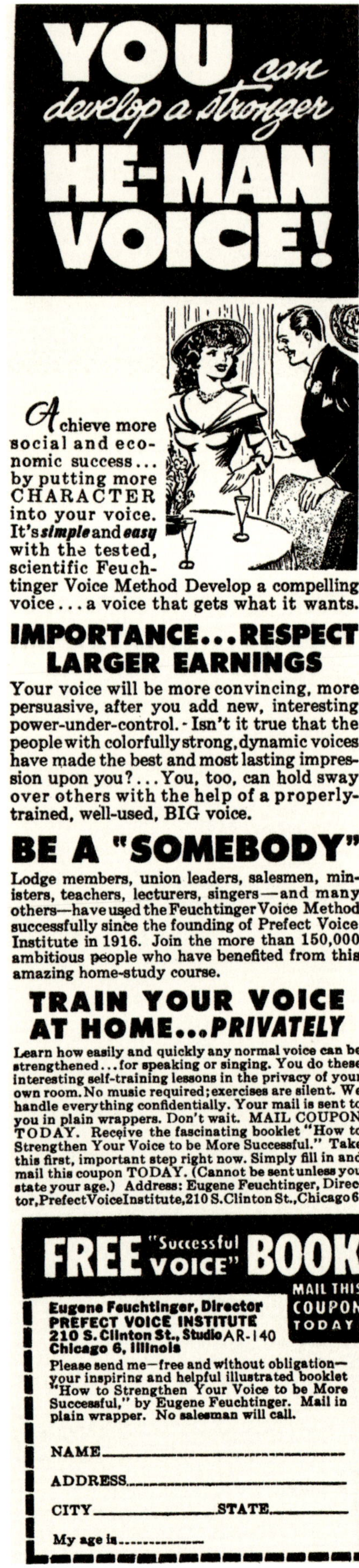
YOU can develop a stronger HE-MAN VOICE!
Achieve more social and economic success . . . by putting more CHARACTER into your voice. It's simple and easy with the tested, scientific Feuchtinger Voice Method Develop a compelling voice . . . a voice that gets what it wants.
IMPORTANCE . . . RESPECT
LARGER EARNINGS
Your voice will be more convincing, more persuasive, after you add new, interesting power-under-control. Isn't it true that the people with colorfully strong, dynamic voices have made the best and most lasting impression upon you? . . . You, too, can hold sway over others with the help of a properly-trained, well-used, BIG voice.
BE A "SOMEBODY"
Lodge members, union leaders, salesmen, ministers, teachers, lecturers, singers—and many others—have used the Feuchtinger Voice Method successfully since the founding of Prefect Voice Institute in 1916. Join the more than 150,000 ambitious people who have benefited from this amazing home-study course.
TRAIN YOUR VOICE AT HOME . . . PRIVATELY
Learn how easily and quickly any normal voice can be strengthened . . . for speaking or singing. You do these interesting self-training lessons in the privacy of your own room. No music required; exercises are silent. We handle everything confidentially. Your mail is sent to you in plain wrappers. Don't wait. MAIL COUPON TODAY. Receive the fascinating booklet "How to Strengthen Your Voice to be More Successful." Take this first, important step right now. Simply fill in and mail this coupon TODAY. (Cannot be sent unless you state your age.) Address: Eugene Feuchtinger, Director, Prefect Voice Institute, 210 S. Clinton St., Chicago 6.
FREE "Successful Voice" BOOK
MAIL THIS COUPON TODAY!
Eugene Feuchtinger, Director
PREFECT VOICE INSTITUTE
210 S. Clinton St., Studio AR-140
Chicago 6, Illinois
Please send me—free and without obligation—your inspiring and helpful illustrated booklet "How to Strengthen Your Voice to be More Successful," by Eugene Feuchtinger. Mail in plain wrapper. No salesman will call.
NAME
ADDRESS
CITY
STATE
My age is

NEW "Pull-Chain" ASH-TRAY & CIGARETTE BOX

$2.98

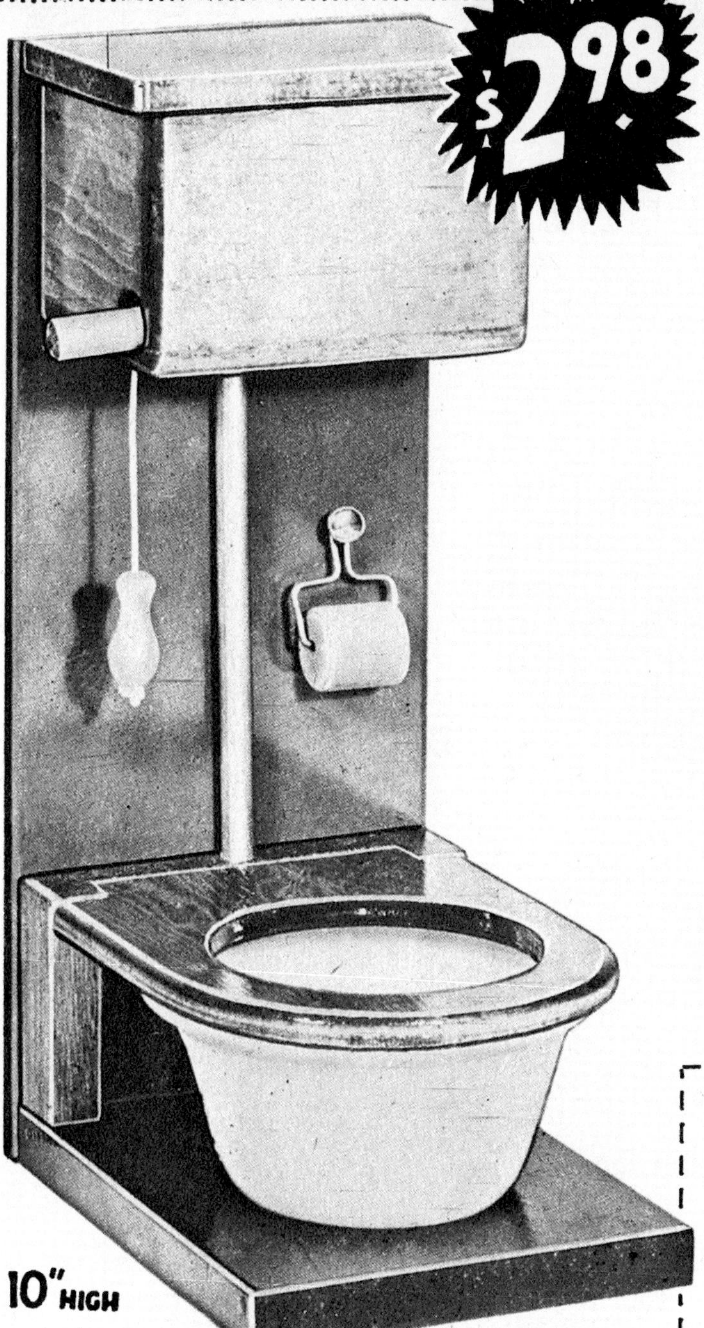

Pull The Chain and Out Pops Your Cigarette

Here's a novelty that will get a laugh . . . everyone will get a thrill when you pull the chain and out comes a cigarette. This novel cigarette dispenser holds plenty of cigarettes and the bowl on the bottom is a deep ash tray which is removable for emptying and cleaning. The picture shows you what a cute and sensational novelty this is . . . at a glance you can see what a laugh it will get from anyone.

EVERY HOME Should HAVE ONE

At first sight, this cigarette dispenser and ash tray looks like a miniature 'privy.' Fools your friends. Pull the chain and instead of a splash out pops a cigarette.

IT'S IDEAL·IT'S PRACTICAL for Den, Office, Bar or Home

This cigarette dispenser and ash tray is beautifully made of wood, stained in an attractive color, with a solid black wooden base. Substantially constructed throughout.

Fully Guaranteed

You take no risk . . . the cigarette dispenser and ash tray is fully guaranteed. You must be 100% delighted or you may return for full refund of purchase price within 5 days.

5th AV. MDSE. MART, Inc., Dept. DM51
150 Nassau Street, New York 7, N. Y.

5th AV. MDSE. MART, Inc., Dept. DM51
150 Nassau Street, New York 7, N. Y.

Please send me my "Pull-Chain" Cigarette Box and Ash Tray. Enclosed find $2.98 in ☐ money-order, ☐ check, or send ☐ C.O.D. I agree to pay extra postage and C.O.D. charges. If I am not satisfied, I may return within 5 days and my money will be refunded.

Name ....

Street ....

City .... Zone .... State ....

what makes a man... a MAN?

The last time you stood nude in front of a mirror, did you like the man you saw there? Was he Vital? Impressive? Magnetic? Was he the kind of man people notice and admire? If not, stop and take stock!
WHAT HAPPENED TO THE MAN YOU WERE?
What happened to: That wonderful feeling of Sexual Power? That brisk pace?
That confidence in your Manhood?

GET BACK YOUR LUST FOR LIFE!

It isn't really gone . . . it still glows deep within you, waiting for you to set it free. You can LOOK alive . . . FEEL alive . . . BE alive . . . **if you are shown how. AND ALL IT TAKES IS FIVE MINUTES A DAY!** YOU DON'T HAVE TO LOSE THE ZEST OF THE MAN THAT WAS. You can bring him back in all his youthful vigor. NOW . . . before another day passes . . . another day of physical weariness and mental fatigue . . . let me show you how. Begin now to add LIVING to your LIFE . . . enjoy new drives, new interests, new desires . . . rekindle the sexual flame . . . become the man you were, **BE THE MAN YOU WANT TO BE!**

NOW YOU CAN BE THE MAN "SHE" ALWAYS WANTED!

Do you feel that you are cheating "Her" just a little . . . because you aren't quite the healthy, vigorous, potent fellow she fell in love with? Don't compromise with life . . . and don't make "Her" compromise. I won't guarantee to turn you into a "Mr. America"; I won't promise you the bulging muscles of a Hercules . . . BUT I DO PROMISE YOU . . . truthfully and unconditionally . . . that in only thirty days you can put "the boy that used to be" back into the "man that is"! I PROMISE THIS . . . **OR YOUR MONEY BACK.** And I'll bet that thirty days from now the letter you write will be one of thanks . . . thanks for the new life you've found and the fun you're having just being ALIVE!

You, Too, Can Vibrate with Manhood!

THIS IS WHAT YOU GET:

- An album of miracle recordings that tells you how to be **DYNAMIC . . . VIBRANT . . . POTENT.**
- An exciting illustrated manual **FREE** that shows you "What Makes a Man . . . **a MAN.**"
- Money-back guarantee. An unconditional guarantee that if you are not a better male within thirty days . . . if your potency as a man hasn't doubled . . . return the album and your money will be immediately refunded.

WHAT YOU DO:

- Give just five short minutes a day to following the instructions in this miracle recording.
- Get rid of drugs . . . tranquilizing pills . . . "pep" pills, diets, and strenuous exercising that can be more **harmful** than **beneficial.**

WHAT YOU CAN EXPECT:

- New sex drives . . . more energy . . . a clearer mind
- Added years to your life . . . happy, potent, vibrant years.
- A return of the confidence of youth.

MAIL COUPON TODAY!

30-DAY *FREE* TRIAL OFFER

C. & L. INSTITUTE, Suite 302
7015 Sunset Blvd., Los Angeles 28, Calif.

☐ Enclosed is $1.00 deposit. Send my album "HOW TO BE A POTENT MALE." I will pay balance of $4.00 plus postage upon delivery. If not completely satisfied, I will return the album within 30 days for refund.
☐ Enclosed is $5.00. Send the album post-paid. Same absolute money-back guarantee.

NAME ____________________

ADDRESS ____________________

CITY ____________ ZONE ____ STATE ________

☐ With my order, BE SURE TO INCLUDE THE **FREE** MANUAL, "What Makes a Man . . . A Man?", which I may keep even if I return the album for refund.

An Amazing Invention—"Magic Art Reproducer"

DRAW The First Day

NO LESSONS! NO TALENT!

Anyone can Draw With This Amazing New Invention— Instantly!

You Can Draw Your Family, Friends, Anything From REAL LIFE— Like An Artist... Even if You CAN'T DRAW A Straight Line!

De Luxe Model Complete for only

$1.98

—With extra high power, extra clear and sharp "reproducer" unit.

A New Hobby Gives You A Brand New Interest!

Yes, anyone from 5 to 80 can draw or sketch or paint anything now ... the very first time you use the "Magic Art Reproducer" like a professional artist—no matter how "hopeless" you think you are! An unlimited variety and amount of drawings can be made. Art is admired and respected by everyone. Most hobbies are expensive, but drawing costs very little, just some inexpensive paper, pencils, crayons, or paint. No costly upkeep, nothing to wear out, no parts to replace. It automatically reproduces anything you want to draw on any sheet of paper. Then easily and quickly follow the lines of the "picture image" with your pencil ... and you have an accurate original drawing that anyone would think an artist had done. No guesswork, no judging sizes and shapes! Reproduces black and white and actual colors for paintings.

Also makes drawing larger or smaller as you wish.

Anyone can use it on any desk, table, board, etc.—indoors or outdoors! Light and compact to be taken wherever you wish. No other lessons or practice or talent needed! You'll be proud to frame your original drawings for a more distinctive touch to your home. Give them to friends as gifts that are "different," appreciated.

Have fun! Be popular! Everyone will ask you to draw them. You'll be in demand! After a short time, you may find you can draw well without the "Magic Art Reproducer" because you have developed a "knack" and feeling artists have—which may lead to a good paying art career.

ALSO EXCELLENT FOR EVERY OTHER TYPE OF DRAWING AND HOBBY!

Create Your Own Design for All Hobbies! Reproduce on anything.

Copy all cartoons, comics.

Outdoor Scenes, landscapes, buildings

Copy photos, portraits of family, friends, etc.

Still life, vases, bowls of fruit, lamps, furniture, all objects.

Copy blueprints, plans.

FREE!

"How to Easily Draw Artists' Models"

This valuable illustrated guide is yours free with order of "Magic Art Reproducer." Packed with pictures showing all the basic poses of artists' models with simple instruction for beginners of art. Includes guidance on anatomy, techniques and figure action.

SEND NO MONEY!

Free 10-Day Trial!

Just send name and address. Pay postman on delivery $1.98 plus postage. Or send only $1.98 with order and we pay postage. You must be convinced that you can draw anything like an artist, or return merchandise after 10-day trial and your money will be refunded.

NORTON PRODUCTS Dept. MTM-12A, 296 Broadway New York 7, N. Y.

FREE 10-DAY TRIAL COUPON

NORTON PRODUCTS, Dept. MTM-12A
296 Broadway, New York 7, N. Y.

Rush my "Magic Art Reproducer" plus FREE illustrated guide "*How to Easily Draw Artists' Models.*" I will pay postman on delivery only $1.98 plus postage. I must be convinced that I can draw anything like an artist, or I can return merchandise after 10-day trial and get my money back.

Name ....

Address ....

City & Zone .... State ....

☐ Check here if you wish to save postage by sending only $1.98 with coupon. Same Money Back Guarantee!

How Many Times Have You Lost Your Chance For Dates

because pimples, blackheads, acne or eczema, externally caused, spoil your looks?

No fun being passed up *all* the time. Maybe you wouldn't if you'd take this pimple, blackhead and blemish problem seriously. Hundreds and thousands of lucky boys and girls have already proved what *you* ought to do . . . let the sensationally successful KLEEREX be your "fairy queen with the magic wand" that gives you the nice looking complexion you want.

KLEEREX is so astounding in its results . . . so quick . . . in clearing up external evidence of pimples, blackheads, acne and eczema rash that you'll be amazed. Often overnight you can see a clearer, softer, smoother complexion as it should be naturally. . . . See yourself more like you want to look. The proof is so overwhelming that the makers offer you *double your money back* if you are not 100% satisfied.

KLEEREX is no smelly ointment, no greasy salve. You brush it over the blemishes. It hides them as it dries them. *More than a million bottles have already been sold*—That's *amazing*. How could anyone bothered with fun-spoiling blemishes put up with them another day after hearing *that?* Don't delay. Mail the coupon right now for special introductory offer of 2 bottles.

KLEEREX CO., Dept.177-SS 2005 S. Michigan, Chicago 16, Ill.

Send No Money—MAIL COUPON

Upon arrival of package, pay postman only $1.00 plus postage. (Cash orders, sent postpaid.) Remember! If you are not thrilled with the different appearance of your skin, return package and get DOUBLE your money back. Mail coupon NOW.

RUSH THIS SPECIAL INTRODUCTORY OFFER COUPON TODAY SURE!

KLEEREX CO., Dept. 177SS
2005 S. Michigan Ave., Chicago 16, Ill.
I want to test KLEEREX to help clear up pimples, acne itch (externally caused). I'll pay postman $1.00 plus C. O. D. postage on arrival with understanding that I may return package for DOUBLE MY MONEY BACK if not satisfied. ($1.00 enclosed with coupon and you pay postage.)

Name...

Address...

City........................ *Zone*.... *State*.........

BLACKHEADS "PET HATE"

Say Men, Girls in Choosing Date

What a "black mark" is the blackhead . . . according to men and girls popular enough to be choosy about dates!

"Nobody's dreamboat!" "Nobody's date bait!" And that's not all that's said of those who are careless about blackheads. But blackheads ARE ugly! Blackheads ARE grimy! And they DON'T look good in close-ups!

So can you blame the fellow who says, "Sure, I meet lots of girls who look cute at first glance. But if, on that second glance, I see dingy blackheads, it's *good night!*"

Or can you blame the girl who confesses, "I hate to go out with a fellow who has blackheads. If he's careless about that you're sure he'll embarrass you in other ways, too!"

But you — are YOUR ears burning? Well, you've company and, sad to say, good company. There are lots of otherwise attractive fellows and girls who could date anyone they like if they'd only realize how offensive blackheads are . . . and how easily and quickly they could get rid of them . . . if they *want* to!

"He-Man" Often Guilty of Blackhead Crime

Take your "he-man" . . . super at track, games, sports of all kinds . . . who thinks that after just a shower he's ready to go anywhere! And won't the girls all admire his muscles!

Sure they would! But not many dance floors are set up for hurdle races! You can't show off your snappy left hook when only cokes are in the ring. The "he-man" who's also clean-cut, will get the breaks wherever he is.

Even Cute Girls Become Careless

Easy, too easy, for a girl to think that if she has the latest in clothes and hair-do she needn't bother about blackheads. A little more make-up, she guesses, will take care of that. BUT MAKE-UP WON'T HIDE BLACKHEADS! Not unless it's plaster of paris, maybe! And even good make-up "slips" at a dance! So don't take chances, cute though you may be!

TAKE THESE TIPS TO BANISH BLACKHEADS

Keep skin clean by washing morning and night with warm, almost hot, water. Use good soap and plenty of it. And finish with cool water.

Extract every blackhead as soon as you see it — with a SAFE extractor. Don't use finger nails. Don't squeeze. That may mean infection, injured tissues, a marred skin.

Just be clean! Be quick! And be safe! That's easy! **And that's ALL!**

FELLOWS! GIRLS!
Keep Skin Clear and Clean!

UGLY BLACKHEADS OUT in Seconds with VACUTEX

NEW! SCIENTIFIC! VACUUM ACTION!

Amazing new VACUTEX is painless . . . safe . . . fast! In seconds you are rid of those ugly blackheads that clog the pores . . . make your skin look grimy and dingy . . . give others such a wrong impression of you. VACUTEX creates a gentle vacuum pressure around the blackhead and extracts it — quickly! — without injury to tender skin tissues. Keep skin always clear this new scientific way. Without painful squeezing! Without dangerous infection from germy fingers! Just place VACUTEX over blackhead and draw back extractor. Blackhead's out! Simple! But you'll be delighted by your instantly improved appearance. Others will notice your clearer, cleaner skin! Try VACUTEX — now!

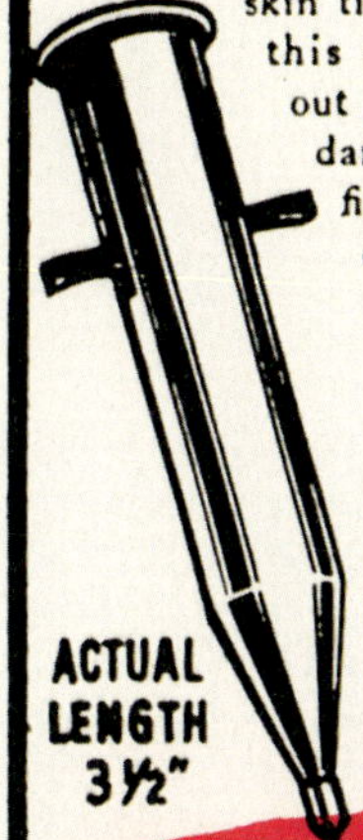

ACTUAL LENGTH 3½"

RUSH COUPON NOW!

No Squeezing
No Infection
No Injury to Skin Tissues!

Just place VACUTEX over blackhead — release extractor — and blackhead's out!

10 DAY TRIAL OFFER

Don't send a penny. Mail coupon and pay postman only $1.00 plus postage. Or save all postage by enclosing $1 with guarantee coupon. If not thrilled to be rid of embarrassing hated blackheads this new quick way — just return VACUTEX in 10 days and get $1 back. Order today!

10 DAY TRIAL GUARANTEE

BALLCO PRODUCTS COMPANY, Dept. 7
19 West 44th St., New York 18, N. Y.

☐ Enclosed find $1.00. Send me VACUTEX postpaid.
☐ Ship C.O.D. I will pay postman $1.00 plus postage.
My dollar will be refunded if I am not delighted.

NAME ____________________

ADDRESS ____________________

SORRY NO C.O.D. OUTSIDE OF U.S.A.

Bibliography

VOLUME II

A listing of every magazine in this volume by chapter, including month and year issued, volume (V), number (N), frequency, publishing company, country of origin and publisher/editor, where known. Note that many men's magazines included little or none of this information to protect the publisher from harassment or arrest, or simply because publishers didn't consider this information vital to its readership.

Cover:
Modern Man October 1959, V8N16-100, monthly, Publisher's Development, USA. Publisher–George E. von Rosen

Timeline
of History with Men's Magazines

Ace June 1958, V2N1, bi-monthly, Four Star Publications, USA. Editor—Ted Gottfried
Ace October 1958, V2N3, as above
Adam April 1953, V1N2, bimonthly, Fawcett Publications, USA. Publisher—W.H. Fawcett Jr., Editor—Ralph Daigh
Bachelor May 1957, V2N3, monthly, Official Magazine, USA. Editor—Bruce J. Friedman
Bare November 1954, V2N5, monthly, D&L Publishing, USA
Bits of Beauty Mar/April 1947, V1N5, bi-monthly, Bits of Beauty, USA
Caper March 1959, V5N2, bi-monthly, Humor Magazines, USA. Editor—Douglas Allen
Carnival Spring Special 1956, Gannet Press, England
C'est Paris November 1950, N904, France
C'est Paris April 1951, N909, as above
Dazzle 1957, V1N1, bi-monthly, Playgirl Publishing, USA. Editor—Walter Hale
The Dude May 1959, V3N5, bi-monthly, Mystery Publishing, USA. Editor—Bruce Elliott
Escape into Bondage, 1950s, Burmel Publishing, USA
Eyeful February 1955, bimonthly, Eyeful Magazine, USA. Publisher—Robert Harrison
Frolic October 1958, V8N2, bi-monthly, Frolic Magazine, USA
Gent September 1957, bi-monthly, Excellent Publications, USA. Editor—James H. Holmes
He March 1956, V2N9, monthly, HE Publications, USA. Editor—Ted Gottfried
Hi-Life June 1958, V1N2, bi-monthly, Wilmot Enterprises, 50 E. 42nd St, New York, NY, Publisher/Editor—Chad Kelly
La Vie Parisienne July 1958, V95N91, monthly, Societe Parisienne d-Imprimerie, France. Editor—A. Rayez
Man To Man 1957 Spring Annual, Picture Magazines, USA. Editor—W.W. Scott
Monsieur October 1957, V1N4, monthly, Monsieur Publications, USA
Paris Life June 1952, V1N6, bi-monthly, Paris Life, USA. Editor—Eugene Tillinger
Rave August 1956, V2N5, bi-monthly, Rave Publishing, USA. Editor—Peter Hamilton
Rogue April 1956, V1N3, bi-monthly, Greenleaf Publishing, USA. Editor—William L. Hamling
Scamp May 1957, V1N1, bi-monthly, Splendid Publications, USA. Editor—Roger Roden
Scamp May 1959, V2N6, as above except, Editor—Ted Gottfried
Sir! September 1956, V5N12, monthly, Volitant Publishing, USA. Publisher/Editor--Adrian B. Lopez
Sir Knight 1958, V1N5, bi-monthly, Sirkay Publishing, USA
Submission in Leather 1958, Burmel Publishing, USA
Swank March 1958, V5N2, monthly, Male Publishing, USA. Publisher—Martin Goodman, Editor—Bruce J. Friedman
Whisper January 1953, V6N4, bi-monthly, Whisper, USA. Publisher—Robert Harrison, Editor—Nils Larsen
Wink April 1955, V10N5, bi-monthly, Wink, USA. Publisher—Robert Harrison, Editor—Harry Roberts

Chapter 1
Robert Harrison's Whirl of Girls

Beauty Parade July 1953, V12N2, bi-monthly, Beauty Parade, USA. Editor—L. Bennett
Beauty Parade April 1955, V14N2, bi-monthly, Beauty Parade, USA. Editor—L. Bennett
Beauty Parade August 1955, V14N4, as above
Beauty Parade October 1955, V14N5, as above
Confidential August 1953, V1N4, bi-monthly, Confidential, USA. Editor—Richard Atkins
Confidential January 1966, V14N1, monthly, By-Line Publications, USA. Editor- Carl King
Eyeful June 1946, V3N1, bi-monthly, Eyeful Publications, USA
Eyeful June 1948, V4N6, bi-monthly, Eyeful Magazine, USA
Flirt August 1952, V5N4, bi-monthly, Flirt Magazine, USA. Editor—Frank Bailey
Flirt April 1952, V5N2, as above
Flirt June 1954, V7N3, as above
Flirt December 1954, V7N6, bi-monthly, Flirt, USA. Editor—Frank Bailey
Titter August 1952, V9N1, bi-monthly, Titter, USA. Editor—Roy Harmon
Wink October 1946, V2N3, bi-monthly, Wink, USA. Editor—Harry Roberts
Wink October 1947, V3N2, as above
Wink May 1949, V4N6, as above
Wink February 1954, V9N4, as above
Whisper July 1950, V4N1, bi-monthly, Whisper, USA. Editor—Nils Larsen
Whisper July 1953, V7N1, as above
Whisper November 1954, V8N3, as above

Chapter 2
Celebrity Sin: The Scandal Magazines

Bare June 1955, V2N12, D&L Publishing, USA
Confidential September 1955, V3N4, bi-monthly, Confidential, USA. Editor—Howard Rushmore
Crime Confessions October 1956, V12N3, bi-monthly, Skye Publishing, USA. Editor—Bill Guy
Glance February 1959, bi-monthly, Cape Magazine Management, USA
Hollywood Confidential 1957, V2N7, Playgirl Publishing, USA. Publisher/Editor—Walter Hale
The Lowdown April 1959, V4N6, quarterly, Design Publishing, USA. Editor—Joel Raleigh
The Male Cry combined with Hollywood Confidential 1950s, V2N9, Playgirl Publishing, USA. Publisher/Editor—Walter Hale
Manhattan Scandals 1940s, N4, USA
Man To Man May 1954, V5N2, monthly, Picture Magazines, USA. Editor—W.W. Scott
Man To Man July 1954, V5N4, as above
Playgirl 1956, V1N3, Playgirl Publishing, USA. Publisher/Editor—Walter Hale
Playgirl 1956, V1N4, as above
Rave March 1956, V2N3, bi-monthly, Rave Publishing, USA. Editor—Peter Hamilton
San Francisco Confidential 1955, V1N1, Dramatic Publishing, USA. Publisher/Editor—Walter Hale
Scandolls 1959, V1N1, USA. Publisher/Editor—Walter Hale
Shock October 1941, monthly, Shock Magazine, USA
Taboo October 1950, USA

Chapter 3
South of the Border: Argentina and Mexico

Argentina:
Dinamita 1956, Argentina
Dinamita 1956, Argentina
Dinamita 1956, Argentina
Dinamita 1956, Argentina
Dinamita 1959, Argentina
Heliópolis February 1938, V2N3, Argentina
Pobre Diablo 1954, N431, weekly, Argentina
Pobre Diablo 1954, N443, as above
Pobre Diablo 1954, N464, as above
Pobre Diablo 1955, as above
Ricuritas 1955, V2N50, Argentina
Ricuritas 1956, V3N66, as above
Ricuritas May 1957, V1N61, as above
Vida Nocturna 1929, V1N1, Argentina

Mexico:
VEA March 10 1939, weekly, Mexico,. Editor—Florian de Oropeza
VEA 1939, as above
VEA December 29 1944, as above
VEA 1944, as above
VEA February 23 1945, as above
VEA March 22 1952, N384, Mexico
VEA 1955, N531, Mexico
Vodevil July 1954, V2N55, Mexico
Vodevil February 1955, N82, Mexico

Chapter 4
John Willie: A Most Bizarre Life

Bizarre January 1946, N2, (actually the first issue) Bizarre Publishing, Canada. Editor—John Willie
Bizarre 1946, N1, (actually the second issue), as above
Bizarre 1946, N3, as above
Bizarre 1946, N4, as above, Canada
Bizarre 1946, N5, as above
Bizarre 1946, N7, as above, Canada
Bizarre 1953, N12, as above
Bizarre 1953, N13, as above
Bizarre 1955, N15/16, as above
Bizarre 1956, N17, as above
Bizarre 1956, N19, as above
Bizarre 1959, N26, as above

Chapter 5
Lenny Burtman: A Yearning for the Exotique

Connoisseur 1950s, N2, Selbee Associates, USA
Extatique 1950s, N3, Tele-Photo Publishing, USA
Exotique 1950s, N3, Burmel Publishing, USA
Exotique 1950s, N5, as above
Exotique 1950s, N8, as above
Exotique 1957, N10, as above
Exotique 1950s, N11, as above
Exotique 1950s, N14, as above
Exotique 1950s, N17, as above
Exotique 1950s, N19, as above
Exotique 1950s, N22, as above
Exotique 1950s, N23, as above
Exotique 1950s, N27, as above
Exotique 1950s, N30, as above
Exotique Photo Album 1950s, #3, as above
Fads and Fancies 1949, N6, Utopian Press, England
Fantastique 1950s, N1, Sheba Publications, USA
Fantastique 1950s, N6, as above
Guys in Gowns, 1950s, Burmell Publishing, USA
Presenting Bettie Page, an Exotique special, Burmel Publishing, USA
Masque 1950s, N1, Selbee Associates, New York, NY
Masque 1950s, N2, as above
Exotique Imitators:
Fantasia 1959, N15, Fantasy House, USA. Editor—John A. Jensen
Fantasia 1960, N16, bi-monthly, Lucian Press, USA. Editor—John A. Jensen

Chapter 6
England: A Long Climb to the Top Shelf

Breezy 1950s, N15, monthly, Bamboo, England
Can Can 1956, V1N3, monthly, L. Miller & Son, England, Editor—L. Miller
Can Can 1956, V1N5, as above
Can Can 1956, V1N6, as above
Can Can 1957, V1N7, as above
Carnival April 1956, V2N4, Gannet Press, England
Carnival April 1957, V3N4, as above
Continental Keyholes 1950s, N8, England
Continental Kuties 1950s, V1N3, Sylvia J. Gough, England Foto 1950s, N2, Axtell Publications, England
Girly 1950s, N17, K&G Publications, England

Girly 1950s, N51, as above
Ladies 1950s, N6, Ben's Books, England
London Life November 16 1940, bi-weekly, New Picture Press, England
London Opinion May 1945, monthly, George Newnes, England
London Opinion December 1945, as above
Lush 1950s, N7, bi-monthly, Modern Fiction, England
Lush 1950s, as above
Magnifico, a Collection of Figure Studies by Rosalinda 1950s, Rosalinda, England
Mam'selle 1950s, N11, Modern Fiction, England
Mirage 1950s, N10, Swanedge LTD, England
Model 1950s, N2, Concord Publications, England
My!! 1950s, N1, Ben's Books, England
Nimbus 1950s, monthly, Fontessa Publications, England
Nu Look 1950s, N6, M.C.G. Publishing, England
Oh!! 1950s, N1, Ben's Books, England
Paris–Vision 1950s, quarterly, Concord Publications, England
Phyllis In Censorland: Photographs by Roye of Phyllis Dixey 1950s, King-Ganteaume Productions, for The Camera Studies Club, England
Silky 1950s, N7, Ben's Books, England
Spot On! 1950s, V1N12, monthly, Hilldon Publications, England
Spot On! 1950s, V2N3, as above
Stag May 1958, V1N5, Pennine Publications, England
X for Men 1959, N6, Warlock Enterprises, England

Chapter 7
The Old Bump and Grind: Post-War, Pre-*Playboy*

Cavalcade of Burlesque Winter 1951, V1N2, quarterly, Burlesque Historical Society, USA. Editor—George Nonamaker
Cavalcade of Burlesque September 1954, V3N4, as above
Cover Girls Models April 1954, V11N12, bi-monthly, Models Publishing, USA. Editor—Peter Goodwin
Follies January 1951, V1N2, bi-monthly, Graphic Magazines, USA
Frolic June 1954, V3N6, bi-monthly, Frolic Magazine, USA. Editor—Luke Bailey
Gala January 1954, V4N5, bi-monthly, Gala Magazine, USA
Gala November 1954, V5N4, as above
Glamorous Models June 1949, V4N2, monthly, Models Publishing, USA. Editor—George Waller, Jr.
Hit! May/June 1952, V8N7, bi-monthly, Volitant Publishing, USA. Editor—Adrian B. Lopez
Hit! November 1952, V8N10, as above
Modern Man November 1954, monthly, Camerarts Publishing, USA. Publisher—George E. von Rosen, Editor—Ben Burns
Night and Day November 1954, V6N10, monthly, Halho Corporation, USA. Editor—A. Lawrence Holmes
Night and Day January 1955, V6N12, as above
Paris Life (American Edition of ***La Vie Parisienne***) Jan/Feb 1952, V1N4, USA. Editor—Eugene Tillinger
Paris Life March/April 1952, V1N5, as above
Paris Life May/June 1952, V1N6, as above
Paris Life Sep/Oct 1952, V1N8, as above
Paris Models December 1952, bi-monthly, Picture Magazines, USA. Editor—Claire Huffaker
Peek March 1948, bi-monthly, Ideal Publishing, USA
Peep Show Winter 1950, V1N1, bi-monthly, Capitol Stories, USA. Editor—Arthur Kass
Picture Show February 1948, monthly, Picture Magazines, USA. Editor—Ana Maher
Picture Show March 1948, as above
Showgirls May 1947, V1N2, bi-monthly, Your Guide Publications, USA. Editor—Eric Gordon
Showgirls September 1947, V1N4, as above
Swagger Jan 1951, V1N1, bi-monthly, Swagger Publications, USA
Wolf Bait 1952, P.A.D. Publications, USA

Chapter 8
Hugh Hefner: Playboy of the Western World

Playboy December 1953, V1N1, USA. Publisher/Editor—Hugh M. Hefner
Playboy January 1954, V2N1, monthly, Playboy Publishing, as above
Playboy February 1955, V3N2, as above
Playboy October 1956, V4N10, as above
Playboy March 1957, V4N3, as above
Playboy August 1957, V5N8, as above
Playboy April 1961, V8N5, as above
Playboy May 1963, V10N5, as above
Playboy July 1964, V11N7, as above
Playboy December 1967, V14N12, as above
Playboy July 1969, V15N7, as above
Playboy September 1969, V15N9, as above
Playboy April 1970, V17N4, as above
Playboy June 1970, V17N6, as above
Playboy August 1971, V18N8, as above
Playboy October 1971, V18N10, as above
Playboy November 1976, V23N11, as above
Playboy May 1979, V26N5, as above
Esquire September 1937, V8N3, monthly, Esquire-Coronet Inc., USA. Publisher—David A. Smart, Editor—Arnold Gingrich
Esquire February 1941, V15N2, as above
Esquire March 1941, V15N3, as above
Esquire November 1942, V16N11, as above
Esquire Christmas 1943, V17N12, as above
Esquire February 1953, V39N2, as above except Publisher—Arnold Gingrich, Editor—Frederic A. Birmingham
Esquire March 1953, V39N2, as above

Chapter 9
"For the Articles": Men's Magazines and Literature

Bachelor September 1961, V3N1, quarterly, Magtab Publishing, USA. Editor—Ted Gottfried
Caper May 1963, V9N3, bi-monthly, Topical Magazines, USA. Editor—Chester Krone
Cavalcade December 1961, V4N4, bi-monthly, Skye Publishing, USA
Cavalier July 1959, V8N73, monthly, Fawcett Publications, USA. Editor—Ralph Daigh
Cavalier July 1962, V12B109, monthly, Fawcett Publications, USA. Editor—Frederic A. Birmingham
Cavalier October 1962, V12N112, as above
The Dude March 1957, V1N4, bi-monthly, Mystery Publications, USA. Editor—James Holmes
The Dude September 1957, V1N10, as above
The Dude January 1958, V2N1, as above
The Dude September 1959, V4N2, as above
The Dude March 1962, V6N4, bi-monthly, Mystery Publications, USA. Editor—Nat Lehrman
Escapade April 1960, V5N3, bi-monthly, Bruce Publishing, USA. Editor—Douglas Allen
Gent December 1956, V1N2, bi-monthly, Excellent Publications, USA. Editor—James H. Holmes
Gent June 1959, V3N5, as above except, Editor—Bruce Elliot
Gent August 1960, V4N6, as above
Gent April 1962, V6N4, as above except, Editor—Nat Lehrman

Nugget May 1956, V1N3, monthly, Nugget Magazine, USA. Publisher/Editor—Michael St. John
Nugget June 1957, V2N5, as above
Nugget December 1959, V4N6, as above except, Flying Eagle Publications
Nugget February 1960, V5N1, as above
Nugget December 1961, V6N6, as above
Nugget April 1962, V7N2, as above
Nugget June 1963, V8N3, as above
Rogue December 1959, V4N9, monthly, Greenleaf Publishing, USA. Publisher/Editor—William L. Hamling
Rogue July 1961, V6N7, as above
Rogue July 1961, V6N7, as above
Rogue August 1961, V6N8, as above
Rogue October 1961, V6N10, as above
Rogue January 1962, V7N1, as above
Swank February 1957, V4N1, monthly, Male Publishing, USA. Publisher—Martin Goodman, Editor—Bruce J. Friedman
Swank January 1961, V7N12, as above

Chapter 10

News and Nudes: The Sleazy Pulp Digests

Behind The Scene June 1955, V1N7, JB Publishing, USA. Editor—William Woolfolk
Bold September 1954, V1N9, Pocket Magazines, USA. Editor—Robert W. Marks
Brief May 1956, V4N3, Male Publishing, USA. Editor—James Collier
Celebrity May 1955, V3N2, monthly, Magnum Publications, USA
Foto-Rama January 1959, V6N3, bi-monthly, Arena Publishing, USA. Editor—Myron Fass
He August1954, monthly, HE Publications, USA. Editor—Milt Machlin
He September 1954, as above
He October 1954, as above
Male Life December 1955, V4N2, monthly, Magnum Publications, USA
Male Life February 1956, V4N4, as above
The Most August 1955, N1, bi-monthly, Minoan Publishing, USA
People Today July 15,1953, bi-weekly, Hillman Periodicals, USA
People Today November 18, 1953, as above
People Today December 16, 1953, as above
Photo Life March 1960, V7N1, bi-monthly, Lux Publications, USA. Editor—Norym Shaf
Picture Digest April 1956, V29N5, bi-monthly, Plaza Digest, USA. Publisher—Allen Stearns
Quick February 1955, V1N3, monthly, Handicraft Publications, USA
Rave June 1953, V1N2, bi-monthly, Rave Publishing, USA. Publisher/Editor—Victor Huntington Howland
Rave April 1954, V1N5, as above
Rave January 1955, V1N9, as above
Rave May 1955, V1N11, as above
Scoop! April 1954, V2N4, monthly, Candid Magazines, USA. Editor—Everett Meyers
Sensation December 1954, V1N9, monthly, Medallion Publishing, USA. Editor—James A. Bryons
She April 1958, V2N2, monthly, Cape Magazine Management, USA. Editor—Charles Sigmund
Show December 1953, V2N4, monthly, Show Magazine, USA
Slick February 1957, V6N2, monthly, Magnum Publications, USA
Tell July 1954, V2N5, monthly, Candid Magazines, USA. Editor—Everett Meyers
Tempo April 5, 1954, weekly, USA
Tempo April 12, 1954, as above
Tempo, April 26, 1954, as above
Tempo May 10, 1954, as above

Chapter 11

Rabbit and Strippers Neck and Neck: The Race to the 60s

21 January 1957, V3N3, monthly, Monogram Publications, USA. Editor—Maurice Schindler
21 August 1957, V3N11, as above
21 February 1959, V5N5, as above
Adam 1958, V2N2, monthly, Knight Publishing, USA. Editor—Lothar Ashley
After Dark December 1950s, V1N1, monthly, After Dark Publications, USA. Editor—Alex Ander
Cabaret September 1956, V2N3, Publisher's Development, USA. Publisher-- George E. von Rosen
Cabaret November 1956, V2N5, as above
Cabaret March 1957, V2N11, as above
Cabaret July 1957, V3N2, as above
Cabaret Yearbook 1956, V1, annual, as above
Caper December 1956, V1N3, monthly, Dee Publishing, USA. Publisher/Editor—David Zentner
Caper April 1957, V1N6, as above
Casanova May 1957, V1N1, bi-monthly, Aries Publishing, USA. Editor--Eugene Tillinger
Dazzle 1957, V1N2, bi-monthly, Playgirl Publishing, USA. Publisher/Editor—Walter Hale
The Dude May 1958, V2N5, bi-monthly, Mystery Publishing, USA. Editor—Bruce Elliot
Escapade May 1956, V1N8, monthly, Dee Publishing, USA. Publisher/Editor—David Zentner
Escapade February 1957, V2N5, as above
Escapade's Choicest Fall 1956, as above
Europe's Top Pin-ups 1957, N3, USA
Europe's Top Pin-ups 1957, N4, USA
Frolic June 1958, V7N6, bi-monthly, Frolic Magazine, USA. Editor—Luke Bailey
Girl Watcher March 1959, N1, quarterly, Bonanza Publishing, USA
Good Humor October 1958, quarterly, Humor Magazines, USA
High July 1959, V1N13, bi-monthly, Periodical House, USA. Editor—Bernard Baily
High September 1959, V1N14, as above
High for that Wide and Handsome Feeling 1959, as above
Hi-Life June 1958, V1N2, bi-monthly, Wilmot Enterprises, USA. Publisher/Editor—Chad Kelly
Hi-Life September 1959, V2N1, as above
Hi May 1957, V1N1, bi-monthly, Periodical House, USA. Editor—Bernard Baily
Ho! 1957 V1N1, as above
Jackpot January 1957, Olympic Publishing, USA. Editor—J.M. Stewart Gordon
Modern Man March 1957, V6N9-69, monthly, Publisher's Development, USA. Publisher-- George E. von Rosen
Mr. March 1957, V1N4, bi-monthly, Mr. Magazines, USA. Editor—Everett Meyers
Mr. March 1958, as above
My Escort March/April 1959, V1N2, bi-monthly, Seeger Publications, USA. Editor—Roy Arden
Night and Day June 1957, V9N6, monthly, Halho Corporation, USA. Editor—A. Lawrence Holmes
Nugget February 1956, V1N2, bi-monthly, Nugget Magazine, USA. Publisher/Editor—Michael St. John
Play May 1959, V1N2, bi-monthly, Lucky Magazines, USA
Plush November 1959, bi-monthly, Plush Publishing, USA
Pose! February 1959, V3N8, bi-monthly, Cape Magazine Management, USA

Relax May 1957, V1N1, bi-monthly, Finesse Publications, USA. Editor—Al Derson
Rex December 1957, V1N3, monthly, Delta Publishing, USA. Editor—Douglas Allen
Venus 1958, V1N1, bi-monthly, Garden of Eve Publications, USA. Editor—Montgomery L. Hooton

Chapter 12
Joe Weider: Of Beef and Betty

Jem August 1957, V1N6, Body Beautiful Publications, USA. Editor—James Kyle
Jem March 1958, V2N6, bi-monthly, Weider Periodicals, USA. Editor—Allen Camelli
Jem April 1959, V3N6, as above
Jem June 1959, V2N7, as above
Jem March 1961, as above
Monsieur June 1957, bi-monthly, Boxing and Wrestling, USA. Editor—Stanley Paley
Monsieur 1957, as above
Monsieur January 1950s, as above
Monsieur July 1959, as above
Monsieur February 1950s, as above
Body Beautiful June 1957, V2N7, monthly, Body Beautiful Publications, USA. Editor—Joe Weider

Chapter 13
Spawn of the Bunny: *Playboy* Competitors' Cartoon Mascots

Buccaneer January 1970, V1N9, bi-monthly, Tempest Publications, USA. Editor—F. Verbel Brown
Debonair March 1966, V2N9, bi-monthly, Textron Development, USA. Editor—William Pickering
Debonair July 1966, V2N11, as above
Debonair January 1968, V4N22, as above
Duke April 1970, V3N2, bi-monthly, M.F. Enterprises, USA. Editor—F. Verbel Brown
Gay Blade May 1957, V2N1, monthly, Bachelor Magazine, USA. Publisher/Editor—Harry Stein
Jaguar September 1965, V1N5, bi-monthly, Jaguar Publications, USA. Editor—Gervin Hayden
Jaguar August 1967, V2N11, as above, except Editor—Herman Petras
Jaguar June 1968, V3N6, as above, except Editor--F. Verbel Brown
Jaguar January 1969, V3N10, as above
Man About Town September 1958, V1N1, bi-monthly, Lucky Magazines, USA. Editor—Lloyd C. Quincy
Mate! March 1961, V1N1, bi-monthly, Agard Publishing, USA. Editor—Larry Reich
Rogue December 1956, V1N7, b-monthly, Greenleaf Publishing, USA. Publisher/Editor—William L. Hamling
Rogue February 1957, V2N1, as above
Rogue May 1957, V2N3, as above
Rogue July 1957, V2N5, as above
Rogue August 1957, V2N6, as above
Rugged February 1957, V1N1, Stanley Publications, USA. Editor—Eric Jonathan
Rugged April 1957, V1N2, as above
Satan 1957, V1N1, bi-monthly, Stanley Publications, USA. Editor—Eric Jonathan
Satan April 1957, V1N2, as above
Satan August 1957, V1N5, as above
Swank February 1956, V3N1, Male Publishing, USA. Editor—Bruce J. Friedman
Tiger August 1956, bi-monthly, Reynard Publications, USA. Publisher/Editor—George Fox, Jr.
Tiger December 1956, as above

Chapter 14
Duke Magazine: The Great Black Hope

Duke June 1957, V1N1, monthly, Duke Publishing, USA. Publisher/Editor—Dan Burley
Duke July 1957, V1N2, as above
Duke August 1957, V1N3, as above
Duke October 1957, V1N5, as above
Duke November 1957, V1N6, as above

Chapter 15
Samuel Roth vs United States of America: How *Good Times* defined Obscenity

American Aphrodite 1951, V1N3, USA. Editor--Samuel Roth
Good Times 1953, V1N1, monthly, Good Times Publishing, USA. Editor—Samuel Roth
Good Times 1953, V1N2, as above
Good Times 1953, V1N4, as above
Good Times 1953, V1N5, as above
Good Times 1953, V1N6, as above
Good Times 1953, V1N8, as above
Good Times 1953, V1N9, as above
Good Times 1954, V2N12, as above
Good Times 1954, V2N15, as above
Hum V1N1, quarterly, Hal Zucker, USA. Editor—Hal Zucker

Chapter 16
The Top 5 American Covergirls

3-D Hollywood Pin-ups January 1954, 3-D Magazines, USA. (Marilyn Monroe)
Adam July 1965, V9N7, monthly, Knight Publishing, USA. Editor—Lothar Ashley (June Wilkinson)
Blush 1950s, N1, USA (Diane Webber)
Cabaret Quarterly 1950s, Publisher's Development, USA. Publisher/Editor-- George E. von Rosen (Jayne Mansfield)
Caper May 1959, V5N3, monthly, Humor Magazines, USA. Editor—Douglas Allen (June Wilkinson)
Earl Wilson's Album of Showgirls, 1950s, USA (Jayne Mansfield)
Ecran 1958, N1429, Empresa Editora Zig-Zag, Chile (Jayne Mansfield)
Escapade December 1955, V1N3, monthly, Dee Publishing, USA. Publisher/Editor—David Zentner (Diane Webber)
Eye August 1953, V3N8, monthly, Mutual Magazine, USA. Editor—Dan Merrin (Marilyn Monroe)
Eyeful August 1953, V10N1, bi-monthly, Eyeful Magazine, USA. Editor—Lee Dawson (Bettie Page)
Fantastique 1950s, Sheba Publications, USA (Bettie Page)
Figure Quarterly 1950s, V9, no info, but apparently from the publisher of Cabaret magazine, USA (Bettie Page)
Focus on Bettie Page 1963, V1N1, bi-monthly, Selbee Associates, USA. Editor—J. King (Bettie Page)
Frolic 1955, bi-monthly, Frolic Magazine, USA. Editor—Luke Bailey (Diane Webber)
Girl Watcher June 1959, N2, quarterly, Bonanza Publishing, USA (June Wilkinson)
Hit Show September 1960, V3N2, bi-monthly, MDA Publishing, USA (June Wilkinson)

Jayne, The Jayne Mansfield Story 1950s, Show Magazine, USA (Jayne Mansfield)
Marilyn Monroe Pin-ups 1953, Maco Magazine, USA (Marilyn Monroe)
Meet The Girls 1950s, V1N3, Riviera Pin-up, USA (Bettie Page)
Modern Man March 1955, V4N9-45, monthly, Publishers Development, USA. Publisher/Editor—George E. von Rosen (Marilyn Monroe)
Modern Man January 1958, V7N7-79, as above (Jayne Mansfield)
Modern Sunbathing June 1961, V31N6-168, monthly, Diamond Publishing, USA (Diane Webber)
Modern Sunbathing November 1961, V31N11-173, as above (Diane Webber)
My Escort 1950s, V1N3, bi-monthly, Seeger Publications, USA. Editor—Roy Arden (June Wilkinson)
Night and Day August 1954, V6N8, monthly, Halho Corporation, USA. Editor—A. Lawrence Holmes (Marilyn Monroe)
Ogle March 1956, V1N1, bi-monthly, True Problems Publications, USA. Publisher/Editor—Myron Fass (Jayne Mansfield)
Paris Frou Frou 1950s, N5, bi-weekly, France (Marilyn Monroe)
Peep Show June 1956, V2N27, bi-monthly, N-E-W-S Publishing, USA (Jayne Mansfield)
Photoplay Pinups 1953, N4, Bartholomew House, USA (Marilyn Monroe)
A Pictorial Biography of June Wilkinson 1961, V1N1, Steele Publications, USA. Publisher/Editor—Samuel H. Steele (June Wilkinson)
Sir! Oct. 1956, V13N10, Volitant Publishing, USA. Editor—Adrian B. Lopez (Marilyn Monroe)
Sunbathing Review Fall 1958, semi-annual, Diamond Publishing, USA (Marilyn Monroe)
Tiger March 1957, V2N1, bi-monthly, Reynard Publications, USA (Diane Webber)
Tonight 1959, V1N1, Studio Publications, USA. Editor—Dave Quimby (June Wilkinson)
The Vagabond Spring 1961, quarterly, Polo Publishing, USA (Diane Webber)

THE HISTORY OF MEN'S MAGAZINES

Volumes III & IV in Stores Summer 2005

Volumes V & VI following Winter 2005!

Volume III

begins with the late fifties' redefinition of obscenity laws and documents the resulting avalanche of sex titles hitting newsstands around the world. The US leads production, but France, Germany, England, Argentina and even Australia all contribute.

Volume IV

traces the roots of "special interest" and under-the-counter publications during this same period, starting in California's San Fernando Valley and ending with a Scandinavian sexual/social revolution that results in the repeal of obscenity laws throughout Northern Europe.

Volume V

covers the newsstands of the world during the taboo-busting seventies. On the one hand we have hippies trying to change the world with magazines based on peace, love and psychedelic sex. On the other hand there're the brash young entrepreneurs who flocked to this publishing free-for-all, typified by *Hustler* magazine's Larry Flynt in the US and his British counterpart David Sullivan, both profiled in this volume.

Volume VI

the final word in this encyclopedic series, is reserved for the most daring and extreme edges of adult publishing. Here you'll peek inside the adult bookstores of Denmark, Sweden, Germany, the US and Japan to see what sexual freedom in the seventies really meant. For the strong of heart, adventuresome of spirit and a spectacular climax to this ground-breaking series.

Each volume contains over 400 pages and nearly 1000 covers and interior images. From the best to the worst, the elegant to the crude, the well known to the obscure. Volume III: Swinging Sixties at the Newsstand and Volume IV: Swinging Sixties Under The Counter document the rise of hippie culture, leg magazines, big hair, California slicks and Swedish sin. They witness the fall of men's adventure, nudists, the French mystique and panties. Mixed in are profiles of quirky publishers, obsessed photographers and the most prolific risqué artist of all time. If you've enjoyed Volumes I and II, III and IV are the natural next step to completing your *History of Men's Magazines* library.

The author: Dian Hanson is a twenty-five-year veteran of men's magazine publishing. She began her career at *Puritan Magazine* in 1976 and went on to edit a variety of titles, including *Partner*, *Oui*, *Hooker*, *Outlaw Biker*, and *Juggs* magazines. In 1987 she took over the '60s title *Leg Show* and transformed it into the world's best-selling fetish publication. Most recently, she authored TASCHEN's *Roy Stuart: The Fourth Body* and *The History of Men's Magazines* Volumes I and II.

Index

VOLUME II

Y

Z

Acknowledgements

Many people made this huge project possible; I never could have done it without every one of you. I've done my best to include you all, but if your name isn't here, please forgive my bad memory. Thanks to Pablo Boraspardo, Kim Christy, Joe Zinnato@erosarchive.com, Jay A. Gertzman, Jutta Hendricks, Richard Jaccoma, Eberhard Kemmer, Stefan Klatte, Eric Kroll, Horst Neuzner and Mark Rotenberg@vintagenudephotos.com.

Special thanks to Benedikt Taschen, Keith Kinsella, Marc Atlan, Geoff Nicholson and to Eric Godtland, collector extraordinaire.

Cover: YEAR: **1959**. TITLE: **Modern Man**. COUNTRY: **USA**.
Backcover: YEAR: **1954**. TITLE: **Flirt**. ARTIST: **Peter Driben**. COUNTRY: **USA**.